# THE COMPLETE SUN SIGN GUIDE

**Bernard Fitzwalter** has been interested in astrology since he was about six, when he played King Herod's astrologer in his primary school nativity play. For the past six years he has been teaching astrology for the Marylebone-Paddington Institute, and for seven years he has had a regular column in OVER 21 magazine. In 1984 he appeared in the first series of Anglia Television's *Zodiac Game*, which prompted the *Daily Mirror* to say that he was 'enough to give astrology a good name'.

# THE COMPLETE SUN SIGN GUIDE

Bernard Fitzwalter

THE AQUARIAN PRESS

This edition first published 1988

British Library Cataloguing in Publication Data

Fitzwalter, Bernard
The complete sun sign guide.
1. Astrology
I. Title
133.5

ISBN 0-85030-777-5

*The Aquarian Press is part of the*
*Thorsons Publishing Group, Wellingborough,*
*Northamptonshire, NN8 2RQ, England*

Printed in Great Britain by Billing & Sons Limited, Worcester

3   5   7   9   10   8   6   4

# Contents

# Introduction

This book has been written to help you find out a little about astrology and a lot about yourself. Unlike most other Sun sign books, it explains the motives and aims that guide your actions and make you do things the way you do; what it does not do is give you a list of things 'typical of your sign' to see if you recognize any of them. You are not likely to be typical anything: you are unique. What you do have in common with others who have birthdays at about the same time as you is a way of using your energy, a way of thinking, a set of motives and beliefs which seem to make sense to you, and which other people, those of the other eleven signs, obviously do not have. This book shows you those motives and beliefs, and show you how they fit in with those of the other eleven signs. The zodiac is like a jigsaw: all the pieces have to be there for the whole picture to emerge.

This book also sets out to answer some very simple questions which are often asked but seldom answered: Questions like 'Why does the zodiac have twelve signs?' and 'What does being a Taurus actually mean?', as well as 'Why are Pisceans supposed to be indecisive? Why can't they be firm instead?' and 'Why don't all the people of the same star sign look the same?' The reason that these questions are seldom answered is because all too many astrologers don't know the rudiments of astrological theory, and what they do know they don't tell, because they think it is too difficult for the man in the street to understand. This is obvious nonsense: astrology was devised for and by people who did not normally read or write as much as we do, nor did they have PhDs or the equivalent. The man in the street is quite capable of understanding anything provided that it is shown simply and clearly, from first principles upwards, and provided he has sufficient interest. Buying this book is evidence enough of your interest, and I hope that the explanations are simple enough and clear enough for you. If they are not, it is my fault, and not that of astrology.

# How to Use this Book

The book is in seven chapters. It is best to read them in sequence, but if you have neither time nor patience then they each work individually. Chapter 2 does not assume that you have read Chapter 1, though it helps. Chapters 5 and 6 make a lot more sense if you have already read their predecessors, but it isn't mandatory. The last chapter, although just as astrologically deep as the other six, is definitely intended as light relief to bring you back to real life gently after some of the more thought-provoking stuff.

The first chapter deals with the theory behind the zodiac; it sets out the principles of astrology and enables you to see why your sign is assigned the qualities it has, how the ruling planet system works, and what all the other signs are like in terms of motivation, so you can compare them to your own. There is a short and very effective method given for assessing the aims and motives of other people. It sounds a bit dense, but it isn't very long, and the answers to most of the questions you ever had about astrology are contained in it. Besides, when you read Chapters 5 and 6 you will need to know a bit about the other signs, as you will be finding out that there is more to you than just the Sun sign part you knew about.

The second chapter describes the essence of the signs. The idea is that you read the chapter from the beginning, and when it branches into twelve sub-sections, you just read the one which applies to you. You will find that the argument carries on as though there were no break. If you don't read the beginning of the chapter first (in other words, if you cheat) you will get lost.

This section also tells you how there are different sorts of people in your sign according to where your birthday falls in the month, and how your planetary energy is displayed in you in different ways and at different ages.

Since you spend the greatest part of your life dealing with other individuals, the way you deal with relationships is treated in some detail. This is the largest part of the book. Though the temptation to plunge in and read the section on yourself and your current partner is strong, please make sure you have read the introduction to the compatibility section first—in this book, Aries with Libra is *not* the same thing as Libra with Aries!

The fifth and sixth chapters show you a different kind of zodiac, and enable you to go into your own life in much greater detail. It isn't complicated, but you do need to think. It crosses the border between the kind of astrology you get in magazines, and the sort of thing a real astrologer does. There's no reason why you can't do it yourself, because after all, you know yourself best.

The last chapter shows you the surface of your Sun sign, and how that zodiacal energy comes out in your clothes, your home, even your favourite food. The final part of this chapter actually explains the mechanics of being lucky, which you probably thought was impossible.

I hope that when you have finished reading it, you will have a clearer view of yourself, and maybe like yourself a little more. Don't put the book away and forget about it once you have read it; read it again in a few months' time—you will be surprised at what new thoughts about yourself it prompts you to form!

## Note

Throughout this book, the pronouns 'he', 'him' and 'his' have been used to describe both male and female. Everything which applies to a male from your sign applies to a female as well. There are two reasons why I have not bothered to make the distinction: firstly to avoid long-windedness, and secondly because astrologically there is no need. It is not possible to tell from a horoscope whether the person to whom it relates is male or female; to astrology they are both living individuals full of potential.

BERNARD FITZWALTER

# 1. The Meaning of the Zodiac
## How the Zodiac Works

### Two Times Two is Four; Four Times Three is Twelve

It is no accident that there are twelve signs in the zodiac, although there are a great many people who reckon themselves to be well versed in astrology who do not know the reasons why, and cannot remember ever having given thought to the principles behind the circle of twelve.

The theory is quite simple, and once you are familiar with it, it will enable you to see the motivation behind all the other signs as well as your own. What's more, you only have to learn nine words to do it. That's quite some trick—being able to understand what anybody else you will ever meet is trying to do, with nine words.

It works like this.

The zodiac is divided into twelve signs, as you know. Each of the twelve represents a stage in the life cycle of solar energy as it is embodied in the life of mankind here on our planet. There are tides in this energy; sometimes it flows one way, sometimes another, like the tides of the ocean. Sometimes it is held static, in the form of an object, and sometimes it is released when that object is broken down after a period of time. The twelve signs show all these processes, both physical and spiritual, in their interwoven pattern.

Six signs are used to show the flowing tide, so to speak, and six for the ebbing tide. Aries, Gemini, Leo, Libra, Sagittarius, and Aquarius are the 'flowing' group, and the others form the second group. You will notice at once that the signs alternate, one with the other, around the zodiac, so that the movement is maintained, and there is never a concentration of one sort of energy in one place. People whose Sun sign is in the first group tend to radiate their energies outwards from themselves. They are the ones who like to make the first move, like to be the ones to take command of a situation, like to put something of themselves into whatever they are doing. They don't feel right standing on the sidelines; they are the original have-a-go types. Energy comes out of them and is radiated towards other people, in the same way as the Sun's energy is radiated out to the rest of the solar system.

The people in the other signs are the opposite to that, as you would expect. They collect all the energy from the first group, keeping it for themselves and making sure none is wasted. They absorb things from a situation or from a personal contact, rather than contributing to it. They prefer to watch and learn rather than make the first move. They correspond to the Moon, which collects and reflects the energy of the Sun. One group puts energy out, one group takes it back in. The sum total of energy in the universe remains constant, and the two halves of the zodiac gently move to and fro with the tide of the energies.

This energy applies both to the real and concrete world of objects, as well as to the intangible world of thoughts inside our heads.

A distinction has to be made, then, between the real world and the intangible world. If this is done, we have four kinds of energy: outgoing and collecting, physical and mental. These four kinds of energy have been recognized for a long time, and were given names to describe the way they work more than two thousand years ago. These are the elements. All the energy in the cosmos can be described in the terms of these four: Fire, Earth, Air, Water.

*Fire* is used to describe that outgoing energy which applies to the real and physical world. There are three signs given to it: Aries, Leo, and Sagittarius. People with the Sun in any of these signs find themselves with the energy to get things going. They are at their best when making a personal contribution to a situation, and they expect to see some tangible results for their efforts. They are sensitive to the emotional content of anything, but that is not their prime concern, and so they tend to let it look after itself while they busy themselves with the actual matter in hand. Wherever you meet Fire energy in action, it will be shown as an individual whose personal warmth and enthusiasm are having a direct effect on his surroundings.

*Earth* is used to describe the real and physical world where the energies are being collected and stored, sometimes in the form of material or wealth. The three signs given to the element are Taurus, Virgo, and Capricorn. Where Fire energy in people makes them want to move things, Earth energy makes them want to hold things and stop them moving. The idea of touching and holding, and so that of possession, is important to these people, and you can usually see it at work in the way they behave towards their own possessions. The idea is to keep things stable, and to hold energy stored for some future time when it will be released. Earth Sun people work to ensure that wherever they are is secure and unlikely to change; if possible they would like the strength and wealth of their situation to increase, and will work towards that goal. Wherever you meet Earth energy in action, there will be more work being done than idle chat, and there will be a resistance to any kind of new idea. There will be money being made, and accumulated. The idea of putting down roots and bearing fruit may be a useful one to keep in mind when trying to understand the way this energy functions.

*Air* is used to describe outgoing mental energies; put more simply, this is communication. Here the ideas are formed in the mind of the individual, and put out in the hope that they can influence and meet the ideas of another individual; this is communication, in an abstract sense. Gemini, Libra, and Aquarius are all Air signs, and people with the Sun in those signs are very much concerned with communicating their energies to others. Whether anything gets done as a result of all the conversation is not actually important; if there is to be a concrete result, then that is the province of Fire or Earth energies. Here the emphasis is on shaping the concept, not the reality. There is an affinity with Fire energies, because both of them are outgoing, but other than that they do not cross over into each other's territory. Wherever you meet Air energy in action, there is a lot of talk, and new ideas are thrown up constantly, but there is no real or tangible result, no real product, and no emotional involvement; were there to be emotional content, the energies would be watery ones.

*Water* is the collection of mental energies. It is the response to communication or action. It absorbs and dissolves everything else, and puts nothing out. In a word, it is simply feelings. Everything emotional is watery by element, because it is a response to an outside stimulus, and is often not communicated. It is not, at least not in its pure sense, active or initiatory, and it does not bring anything into being unless transformed into energy of a different type, such as Fire. Cancer, Scorpio and Pisces are the Water signs, and natives of those signs are often moody, withdrawn, and uncommunicative. Their energy collects the energy of others, and keeps their mental responses to external events stored. They are not being sad for any particular reason; it is simply the way that energy works. It is quite obvious that they are not showing an outgoing energy, but neither have they anything tangible to show for their efforts, like the money and property which seem to accumulate around Earth people. Water people simply absorb, keep to themselves, and do not communicate. To the onlooker, this appears unexciting, but there again the onlooker is biased: Fire and Air energies only appreciate outgoing energy forms, Earth energies recognize material rather than mental energies, and other Water energies are staying private and self-contained!

We now recognize four kinds of energy. Each of these comes in three distinct phases; if one zodiac sign is chosen to represent each of these phases within an element, there would be twelve different kinds of energy, and that would define the zodiac of twelve, with each one showing a distinct and different phase of the same endless flow of energy.

The first phase, not surprisingly, is a phase of definition, where the energies take that form for the first time, and where they are at their purest; they are not modified by time or circumstance, and what they aim to do is to start things in their own terms. These four most powerful signs (one for each element, remember) are called cardinal signs: Aries, Cancer, Libra, Capricorn. When the Sun enters any of these signs, the seasons change; the first day of the Sun's journey through Aries is the first day of spring, and the Spring equinox; Libra marks the Autumnal equinox, while Cancer and Capricorn mark Midsummer's Day and the shortest day respectively.

The second phase is where the energy is mature, and spreads itself a little; it is secure in its place, and the situation is well established, so there is a sort of thickening and settling of the energy flow. Here it is at its most immobile, even Air. The idea is one of maintenance and sustenance, keeping things going and keeping them strong. This stage is represented by Taurus, Leo, Scorpio, and Aquarius, and they are called, unsurprisingly, fixed signs. These four signs, and their symbols, are often taken to represent the four winds and the four directions North, South, East and West. Their symbols (with an eagle instead of a scorpion for Scorpio) turn up all over Europe as tokens for the evangelists Luke, Mark, John and Matthew (in that order).

The final phase is one of dissolution and change, as the energy finds itself applied to various purposes, and in doing so is changed into other forms. There is an emphasis on being used for the good, but being used up nonetheless. The final four signs are Gemini, Virgo, Sagittarius, and Pisces; in each of them the energies of their element are given back out for general use and benefit from where they had been maintained in the fixed phase. It is this idea of being used and changed which leads to this phase being called mutable.

Three phases of energy, then; one to form, one to grow strong and mature, and one to be used, and to become, at the end, something else. Like the waxing, full, and waning phases of the Moon.

The diagram on page 16 shows the twelve signs arranged in

their sequence round the zodiac. Notice how cleverly the cycle and phases interweave:

(a) Outgoing and collecting energies alternate, with no two the same next to each other;

(b) Physical ebb and flow are followed by mental ebb and flow alternately in pairs round the circle, meaning that the elements follow in sequence round the circle three times;

(c) Cardinal, Fixed, and Mutable qualities follow in sequence round the circle four times, and yet

(d) No two elements or qualities the same are next to each other, even though their sequences are not broken.

The interweaving is perfect. The zodiac shows all forms of energy, physical and mental, outgoing or incoming, waxing or waning, harmoniously forming a perfectly balanced unity when all the components are taken together. Humanity, as a whole, contains all the possibilities; each individual is a component necessary to the whole.

All this can be a bit long-winded when what you want is some way of holding all that information for instant recall and use, which is where the nine words come in.

If a single word is used for the kind of energy flow, and another two for the element and quality, then they can be used to form a sentence which will describe the way the energy is being used.

As a suggestion (use other words if they are more meaningful to you), try 'outgoing' and 'collecting' for the energy flows.

Next, for the elements:

| | | | |
|---|---|---|---|
| Fire | : | activity | (Aries, Leo, Sagittarius) |
| Earth | : | material | (Taurus, Virgo, Capricorn) |
| Air | : | communication | (Gemini, Libra, Aquarius) |
| Water | : | feelings | (Cancer, Scorpio, Pisces) |

And for the qualities:

| | | | |
|---|---|---|---|
| Cardinal | : | defining | (Aries, Cancer, Libra, Capricorn) |
| Fixed | : | maintaining | (Taurus, Leo, Scorpio, Aquarius) |
| Mutable | : | using | (Gemini, Virgo, Sagittarius, Pisces) |

Now in answer to the question 'What is a Gemini doing?' and answer can be formed as 'He's outgoing, and he's using communication', which neatly encapsulates the motivation of the sign. All that you need to know about the guiding principles of a Gemini individual, no matter who he is, is in that sentence. He will never deviate from that purpose, and you can adapt your own actions to partner or oppose his intention as you please.

A Scorpio? He's collecting, and he's maintaining his feelings. An Arian? He's outgoing, and he's defining activity. And so on.

Those nine words, or some similar ones which you like better, can be used to form effective and useful phrases which describe the motivation of everybody you will ever meet. How different people show it is their business, but their motivation and purpose is clear if you know their birthday.

Remember, too, that this motivation works at all levels, from the immediate to the eternal. The way a Taurean conducts himself in today's problems is a miniature of the way he is trying to achieve his medium-term ambitions over the next two or three years. It is also a miniature of his whole existence: when, as an old man, he looks back to see what he tried to do and what he achieved, both the efforts and the achievement, whatever it is, can be described in the same phrase with the same three words.

# The Planets and the Horseshoe

You will have heard, or read, about the planets in an astrological context. You may have a horoscope in a magazine which says that Mars is here or Jupiter is there, and that as a consequence this or that is likely to happen to you. Two questions immediately spring to mind: What do the planets signify? How does that affect an individual?

The theory is straightforward again, and not as complex as that of the zodiac signs in the previous chapter. Remember that the basic theory of astrology is that since the universe and mankind are part of the same Creation, they both move in a similar fashion, so Man's movements mirror those of the heavens. So far, so good. If you look at the sky, night after night, or indeed day after day, it looks pretty much the same; the stars don't move much in relationship to each other, at least not enough to notice. What do move, though, are the Sun and Moon, and five other points of light—the planets. It must therefore follow that if these are the things which move, they must be the things which can be related to the movements of Man. Perhaps, the theory goes, they have areas of the sky in which they feel more at home, where the energy that they represent is stronger;

there might be other places where they are uncomfortable and weak, corresponding to the times in your life when you just can't win no matter what you do. The planets would then behave like ludo counters, moving round the heavens trying to get back to a home of their own colour, and then starting a new game.

The scheme sounds plausible, makes a sort of common sense, and is endearingly human; all hallmarks of astrological thought, which unlike scientific thought has to relate everything to the human experience. And so it is: the planets are given values to show the universal energy in different forms, and given signs of the zodiac as homes. Therefore your Sun sign also has a planet to look after it, and the nature of that planet will show itself strongly in your character.

The planets used are the Sun and Moon, which aren't really planets at all, one being a satellite and the other a star, and then Mercury, Venus, Mars, Jupiter, and Saturn. This was enough until the eighteenth century, when Uranus was discovered, followed in the subsequent two hundred years by Neptune and Pluto. Some modern astrologers put the three new planets into horoscopes, but it really isn't necessary, and may not be such a good idea anyway. There are three good reasons for this:

(a) The modern planets break up the symmetry of the original system, which was perfectly harmonious;

(b) The old system is still good enough to describe everything that can happen in a human life, and the modern planets have little to add;

(c) Astrology is about the relationship between the sky and a human being. An ordinary human being cannot see the outer planets on his own; he needs a telescope. We should leave out of the system such things as are of an extra-human scale or magnitude: they do not apply to an ordinary human. If we put in things which are beyond ordinary human capabilities, we cannot relate them to the human experience, and we are wasting our time.

In the diagram on page 20 the zodiac is presented in its usual form, but it has also been split into two from the start of Leo to the start of Aquarius. The right hand half is called the solar half, and the other one is the lunar half. The Sun is assigned to Leo because in the Northern hemisphere, where astrology started, August is when you feel the influence of the Sun most, especially in the Eastern Mediterranean, where the Greeks and the other early Western civilizations were busy putting the framework of astrology together in the second millennium BC. The Sun is important because it gives light. The Moon gives light too; it is reflected sunlight, but it is enough to see by, and this is enough to give the Sun and Moon the title of 'the Lights' in astrology. The Moon is assigned to Cancer, so that the two of them can balance and complement each other. From there,

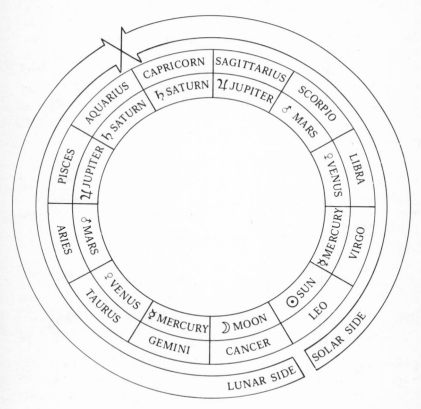

moving away from the Lights around the circle on both sides, the signs have the planets assigned to them starting with the fastest mover, Mercury, and continuing in decreasing order of speed. Saturn is the slowest mover of all, and the two signs opposite to the Lights are both governed by that planet. The reasons for this apparent assymmetry will be explained in a little while. This arrangement is, of course, the horseshoe of the title to this chapter.

The Sun and Moon work in a similar fashion to the outgoing and collecting energies we noted earlier with the twelve signs. The Sun is radiant above all else; energy comes outwards from it, warming and energizing all those around it. Leo people, whose sign is the Sun's, work like this by being at the centre of a group of people and acting as inspiration and encouragement to them all. The Moon reflects the Sun's light, and energies of a lunar kind are directed inwards towards the core of the person. The two energies are necessarily linked; lunar people would starve without the solar folks' warmth, but the solar types need someone to radiate to or their purpose is unfulfilled.

The planets on each side of the horseshoe display their own energies in a solar or lunar way depending on which side of the pattern they are on.

Mercury and Venus form a pair, representing complementary but opposite ideas, which should be familiar by now. Mercury represents difference, and Venus stands for similarity.

Wherever anything new forms that is distinguishable from the background, then Mercury is there making it what it is, highlighting what makes it different. Anything separate is Mercurial, and words, since they are separate and can be strung together into millions of different combinations, are Mercurial too. Mercury is not a long-term influence; it notes things as being different for an instant, and then they become part of the establishment, and something else is new elsewhere. Because 'new' is an instantaneous state—that is, something can only be new once, and for a moment—Mercury is not associated with anything lasting, and its rapid motion as a planet leads to its being associated with the idea of speed. Virgo, Mercury's solar sign, is concerned with the changing of the shape of things ('collecting, using material' in our keyword system), while Gemini, the lunar sign, is concerned with reading and writing, and getting new ideas ('outgoing, using communication').

Venus does the reverse; it looks for that which is similar, finding points of contact to make relationships between common interests and energies. It likes to preserve the harmonies of life, and resents anything which might interrupt them. Love and affection are naturally Venusian, but so is music and all of the Arts, for the harmonies they contain. Expressed in a solar way, Venus is Libra, the maker of relationships; its lunar face is Taurus, emphasizing food and furnishings as things which give pleasure to the individual.

The next pair are Mars and Jupiter. Mars applies force from the outside to impose structure on a disordered universe, while Jupiter expands forcibly from the inside to give growth and wealth, inviting everyone else to join in.

Mars is pure force, energy in a straight line with a direction to go in. Anger and passion are both Martian, and so is lust, because they are all examples of great energy directed towards a given end. Note that Martian force is not necessarily strength, wealth, or know-how, just pure energy, which often boils over and needs controlling. Mars is the power in an athlete, and in an assassin too. It is also the power in a lover, because the urge to create is also the urge to pro-create, and if that energy fulfils its purpose then that creation takes place. Scorpio is its solar side, the power to control and create; in lunar form it is shown by Aries, as energy enjoyed for its own sake by its owner, with no purpose except to express it.

Jupiter is the spirit of expansion from within; not only does it oppose Mars' force from outside, it opposes Mars' physicality with its own mental emphasis. Jupiter develops the mind, then. As it does so, it develops all natural talents of an academic nature, and encourages movement, enquiry and travel to broaden experience and knowledge. The Solar expression of this is Sagittarius, where the centaur symbol is both a wise teacher and a free-roaming wild horse at the same time. Jupiter in a lunar sense is Pisces, where the imagination is developed to a greater extent than anywhere else, but used to provide an internal dream world for the owner's pleasure. Great sensitivity here, but the lunar energies are not of the sort to be expressed; rather other energies are *im*pressed on the Piscean mind.

Saturn is the last of the five planets. He stands alone, and if it is necessary to consider him as paired with anything it is with the Lights as an entity together. The Lights are at the centre of the system; Saturn is at its edge. They are the originators of the energies of the zodiac, and he is the terminator. Everything to do with limits and ends is his. He represents Time, and lots of it, in contrast to Mercury, which represented the instant. He represents the sum total of all things, and the great structures and frameworks of long-term endeavour. In solar form he is Capricorn, the representative of hard work, all hierarchies, and all rulers; in lunar form he is Aquarius, showing the horizontal structure of groups of people within society at different levels. Here he denies the activity of Mars, because society is too big for one person to change against the collective will, and he contains the expansion of Jupiter within himself. Venus and Mercury can neither relate to it nor make it change, because it is always the same, in the end.

The planets show important principles in action, the same as the zodiac does. You have probably noticed that the horseshoe of the planets and the ring of the zodiac say the same thing in a different way, and that is true about most things in astrology. It may be that the two systems interrelate and overlap because they are from the same source: after all, $3+2+2=7$, which is the planet's total, and $3x2x2=12$, which is the signs'. How you assign the elements and qualities, pairs of planets and lights is for you to decide. The joy of astrology, like all magic, is that it has you at the centre, and is made to fit its user's requirements. Now you know the principles, you can use it as you please, and as it seems relevant to you.

# 2. The Essence of the Signs

All the energy in the zodiac is solar, but that solar energy takes many forms. It is moderated and distributed through the planetary energies until it finally shows in you, the individual. You will be motivated by, and behave in the manner of, the energies of your ruling planet. Remind yourself from pages 20-23 which one is yours. Remind yourself also of the way your sign uses its energy from page 17. Now we have to see how those essential principles work when expressed through a person and his motivation.

## What it Means to Belong to Your Sign

You know what it is to belong to your sign, and to be you; but you probably don't know what it is that makes your sign the way it is, because you cannot stand outside yourself. You would have to be each of the other eleven signs in turn to understand the nature of the energy that motivates you. This essential energy is in everyone of your sign, but it shows itself to different extents and in different ways. Because it applies to so many people, it is universal rather than specific, and universal ideas tend to come in language which sounds a little on the woolly side. You will think that it isn't really about what makes you who you are, because you don't feel like that every day—or at least you think you don't. In fact, you feel like that all the time, but you don't notice it any more than you notice your eyes focusing, yet they do it all the time, and you see things the way you do because of it.

The first thing to note is that the zodiac is a circle, not a line with a beginning and an end. If it were a line, then we could see how far along it you were, but that would be to miss the point; if the zodiac is a circle, then your sign is a stage in an endlessly repeating cycle, and we will get a much better idea of what it is if we look to see where it came from, and where it is going.

Secondly, each of the zodiac signs is divided into degrees, like an arc of any other circle. Since a circle has 360 degrees, then each sign must be 30 degrees, since there are twelve signs. Each of the signs is further split into sections of ten degrees, called decanates. There are three decanates in each sign, and the one that your birthday falls in will tell you a little more about how your particular Sun sign energy actually works in you as an individual.

# Aries

The sign before Aries is Pisces. Pisces represents the dissolution of all that is definite, the breaking down into component parts, and further down into elements. All things are possible in Pisces at a universal level, but nothing has any form. Nothing exists, or does not exist; nothing has direction, shape, or connection with anything else. From this primeval soup of endless possibility, energies meet and coalesce; possibility becomes probability; direction and purpose are drawn together. Finally, they become a single point of focused energy—the beginning of separate existence. This energy must start the new cycle of things. It must be strong enough to be the initiator of other processes which will take up where it leaves off. It must be sure of its own purpose, for it has to make new things from nothing, using only itself. It is sure, like nothing else is, of its own existence, and confident of its own strength; it can say 'I am myself' when everything else in the universe is unformed and without direction. This is the spirit of Aries, the beginning of the cycle, the spark of creation.

Biologically it corresponds to a spermatozoon and the moment of conception; a package of possibilities made definite at a single point, a living thing whose sole purpose is to make a beginning.

An Arian does not feel particularly spiritual; other signs have time for reflection, but the Arian does not. You know simply that you are, and that you are individual. You need to do what you feel you would like to do; this is not through some wayward urge to be different, although later social contact and conditioning may make it so, nor is it from a desire to be seen to be doing something others could not, and thus acquire glamour and notoriety, though it may be a convenient face to put on things, if people seem to view it so. The desire is much too simple for that; it is simply a desire to exist on your own terms. You do not need to create or maintain anything, because that would put your energies into something which is not yourself, and suggest that there are more important things to you than your own existence. You do not need to break things down and re-create them to be the way you want them to be, because that involves spending some of your existence ensuring the non-existence of other things. You have no need for that; you are not threatened by any other thing that is, because you know that you are yourself, untouched by other forces.

Completion and maintenance are not part of the Arian vocabulary; seeing a project grow to completion and fullness of form does not concern you, any more than keeping it going and continuing its purpose. Beginning is what you are best at. You have almost no concept of time; you may grow one to enable you to understand others, but the pure energy of Aries lives in an eternal present, where tomorrow is a long time away, next year almost impossible to believe, and yesterday doesn't matter any more.

This sense of immediacy extends to your own experience, which must be actual for you to appreciate it. In other words, you have to do it for yourself. Reading the instruction book is not something you do; you switch on and push all the buttons to see what happens for yourself. This tendency to rush in and touch, to make things happen with your own hands, leads to a lot of accidents, especially on those days when the energy flow isn't quite as strong as you remember it being. Blades and other sharp things seem to have an affinity for you, and you discover how sharp they are time and time again, confident either in your ability to avoid accident or in your desire to see just how sharp they are. You are usually mistaken, and it is something you learn again and again.

Arian energy flows through the whole of the body, and therefore you think in terms of its use all the time. Where the Gemini, for example, thinks nothing of his body, but lives in his mind, you are the other way round; you use your body for everything, and gain satisfaction from doing so. Sports and any kind of exertion are a pleasure to you. The idea of laziness, as in a disinclination to do anything physically, is alien to you. You may well be disinclined to do something because you are not interested in it, but not because you don't like exerting yourself. Arians get dubbed 'pioneers of the zodiac', a title which suggests a sort of hardy, self-denying loner driven on to new horizons by a desire to be first. All this is true to some extent, but it is misleading. You are not driven by anything to do anything; you do what appeals to you, and you use all your energy in a direct and physical way to achieve that, without thought for what happens later. A good example is a footballer heading the ball; all his thoughts go into using his head to direct the ball. He does not care, as he leaps to make the shot, where he lands after his head has hit the ball; he will only become aware of a need to land somewhere after his head has hit the ball. That's how Arians work.

Aries corresponds to the head of the body. Arians have big heads, sometimes, and strong skulls with noticeable eyebrows. The head leads the rest of the body, and Aries leads the rest of the zodiac. The head is where most of your sense organs are located, and Arians like to feel things directly. Arians also get headaches and similar problems when they are under stress, but in matters of health there are other considerations, and some of them will be examined later.

Sexually, an Arian again expresses his energy physically. A sexual relationship for an Arian is based on physical sensation more than anything else. Sexual satisfaction does not come to an Arian through togetherness or mutual affection, nor through intellectual rapport; it is found entirely in the physical sensations of using the body to express desire, and enjoying the sensations felt by the body in return for that energy output. Pure, and simple; uncomplicated, unaffected by other considerations, it is simply a person whose body is his most important possession using it to communicate desire to another body.

To sum up, if you want a single adjective to remind you how an Arian has to do things, it is 'headlong'. Head first, at full speed, completely absorbed in the experience of the action, and without a thought for his own safety or the consequences— that's how Arians do things, like the Ram which represents the sign.

## Early, Middle or Late? The Decanates

*First decanate (21–30 March)*
This is the purest form of Aries. There is a double helping of Martian energy here, expressed as an irrepressible form of outward-looking, enthusiastic optimism. You will have a special zest for life; you will feel that you are in some way special and different from everybody else, because you have that spark of independence which knows that nothing is ever going to go wrong for you. What you don't do is share yourself in any way; you are too involved in the action itself to think of companionship when you really think about it. Thinking about it doesn't happen very often either; such is the speed and the passion of your way through life, that you seem never to think things through; you may say that you don't need to, and you would be right to some extent, but there is an appreciation which comes from examining things after the event to see what they can teach you, and this you will never see. Nor do you bother to see how much, or how well, you can do things; to you, the action itself is enough, and you trust your own abilities; there may be other abilities which you will never discover, or improvements on your known talents which you will never make. That's double Mars for

you—it never looks back, and it never has time.

*Second decanate (31 March–9 April)*
Here Aries is moderated a little and the Sun helps Mars to turn some of its boundless energy into warmth rather than movement. You will be keen to develop your personality and your talents, where the earlier decanate does not. You will still be dashing and full of life, but somehow there is a warmth to you which others find inspiring, and you enjoy being a leader to some extent, whereas the earlier decanate is very much a loner in essence. You will be keen to do as much as you can with yourself, and wherever you think you have some ability you will take care to develop it, thinking as you do that it is better to be able to do things yourself than to have others do them for you, and better yet to do them *well* yourself. Much more of your energy will be put into showing what you can do; your achievements are somehow more visible than those of other Arians. People like being near you; your flair and enthusiasm seem to transfer to everyone.

*Third decanate (10–19 April)*
Aries' Martian energy works through Jupiter in the final section of the sign, bringing thoughtfulness to bear on the immense power of Mars, and spreading it out a little rather than concentrating it. There is also a change of emphasis from the strictly personal to the more general. The Arian here feels that he is indeed uniquely gifted with a capacity for effective action, but that he ought to use this carefully and to the best effect. He thinks before he acts, and he uses some of his direct energy in his thinking processes, giving a clear and decisive mind not always found in the other Arians. He also thinks that he must consider the impact of his actions on others, and if possible act to their benefit. Sometimes this gets stuck in his mind and a preoccupation with some consideration or other arises—a sort of 'one-track mind' caused by the Arian simplicity of approach coupled with instant decisions and the usual Arian inability to wait for things to happen—but at least the intention is good.

This is the only Arian to consider using his energy for anything other than a personal, and short-term, goal; the way he uses his energy contrasts sharply with the first decanate, where the energy almost uses the person.

## Three Phases of Life: Aries as Child, Adult, Parent

*The Arian child*

Arians seem to be the most lively children, and thoroughly enjoy their childhood. The problems come later, when they show a marked reluctance to stop being children and adopt adult behaviour patterns.

As children, they are bouncy and energetic, full of energy and into anything and everything. They adore being outside where they can run, climb, swim, play games, and generally tire themselves out; the next day they are ready to do it all again, as though each day was the first time they had ever experienced such delights. To a certain extent it is, because they are slow to build a sense of time or accumulated experience. The girls are just as active as the boys, and favour the same kind of activities. When they are put into a classroom, they work hard and well as long as their attention is kept, but that is not often for long. Because they get bored so easily, and have no sense of anything being necessary as well as no sense of time, they do not concentrate for as long as some oher children. As a result, their schoolwork can be a bit haphazard, both in the quality of presentation, and in the depth of understanding behind it. They are at their best where they are allowed or encouraged to show their own thoughts—English essays will be fast-moving and amusing, though they could end abruptly, showing that something else has disturbed the creative flow and diverted interest elsewhere! They need to learn to consider other people than themselves, which they find difficult, and some degree of tidiness and organization for later life, though any parent who hopes to get an Arian child to develop much of this is fighting a losing battle. It is not possible, and not desirable, to suppress the Arian child's energy, but you can channel it constructively.

## The Arian adult

The Arian adult retains most of the child's characteristics; this is in direct contrast to the Capricorn adult, who seems to be born as an adult, and seems never to display any childish qualities, even as an infant!

The desire to suit himself is still there, as is the lack of organization. Although he is decisive, the decisions are usually not based on careful consideration, but on the first solution that comes into his head, according to the theory that any action is better than no action. It never occurs to him that other people might have better solutions, or cheaper ones. It also never occurs to him that other people might not be in agreement with the solution adopted, so he does not bother to ask them. He is completely without regard for risk or danger, and this can lead to accidents. An injured adult Arian is sometimes an amusing sight: like a child who has fallen and grazed his knee, he is in complete amazement that such a thing could ever have happened to him, and tearfully blames Fate for this wicked and unmerited mishap which has completely and irretrievably shattered his faith in the world. For five minutes, that is, until something else has taken his mind and interest away from it all.

Arian adults need to find a physical outlet for their energies, and most of them play some sort of sport, the more demanding the better. They are not particularly good team athletes, because their energy centres around themselves; they are much more suited to individual competition.

Having unstructured thought processes which change every few minutes makes Arians original and opinionated, though not particularly profound thinkers. Often their capacity for saying what they think at the moment that it occurs to them makes for some biting humour, and they tend to develop a sharp sense of humour which enjoys satire and cynical one-liners. They do not enjoy sophisticated humour or verbal wit; if it is funny immediately and without having to think about it, then they laugh. That said, they like puzzles, but only if they can solve them without too much difficulty; like children, they appreciate finding something for themselves, but they won't try very hard to get it.

## The Arian parent

Arian parents are both very pushy, because the Martian energy pushes through them into the children; just how they are pushy depends on the sex of the parent.

An Arian father wants the child to be like him, to be an extension of the things that he has chosen to do. He also wants the child to be Arian because that's all he himself knows how to be, and he can't imagine life any other way. If the child is Arian, or at least has the Sun in a Fire sign, then he might fit in well with his father's wishes, but if he is of a different, gentler, nature, such as a Piscean or a Virgoan, then there will be problems because the Arian father will not be able to understand his way of thinking. It is, of course, a mistake for the Arian father to insist that the child do Arian things in an Arian way. Considerable care and tolerance is needed on both sides to make this relationship free of stresses.

An Arian mother does not want her child to be like her, but she does want her child to be as effective and successful as she is; she wants her child to be number one and at the front, in a very Arian way, at whatever the child does. Children are an extension of herself, to an Arian mother; if they are hurt, she is hurt. At school, if the child is unfairly treated or injured in any way, the Arian mother is there to complain to the headmaster, as though she herself had been hurt. Whatever talents her child shows, which may not of course be Arian ones, will receive full support from the Arian mother, so that every talent can be fully and energetically expressed. The only problems are that she is sometimes interested only to develop talents in the child that she herself has, or wishes she had (her child may not choose to do anything with these abilities), and that she sometimes feels that only she can direct and aid the child's progress, becoming too dominant for the child's good. When the child does grow up and away, she is left feeling cheated of something she regarded as hers for all time, which, of course, was not true.

# Taurus

The sign before Taurus is Aries. Aries represents the start of all that is new; it is the initial surge of energy that defines and gives life to any new organism. Everything has to start somewhere, and as it starts—is shaped, forged, or born—it is partaking of the Arian phase of its existence. Aries gives no thought to how anything should continue or maintain itself, not even to how it should grow; initiation is all. Once started, however, the organism needs to sustain itself, protect itself, and feed itself. In short, it needs to ensure that its own requirements are met, and to provide a safe environment for its continued existence.

This self-protecting, self-nourishing, growing phase is what Taurus is all about. Taurean energies are those directed towards providing security and nourishment for the self. Only when this phase is fully completed, and all is secure, can the organism start to take an interest in the world outside, and consider communicating with other organisms—and that communicative phase is Gemini.

From this sequence of signs you can see how the Taurean has his place in the cycle, and you will no doubt recognize a few of the deeper facets of the Taurean character in the sequence too. Taureans would rather do anything than give up and start again. Starting things is the last thing they want to do, and the last thing they will ever consider as a course of action. It is because the idea of starting is Aries, and it is behind them in the cycle; they feel that starting over again would be a backward step. As a last resort they will consider it. Every sign considers the activities of the sign behind it as the emergencies-only, against-their-better-judgement course of action. Conversely, Taureans aren't usually very good at putting their thoughts into words, and would dearly love to have the verbal dexterity of the Gemini. To all signs, the qualities of the next sign on in the cycle seem irresistibly glamorous. It's not that Taureans don't think much; it's rather that they don't talk much. Sometimes they don't know what they think, but they know what they feel, which is an organic process, done with the whole body, rather than just inside the head.

The Taurean measures himself by what he can touch or feel. His instrument of discernment is not his mind, but his five senses—in particular taste and touch. When you are surrounded by things which you know are yours and are likely to remain so, then you are comfortable. A Taurean likes to know where his next meal is coming from, and where he is likely to rest his head this evening—in fact, they are his main concerns. An ever-changing world where things are never the same twice, and where the most recent things become rapidly out of date, is upsetting for the Taurean mind.

Let us look at the Taurean approach to the world from three key points of view. Taken together, they will show you the whole of what a Taurean tries to do with his world. These points of view are stability, possession, and nourishment.

*Stability* is absolutely essential for your happiness, Taurus. As the first earth sign of the zodiac, your roots and where you live are of prime importance to you. You can reassure yourself about the rightness of your existence if you know where you are; familiar surroundings enable you to orientate yourself properly. If you are in strange surroundings, or for some reason your usual routines are disrupted, then you start to worry, and the old uncertainties about where your next meal is coming from start to surface. You define yourself in relation to your surroundings, so if the surroundings are unfamiliar to you, then you don't know who you are. It's as simple as that.

You are obviously going to try to maintain stability in your life and circumstances, if only to maintain some sort of consistency in your view of yourself. Don't forget that you are a fixed sign, and they are the ones which like to keep things, as far as possible, just the way they are, even if they are not particularly favourable; change is always seen as something to be avoided (yet at the same time rather dangerous and exciting, because it is a quality of the next sign on, as we noticed earlier). This desire to be rooted in the earth, to be in the same place for ever, like a tree, can lead to some problems in itself. You could get blown over by a wind, killed by a drought, or cut down by a woodcutter; in other words, you cannot adapt to changing circumstances, nor do you

move when it would be in your interest to do so. Other people see
this insistence on stability as sheer stubbornness, though on
good days they will be quick to label you as constant and
dependable, too.

   *Possession* follows on from the desire for stability. The best
way to make unfamiliar things familiar is to own them; over a
period of time you can get used to them, and feel secure in their
possession. If they are yours, they are not likely to be taken away
again or wander off, and this adds to their stable status in your
mind. Consequently, a Taurean likes to acquire things, and
enjoys the things he owns. Since you see yourself in the things
you own, and since you define yourself by your surroundings,
you are likely to have a very comfortable and well-furnished
home, and enjoy being in it. Other zodiac types use their homes
to live in or to work in, but only you use it as an extension of
yourself. You are like your home, and it is like you; friends and
guests will be able to see your character very clearly from the
decoration and furnishings, which they cannot so easily do in a
non-Taurean house. Of course, you are equally keen to possess
and make stable all the intangibles in your life, too; this means
that you are very possessive of your loved ones, and will be
deeply wounded by any separation. If someone in whom you
have placed a lot of trust and affection goes out of your life, you
feel insecure, because things have become unstable again, and
your emotional stability and nourishment have been interrupted.
As you no doubt know, this can grow into jealousy and a
suffocating possessiveness; on the other hand, your loyalty,
devotion, and unwavering constancy are the envy of anyone
who wishes that love was, for them at least, for keeps. It certainly
is for you.

   *Nourishment* is essential to the Taurean. Where the Arian uses
his body as a vehicle for his energy, the Taurean uses his body to
live in; it has to be kept going, and all its requirements met. Food
is more than just something to eat; for you, it is a reminder that
you have a physical existence, and that you are maintaining it.
This in turn is reassuring, and so the feeling of stability and
security is reinforced. You eat well, and you like eating; not

surprisingly, you take great interest in food, and make it reflect your opinion of yourself, as you do with everything you own. After all, if you ate rubbish, it would show what a low opinion of yourself you had, wouldn't it? To reassure and remind yourself, you make sure that what you eat is to your taste, and of high quality. Emotional nourishment is attended to in the same way, as are bodily comforts. Taureans like to be liked; it provides emotional nourishment, and a form of reassurance.

You can see how stability, possession, and nourishment all work together to the same end—security. Whatever a Taurus does is towards this ultimate end.

Physically, the sign corresponds to the throat and neck. This seems a little odd until you think about it. The neck supports the head, which is the important bit of your body; the idea of support is very Taurean. The throat contains the tubes through which you take in food, water, and air; nourishment of every kind, in fact. There you will find also some of the glands whose work is to stabilize and maintain the whole of the body as it grows. All very Taurean. Glandular diseases are, not surprisingly, common to Taureans who have to deal with too much instability at once. There are other considerations to take into account when discussing diseases, though, and some of them are examined in 'The Year within Each Day' (p.437).

Taureans often have thick necks, but they also have lovely voices, because that's where their larynx is. Many of them sing well, and most of them are musical, because music is soothing to listen to; a familiar aural environment, this time!

To sum up, if you want a single picture which encapsulates the spirit of Taurus, look no further than the zodiac picture of the bull. Fierce when roused, very territorial, but quite content to live in his field and munch the grass unless disturbed. Leave him alone and he's very happy with things as they are.

## Early, Middle or Late? The Decanates

*First decanate (20–29 April)*
This is the purest form of Taurus, where there is a double helping

of Venus's energies, seeking everything that is amenable and pleasant. Early Taureans are the most comfort-loving of the sign, and the ones with the greatest liking for anything soft. Soft clothes in soft fabrics which have a pleasant feel to them are appealing to you; it is the direct, tangible reassurance of a comforting substance which Venus would like you to appreciate. You are also the most artistic and discerning in your tastes, compared to the other two decanates. Taureans have a very good sense of colour and design, and the influence of Venus is going to make sure that you never have two clashing colours close together. Venus will also make you the Taurean who is the most appreciative of his food; you will spend much time in its preparation.

Emotionally, you are likely to need a lot of reassurance, and will be overly fond of anyone who offers you comfort and companionship. You don't like arguing with people, even if you know that you are right, and will not be swayed from your point of view; the emotional disturbance generated by an argument of any kind is something which you just can't bear.

*Second decanate (30 April–10 May)*
This time Venus gets a little help from Mercury, and the intense feeling of softness and vulnerability is moderated to some extent. Mercury will help the mind and wit of this Taurean, so that these middle-of-the-sign bulls are the clearest-thinking of the sign, as well as being the ones with the best-developed sense of humour. Taureans aren't very verbal people at the best of times, but here those faculties are given a helping hand. The voice of the Taurean is at its best here, too.

Taurus is an earth sign, of course, and any material whatsoever is earthy by element. In this section of the sign, skills in working with any material come to the fore; Taureans who work with wood or metal, or those who like to use their Venusian sensibilities and work with food or furnishings, have an extra talent and facility given by Mercury in the central decanate of the sign.

Money is important to Taureans, too: it is something to

acquire in itself, it can be used to acquire other things, and its possession gives security. Skill in the handling and acquisition of money also comes from Mercury to this decanate.

*Third decanate (11–21 May)*
The first decanate was receptive and comforting—the 'nourishment' mentioned earlier. The second decante is to do with acquisition and possession, and the use to which material is put. The last one is to do with possession and stability, and the maintenance of things in their positions. It is Taurus at its most solid and powerful; people with the Sun here don't need the comfort and reassurance that the earlier ones do, but they will do everything they can to hang on to whatever it is that they have. These are the Taureans who suffer long and hard rather than give up or change direction; these are the ones it is dangerous to goad into eventual action, because they are strong and angry defenders of what they see as their own. They take life seriously, with a strongly developed sense of duty. They get on with what they have to do without complaint, and when offered something different by way of diversion or entertainment, they will make sure that they have finished all their work first, and that all is secure and taken care of before they let themselves relax a little. Perhaps it is because they are at the end of the sign that they feel they have so much to do before the next sign comes along!

## Three Phases of Life: Taurus as Child, Adult, Parent

*The Taurean child*
The Taurean child is the one who gave rise to that overworked description of the moderate achiever at school—'he is a plodder'. It is true that Taurean children do plod, but they are thorough, and what they have learned, they remember for ever. They cannot be rushed; they assimilate things at their own pace, and do not move on to a new subject until the old one is thoroughly familiar and well known. Until the Taurean child feels that a certain technique or piece of knowledge has been

examined from all angles, is familiar, and is unlikely to offer him any surprises when he returns to it, he will not move on. This rate of progress makes him a little slower than the rest of his class, but his sense of duty keeps him working in an attempt to keep up—hence the title of plodder, since he will always appear to be working very hard, yet will never make the rapid progress that other children do from time to time when a subject really interests them.

Taurean children are apt to be heavily built, and this can lead to some teasing at school. Unfortunately, since they represent by their very youthfulness the beginning of the sign (see first decanate, above, for the qualities peculiar to this end of the sign), they will compensate for their emotional discomfort by overeating, which can lead to health problems. Their heavy physique means that they seldom excel at individual sports, but their sense of duty, solidity, and support can make them useful members of sporting teams—they make very good second-row forwards in rugby!

Any artistic talents must be encouraged. All Taureans have them, and they must be noticed and nurtured when they show in the child.

These children are possessive, like their parents. They are unwilling to share their toys, books, or money with their friends, and they can get very jealous and resentful of affection transferred from them to a sibling or friend. They should be encouraged to be more open and generous—you won't change their essential nature, but you may stop them becoming obsessive at an early age!

*The Taurean adult*
The Taurean adult is solid and reliable, but never innovative or a motivator of others. He is careful to weigh things up before he makes a decision, and when the decision is made, he knows that it is based on all the available information. All this seems most laudable, but outsiders should note two things: firstly, the course of action decided upon will be the one which introduces the fewest new elements or procedures into the Taurean's

established routine, and which involves him in no loss of position or possession at all; and secondly, the course of action decided upon is not modifiable in any way at all, even if new circumstances merit a serious rethink. The Taurean will admit neither of these things, but they need to be taken into account.

A resistance to change, and an unwillingness to modify their point of view, can mean that they are rapidly overtaken by events, and are not really at home in situations where they have to think quickly to react to a constantly changing challenge. They will make their own territory wherever they are, and do their job in it in their own way, oblivious of any new developments outside. The routine that they generate for themselves is itself a form of security for them. Anything which requires a steady effort over a long period is ideal for the Taurean; he possesses a stamina and an ability to apply himself over the long period which no other sign can match, and easily outlasts the Fire and Air signs.

Although not mean or miserly, Taureans do not throw money away. They spend it freely, but it is to their own benefit rather than anybody else's. When they keep money, it is for their own security rather than so that the world can see how rich they must be. Taureans enjoy their wealth directly and for themselves, which is what sets them apart from Capricorns in this respect.

### The Taurean parent

A Taurean parent is very protective. He tries always to provide a stable and comfortable environment for his child, where every one of the child's needs are met. Since the adult knows how important it is to him to have the security of his home and surroundings, he feels that the child must surely have these needs too and it is his duty to provide them. He also wants the child to appreciate all that his parent has done for him, a process which he sees as emotional reassurance for both of them. If the child rebels at all, or spurns the parent's generosity, then it is the parent who is upset, because there is an immediate instability as the child leaves, coupled with a loss of possession as the child takes with him all the time and emotional energy the parent invested in him. These displays of independence are usual in any home, but they are devastating to the Taurean parent, who needs to tell himself that this is only to be expected, and a natural process.

Taurean parents spoil their children with material comforts, and feed them handsomely: 'mother's apple pie' is really something if your mother is Taurean. As they get older, Taurean parents become more and more accustomed to their home routines, so the noise and disruption generated by teenage children is very wearing on them: they find children as infants much more rewarding. Letting go of their children when they have had them for so long, so to speak, is the hardest thing Taurean parents ever do.

# Gemini

The sign before Gemini is Taurus. The Taurean individual is concerned to maintain himself in his environment by making sure that his physical needs are met. He makes sure that he has food, shelter, money enough for his needs, and by using his five senses, defines himself in terms of his surroundings. All activity is directed inwards—'collecting', as we said when considering the zodiac. When these needs are met, and the individual is no longer concerned with his physical survival to the same extent, he begins to take note of whatever else there is in the world. He becomes aware of his ability to deal with more than one project at a time, and how his viewpoint changes if he himself moves around. This business of mental assessment and movement is what characterizes Gemini. In addition, he becomes aware of other people, and recognizes them as different from himself. He can impose his thoughts on their way of thinking, and vice versa—by speaking to them. This interactive process of thought and word, the whole concept of communication, is also at the core of Gemini. As time goes on, the individual will develop a series of opinions about things, built up from the responses gained from his questions and conversations. These opinions then shape his perception and guide his emotion: personality becomes apparent where there was none before. This stage, the formation of emotional response, is what Gemini grows into, and is the business of the next sign, Cancer.

From this sequence of signs you can see how the Gemini has his place in the cycle, and perhaps understand why the Gemini behaves as he does. He has no need to see things through to the end, because his concern is the assessment of the idea, and its communication. Concrete results, or the final stages of anything, are not what he is about. The need to compare one thing to another, to see the other point of view, is what makes the Gemini interested in more than one thing at once, and always interested in something new. Unless you have two things to compare, you cannot function properly, and it is worth remembering that. You work by contrasting two or more points of view. Your mind is like a hologram, taking in all sorts of information from all sorts of sources, and then selecting parts of it to build a full picture from a given point of view.

Biologically, Gemini corresponds to the logical part of the brain, the nervous system, and the respiratory system. You can see Mutable Air in the action of the lungs; oxygen in, carbon dioxide out. The assignment of the brain and nervous system to Gemini isn't hard to understand either. Movement and thought are the keys to Gemini existence; the nervous system links the two. An individual always functions in a similar way to the parts of his body assigned to his sign: again, this is worth remembering.

How does all this show in daily life? Primarily through your communicative abilities. Only you can speak with such speed and fluency. Speech is a form of exercise for you: it gives you a chance to use your brain. Perhaps surprisingly, your memory isn't as good as that of some other signs, and this is because you need new information all the time, rather than holding the old stuff. Unless a thing holds your interest, you cannot remember it, and you have made sure that nothing holds your interest for very long by actively seeking new input the whole time. At any given moment, you are very interested indeed in whatever you are doing; indeed, you give it your fullest attention, which is a lot more than most people think of, as we will see in a little while.

Like a newspaper, you are loud and passionate on the matters of the moment, but have no interest at all in what happened yesterday. Tomorrow interests you greatly, because it promises to be new and different from today, but only for that; the idea of planning for tomorrow suggests forethought, and you have none of that either. Like the Arian, you are an instantaneous person, living in the present instant, like a single nervous impulse from your brain to your muscles. Nerves carry thought, but they don't have memory, and they don't remember what they did last time—at least, not often.

Gemini is a double sign. There are two twins in the picture in the stars, and I have lost count of the number of Geminis who have said to me 'I'm a Gemini; there are two of me—I must be schizophrenic!' This well-worn quip brings out two more facets of the Gemini mind. Firstly, that Geminis do have more than one way of seeing things the whole time, and secondly, that they don't think much of astrology. There are two reasons for this, too: astrology can seem to suggest a world where everything is known beforehand. A Gemini wouldn't want that, because it would remove the possibility of novelty, and seriously disrupt the way he performs his thinking. If he couldn't think, he couldn't live. Secondly, astrology is quite complicated, and requires some study. A Gemini wouldn't like that either, because he finds the process of hard learning tedious. There are no changes in something you learn by heart—obviously, because that's why you do it—but that is precisely why it is so hard for the Gemini to do. He hates the idea of repetition, and of being static; hard learning sounds like both at once to him.

The idea of communication, especially argument, where the same idea is modified as it goes back and forth, is ideal for the Gemini mind. So is something that works as a communication on more than one level, and even more so if the second level reverses the direction of the transaction, as in, for example, cheating at cards. As a result of this, all forms of buying and selling are Geminian, and the Gemini's mind seems to be able to work simultaneously on all the levels of the process. It is being able to see the deal from both ends at once that amuses him so—

especially if, as in a dishonest agreement, he is in effect being paid twice for the same sale. This delight in the underhand, with its accompanying skill in all forms of deception, is what gives rise to the popular accusation that all Geminis are liars and criminals, and that even the honest ones are schizophrenic. It isn't so: but considerable effort is needed by the other eleven signs to understand how the Gemini's way of thinking actually functions, and it is frequently misunderstood.

Mental arithmetic is, of course, easy for this sort of mind. What isn't easy is anything like a considered response, or any expression of the emotions. The Gemini assesses things mentally with himself as the assessor, impartial, and to one side; he never develops a personal opinion about what he experiences. Emotions are therefore at rather a low level, and are mistrusted because they can't be neatly analysed like numbers or words; also, they imply belief, which is something that comes over time, and the Gemini refuses to give time to things in case he gets set in his ways. Lack of practice with his emotions makes him clumsy and uncomfortable with what emotional responses he has, and they do not develop the strength and power of those of the other signs. Emotions seem untrustworthy things to a Gemini; fascinating, and worth thinking about, but too suggestive of caring and staying put, which are, of course, Taurean traits. Every sign hates being like the sign before; it makes you feel as though you're not making any progress! This lack of skill in his emotional life makes the Gemini rather cool sexually; he would rather have a lively intellectual friendship. After all, it's not his body that his energy acts through; it's his mind.

The Gemini makes sure that he is in circulation. He likes to be with young people rather than old, and with people who talk readily rather than quiet types. What he is doing is to ensure that he gets plenty of new material to think about, and can change that into his own opinions for later communication. This process is very much akin to the function of the lungs in breathing, and the Gemini has to work this way. If a Gemini cannot circulate properly, then he develops lung trouble, because the body system that is related to his planetary energy will be the first to show any difficulties in properly expressing that energy. There is some more about this in 'The Year within Each Day' (p. 437).

In short, a Gemini looks, reads, listens; thinks; and says what he thinks. If he cannot do these things, he cannot function properly. He cannot, and will not, do anything more, or anything less.

## Early, Middle or Late? The Decanates

*First decanate (22–31 May)*
This is the purest form of Gemini. There is a double helping of Mercury's energy here, and so the energy in this third of the sign is concentrated in those areas where Mercury acts best: mental activity and verbal processes. All forms of rational thought are highly developed if you are from this part of the sign, and you will have a great talent for any kind of analytical activity. Have you ever thought about being a lawyer? Do you like arguing about the finer points of the rules, applying them to this or that situation? Do you always argue about the offside rule when watching Match of the Day? It is all the same thing; Mercury is showing you how to examine the point at issue, and making sure that you win your argument. Teaching is to do with this section of the sign, too, and school of any kind, whether as pupil, teacher, or even the building. The Gemini link is obvious: transmission of knowledge. Early Geminis seem to like a school atmosphere; many of them find themselves involved in a teaching or training role in later life, because it is so suited to their Mercury energies.

This early part of the sign concerns itself with any short-distance communication or transaction; therefore shops, trading, and the mechanics of buying and selling anything are at their peak here, where Mercury is doubled. It is worth noting that all these double-Mercury activities are empty of emotional content, and can be performed effectively without getting involved in a personal sense. Compare them to the next section to see what I mean.

*Second decanate (1–10 June)*
Here the purely mental faculties of Mercury are modified by the influence of Venus, and the Gemini mind turns away from noting the differences in things, to note the similarities instead. This is the friendliest section of Gemini, the one which is keen to meet and chatter to as many people as possible, so that every day has some conversation (and some gossip) in it. This is also where Gemini becomes involved with his immediate family, especially his brothers and sisters. Siblings, as opposed to your parents or more remote relatives, are particularly assigned to Gemini in astrological practice, and those of you belonging to this section of the sign will find that your brothers and sisters play an important role in your life. For those of you in business, this section of the sign is best suited for making agreements and contracts rather than buying and selling. It's to do with finding similarities rather than differences again.

*Third decanate (11–20 June)*
Here Mercury is joined by Saturn to give a forward and outward looking frame of mind, coupled with an interest in technology and a sense of space and distance. If you want a mental image for this decanate, it is either the international telephone system or an air mail letter. Long-distance communication is in this sector, and the distance can be in time as well as space: creative Geminis, communicating to people they may never see, are here, including a few composers and poets – Richard Strauss and W. B. Yeats, the actors Basil Rathbone and Errol Flynn, whose work and reputation survive them, and quite a few who made their name in publishing. Radio and television are part of this sector of Gemini, too; wherever there is an opportunity to speak to lots of people at once, the late Gemini finds himself at home. Unlike the first two decanates, here the scale of the operation is important; the more, the merrier.

# Three Phases of Life: Gemini as Child, Adult, Parent

*The Gemini child*

A Gemini person, of any age, never stops being the Gemini child. Childhood, as opposed to infancy, is very much a Gemini time of life, and the adult Gemini will always be a schoolboy at heart. Gemini children are quick to learn, but slow to remember; they enjoy anything that is new, but they never seem to have the patience that is necessary to master things fully. The Gemini ability to do more than one thing at a time is almost constantly on display in this child, who can eat, read a comic, watch television, listen to a record and have a conversation with his sister all at the same time — and really follow each of those activities, which many adults never understand. A problem from the parent's point of view is that children have a much shorter attention span than adults, and Mercury's speed makes the Gemini child bored with any one activity in a matter of minutes. If not channelled, Mercury's energy can lead to tension and strain in the child. In many ways, the child must sort this out for himself; as he gets older, he will find his own ways of providing the mental stimulation he requires. Emotional problems in a child with a highly placed Mercury influence, such as a Gemini, often show through Mercury's organs, the lungs; asthma is common.

Linguistic ability is very high, so this should be encouraged; patience and stamina are very low, and while some emphasis should be placed on these qualities to help them develop, it is useless to pretend that a Gemini can be taught to do things slowly and steadily. They can't, and it is unnatural for them to try to do otherwise. They work in fits and starts, progressing quickly when the mood takes them; they never do things any other way.

*The Gemini adult*

The Gemini adult, like adults from the other eleven signs, spends his life trying to arrange the circumstances of his life to suit his essential planetary energy. This leads him to develop, more than anything else, his ingenuity.

Gemini needs a number of things to keep him busy. If he has a full-time job, it will be one where he has to think a lot, and where the problems are constantly changing. Even if it is always the same kind of problem, then there need to be a lot of them to solve for the Gemini to feel happy. If the job tends to move in slow phases, with each stage of the project taking several months, then the Gemini will soon be looking for something a little faster-moving. Ideally he would like a job where he thinks a lot, chats a lot, where each phase lasts about a fortnight, and where he has plenty of time left over, somehow, to do other things which interest him.

If this isn't possible, then a part-time job, or, much better, two part-time jobs, will delight him. Even then, he is likely to want something to fill in the spare moments, so an absorbing hobby will be found. In time, this will be adapted so that it makes money (the idea of being paid for enjoying yourself amuses the Gemini; it is no effort for him, and the fact that money changes hands interests him greatly) to supplement whatever he makes normally.

What Gemini needs is variety and mental exercise, and he usually knows how to provide them. What most people don't notice is how hard he tries to avoid either being personally involved with his work, or having responsibility. Geminis only achieve high office, as a rule, by working for themselves; they are not really 'company men'. This is because responsibility, to them, suggests lack of variety, and lack of movement. So they avoid it.

Our society congratulates those who achieve prominence in large organizations, while passing over those who do not; it never occurs to anyone to look for those who deliberately take the opposite track. This suits Geminis fine: they are trying to amuse themselves, not anybody else, and they remain invisible while doing so, not to mention quite well paid. Ingenious, yes?

*The Gemini parent*
Gemini parents suffer from a reverse generation gap. They are so interested in what their children are doing, and so eager to join

in, that the children resent it.

Children need to feel that their parents are at a considerable distance from them, both in speed of mind and in their interests too. Astrology thinks of children and parents in terms of Mercury and Saturn, not two Mercuries! (Page 23 will remind you about Saturn.) Gemini parents feel that they are just the same as their children, which the children, especially if they are not Geminis, will be at pains to disprove.

The Geminian parent provides plenty of activity for his children to be involved in, but becomes dissatisfied if the child doesn't want to join in. Perhaps the child is a little slower than the parent; if the child were a Taurus, for instance, then this would be the case. A Gemini parent will be exasperated by any apparent disability on the part of the child to do with reading and speech. There are other talents, you know. In addition, Mercury will make the parent analyse and criticize the child's efforts; it is far harder for a Gemini to express approval of something as a whole than to pick out some flaw in it, but that is what a child needs from its parent quite a lot of the time.

Finally, those about to become Geminian parents should not forget that Gemini is the sign of the twins; you may need to buy two of everything!

# Cancer

The sign before Cancer is Gemini. In Gemini, the individual is concerned to notice things, think about them, and communicate his thoughts; he is eager to express the fact that he can think, and is able to assess his surroundings. He has noticed that there are other people in the world than himself, and he wants to see what they think about things, hence the communication that Geminis hold as their own special talent. Cancer is the next stage: assessing the reply. When the responses have been assessed, the individual is able to see how they affect his point of view: he forms an emotional response to his surroundings. After a while, he relies on his feelings more than his thoughts, and trusts to intuitive processes more than rational ones. This is

Cancer. For Cancer, it is the emotions which are used to define the world. Emotional nourishment is needed, and actively sought. Relationships with the immediate family are used to provide a secure base for all the emotional requirements, leading to the development of feelings of caring, nurture, and belonging. All of these are the essential business of the Cancer phase of the zodiacal circle.

When the emotions are secure, confidence builds, and then the individual can act as a source of sustenance in himself for those around him. This is Leo, the next sign on from Cancer. As you can see, the sequence is one where emotions are formed and recognized, later to be output to others (in Leo); and where the sphere of interest widens from one individual, or perhaps two (Gemini) through a family group (Cancer) to a social group (Leo).

A Cancerian, you will remember from page 17, is 'collecting, and defining emotion'. There seems to be a paradox here: how can something as intangible as inward-flowing emotional energy (which is how we defined the element Water) have such a powerful and assertive word as 'defining' applied to it? Easy: the water springs from inside. It is the Cancerian who is the source and origin of the emotions he feels; everything that he comes into contact with causes more emotion to well up. It is not communicated; it does not flow in steady streams for the benefit of everybody else at large, but is kept inside until needed. Cancerians worry a great deal: to follow the analogy of the water, it is stored in underground reservoirs. Where the emotional energy is released, it appears as a caring impulse, the maternal instinct.

Biologically, Cancer corresponds to the stomach, and to the early stages of digestion (where food is responded to by gastric juices), and to the breasts. The relationship between the maternal urge, an outflow of self-generated emotion, the element of Water, and mother's milk isn't hard to understand.

There is a possessive side to a Cancerian; they are supposed to be moody and sensitive to hurt, yet they are also said to be protective and difficult to understand. All of these observations become more credible if the underlying motivation is examined.

Since the Cancerian is seeking emotional stability and nourishment, he is bound to be protective of himself and his family,
since they are what comforts him, and they need him to protect
them in return. The flow of emotional interdependence round a
family group is as real as the flow of the bloodstream to a
Cancerian, and he needs emotional input of the reassuring
variety as much as he needs to be able to output that energy in
caring for something. The water flow needs to be maintained.
Anything from outside which threatens to interrupt these
essential activities is resisted. It is not in the Cancerian nature to
counter-attack; the energy flow would have to be outgoing for
that to be the case. Instead, there is absolute resistance. Once a
Cancerian is resisting, then there is no way to move him other
than by destroying him. You can't get into a crab except with a
hammer, and that destroys the crab.

The Cancerian, then, is very possessive, but not of material
things. It is important to realize this. There will be many material
things to which he is very attached, but their value is not in what
they are or what they are worth, or even what their use is, so
much as the sentimental value they hold. The Cancerian is not
what he owns, like the Taurian, or what he is seen to own, like the
Capricorn, but what he feels. He will sacrifice all his belongings,
if he has to; he will not sacrifice the people he loves.

Cancerian moodiness and over-sensitivity is simply due to an
instinct for self-preservation. If every outside influence is
known to produce an emotional response in the Cancerian, then
he stays away from those things which affect his emotions in a
way that he doesn't like. It is exactly the same as not eating those
things which you know will upset your stomach.

One of the keys to understanding the way a Cancerian thinks,
and how private he is, is to think of him as a box, or container.
Whatever is inside the box, he regards as his, and cares for it. In
return he is given emotional nourishment by the familiar and
friendly responses of those he cares for. Everything that is
outside the box he will resist, presenting an impassive and
enduring exterior to the world; he is both protecting his own
possessions and resisting any unwanted intrusions into his

security and privacy. From the outside the box can look uninviting and uninteresting, especially to the outgoing signs, who tend to like organisms which, like themselves, radiate their energy to others. The inside of the box is warm and cosy, full of life and love. The alternative use of the box, where the outside is highly decorated, but the inside is empty, is found in Capricorn, the sign opposite to you.

To sum up, the Cancerian really is a lot like the animal in the zodiac picture, the crab. He is armoured against the world on the outside, to protect the essential parts within, which are soft and vulnerable. He is snappy when threatened, but unable to move very quickly to turn the situation to his advantage. When he does move, it is sideways, to avoid direct confrontation and action. Like the hermit crab, he is tied to his home environment, and likes it that way. His environment is water; it passes through him and around him the whole time, and he takes his nourishment from it.

## Early, Middle or Late? The Decanates

*First decanate (21–30 June)*
This is the purest form of Cancer. There is a double helping of lunar energy here, and the emphasis is very much on the intuitive side of things. All sentiment and memory, plus combinations of the two, such as nostalgia, spring from this sector of the sign, and if your birthday is here, then the sentimental side of your character should be strongly developed. Allied to this is the sense of belonging and security that comes from being safe at home; this decanate is also assigned everything to do with hearth and home, so your own home is probably very cosy and much loved, somewhere that you feel is your retreat from the rest of the world. Motherhood and the feminine side of one's nature is, of course, a lunar thing, so with the Moon doubly active here, you should feel the urge to care for things and look after their needs as one of the most powerful you have. Do you look after stray kittens and sparrows with broken wings? On a slightly higher level, this lunar influence will show

in an intuitive way of thinking, and a defensive attitude to go with it. That means that you know when you are right, because it feels right; but you don't know why it is so, though you're going to do it that way anyway. No amount of persuasion will deter you from these intuitive, internal, decisions. That's lunar energy.

*Second decanate (1–11 July)*
Here the lunar energy is modified by that of Mars, giving a different frame of reference for all those internal emotions. There is a great feeling of tradition, history, and family in this decanate; the feeling that you are responsible for the creatures in your care is replaced by a feeling that you are responsible for the care of the traditions, history, and belongings of the family. You are likely to feel that you are the present holder of the office, so to speak, and that the care and continuance of the family's history is up to you. You are probably fascinated by what your grandparents did. Perhaps your home is furnished with some pieces of furniture from your mother's house, or your grand-mother's; the sense of the family going back over the years is important to you, and provides both a sense of identity and a purpose for the future. You have a high regard for history, and particularly value old family possessions.

The Cancerian caring impulse here is not limited to the individual mother-and-child relationship of one generation, as it was in the first decanate; it is extended throughout time, both backwards into history and forwards into the future. These Cancerians are also fascinated by death and the processes of the end of life; to them, it is one of the joining links between generations of the same family—the other link being birth, of course, which is again a Cancerian matter.

*Third decanate (12–22 July)*
The final decanate has the Moon's energies blended with those of Jupiter. Instead of extending the range of the caring impulse in time, as in the second decanate, it is extended in space. It looks to structures and properties; to organizations and large groups, especially large family groups; and to all definite

structures and sets of rules. This decanate, and the people whose birthdays fall in it, looks upwards rather than down, whereas the first decanate looked inwards, and the second looked back rather than forwards. Here the Cancerian mind is trying to protect against unknown future threats by making solid defences. The Law, or any set of rules, is part of this way of thinking: if everybody keeps to the rules, then nobody should get hurt, and the Law is there to protect the helpless from harm. That's how the late Cancerian sees it. There is a need to see that things are properly and fairly set out, so that they will last, and be both secure and protective to their users—this is the prime concern of those born in this decanate. They take pride in their houses, especially their foundations: by now you can see why.

## Three Phases of Life: Cancer as Child, Adult, Parent

### The Cancerian child

The Cancerian child can look after himself, and in fact always does so—but in the opposite way to what that opening phrase implies. He goes through his early years carefully testing and feeling his way through life, with a deep distrust of whatever is new and potentially harmful to him. He is not at all adventurous— it is not in his nature to be so—and he sometimes has to be made to leave the house to go outside and play. He is always going to be concerned for his own security, and will flinch from anything which makes him at all uncertain of his safety or of whether he is going to like it. Cancerian children worry a great deal, mainly because early life offers so much that is new and different, with so many situations and behaviour patterns to be learned. If you remember that the Cancerian child will always try to give the right replies so that a positive emotional response is gained, then you will appreciate the difficulty in learning so many at once. The Cancerian child cannot 'play it by ear' or 'just be himself'; he is acutely conscious of what others think of him, and of the reaction they show to him. When troubled or unsure, he will always try to return to a familiar situation; often this means at home, close to a parent, and with a favourite object.

The older Cancerian child makes a perfect watchdog for his younger brothers and sisters; he can always see the danger in a deep pond, for example, or a busy road, and will make sure that the younger ones come to no harm, if only because he himself would not take such risks.

At school, Cancerian children are good at subjects which require retention, poor at those requiring expression; on the whole, then, they are good at history, poor at art and drama. They are not great team sportsmen; boisterous physical contact sports, such as rugby, may seem too hazardous to them.

### The Cancerian adult

By the time he is an adult, the Cancerian is quite practised at maintaining the ebb and flow of his emotions. Most of the time he keeps his emotions down under the surface, showing them only to those few individuals whom he trusts, and for whom he cares. He finds these people to be both a source and an outlet for emotional energies, and they are necessary for his continued health and well-being. He has a range of activities in which he feels 'comfortable'; by this he means that they are satisfying, that he can manage them without too much trouble, and they do not either threaten him or demand an excessive emotional reaction from him. If these needs are met, there is no reason for a Cancerian to seek out anything new to occupy him; if he does so, it is because he is being pushed. The push can be from external influences, or, if apparently self-motivated, from other planetary energies beside Cancerian ones; but the pure Cancerian would never seek outside challenge from a sense of adventure or boredom. (There is no such thing as a pure Cancerian, of course, nor a pure example of any other sign; when the Sun was in Cancer, the other planets were in other signs, making you an individual mixture; see the fifth part of the book.)

What the adult Cancerian looks for in his life is a secure situation that he can put roots down into and make his base. He tends to find this in a large organization; Cancerian entrepreneurs are rare indeed. Once in that organization, they work well; they abide by its rules, acquire areas of influence for themselves, look after those who are beneath them, and generally rise fairly quickly. They are the perfect company employees, and are often the ones who go from tea-boy to Managing Director within the same company. There are a surprising number of Cancerian generals and admirals: it is true that the armed forces are not exactly a caring profession, but they have a well-defined structure, and usually have a plan for any eventuality—and it is this internal security which attracts the Cancerian.

## The Cancerian parent

Cancerian parents are very caring and loving; they need little instruction in how to look after anything. They are masters at creating the warm home environment a child needs in his early years, and the child will never be deprived of affection and protection from parents such as these.

As the child grows, the Cancerian parent finds himself in a rather difficult position. He is still extending feelings of love and care towards the child, and will always do so, but he is threatened by the child's growing sense of individuality and independence. Cancerians always want things to stay in a stable pattern, and regard the home as the one place that this can be guaranteed to occur; a child who has his own ideas is a source of disruption to this pattern from within the home—a very worrying problem for the Cancerian parent. Cancerian parents worry as much for their children as they do for themselves; it always seems to escape them that children are fairly indestructible items with a strong instinct for self-preservation. Indeed, if this instinct is switched off by an over-protective home environment, then the child of Cancerian parents is considerably more at risk when outside the home than other children.

Cancerian fathers stabilize their emotional responses and opinions early, and so there is considerable 'generation gap' difficulty with teenage children. Cancerian mothers are rather better at this, identifying with the home rather than with the child and becoming serene matriarchs as the generations of their families unfold below them.

# Leo

The sign before Leo is Cancer. Cancer represents that stage of a person's existence where they want to be sure of themselves, and do everything possible for reassurance, or to guard their personal security. They feel that they are likely to be attacked, confronted, or asked to do impossible things at any moment, and they are sure that they will find such tasks beyond their capabilities. Only when the individual is quite secure in himself, and confident in his abilities, does the next phase begin; this is Leo.

Leo has the confidence in himself that the Cancerian lacks. He knows he can do things, and knows, too, that he is the best person to do them. He makes himself the centre of things, and makes sure everybody knows his position, then proceeds to play things his way.

The Leo phase is concerned with being in control, but also with being the instigator as well. It is the difference between being a commander and being a mere manager; words that imply a sense of action, command, and being the principal person are all Leonine in their feeling. Leos are kings, rulers, generals, emperors; they are leading lights, superstars, grandmasters, conductors of the orchestra. It is an essential part of the Leo experience to be addressed in terms of respect, using a title which shows recognition of the Leo's place at the centre of things.

The orchestral conductor is a particularly good example. The conductor is the one whose interpretation of the work is being expressed by the musicians. He organizes, leads, and conducts them, but he does none of the actual playing. He is seen as the focus of the performance: the applause is directed to, and received by, him. He inspires the performance; he is its originator, centre, and focus. What he does not do, however, is write the music (for this example, anyway) or play any of the instruments. Yet the players address him as 'Maestro', and his name is given billing of equal magnitude as that of the composer, if not more.

Why? Because he is taking the role of the Leo. He takes an existing situation (the music) and makes it his own. He is the heart of the performance. Energy radiates out from him as he inspires the other performers to work together in the expression of his vision of the music. Leos are always the inspiration of their group. They can put enthusiasm into others. They know it will all be worth it in the end. They have confidence in themselves, their abilities, and their vision.

The sheer radiance of a Leo's energy makes it difficult to see behind the source of the light: being dazzled is all too easy. Careful thought, though, shows up one or two things. Leos are quite confident about what they can do, but they are nothing like so confident about things that they haven't tried; this leads them to stick with the things they know well, and to dismiss new ideas as unimportant, as long as they think they can get away with it. As a Leo, you will have been enraged by the last sentence: how dare I suggest that there is anything you can't do! Everybody is wary of unfamiliar things, you will say. Not so: even among the other Fire signs, Sagittarius will try new things from pure curiosity, without thinking about whether he can succeed or not, while Aries will attempt anything at all, simply because the idea of not succeeding does not enter his head. *You* have to be sure that you will still be able to be the centre of appreciation after the event, and this makes you wary.

Still reading? I hope so. We both know that Leos are sensitive to being teased: the difference between us is that you don't tell everybody. The reason for this inflexibility of approach and avoidance of new adventures is that you are a Fixed sign. You have to maintain what you have, and to put your own energy out into your surroundings: in other words, you have to have life liveable *on your own terms*. You are doing this for yourself, in the only way you know how. It is not in your nature to do things for the benefit of others rather than yourself, and it is not in your power to change the nature of things through your own efforts. Both of these things you might like to do, and privately wish you could, but they are the province of the next sign on from yours, Virgo, and for the moment you must stay where you are. You cannot create things from your surroundings, you can only create things from yourself. When you create from yourself, you create an active force that others can use; they will do things for you, and then give you the credit for your inspiration and encouragement. You are the heart of their activity, and they do the circulating for you. Heart and circulation: a life-giving system together.

Leo corresponds to the heart in the body at all levels, from the individual to the collective. Your function in any group is to pump out inspiration and warmth; a group of people feels livelier, happier, and more active when you are at its heart. They have to do things at your rate, though; when someone challenges your authority, you cannot function. If you are rushed or flustered, you lose your power, and do odd things in an attempt to regain your rhythm. The last thing any group of people needs is a palpitating heart, or for some outsider to bring on a heart attack. No joke: all the 'heart' phrases apply to a Leo as he goes through life. You are naturally good-hearted and even great-hearted, but if there is nobody to receive your light and tell you how they appreciate you, you are down-hearted, faint-hearted, or even broken-hearted.

Leo is the sign of the Sun; like the Sun, you are a radiant centre to a whole system of satellites. People move around you, grateful for your stability and warmth. If you were to move or be displaced, the planets would be thrown out of orbit, and chaos would result. As you see, staying still and being warm is what you are best at.

Like the Sun, a Leo's essential function is to convert material resource into heat and light, and then to radiate this outwards. This makes you a motivator of others; you supply that energy which others need to make things happen. You change things from a static state to an active one, and you place yourself at the centre of the activity.

This radiance of personal warmth gives you a reputation for generosity, which is true, but what the other eleven signs don't realize, especially the six 'collecting' signs (page 12), is that you can't help it. You can't *not* give out, in fact, which seems genuinely altruistic to others, because they have to get something in return if they are to give something out. What you do need, and they don't realize, is to be appreciated for the role you play at the centre of things. You know that when things aren't quite going your way you slip away and do something else to draw attention back to yourself; now you know why you do it. It's to re-establish yourself at the centre of things.

The rest of mankind is naturally attracted to your kind of warmth and light; without it the race would never continue. Literally, as it happens, because Leo is the sign given to the process of having chidren. The obstetric side of this is actually assigned to Cancer, but the child itself is Leo, because it represents a person's own energies put outside himself and made into physical form. The new individual can thus maintain (Fixed signs maintain, remember?) the activity (Fire sign) of his parent, and the line is extended for another generation.

Everything which is an expression of personal warmth is assigned to Leo. Children in all forms, not only the individuals, but also the processes of creating them, and all the happy and warm activities in life like love and laughter. Gambling is Leonine too, but only in that it is an extension of personal will in an attempt to influence chance. Wherever there is warmth and a feeling of wellbeing, wherever there is optimism and confidence, there is the spirit of Leo.

The lion of the sign is well chosen. Like the animal, Leo people are proud, confident, majestic, lazy, generous to their friends, and an inspiration to us all.

## Early, Middle or Late? The Decanates

*First decanate (23 July–1 August)*
This is the purest form of Leo. There is a double helping of solar energy here, expressed without any other planet to give it shape or direction. This is pure radiance, where the energies of the person are used to glorify the self, and to write the joy of being a Leo large enough for the world to read it. There has to be one decanate of the thirty-six where the individual celebrates

himself to the exclusion of everything else, and this is the one. The things attributed to this part of Leo are all things to be proud of: you probably find almost all of them to your taste. Children and births generally are here, because they are the pride of their parents, the joy of their family, and a Leo's creative ability made real. Here too is that other sort of child, the brainchild; it does not matter whether it is a novel, a painting, or just a good idea taken up and put into practice—each is a real thing born of the Leo's self-expression, reflecting his creative ability. Fashion and clothes are in this first decanate too, because they are an expression of the wearer and his personality. So is anything spectacular or showy; spontaneous displays of energy for their own sake are showing their solar side by giving out rather than taking in. Perhaps, on the human scale, you sometimes make grand gestures or give lavish parties just because you feel like it. And, of course, the heart of anything, whether literally or figuratively, belongs in this early third of Leo too.

*Second decanate (2–11 August)*

Here Jupiter adds its distinctive sense of size and humour. 'Jumbo' seems to be a good word for Jupiter: everything it touches is larger-than-life and fun. With Jupiter to moderate its radiance, the solar energy of the middle Leo is turned towards the intellectual and the spiritual. Education and school-days are given to this decanate sometimes; perhaps you enjoyed the cheeriness and the sense of all being best pals which never seems to be carried on into later life no matter how hard you try.

Jupiter has much to do with the good life: in this section of the sign the Leo is likely to enjoy good food and wine, and to see them as a natural expression of himself. Jupiter is also the alcohol in the wine, you see. The Sun and Jupiter together give an emphasis on 'good things gathered in': this can be natural produce like food and wines, but it can just as easily be profits from business, which will be displayed and enjoyed just as fully by the Leo in the form of the plush offices, big cars, expensive suits, and things like that which are an expression of a full and profitable life. The profits don't have to be earned, though; Jupiter is also the planet of strokes of sheer luck in return for trusting to fortune. Hunches which pay off, pools wins, successful days at the races are all part of this sector of the sign, and the Leos who receive the rewards offered to them usually enjoy them to the full. In short, this decanate is for people who not only enjoy the best that life has to offer, but who like to be seen to do so.

*Third decanate (12–22 August)*
The final decanate has Mars as its co-ruler; joined with the Sun as it is, the emphasis is on the physical expression of the self. Here are the Leos who like to take an active part in things, and of course like to win, as all Leos do. Not surprisingly, sport in all forms is assigned to this decanate. The ideas of asserting yourself in competition, showing the other players just what you can do, and winning, are very much of the flavour of the Sun with Mars. Military conquests are here, too: any wargamers amongst you?

Leos from this decanate are likely to draw attention to themselves with the sort of equipment they own—the best golf clubs, the fantastic car stereo with six speakers, the gold watch with a stopwatch and tachymeter. The emphasis is on performance where the previous decanate concentrated on luxury, but in both cases the idea is to express and draw attention to the owner's personality.

Mars has an almost infantile emotional quality to it at times, and a fierce passion, too: these last degrees of the sign give Leos who fall blindly and powerfully in love, giving everything in the hope of being recognized in their devotion by the object of their affections. This is as close as a Leo will get to the self-sacrifice which characterizes the next sign in the cycle, Virgo.

# Three Phases of Life: Leo as Child, Adult, Parent

*The Leo child*
The Leo child is a boisterous creature, full of confidence and

energy. He is often a little bigger, physically, than his classmates, and if he is allowed to indulge his hearty appetite to his heart's content, may well become rather too heavy for his age. Being big gains him the attention of the other children he mixes with, and he likes that: it is a habit that continues through life, and is the reason that many adult Leos are overweight.

If there is a position with a title attached to it the Leo child will make sure he gets it; the status of being Prefect or Year Captain appeals to him enormously. It is nothing to do with the responsibility of the post, but simply the status which goes with it. Similarly, if there is a school play or something similar, the Leo child will want to be the star—and will fill the role admirably if given the chance, for all Leos are at their best when there is an audience.

Generally speaking Leo children enjoy their childhood and schooldays very much indeed, probably because of the generally lively atmoshpere that most schools have. This is not so obvious a statement as you might think: Cancer and Capricorn children, for instance, treat school very seriously, and sometimes need reminding to smile occasionally. There are two things which the Leo child needs to learn in his early years which do not come easily to him at all, and any personal difficulties he has are usually due to one or the other of them. The first is that he has to realize he is not (except in very rare instances) the best scholar/athlete the world has ever seen: not being the best as a matter of course is hard on a young Leonine ego. The second is that respect is sometimes due to those in authority over him: Leos never really grasp the idea that respect is something given, not always received.

*The Leo adult*
The Leo adult has one immense advantage in life—it is almost impossible for anyone to dislike him. All the enthusiasm of his childhood is there, added to a generosity which seems to increase with age; even when he is being stubborn and refusing to see another point of view, he is a likeable, even lovable, character.

It is not the Fire-element side of Leo that causes any friction, it is the Fixed-quality side. Leos will have their own way at all costs, and they will not move from their position. The reasons for this are simple: the Leo genuinely believes that he knows best, and that the person most suited to do what he knows is right is himself. Anybody else must be misinformed, and there is no advantage in changing a system that works very well as it is. That, at least, is the explanation a Leo gives to himself. He is less likely to consider that adopting another person's viewpoint would move him away from the centre of activity, and divert attention from himself, but these are motives every bit as powerful as the ones he admits to, and possibly even more so.

There is a good side to this fixed-ness, of course; Leos have loyalty and stamina, of the sort which keeps them dedicated to the support of their dependants and the pursuit of their goals no matter what. They are not the sort of people who are interested in one thing one minute, and another the next.

Like all adults, Leos arrange their lives so that they can spend most of their time in a situation which is a comfortable outlet for their zodiacal energy.

This means that they fix things so that they are always at the centre of whatever is going on; so that they are always the focus of attention; so that they can be a source of creative ideas for everybody else; and so that this situation can continue. The disadvantages for the outsider are that other opinions are likely to be dismissed; that no real change in the situation is ever likely to take place; and that he is likely to find the Leo pompous and opinionated rather than warm and generous.

Forcing change on an adult Leo by changing things around him and then showing him how much he is out of touch with reality is very damaging to him. He can be deeply hurt by this, and the damage to the group from the resulting loss of warmth and goodwill makes it an exercise of dubious value.

## The Leo parent

Leo parents have one great talent, and one great disadvantage. The great talent is the love, warmth and generosity that flows freely from all Leos, and which is especially true in the case of their own offspring. No child of Leo parents ever suffers from not being loved and cherished. A Leo parent identifies with his child to an extent not found in many of the other signs—he can remember what it is to be a child, and enjoy his child's little triumphs and catastrophes with all the vividness of the child's imagination.

The big disadvantage is that he may be too imposing and demanding. Leos are proud of their children, and want their children to be a credit to them. They want their friends to admire their children as an extension of their Leonine selves, which they are, of course. Children, however, are rarely the paragons required for this sort of activity, and the result is that the Leonine parent becomes over-corrective of minor behaviour faults in the child, seeing them as affronts to his own self-respect.

Leo parents are dominant in their own homes; they 'rule' them like the kings the sign represents. They decide who does what, and this can mean that a child is forced to pursue some activity which the Leo parent thinks would be good for him, but in which the child has little interest. Children are individuals, and must develop their individuality; but if they have Leo parents they must recognize that it is the Leo who is the dominant personality in the household, and they may have to wait until they leave home before they can develop their own interests and talents.

# Virgo

The sign before Virgo is Leo. Leo is where an individual expresses himself in a very simple and direct manner, pouring his energies out from himself in any way that takes his fancy. In some respects, it is uncontrolled, but then Leo energy doesn't have to be controlled; as long as the expression is there, good and strong, then the Leo purpose is met. It never occurs to Leo to do anything for any other purpose than to please himself. He isn't selfish, at least not in the usual sense of the word, but he *is* self-centred, and he needs to be; his ruling planet, the Sun, requires him to be that way.

Virgo is one stage further on from Leo. Merely expressing energy isn't enough. Virgo has to make the best use of his energy, get it to do things. There are some terribly wasteful procedures in the way a Leo acts, and the Virgo mind is concerned to remove these. Leo makes grand gestures, but they are often too personal in their expression to be useful to everybody; Virgo tries to trim the excessively personal element from his actions so that they are more accessible and useful to a greater number of people. When this process is taken to its logical conclusion, the result is the complete absence of individuality, replaced by something which is suitable for everybody, and perfectly balanced. Strictly speaking, that is the province of the next sign on, Libra, but the Virgo sees it as the direction he ought to be going in, and works towards it none-the-less.

The expression of Leonine energy is seen in the way they do things. The important word there is 'do'—the action itself is the key to the sign.

The function of Virgoan energy is seen in the way they do things. The important word there is 'way'—the technique used is the key to the sign.

Have a look at those sentences again. Leos express; Virgos function: it's a different sort of energy. It is, of course, the moderation of solar energy via Mercury (page 21). 'Function' is a much more precise sort of word in its connotations; it suggests precision and fine detail. These are important concepts for a Virgoan; they need to know the details of things, and they need to get them right.

One of the best ways to see how a sign really works is to look at the organ of the body which the sign looks after, and then compare its function to the way the individual deals with his life. Each sign of the zodiac has an area of the body assigned to it, and in the case of Virgo it is the intestinal system.

So what does the intestinal system do? It digests things. It breaks down the material that is handed to it, right down to enzyme level, reducing it to its component substances. Then it uses those substances to meet the needs of the body, making the most efficient use of what it has at its disposal to keep the body at its best.

On the large scale of daily life, the Virgoan works in the same way. He breaks down and examines everything that is presented to him, finding out what it actually consists of, making sure that he is completely familiar with its working in every detail. Then he puts this to the best possible use he can find, usually for the benefit of somebody other than himself. He takes care to see that things are done properly and well; he makes a little go a long way, and doesn't waste anything. The result is that both the Virgo and those around him are looked after in the best way possible.

Mercury's energy works best on a small scale. Virgoans are often portrayed as fussy and critical, but this is a misunderstanding of the way they function, even though it might be true to some extent. Mercury notices that which is different, or out of place; it also notices things on a small scale. An article of clothing left lying about by its owner will be noticed at once by a Virgo because it is out of place, and because it is a small-scale event. What happens next is that the Virgo analyses and digests the situation, comes to the conclusion that the best and most effective action would be to put it where it belongs in the wardrobe, and proceeds to do so for the benefit of the owner. Then, because Mercury is a communicative planet, the Virgo tells the owner what has happened, so that he will know where his clothes are when he next wants them. Now, *from the other person's point of view*, it looks as though the Virgoan is being critical of the way he leaves his clothes lying about—but it is not actually the case. Most non-Virgoans work on a larger scale of thought, and are annoyed when forced to examine small details which are usually not important to them. Virgoans cannot believe that there are actually people who do not mind not being able to find things, and who can't remember when they last saw their house keys. In the small-scale vision of the Virgoan reality, keys look big; in the impressionable world of, say, the Sagittarian or Piscean, keys are unimportant trivia.

It is impossible for the Virgoan to see the whole picture until he has mastered the detail—a fact that both Virgoans and those of the other eleven signs would do well to remember. It is similar to doing a jigsaw puzzle; until every piece has been inserted, the picture is incomplete. Other signs have to wait for the Virgoan to complete the jigsaw before they can discuss the implications of the picture—and even then, they will find that the Virgoan is much more interested in the discrepancies in printing and cut that he noticed when assembling the pieces of the puzzle than in the content of the picture. Always it is the physical and practical aspects of things that capture his attention.

Unlike the other Mercurial sign, Gemini, Virgos aren't really very good with ideas. They are much more at home with the material world, like the other Earth signs, Taurus and Capricorn. What makes Virgo special, though, is the emphasis on using the material, and on the skills and techniques that implies. Being able to do things for yourself, to be able to work with the actual materials at hand, and to be master of these crafts, is very Virgoan. The hands are a Virgoan part of the body, and being able to use them to work and fashion things to be the way you want them is important to you. One of the most Virgoan activities imaginable is planing a piece of wood: it is a manual process, one that gradually changes the material to a new shape by removing little parts of it by a repetitive action, but an action which is never quite the same twice. Most people find this process a chore, but not a Virgoan. The idea of practice, of improving skill and understanding by repetition and re-familiarization, is one which this sign understands instinctively. It is all to do with 'using material', as we noted on page 17.

## Early, Middle or Late? The Decanates

*First decanate (23 August–1 September)*
This is the purest form of Virgo. There is a double helping of Mercury's energy here, so there is a tendency to do things at levels of detail within levels of detail, if you see what I mean. Centuries ago, this decanate was said to be associated with servants, because they were the instrument you used to get things done for yourself; perhaps nowadays people born here

find that their lives involve being of particular service to somebody else in some way. Certainly the decanate emphasizes the means used to do things; all tools, their makers and users, are here. You will find that you tend to concentrate more on the technique you are using to produce your desired result than on the result itself. Are your bookshelves full of 'How-To-Do-It' books? Do you have a kitchen full of things that are exactly right for the job, but for one job only, such as a cherry stoner, or a lemon slice press? If so, you can see that to you, the fun of solving a problem is deciding what techniques are required, learning those techniques, and using them with the right tools to get a perfect result. What you do with the result has relatively little interest for you.

For some reason now lost in the past, this decanate is associated with domestic pets of all kinds. Perhaps they replace servants in the modern household as creatures who are wholly dependent on their master.

*Second decanate (2–11 September)*
Here Mercury's careful and analytical powers are mixed with those of Saturn. The emphasis moves away from pure technique, and centres on keeping things up to scratch, caring for things, and making sure that there is something in reserve when needed. These middle Virgos are careful folk, who like to save a bit if they can against the proverbial rainy day. It is all to do with the idea of making efficient use of what you have, and of not wasting any resource in case it is needed later. There are other things besides rainy days that can limit your effectiveness, though, and the most common is illness. Virgos are very concerned for their health, and usually keep a stock of remedies to hand in case they should be taken ill. Perhaps it is because little symptoms seem bigger to their way of seeing things than to people of other signs, or perhaps it is because they realize that the most precious resource they have is themselves, to be looked after and used in the best way possible; whatever the reason, Virgoans of the middle decanate are the hypochondriacs of the zodiac. This is connected with the way Saturn works on Mercury;

it makes the individual realize just how much he really does have at his disposal, and how finite is the time he has in which to use it.

*Third decanate (12–21 September)*
The third decanate sees Mercury's influence blended with that of Venus, and the result is much lighter in feel than the previous one. The influence is less on looking after your health when it has failed, and more on preventing its failure. This is done, as always with a Virgo, by adopting the appropriate technique. In this case, again predictably, given that the Virgo looks after the intestinal system, that technique is proper nutrition. If you also take into account that Venus looks after food generally, there is no other interpretation really, is there? Late Virgoans, then, are careful about what they eat. Some of them are serious about it, becoming extreme vegetarians or adopting a macrobiotic diet, but even the moderates will find themselves considering wholegrain bread and tea without sugar.

The great thing about Virgoan thought is that it is so sensibly logical. The interest in food springs from wanting to maintain the body at its best by giving it the best material to work with; since there is always an interest in doing things personally, by hand if possible, many late Virgoans take a great interest in cooking, finding great satisfaction in mastering the skills of baking bread and suchlike. It's all to do with 'using material' again.

## Three Phases of Life: Virgo as Child, Adult, Parent

*The Virgoan child*
Virgoan children are just what many people think the ideal child should be like; they like being helpful, they like doing little jobs, and they are not usually in the way. They are quiet, they are studious, and they don't leave everything they own scattered behind them as they go. On the other hand, they are not particularly adventurous, and they are often quite happy to stay at one level of proficiency and abilities. It is an early sign of their

preference for seeing the detail of things rather than the larger view.

Virgo children like to know how things work. They need to see the inner workings of things, especially mechanical things, and indeed will develop an aversion to using anything which they feel less than fully knowledgeable about. They ask endless questions of anybody available, seeking always to discover the reasons for things being as they are. If they feel that the answers they get are too general, they will continue to ask until they are satisfied.

Virgoan children are model pupils in their early years at school. They are good readers and writers, and their natural neatness means that they excel at primary school, where literacy and numeracy are the goal, and tidiness of presentation is usually highly thought of. They get a lot of pleasure from being punctual, and they are never late for a lesson. At the same time, they feel a need to comment on the unpunctuality of others. All that is happening is that the Virgoan is communicating the inconsistency he has noted; it is an attempt at conversation, nothing more, though it may lead to the child acquiring the reputation of being 'Teacher's Pet' or some similar title.

### The Virgoan adult

The Virgoan adult needs to guard against being too highly-strung. It is so easy for him to think that he can do things better than anybody else, and that it might be better if he did (Here, let me do that for you; it won't take five minutes, and it isn't any trouble'), that he ends up doing everything for everybody, and wearing himself out in the process.

Not everybody has Virgoan standards of finish and quality; you think that people would like to be reminded of ways in which they could do things better, because you are helping them make better use of the material at their disposal, but this is not so. Some people are not as concerned with presentation and cleanliness either, and your noting the inconsistencies is even less well received than before, since you don't even have the excuse of helping them make better use of their talents.

Being seen as critical upsets you, and you will see it as a failure of technique on your own part, an indication that you have somehow been doing the wrong thing. You will think about the situation, and resolve to try even harder next time. As you will, I hope, see, this is a vicious circle, leading to unhappiness all round.

One of Mercury's less-appreciated qualities is its lack of emotional warmth. In the other Mercurial sign, Gemini, it shows as an amoral outlook which sees no wrong in changing the truth a little if it suits the mood of the moment, and in the Virgoan character it shows as an aloofness of attitude, a feeling of not being deeply involved *personally*. It is a difficult thing to define precisely; you are definitely involved, but you are not personally involved: your interest is there, but your emotions aren't.

The tragedy of the adult Virgo is that you are too much of a specialist, and that you really try too hard. You are really concerned for others' welfare, but are seen as uncaring and clinical. You take an interest in the things you see, but are seen to criticize instead. Luckily, the service you render the community is both genuine and practical, and the worth of what you do is recognized as such, even if your personal qualities are mis-interpreted.

### The Virgoan parent

As a parent, the Virgoan is at his best with children who have grown past infancy. When they want to know things, he is there to inform; when they want to try things, he is there to encourage and teach. If there is a drawback to this, it is that he will want the children to do things the way he does them, and will not want to see them 'wasting their time' doing things their own way.

Certainly the child of a Virgo parent is well cared for in a material sense; it is likely to be properly fed, well-clothed, healthy, and clean. Despite this obvious care, though, there may be a certain lack of emotional involvement with the child, and if this is coupled with apparent criticism in the usual Virgo fashion, then difficulties can arise. Children need pure praise from time to time, deserved or not, rather than criticism, however well-meant; Virgo parents need to think about this.

The best thing about a Virgo parent is his willingness to do things for the child; the only thing he needs to be aware of is the dividing line between support and restriction.

# Libra

The sign before Libra is Virgo. Virgo represents the individual making best use of all the talents he has, developing each one to its utmost. The zodiac is the story of a person's life and development, told in symbols; the stage represented by your sign shows an area of activity which will preoccupy you for much of your life. In a way, you are representing that stage for society as a whole; other people with different birthdays represent the other stages. The individual who starts as an infant in Aries has completed the stages of learning about himself by the time the Virgo stage is reached, and so he turns his attention outwards towards the rest of society to see what it can offer him, and what he can offer it. To do so, he must form relationships with others—not just personal relationships, though they come in all flavours and strengths from acquaintances to marriages, but working and professional relationships too. This whole area of activity, the forming of relationships, is what Libra represents. Therefore it follows that as a Libran, much of your time will be spent talking to other people, forming and sustaining friendships, and generally being social. It doesn't sound much, but it is what you do best, and what you like doing best; in fact, you can do it better than all of the other signs, and you need to do it more than they do, too. Some of the other signs don't need friends in the same way that you do, and don't really care if they are left on their own: Aries and Capricorn are often like this. Aquarius likes the social scene as much as you do, but he prefers larger groups; he doesn't have the personal touch that you do, and is uncomfortable in a one-to-one situation, where you are at your best. So, you see, personal relationships are the specific concern of the Libran: it's your *job* to be nice to people.

For you it is enough just to be with someone you love; you

don't need to control their whole life, dictate and arrange what they do or what happens to them, or anything like that. You might want to, but it's really the concern of the next sign on, Scorpio. His job is to control and maintain things for whole groups of people, but yours is just to make contact and to get people talking.

You can see how your position in the zodiac gives you a role to play in society, but to see how you go about it we must take another look at Venus, the planet behind the sign. Incidentally, don't worry if I seem to change from talking about Librans on an individual and personal level, to talking about them as a group within society: astrology sees them as both the same thing, working on different levels and scales but in the same way.

Venus is the planet of attraction; its energies are used to bring things together by finding things that they have in common and uniting them. This works at all levels, from magnets to people in love. Librans use Venus' energies to unite things too.

Libra is an outgoing sign, and a Cardinal sign. Therefore the Libran is going to make things happen, rather than accept what he's got or wait for things to come to him. Since Libra is an Air sign too, what the Libran is going to do is to contact people and give them his ideas. In other words, talk to them, see what they're like, let them see what he's like in return. Everybody likes talking to a Libran, because they are so nice, or so people say: why should this be?

You already know the answers, if you think about it. A Libran is always going to be able to find something he has in common with the person he's talking to; Venus will help him spot it at once. Perhaps it is a shared interest ('We must have a round of golf together sometime'), or just a conversational opening line ('I do like that sweater you're wearing'); but whatever it is, it's nice to think that the two of you have something in common, something to unite you, before the conversation even gets started. Clever, isn't it? If you think that all conversations are conducted this way, Libra, try talking to a Virgo or a Gemini: they will open a conversation by noticing what isn't quite right ('You've got a mucky mark on your jacket, look') which gives them an instant reputation for being critical.

If a Libran is the one to start the conversation, which is likely, because it's a Cardinal sign, remember, then the other person is bound to be impressed. Somebody who is actively trying to get to know you and is putting all the effort in, and is finding points you have in common at the same time, is likely to be popular. Everybody likes Venusian energy—it soothes, restores, puts you back in one piece and makes you feel good—and Librans give it out for free.

What do you get out of it? You get the pleasure of relationship. It doesn't matter how the friendship develops as long as it is there, in your view. There has to be more than one of everything in your world, so that you can enjoy the relationship between them; singularly, the state of being only one, is what you are trying to avoid. In a relationship, you are satisfied; out of a relationship, you make a new one to be in.

To you, the best relationship is a balanced one, where the qualities of one thing are balanced by those of the other. An interest in, say, politics, is balanced by a similar interest in another person, and the relationship thus formed interests you in itself. The fact that one person loves cricket and the other doesn't is ignored by you as far as possible, because there is no balance, no point in common. Venus attracts you towards those things you like, or feel an affinity for, and turns you away from those things you don't. This often gets you an undeserved reputation for laziness, but you are being misunderstood. It is simply that you would rather do the things you like than those you don't, and your attention is always attracted (Venusian word again) to something you would like; as a result you never get round to the things you don't like, and people call you lazy.

An ability to find affinity with something in everybody, coupled with a desire to find balance and restore harmony, leads you to be indecisive. After all, if you can see both sides of an argument, how can you decide? You could follow your own interests, of course, but since your own interests are those of your friends by definition (if you were on your own, you'd hate it) you're no further forward.

Your employment of relationships extends beyond people; it runs through everything you own or come into contact with. Librans are renowned for their refinement and taste; it's all true, but it isn't difficult to see how it got that way. The pleasing arrangement of things like pictures and furnishings in a house depends on the relationship of their relative positions, and you can see what's right and what isn't at once. You'll soon put things right if they're not (Cardinal action again). Colours work the same way, and shapes too; this gives you superb artistic taste, and a pleasing dress sense. Everybody else has to think about whether something is or isn't in balance, but you can do it instinctively. Music is a similar area; harmonies and balanced sequences of rhythm and melody are the very essence of Libran thought patterns. You should find that music does much to relax and reassure you.

Each zodiac sign has a part of the body associated with it, and for Libra that is the kidneys. Kidneys are the body's filters—they take all the rubbish out of your bloodstream, and keep things clean, balanced, and circulating. You work in a similar way—life with the lumps taken out is your aim. If an argument can be resolved, or a better balance made, or if life can simply be made nicer for you, then you'll do it. Librans are the kidneys of society—and by golly it needs you!

Libran energy, then, works constantly to restore unity and to find points of contact. It wants to achieve balance—not surprising, since the picture for the sign is exactly that: a balance.

## Early, Middle or Late? The Decanates

*First decanate (22 September–2 October)*
This is the purest form of Libra. Here there is a double helping of Venusian energy, and people from this part of the sign are very soft and romantic in their approach to life. Unions of all kind seem desirable, and you seem to be devoted to finding a matching partner to everything, including yourself. Marriage is supposed to be to do with this part of the sign, and it's not hard to

see why: to you, the establishment of personal relationships is the most important thing there is. Because you are at the beginning of the sign, you work on a more immediate and intimate level than the other Librans; they can think of relationships in the broadest of terms, and of universal relationships such as peace between nations, but you are strictly one-to-one. Your world is that small world between two people. You exist in a series of intimate one-to-one relationships, a close personal friend of everybody you know—separately!

An offshoot from this is that you know yourself better than any of the other Librans; you have some ability to assess yourself as others see you, which is, of course, different from how you see yourself. You are then able to form a relationship between these two sides of yourself.

Your sense of balance is more finely developed, too—to such an extent that you probably stand with your weight on one foot for a few minutes, and then the other, in turn; even the books and ornaments in your house are probably arranged in exact symmetry. Have a look and see.

*Second decanate (3–12 October)*
Here the energies of Venus are given Saturn's influence as well. Saturn adds weight to anything it comes into contact with, and at the same time prolongs its effects. It will lengthen the time-scale of your relationships, for a start; you will be concerned with those partnerships which last for years rather than days. Venus and Saturn together will also lead to the formation of relationships which are hard in some way, and need considerable effort to be adequately managed. Some of these will be ordinary working relationships, especially if you are in a position of responsibility, like the one a doctor has with his patients. Some of them will be long-running feuds; enemies and wars are usually assigned to the middle degrees of Libra. Some of them will be relationships that are ended: by divorce, for instance. Being born with the Sun in this decanate means that the parts of your life which will be most important for your development, and most satisfying to you in the long run, will be those that are concerned

with relationships where difficulties are encountered.

A talent unique to this decanate, which, of course, you will have, is a strong sense of fair play. It comes from having the balance-and-bring-together principle of Libra raised from the personal level up to the social level. The idea of everyone having a fair turn, and having to take the bad with the good, is one which is strong in you.

*Third decanate (13–22 October)*
The last decanate finds Venus having to work with Mercury. Here the principle of balance-and-bring-together is raised beyond the personal and the social into the universal, taking the idea of fairness with it; the result is the law, as represented by all rules and regulations, and all courts, judges and the like. If you have your Sun here, perhaps legal processes will be important in your life. Or perhaps you will be trying to apply your principles to a large section of the community, by being in a political movement, or fighting for the rights of a particular group. Whatever it is, Mercury is the planet of speech, and Libra is an Air sign, so the idea of saying what you believe is in here. This decanate produces the best Libran talkers, and they always talk for a purpose, because the sign is Cardinal; there is usually some aim or principle you want people to adopt. You could be trying to bring two sides together; that would be very Libran.

There are one or two odd little things which are given to this sector of the sign which are perhaps best not examined too closely: they include theft and similar crimes. At the same time, it must be remembered that Librans aim not only to do things in a balanced way, they aim also to create or restore balance in an unbalanced situation. If we change that phrase to 're*dress* the balance', we get a sort of 'Robin Hood Principle'. If this affects you at all, you will know what I'm talking about.

## Three Phases of Life: Libra as Child, Adult, Parent

*The Libran child*
Libran children are very appealing creatures; they are kind-

natured, easy to get on with, frequently very talented in an artistic way, and utterly charming. They learn early on that adults, especially relatives, find them charming, and develop a repertoire of coy expressions and appealing gestures which they will gladly perform when they feel the occasion warrants it. As they grow older, this becomes more subtle in its use, but is never entirely discarded; it is, of course, the development of the use of Venus' energies in giving the other person what he likes to see.

At school the Libran child is good at anything artistic or musical, where his inbuilt sense of colour, shape, and harmony helps him excel at the elementary level required of a primary schoolchild. Of course, his talents will help keep him that little bit ahead of his peers throughout his school life—where they have acquired skills, he has a natural aptitude. What the Libran child isn't good at, though, is anything he doesn't like; Venus' energies will turn him away from things which bore him, and he will sit in class without listening or learning. Subjects likely to have this effect are the ones usually most prized in later life, such as mathematics; to the Libran child they don't have sufficient visual content, or enough personal qualities, for his Venusian energies to work on.

As he learns to project his character in forming relationships, the teenage Libran finds that his social life develops in advance of that of his contemporaries; he is eager to find friends of the opposite sex, and to practise creating partnerships, as all Librans must.

### The Libran adult

The Libran adult is governed by a need to live a balanced and harmonious life. Most of the time he can achieve this, using the tricks he learned as a child, but he will also have brought with him from childhood more than a few weaknesses, and these will ensure that he never quite gets the harmonious existence he strives for.

Easily the most troublesome of these weaknesses is indecisiveness. An inability to choose a course of action is not a great failing in a child, because an adult is usually on hand to make the decisions for him; in an adult world there are many decisions to be made, and the Libran is always unwilling to take any option which precludes him taking any others. In other words, Librans want to have their cakes and eat them; what's more, they would like things to be so arranged that there will be a choice of cakes available, and eating one will not rule out being able to choose another one for later.

Linked to this is the inability to concentrate on things which hold little appeal, for the usual reason (Venus' energy). The consequence is that many Librans find themselves dismissed as rather lightweight individuals, not capable of handling serious responsibility and hard work. This unfortunate state of affairs has more to do with the Capricornian values held in a business-oriented society than any deficiencies on the Libran's part, but it works out that way nonetheless.

Obviously, the answer is to be more effective without having to take quick decisions. The way to do this is to give yourself plenty of time. Time is something of a Libran commodity anyway; when used properly it enables you to do things in a relaxed, graceful, and satisfying way, without feeling rushed or thrown out of balance; it also allows you time to think, and practically takes the decisions for you, if you wait long enough. If the adult Libran can avoid being rushed, he can achieve the relaxed and elegant lifestyle he always longs for.

### The Libran parent

Libran parents have two sides to them, as their children soon discover. Like the two pans on the set of scales which represents the sign, they are different but complementary, and if you overload one the other rises.

The first side is the soft side. Venusian energies are naturally kind and indulgent, and a child has only to ask a Libran parent for its wish to be granted. Children are easily spoilt by Libran parents. Librans like to be liked: perhaps the parent enjoys the thanks offered by the child, even if they don't last long.

Libran parents look after the appearance of their children very well; their sense of visual balance and hatred of anything unseemly or untidy makes sure that their offspring are scrubbed and polished, and that their clothes are neat.

The other pan of the scales is the 'fair-play' side. If the Libran parent thinks that somebody is having things too much their own way, then action is taken to restore the balance. It works both for and against the child: if the child is unfairly treated at school, the Libran parent will be a loud complainer to the headmaster, but if the child is having too much of his own way at the expense of the parent, then the parent will make his feelings known.

Libran parents are indulgent, yes, but they won't suffer themselves to be unappreciated; when it looks as though their own balance and enjoyment of life is being upset, they act. Their action is effective; being a cardinal sign sees to that. It really depends on how much can be loaded into one pan of the scales before the whole apparatus starts to tilt; these parents exist for themselves as well as for their children, and of course, for the relationship which links them.

# Scorpio

The sign before Scorpio is Libra. Libra represents the individual's concern to form relationships with others, and it does this by offering itself in friendship. Libra is the initiator of all relationships, and is more than willing to change its point of view, or make the odd adjustment here and there, if the end result is helpful to the relationship. To a certain extent, this makes Librans pliable, but only because they have to be to achieve their ends. At all times they are concerned that the energies of the situation be balanced. Not necessarily static, but balanced, which is how they would like to see it.

Scorpio is a development from that stance. Where Libra started the relationship, and sent out the invitations, so to speak, then Scorpio has to handle the returns, evaluate the responses, decide on his responses in turn, and do what he can to keep the situation under control and growing nicely. Where Libra gives out an idea, Scorpio collects the reply, or the feeling it generates.

Scorpio collects all that there is about a situation, and makes sure that it is all going the way he wants it to. Nothing is left to chance: interpersonal relationships are a minefield, in the Scorpio view, best handled by a professional such as himself.

There will come a time, possibly, when Scorpio is so much in control of things that he will cease to consider the possibility of anything going wrong. He will know that he can cope with anything, and he will be well enough informed about virtually everything to be able to give help and advice to others, without having to worry about himself. When he reaches that stage of confidence, he will have left Scorpio and become a Sagittarian, the next phase in the cycle. For now, however, we must concentrate on the Scorpio's existence as he devotes himself to controlling the situation Libra left him in.

If we go back to the basic structures of astrology, we see that Scorpio is a collecting sign rather than an outgoing one. This means, Scorpio, that you are taking things in from your situation, rather than contributing to it. You react to the things around you, and especially to the people you contact. Scorpio is also a Water sign; this means that the world you choose to operate in is not a material one, but a mental one. Impressions, emotions, feelings; motivations, desires, needs; jealousies, revenges. These are the features of the Scorpionic landscape, the features of your daily existence that are prominent landmarks, and which you recognize and navigate by. This emphasis on the mental world makes you intelligent, and naturally so: Nature sees to it that animals get the equipment they need to suit them for their environment. Taureans are Earth creatures and have the strength and stamina necessary to exist in a material world; you have the intelligence and cunning necessary to exist in a world of feelings and emotional responses.

Scorpio is also a Fixed sign: you like your environment, and you find that you can manipulate it or work with it so that you can gain profit from it. You feel safe and familiar among the hopes and fears of others; you know that with a little bit of effort here, and a bit of care there, you can make them grow the way you want. Like the gardener who makes his vegetables grow bigger with care and attention, so you work with the motivation of your companions. What you want out of it is the security of being in control: the idea of not being in control terrifies you.

What you are trying to do is to maintain your emotional responses to things at the level they are now at. You think, somehow, that if you get over-emotional about things you will lose precious emotional energy, which must be kept intact. You are right, to some extent; you have a very great deal of emotional energy, but you are not a generator of it, as the Cancerian is, nor does it benefit you to let it loose and be swept away on it, in the Piscean manner. To do so would be contrary to the nature of your ruling planet, Mars; Mars gives things firm direction. Letting things loose is not Martian.

So, to maintain your emotional response, you make sure that you are familiar with what's going on. That way nothing will surprise you, shock you, sneak up on you, or in any other way cause an uncontrolled emotional reaction. To do this you need to anticipate everybody's moves. You have to find out about everybody else and be able to see what they're going to do *before* they do it. You also have to maintain control of the environment, so that nothing unexpected can occur from outside so change people's anticipated response. This is going to mean a lot of work, but you know that it is the only way, and so you do it. Total control, of yourself, your surroundings, and everybody else. When you've got that, you're happy. You will have picked up, en route, so to speak, the skills of a detective, a psychiatrist, and the secret police, as well as the organizational and financial skills of a business analyst and investment consultant; but these are actually secondary: the prime aim is to maintain control of your own emotional responses.

It needs a lot of energy and determination to do all the things you have set for yourself, and to do them at the deep levels necessary for your purposes; luckily, Mars gives you that. Mars is the energy you use to investigate things, find out how they work, and (most importantly) how they are likely to affect you. Mars is also the destructive power you unleash on your enemies, hurting them before they can hurt you. Your are better than they are at plotting and scheming, because you are at home in the world of the imagination, where they are probably not, and their passions and jealousies are easily recognized by you as more emotional energy for you to collect and use. You don't leave them anything like so easy a way into your own way of thinking: you have it under control, of course.

The Scorpio is a creature whose impact in the imagination is much bigger than his physical presence and capabilities. He induces fear and fascination in the onlooker, and seems to enjoy it; when disturbed he is lethal. He is difficult to see the inside of, because he armours himself against intruders. Only when the situation is completely beyond his control will his reserve break, and then his anger is as likely to be directed against himself, for letting the situation get like that, as against his enemies. All of these things apply to the animal after which the sign is named just as much as to any Scorpio individual—there is no better picture of a Scorpio than a scorpion.

## Early, Middle or Late? The Decanates

*First decanate (23 October–1 November)*
This is the purest form of Scorpio. There is a double helping of Martian energy here, giving a particularly intense desire to exercise a controlling influence. Scorpio is the sign associated with beginnings and endings; where the essence of things come from, and where they go, is a spiritual question rather than a physical one, and in astrology the Water signs deal with spiritual energies for the most part. Scorpio is the deepest Water sign, and so all the unknown answers to the great mysteries are in it somewhere. This section of the sign, then, is concerned with the processes of life and death. Perhaps you will be literally concerned with them; undertakers and obstetricians both have a Scorpionic role in life. Perhaps your own life will be played out in separate sections, with each episode having to be completed before the next can begin. Such people have no lifelong friends, and no real roots, because they must surrender them all at the end of each stage of their life. Scorpios are particularly good at

making new beginnings, and this end of the sign emphasizes that characteristic. It is all because of the Martian energy: Mars defines and delimits, being both energizer and executioner.

*Second decanate (2–11 November)*
Here the energy and capacity to give and take life, symbolized by Mars, is blended with the energy of Jupiter, which causes it to spread and dissipate. None of the energy is lost, and the energy is not lessened by its being spread over a greater area: if you want a mental picture, imagine a drop of ink falling into a glass of water, spreading out to mingle with the clear liquid, turning it to its own colour. The fact that it all happens below the surface is of interest, as is the fact that the ink permeates the water completely, leaving none of it untouched. The Scorpio from this decanate is interested in the underlying causes of things and likes to penetrate beneath the surface of what he sees, to discover their true identity. He spreads out, too, until he has discovered and examined every part of the origins of things. The early decanate Scorpio is publicly visible, but this one keeps a very low profile indeed.

There are one or two things assigned to this section of the sign which may remind you of the ink in the water, and may prove to be suitable symbols for events in your life: among them are all mutations, irreversible changes, and transformations, and all forms of poison or venom.

*Third decanate (12–21 November)*
The last decanate of Scorpio finds the energies of Mars mixed with those of the Moon. This is a very unusual combination, for these two planets are usually particularly averse to each other's company. The powerfully individual energy of Mars becomes reflected outwards by that of the Moon, and is put to use for the benefit of others. Often this takes the form of things handed on from one generation to another; you may be involved in handing something on, or you may be the recipient of such a legacy. The extension of a family, as it descends from one generation into another, is to do with this end of the sign; your position in the

dynasty, so to speak, may be important to you if your birthday is here.

Scorpio knows that making the best use of all the resources at his command is his special talent, and he knows, too, that things go in stages, often with no possibility of keeping things from one stage to another. So he is quite willing, in this decanate, to put his talents to use for the benefit of those whom he may never meet. Bankers, and others who handle other people's money, are assigned to this part of the sign, not surprisingly; it is all to do with controlling resources *on behalf of other people* – an interesting change of emphasis as the zodiac prepares to leave Scorpio for Sagittarius.

## Three Phases of Life: Scorpio as Child, Adult, Parent

*The Scorpio child*
Perseverance and determination are not usually the qualities expected of a child, but a young Scorpio has plenty of both. When he finds something to take his interest, he will spend a great deal of time with it; this is not the sort of child whose interest span is only a few minutes, and who is always looking for something new. Even if there are difficulties in mastering the activity in question, he will stay with it until he has control of it.

Scorpio children are deeply curious. They need to know all that there is to know about the things which interest them. All children are curious, of course, but where the Virgo child likes to know how things work, and the Sagittarian child just likes to know lots of things (the scope matters more than the depth to him), the Scorpio child wants to know the underlying reasons why. It's not the knowing that he particularly enjoys; it's the finding out. Scorpio children, therefore, love mystery stories, and, when they are a little older, detective fiction.

Once he has established a way of doing things to his satisfaction, the young Scorpio is very unwilling to change. He will be quite sure in his own mind, no matter how young he is, that he has covered all the eventualities, and is going about things in the most effective and productive way. Having to abandon his routines, therefore, results in a display of stubbornness. Often labelled sulky, moody or spiteful for their behaviour, Scorpio children are none of these; what is being described is determined and purposive behaviour on a child's scale, seen from an adult's viewpoint.

The young Scorpio practises self-control, which is such a feature of his adult life, from a very early age. Consequently, he recognizes, and appreciates, any behaviour-controlling environment. In other words, he actually flourishes under a strict upbringing, unlike virtually every other zodiacal youngster of the twelve.

*The Scorpio adult*
Scorpio adults are getting to be more and more effective as this century goes on. Let me explain. Now that most European societies are highly developed, and most of us live in cities, there isn't a lot of space. The most successful individuals are going to be the ones who don't have to wave their arms about to be effective, and who don't find the prospect of a lifetime working in the middle ranks of a large company too depressing for words. These well-adapted individuals are going to have to be very good at handling people, very good at getting their own way despite the opposition and apathy of the world at large, and practically invisible: Scorpios are all of these.

No zodiac sign has more stamina than Scorpio. Mars gives power to Aries too, but the Arian's actions are based on explosive release of energy, while the Scorpio's are based on concentrated application. It's the difference between dynamite and a cutting torch; they both open safes, but one is more controlled, although the other's faster.

Scorpios do not waste time. Time, like money, is a resource, and is therefore to be used effectively and sparingly, in your way of thinking. You decide what you want, think round it until you are fully conversant with every possible aspect of it, including what might happen if things go wrong, and then use the means at your disposal in the most effective and concentrated way to achieve your purpose. What you don't know is that other signs just don't have that degree of intensity, that capacity for concentration, or that kind of sheer power.

You build your life in a series of little steps, each one with a goal to be achieved or a target to be met. When you have succeeded (only a matter of time), you can go to the next. You fit very well into large organizations; their restrictive structure is a familiar framework of control to you, and you direct your energies through that framework so that your way of working is its way of working. This means that you probably rise quickly through the organization; if you do not, it is because you are satisfied with whatever you have found at the level you have reached, and are unwilling to change.

Whatever you do, and wherever you do it, you are always in control; you will venture nothing which might involve you not being in control, not even for a minute. That's the key to the adult Scorpio: the controlled application of concentrated energy. Everything else follows on from that.

*The Scorpio parent*
Scorpio parents have only one fault—inflexibility. They are very proud of their children: they have a fondness for them, which comes from being a Water sign, and they are thrilled to think that the family is continuing and growing, which comes from being a Fixed sign. They provide a carefully controlled environment for their children to grow up in, but the children themselves, unless Scorpios like their parents, may find this too restrictive.

Children usually like to do things their own way, and it is here that the inflexibility of the Scorpio parent shows. He is unable to see that his carefully considered and proven ways of doing things hold no appeal for his children, and of course, the more he tries to force his point of view, the worse things get. The sense of injury to the parent is twofold: firstly, he is upset to think that his own efforts are not fully appreciated by the very audience whose approval he most desires, and secondly, he is aghast to think of the waste of time his children are about to embark upon to come to the same conclusions he came to years ago. The realization that his own way is only best for *him* would help a great deal.

# Sagittarius

The sign before Sagittarius is Scorpio. Scorpio represents the individual maintaining control over everything and everybody he comes in contact with. To a Scorpio, if there is no control, the value of things might be wasted and lost; there is also the possibility that the Scorpio himself might be put at risk if he were to let too much slip. There must come a time, though, when he is completely sure of himslf, and knows that he is strong enough to resist most of what the world can throw at him. He will have acquired a great deal of knowledge and information—too much, in fact, to keep to himself. The only thing he can do, then, is to give some of it out again. This is the next stage in the cycle—Sagittarius.

Sagittarius has confidence in his own abilities; even if he has not met a particular problem before, he is sure that he can resolve it somehow, and equally sure that it is unlikely to injure him in any lasting way. He transfers his confidence to others, by telling them what he knows, in the belief that they will be the same as he is once they have been taught. The end result of his being so useful to society is that his reputation is increased; if that increase in reputation were to be translated into measurable quantities, such as being appointed to some prestigious post, or being paid large amounts of money for his knowledgeable advice, then he would have reached yet another stage in the cycle, that of Capricorn. For the moment, though, we must stay with Sagittarius—a strange mixture of curiosity, knowledge, and blind optimism, a creature who is eager to show what he can do, but who seldom considers being paid for it.

Sagittarius is the last of the Fire signs, the final version of that creative force which is so athletically displayed in the Arian, and so warm and cheerful in the Leo. A Sagittarian is a little of both of these, and more besides. Aries uses his energy for direct physical action; he decides on a course of action, and goes to it at once. Unless he is actually doing something, he is unhappy. Sagittarius works in a similar way, but his preferred work area is that of ideas in social context. He likes to know what everybody else knows.

He likes to hear everybody else's opinion. He can see at once what they really mean, even if that's not what they actually say, and he will tell them so—at once, face to face. Direct, open, perceptive, inquisitive; this is Fire energy at work in the world of ideas and beliefs. What it is looking for is truth; it will burn away anything which has been built up to obscure or disguise the truth, until the essence of the argument stands there naked for all to see. Notice how similar Aries and Sagittarius are; one is a physical energy, and the other is an intellectual energy, but they share the qualities of Fire—they are effective, direct, and pure.

That piercing flame has already made the Sagittarian well aware of what he is; he knows all his own motives, and he is honest with himself. He has nothing to fear, either from himself or from anybody else, and he knows it. Because of this, he can be honest all the time, and he is. There are social disadvantages to being both absolutely honest and accurately perceptive at the same time, although the Sagittarian will not see them; to him, it is the only way to be. His friends bear the scars of his wounding remarks, but they forgive him because they can see that he really is as honest as he says he is, and he has no malice in him. He is only concerned with the truth that lies at the heart of things. Scorpios often dig down to the heart of things, too, but what they want is the answer, not the truth; they are very different things.

Sagittarius does not just acquire truth for its own sake, collecting it like something antique and valuable. He is a Mutable sign, and that means he wants to use things. In his case, he wants to use what he knows to be true, distributing the ideas to as large an audience as possible, so that everybody can put them into action, and so produce real results to the benefit of all. It all sounds very noble, and for the most part it is; but as any Sagittarian will immediately see, it gives the Sagittarian what he wants at the same time. As the ideas circulate, they change: they mutate, in fact. This is what a mutable sign needs to see— change, providing him with new combinations to examine all the time, nothing ever quite the same twice.

Sagittarius is ruled by Jupiter, and it is this which drives the Sagittarian to seek ever wider horizons. Sagittarius is the only

Fire sign ruled by a planet whose energies are those of outward movement. The combination of Fire and expansiveness produces an irrepressible optimism; the outlook must always be onwards, outwards, and upwards. Looking inwards, downwards, or back is something a Sagittarian finds most unnatural, and he cannot really understand why many people do.

Each zodiac sign has a part of the body associated with it, and somebody born under that sign will find that their life is led in a way parallel to the action of that part of the body. In the case of Sagittarius that part of the body is the thighs. Here are the biggest muscles in the body, the ones used when you run and jump. Mobility is very important to Sagittarians; when they stop moving, they are ill at ease. It is their enjoyment of movement, coupled with the sense of fun they get from Jupiter, which leads to them being described as 'sports-loving' in many astrology books. Mobility combines activity with change of circumstances, which is what the sign really needs.

Sagittarians jump in a figurative sense, too: they jump from one idea to another. They are capable of enormous leaps of imagination and perception; there is no idea or concept that they cannot master, and they love coming across a new one, especially if it influences a large number of people. For this reason, Sagittarians are often very interested in the Law or organized religion; in both cases they are able to deal with a large body of ideas that influence a great number of people.

Finally, Sagittarians jump in the popular sense, as well. They have simple but strong sexual appetites, and are usually very attractive sexually. Many find it difficult to reconcile the intellectualism of the sign with its basic sexual nature, and often conclude that the intellectual side must be some sort of a pretence. It is not so: what is happening is that the Sagittarian is trying to express his own energy, and to give himself to others in a way that will have some sort of a useful result. All the Fire signs are like this.

Sagittarius does have two sides to him, in any case. A look at the symbol of the sign is often useful, and in this case it is particularly illuminating. The centaur has the top half of a man, and the bottom half of a horse; the mixture of the intellectual and the animal is there for all to see. Notice also the fact that the Sagittarian centaur is an archer; his arrows are his piercing intellect, shot into the sky to symbolize his interest in higher ideals, such as Truth. He has no idea where the arrows fall, and he doesn't care; he has plenty more where they came from. He has four hooves; they carry him further, and faster, than the feet of ordinary men, but they also mean that he will kick if he is tied down or denied movement. And last, but not least, there is something about a horse, at least in the popular imagination, which makes you want to stroke it, talk to it, and feel reassured by its presence. A Sagittarian is a horse which can talk back.

## Early, Middle or Late? The Decanates

*First decanate (22 November-1 December)*
This is the purest form of Sagittarius. There is a double helping of Jupiter's energy here, expressed as a mind interested in matters on the largest and most far-reaching scales possible. Religion is assigned to this part of the sign, not in its role as a personal faith, but as the beliefs held by great numbers of people. All beliefs, including every kind of moral philosophy, are here. Do you have very strong views on things, a set of guiding principles that shape your opinions? All legal processes in an abstract sense are here; that is to say, the Law rather than the judge. There are a very great number of Sagittarian lawyers, though it is hard to say whether they do it from a belief in justice or from love of a clever argument. All things which are to do with looking upwards and outwards are here, such as astronomy, and probably astrology too; clairvoyance, a product of far-reaching thought if ever there was one, is in this section of the sign too. Are these the sort of things you feel an affinity with? If not, perhaps you are more interested in straightforward commercial life, though even there you cannot resist the double Jupiter influence. Foreign trade, as opposed to local or domestic, is given to this part of the sign. Whatever you do, you will find yourself drawn to the far-reaching qualities of things if this is your decanate.

## Second decanate (2–11 December)

Jupiter's expansive influence here is concentrated and given purpose by the influence of Mars; these Sagittarians are much more concerned to see definite results for their efforts. The first decanate was happy to consider philisophy for its own sake, almost, but this one wants to do something with it, and its concerns are much more down to earth. Mars gives a need for physical involvement, wherever he is found; and so in the case of the Sagittarian he will redirect the need to explore new things down onto a physical level and away from the mental and spiritual one. The people of this decanate are the travellers and explorers; Mars and Jupiter keep them hungry for new places to see, new roads to travel, new people to meet and languages to speak. All sorts of exploration and adventure find themselves assigned to this part of the sign; air travel and sea voyages are here too, because they are usually over long distances and involve some degree of risk (Mars for danger, Jupiter for confidence). If your birthday is here, you probably like travelling for its own sake, and would willingly go anywhere just for the experience, especially if the means of transport were itself interesting or unusual.

## Third decanate (12-21 December)

The final decanate sees the expansiveness of Jupiter allied to the warmth of the Sun: an excellent combination, but one that limits the sense of movement normally found in the sign. The energy of the individual in this case is not devoted to grand ideals as in the first decanate, nor physical experience, as in the second, but to individual mental development. People with their birthdays here think very carefully about things. They come to personal conclusions rather than general ones, and are often entirely original in their thinking. Inventions and scientific thinking are attributed to this part of the sign, but so are acts of faith, and mysticism; they don't sound as though they have a lot in common, but if you think for a few moments you will see that they are all products of deep thought on an individual level, applied to universal themes. The development of ideas is a

Sagittarian process; this section of the sign specializes in it. The movement and exchange of argument, so easy to see in other Sagittarians, is conducted internally in the people of this decanate. They may be less noisy than the other Sagittarians, but they are still searching for the truth just the same.

# Three Phases of Life: Sagittarius as Child, Adult, Parent

## The Sagittarian child

Sagittarian children are wise beyond their years, and often behave like little adults; Sagittarian adults, though, are eternal children. How does this come about? It is to do with Jupiter, as you might expect. This big planet gives a bouncy energy and a sense of inquisitive adventurousness to the young Sagittarian, and this is seen as a good thing by his parents. He will always be asking 'Why?', and wanting a better explanation than 'because they are, that's why'. His attention span isn't very long, but it isn't because he can't concentrate; on the contrary, it is because he understands the essence of things very quickly indeed, and is eager to learn something else as well. To this child, the world is full of new and interesting things, and each one captivates him completely—for a few minutes. Of course, these traits are not going to vanish overnight; once a Sagittarian, always a Sagittarian. Consequently the fascination, the curiosity, and the delight in new discovery is there in the adult too: hence the 'eternal child' epithet.

The clear perception of the real reasons for things which is part of the Sagittarian character is considered a valuable talent in an adult, but somewhat precocious in a child. When told by his parents not to play by the river, the Sagittarian child knows at once that what they really mean is that they are frightened lest he fall in and drown. Since he knows that he will be careful, and knows that the river could be dangerous, he feels that he need not take his parents' warning literally. When he is later punished for disobedience, he explains his thinking, but is not taken seriously. The same happens at school, and with his friends: he will have to wait until he is considerably older before his perceptive mind is given the credit for being what it is.

### The Sagittarian Adult
Most people from the other eleven signs find Sagittarians easy to understand, or so they think. In fact, they have usually *mis*understood. The six 'collecting' signs (page 12) are quite convinced that the Sagittarian's optimism is some enormous confidence trick, and that underneath there is some shy and frightened animal nearly dead from worry. It must be the case, they say: how can a single person have all that energy and confidence otherwise? Nobody said anything about the zodiac being fair; it is balanced, when taken as a whole, but individual sections of it needn't be particularly fair, and they aren't. Sagittarians have confidence, imagination, optimism, and luck, and they're not making any of it up, either. So how come, say the other eleven signs, and probably a few Sagittarians as well this time, that with all that going for them, Sagittarians aren't more successful?

Easy. They give it all away. To know a thing is enough for a Sagittarian; actually doing it isn't interesting, unless in doing it he can show it to somebody else, and they can then do it for themselves. They are teachers, discoverers, thinkers; not workers, hoarders, or bankers. 'Success' is a material thing, described in Capricorn/Taurus, Earth element terms: how can a Fire element person find that attractive? Besides, success means responsibility, and responsibilities tie you down; a Sagittarian wouldn't allow that to happen. Freedom of movement means more to him than a big pay cheque, and the trappings of success are too heavy to travel with; they don't permit flexibility or change—more Sagittarian essentials.

Sagittarians already know more than most people can ever imagine learning; they can see in an instant what it takes many people years to see. They are never upset by obstacles, and bounce back after the most crushing setbacks as though nothing has happened. In addition, they are genuinely lucky. None of this matters to them; what matters is that they are not tied down, and that they can put their enormous knowledge to general use. No wonder the other eleven signs don't understand them.

*The Sagittarian Parent*
Being a parent is a natural thing for a Sagittarian. For a start, they have the child's vision of the world, where everything is new and interesting, and they never lose it. They are also natural teachers; when a child wants to know why something is the way it is, the Sagittarian parent knows the answer, and is delighted to be asked. Sometimes he doesn't even need to be asked—and sometimes even the most inquisitive child can find the constant flow of answers more than he really wants! Sagittarians see the job of being a parent as one of talking, teaching, and playing— and they love doing all three. The idea of the responsibility of parenthood, or of an investment in the future, isn't really Sagittarian, nor is the idea of instilling a sense of discipline and duty into the child. Here is the drawback to the Sagittarian approach: they have little regard for rules and formal behaviour themselves, and so it never occurs to them to instill it in their children. Like father, like son, really.

# Capricorn

The sign before Capricorn is Sagittarius. Sagittarius represents that stage where being sure of yourself produces the confidence to give yourself to others without fear of losing anything. It is similar to the process of teaching, where information and skill is passed on to a wider group for the good of the group rather than the good of the teacher. It is to do with putting ideas out to a wider audience. When those ideas are put into action, and made to produce results, then that is no longer Sagittarius. When the teacher's reputation increases, and he is recognized as a person of importance because of what he knows, that is not Sagittarius either. When a group of ideas become fixed into a set way of doing things, a routine if you like, then they are no longer Sagittarian. Whenever knowledge or ideas are changed into visible results, Sagittarius becomes Capricorn.

The ideas of Sagittarius become the achievements of Capricorn. The outward energy of the Fire sign idea becomes collected and set in the form of the Earth sign object. Capricorn energy is nearly always in the form a visible object; it tries to encapsulate all the time, effort, ideas, money, planning, dedication, and heartache that went into something by having a visible object by which the achievement is measured. Capricorn people buy themselves big cars and big houses as a reward to themselves for their achievements; they say 'I wanted to have something to show for it all'. How right they are: Capricorn must not only have visible results, but it likes to show them off, and it likes to be admired, too. The recognition and the reputation that goes with it are absolutely vital to Capricorn thought: if it doesn't add to your reputation, it isn't worth doing.

It sounds rather selfish, and it is, though to be fair it is actually self-centred, which is a different thing. All of the collecting signs are self-centred, but only two of them (Cancer and Capricorn) are Cardinal as well, so only these two are so noticeable in the way that they look after themselves first. Eventually the wealth and achievement of Capricorn is shared with others, and used for good causes in an attempt to improve the chances of those less fortunate. To use the wealth of the individual for the good of society is the activity of the next sign in the cycle, Aquarius, which takes us further round the zodiac than we want to go for the moment; let's return to Capricorn.

Capricorn's ruling planet is Saturn, as we have already noted. Saturn is the last planet of the traditional 'seven stars'; after all the growth and change that the energies of the other six have made possible, Saturn puts the lid on, and gives things their final form. He is the planet of frameworks and containers; he is the much-quoted 'bottom line' of long and involved contracts. When all the fancy words and promises have evaporated, the reality of the affair is Saturn. The hard work necessary to keep things going is Saturn. The rules and regulations necessary to stop the whole thing falling apart are Saturn. Hard work, duty, being serious, getting results, being disciplined, keeping to the rules, putting in the hours necessary: all of these are the energies of Saturn, and it is these that the Capricorn is concerned with. Not that it is all bad: hard work and patience usually bring promotion, doing your duty usually gets you a medal, you are usually paid for putting in the hours; all of these are visible rewards, and as such appreciated by a Capricorn. Saturn is lord of structure and time; he puts things in their places, and keeps them there for ever. A Capricorn person, with Saturn's energies in him, enjoys finding things in their places, and keeping to his. He has enormous stamina, because Saturn will give him both strength and time together. He is not as explosively powerful as Mars' people, or as creative as Jupiter's, but he can maintain his efforts over a long period, which other planets' people cannot.

Perhaps the greatest advantage a Capricorn has is his facility for turning time and energy into money, and from there into tokens of success, such as big cars and houses. 'Advantage' and 'facility' are perhaps the wrong words—a Capricorn can do nothing else *except* turn time and energy into money, but it is a feature of our society that we treat such a thing as being desirable, and define success as being that very process.

Capricorns, then, are the successes of society; when we think of material wealth and achievement, we are thinking in a Capricornian way, and all our status symbols are products of Capricorn thought. Each sign contributes its role to society— Arians provide the initial impetus, Virgoans the crafts and skills; Capricorns are the workers, the builders, the achievers.

Seeing the Capricorn in that way, like an organ in the body of the nation, leads to an interesting thought: if astrology maintains, as it does, that things exist in the same way at different levels, then is here a Capricornian organ in the body which functions in the same way for the individual as the Capricorn himself functions for society? The answer is yes, though in the case of Capricorn the parts of the body are not strictly organs. They are your bones and your skin.

Bones and skin are wonderful symbols for how a Capricorn thinks and works; one is the framework on which your body is built, and the other is what people actually see of you. Compare that to the Capricorn's liking for structures and rules, so that he knows where he is and what he has to do. Compare also the structure of bone, dry and hard, to the no-nonsense, serious, and sometimes rather pessimistic view of life that the Capricorn displays (not to mention his sense of humour, which is very dry indeed). Compare the function of skin as an outer covering to the Capricorn's desire for his achievements to be recognized, and his love of status symbols. Saturn, of course, represents both parts of the body at once. It is the outer envelope of the seven-planet solar system, as the skin is the outer envelope of the body, and it is the planet which gives structure, as the skeleton does. There are all sorts of phrases in everyday use which show how people have recognized Saturn and Capricorn over the years— 'all skin and bone' suggests an animal which has had a hard time, and 'having old bones' is used by somebody who realizes his age. You can probably think of a few more.

The essence of the Capricorn, then, is about defining the structure of things, and working hard within the rules to achieve, and be recognized for, material success. Organized structure and reputation—bones and skin.

If the idea of bones and skin doesn't appeal as an image for your activities, then look to the animal symbol of your sign. Capricorn goats are tough and hardy beasts, with endless stamina. They keep on going, and they don't eat much—unlike sheep, who are much less determined and ambitious, and will opt for an easier life if they can. What goats really want is to get to the top of the mountain, to stand alone on the highest point of all, so that everyone else can see that they have made it to the top.

The Capricorn goat in the sky is actually two animals in one— he has the tail of a fish. Anything aquatic in astrology is a reference to spiritual and emotional values. In this case, because Capricorn is so practical, the message is not about ethereal or philosophical values, but about the wisdom of experience which Capricorns build up over a period of time. Capricorn doesn't just chase money and a bigger house—he acquires them on the way, but all the time he is thinking about the structure of things, appreciating the reasons why things are the way they are. A Capricorn is conventional, sure, but not from lack of thought; he wants things to continue as they are because in his opinion it would be better for everyone if they did. That's part of why the goat has a fish's tail.

## Early, Middle or Late? The Decanates

*First decanate (22–31 December)*
This is the purest form of Capricorn. There is a double helping of Saturnine energy here, expressed as an appreciation of all hierarchies. To you, chains of control and command are good and necessary things, a belief which you will have considerable trouble explaining to any Sagittarian or Aquarian. To you, a pyramidal power of structure, with the boss at the top, then the managers and executives, and the juniors at the bottom, is the natural way of things. You feel at home in such a system, and you can use its rigid structure as a ladder to help your own progress upwards; each step is clearly defined, and unlikely to move under your feet.

The government of a country, not surprisingly, is assigned to this part of Capricorn; perhaps you will find yourself attracted to government as a career. There are lots of Capricornian politicians, and even if you don't want to be in the public eye there are thousands of Capricornian civil servants and local government officers, all of whom appreciate the firm and definite structure of their respective organizations. The same goes for banks, and in fact virtually any large corporate structure: they are all Capricornian if they have a defined hierarchy, and if you are from this sector of the sign you will be able to identify with that.

There are family hierarchies, too: this part of Capricorn is concerned with your parents, and you will probably find that a large part of your life is taken up with your duty to them. Perhaps you go into your father's business, or take up a trade which he would like to see you in.

The business of Capricorn is to work to improve your position and reputation; in this decanate the position matters to you more than the reputation.

*Second decanate (1–10 January)*

The second decanate sees the influence of Saturn softened by that of Venus. The appreciation of structure and material is still there, of course, but the emphasis on hierarchy and your position within it has gone. What you are concerned with is the rewards for your effort. All forms of recognition for effort are in this part of the sign. Public honours are here, like knighthoods and MBEs, and so are status symbols, like black BMWs and Porsches. That doesn't mean that in every case if your birthday is here that you will be knighted, but it does mean that such things are important to you, and most of your energy is directed towards gaining some kind of public recognition for your efforts.

You are not the sort of person who wants to struggle through life, gamely plodding on doing something for duty's sake and not enjoying a single moment of it. You're not afraid of hard work, but you want to work hard at something you like, and to be handsomely rewarded for it. You would like to work hard at enjoying your rewards, too, and be appreciated for what you've attained in life. There's no virtue in having power and money if you don't use it, according to you, and there's certainly no use in having a limousine in your garage if you don't take it out and drive it now and again. You're not the sort to apologise for taking a limousine to the supermarket: you want to enjoy your car, and you want to enjoy people noticing that you've got one.

This is the decanate of the self-made man, who gets to the top through pure hard work, and enjoys being there. The goal is not the position itself, because hierarchies don't interest you; what matters is the prestige, the public recognition.

*Third decanate (11–19 January)*

In the final decanate the power of Saturn is mixed with Mercury's influence. In this section the position and the recognition are simply distant goals; what matters is the work itself. Mercury always deals on a small scale: with Saturn to keep its nose to the grindstone, so to speak, the result is a concentration on working, working in an effective, controlled, and practical way.

Saturn and Mercury together are the signature of rational thought; if your birthday is here you probably have a very cool and rational way of looking at things. You won't think of yourself or your preferences, just of the job that has to be done, and how it should be approached. The effect is one of logical practicality and disciplined application—imagination and originality are nowhere to be seen in this sort of process, and neither is any personal or emotional bias. It's not a cold way of thinking, as in ruthless and cruel, but it is a dry one, as in unfeeling and inflexible.

If Capricorn is to be able to turn ideas into objects, which is its purpose, then the way it works is important. This is the part of the sign which cares about the actual way things get done. Rules and regulations are given to this part of the sign, including Acts of Parliament and other such ways in which the Government, as a Capricornian institution, performs its function. If your birthday is here, the way things get done is more important to you than what you are doing them for; that things are done properly and effectively, in accordance with the rules, is often more important than anything else. What you can't stand is people who cut corners in their rush to get things finished, and people who want the glory of achievement without necessarily doing all of the work—as often occurs with people from the other two decanates, in fact.

# Three Phases of Life: Capricorn as Child, Adult, Parent

### The Capricorn child

Capricorn children are apt to be quiet and careful. When very young, they make sure that they are not in any sort of a danger: they look at things like high trees and rivers and think about them rather than fall out of them or into them as other children do. Saturn gives a naturally cautious approach and a strong sense of self-preservation, and as a consequence Capricorn children manage to avoid the physical accidents which seem to feature in the lives of, for example, Fire-sign children.

At school, they are never very creative, nor expressive; they much prefer learning about things which have no element of personal expression in them, such as mathematics and science. Poetry and art, or any other activities where imagination and self-expression are called for, become something which the Capricorn child hopes to get through with as little fuss as possible, preferably without being asked to contribute something in front of the whole class. The reasons for this are simply that such activities are unstructured, and the Capricorn child is much better at following the rules than relying on his own creativity.

He will react very positively to praise from an early age. It is as though he doesn't know how good he is until somebody tells him, and the procedure of hard work followed by recognition of his efforts is one which he will continue to enjoy for the rest of his life.

Capricorn children are often given positions of responsibility at school, such as being made prefect or something like that. Because there is something of the old man in every Capricorn (Saturn showing itself again), they often seem mature and reliable to their teachers, and this may help them to win such promotions, but there is more to it than that. What actually takes place is that the Capricorn child quickly identifies the command structure within the school, and learns, too, what sort of behaviour is appropriate for progress up through that structure. It is an instinctive thing, in the same way that a vine will climb a trellis.

*The Capricorn adult*
Climbing the trellis is the essential activity of the Capricorn adult's life, too. Capricorns and big organizations were made for each other. The Capricorn shows that he recognizes the importance of the organization by seeking to climb it, and the organization shows its recognition of his efforts by rewarding him with promotion. The organization sees no harm in this: after all, it is trying to maintain itself, and to take on board people who sincerely believe in the system itself must be good for the

system. The organization knows that as the Capricorn rises through the hierarchy he will do all that he can to maintain and care for the system beneath him, because it is that which gives him his position; both sides benefit from this, and everything works very well.

An adult Capricorn will try to avoid anything that is new, untried, irregular, unconventional, or just plain revolutionary, and it is not because he fears for his safety; no, he learned how to avoid physical risks as an infant, and he doesn't have to think about it now. What he fears is the loss of his position. Anything which undermines the system brings with it various side-effects which the Capricorn would rather avoid. It could be that somebody takes a shortcut to the top; this would suggest either that the existing hierarchy is irrelevant, or that hard work isn't necessarily the best route to the top—both very upsetting ideas from a Capricornian view. At the very least, it suggests that the intruder is out of his proper place, acting above his station—another un-Saturnine idea. Then again, it might be that revolutionary changes might sweep away all the people who are in an inferior position to the Capricorn, which brings him down to ground level again, and removes the prestige attached to his progress so far. Again, such things are un-Capricornian.

The older he gets, and the further up the ladder, the less adventurous and more conservative the Capricorn becomes; he has more to lose than he could possibly gain by being innovative, so he stays with the structure as it is. What he wants, at the end of his day, is to have finished with more than he started with, and for his achievements to be recognized. The Capricorn's ultimate achievement is to build something which will have his name on it for all to see, and which will continue to embody his achievement long after he has gone.

### The Capricorn parent

Capricorn parents work hard for their children's benefit, but they expect their children to work hard for them in return. To the Capricorn parent, the child is the next stage down in the family hierarchy; those qualities which the parent admired in his parent are to be instilled into the child, so that the family continues in the traditions of achievement and excellence. The parent also expects the child to recognize the achievements of the parent, and to be suitably respectful; alas, children are seldom interested in traditions of excellence, and must usually reach the age of the parent themselves before they realize what it was that their parents wanted them to do.

The thing that children usually seem to bring out in a Capricorn parent is inflexibility. Capricorns think along fairly traditional lines, and by the time they are parents are usually quite set in their opinions; children think differently, and much more quickly, which shows the parent as inflexible by comparison.

Capricorn parents will make sure that their children have a better standard of material wealth than they themselves had. Partly this is because if they didn't, it would seem as though the family was making no progress over the generations, and partly it is because the parents want admiration for their children too, and the best way they know to do that is through status symbols. They don't always give their children as much pure affection as they might, which is one of the failings of the sign; any kind of energy, emotional included, gets transformed into material wealth by a Capricorn sooner or later. Saturn isn't a warm planet anyway, so its people can't be as demonstrative or as intimate as the other signs even if they try.

# Aquarius

The sign before Aquarius is Capricorn. Capricorn represents the peak of personal achievement in a material sense. It is where all the effort that you put into your career pays off; it is where your work and worth is recognized and rewarded; it is where you can see and touch your success in terms of money and possessions. The trouble with being at the top, though, is that from there onwards everything is down. To go down by the route you came up is a very disappointing and unsatisfactory procedure, so the only alternative is to take another route down from the top, one whose challenges and rewards are of a different kind.

Because Capricorn represents the individual at his most successful, and because Aquarius is beyond that (in the zodiacal sequence), Aquarians don't need to direct their energies towards their own success: they are past that stage. If they aren't concerned with themselves, therefore, they must be concerned with everything that isn't themselves, or society in general. And so they are. Capricorn found himself interested in the structure of his personal existence, and how he could get to the top of it; Aquarius find himself interested in the structures of the society he is part of, and wants to know what it is that links groups of people together. If his interests continue to grow, eventually he may see that society is not only linked, it is interlinked, such that everybody is part of a single whole, containing within itself all possible eventualities, which may or may not choose to take shape. This mind-boggling vision actually belongs to the final stage in the cycle, Pisces: for the moment we must return to Aquarius.

Aquarius is an Air sign, like Gemini and Libra. For all of these signs, the prime energy is mental; ideas, words, and speech are what keeps them going. Aquarius is also a Fixed sign, so here the words and ideas have somehow to be slowed down, kept still. It is the business of Fixed signs to look after what comes their way, caring for it, making it strong and firm, but not adding to it or changing it in any way. How can you do that with ideas?

Like this. When an idea is first created, it is open and flexible. When it is repeated and kept in the same form, it becomes an opinion, something that can be held and quoted by many other people than its creator. If they all decide to keep it as it is, it becomes a belief or a principle of behaviour. If it grows in strength and complexity, it will eventually become a social code of political system, like, say, Marxism. Aquarius is interested in, and feels at home with, this process; it follows the flow of his planetary energies very well. He is interested in any idea or principle which applies to a large number of people at once. In the same way, he is interested in what large numbers of people have to say, or what they feel, rather than the single voice of an individual. Many Aquarians are drawn to politics for these reasons. Many others take up humanitarian causes, such as those of the underprivileged, or perhaps ecological causes, because they are interested in applying a belief, or an ideal, to the whole of humanity, the largest group imaginable.

Not all Aquarians are activists, of course, but they do tend to gather where ideas are kept fixed, stabilized, and prominent. Many are attracted to Science; indeed, it is usually said that the rise of modern scientific thought, and the technology it has brought us, is an Aquarian phenomenon. Possibly so, but what is important about Science is its insistence on provable truth. The idea of a hard, unalterable truth about matter, which will apply to everything, is very Aquarian: it is an idea made fixed, and applied equally to everything; that is, to the widest possible group. Ideas crystallized into principles and then applied to everything are of course rules, as in rules and regulations; they are used to guide the actions of large numbers of people, and usually (it is hoped) for their benefit. All of this is Aquarian thought.

Aquarians care for the world at large, not for themselves. They care for those who have less than the rest, because they sincerely believe that everybody should be equal. They are interested in, and feel comfortable in, any social group; yet they are somehow loners in every group they join, individualists who never quite fit, and noticeably cool in personal relationships. It sounds contradictory: how can it be so?

The answer lies in the horseshoe of the planets, which we looked at earlier on page 18. Aquarius is ruled by Saturn, but is on the lunar side of the horseshoe. Therefore it must be completely opposite to the sort of thing that Capricorn represents, which is on the other end of the horseshoe, yet they must be related in some way because they are adjacent signs in the zodiacal circle, and because they are both expressing Saturn's energy. Saturn will always form structures, and it will always limit expression, because it is opposed to the sources of Light, the Sun and the Moon. These are points worth remembering. Remember, too, that anything which is solar in its nature is personal and individual, whereas anything lunar is general and public. Capricorn's form of structure, then, is a vertical one, a personal ladder to the top of his career; Aquarius's structure is a horizontal one, a firm network of ideas and principles which he uses to help society. Notice that Aquarius's structure is just as rigid as Capricorn's; anybody who protrudes through the network by being higher than his neighbour is seen as a bad thing— Aquarius enforces his horizontality on others, laying low the mighty, elevating the oppressed, until everybody is on the same level. There's militant democracy for you!

Because Aquarius is the lunar version of Saturn, the energies are always applied for the public good, and in a compassionate manner. Lunar light is a caring light, though it is not a light source in itself—it reflects the light it receives from elsewhere. Thus Aquarius needs other people around him before he can exercise his social principles, and so he makes sure that he always has plenty of company. On an individual level, though, Saturn will restrict his response; cool moonlight made even colder by Saturn does not generate personal heat, and Aquarians are thus cool and unemotional creatures at times.

Each sign of the zodiac has a part of the body associated with it, and it is often instructive to think of yourself as functioning generally in the same manner as that part of the body; you provide the function of that organ for the body of society, so to speak. In the case of Aquarius, it is not only the lower leg, symbolizing walking and social activity, but also the nervous system, which is a very close parallel to the systems of social rules which govern our behaviour. Aquarians, then, keep society moving, but they also tell it what it ought to be doing for its own good.

## Early, Middle or Late? The Decanates

*First decanate (20–29 January)*
This is the purest form of Aquarius. There is a double helping of Saturnine energy here, expressed as a very strong denial of the individual. Almost all of the energy is turned outwards, away from the person, and towards society at large. Not surprisingly,

all forms of politics are assigned to this part of the sign, especially those where the views of the majority are the important ones. Hence, democracy in all its forms, from the House of Commons to a revolutionary Socialist party somewhere in the Third World, belongs here. Where the views of only one person matter, such as in a monarchy or under dictatorship, then astrologically that is assigned to Leo, and this part of Aquarius is of course directly opposed to that. If you were born in this decanate, you are likely to have very firm political views. You may not express them openly, but you will have your own ideas on the way things should be done, and you will be very angry with people who, in your view, are doing the wrong thing. There is a tendency for you not to see any point of view but your own— an 'unusual thing for an Air sign, but if anything can restrict communication, double Saturn can. What matters to you are principles—individual excuses or failures to serve the cause don't concern you at all. You can be hard on yourself for the sake of something you believe in, so you don't see why other people can't do the same.

## Second decanate (30 January–9 February)

Here the harsh energy of Saturn is mingled with the lighter and faster energies of Mercury. Mercury will always insist on communication of some kind, wherever it is, and it is at its best in the exchange of ideas. It also works at close range; it doesn't usually have enough power to be effective over great stretches of time or distance. As a result, the energies of the Aquarian from this decanate find themselves working on the level of personal friendships rather than on the grander scale of political theories. All forms of personal friendship are given to this decanate; if your birthday is here you will be a firm believer in the theory of 'It's not what you know, it's who you know that matters'. You will have lots of friends, in lots of different circles—each one of them gives you an opportunity to make a different kind of association, and you will like that. 'Association' is a very Aquarian word, and it applies specifically to this part of the sign. There are two sorts of association: the first is any group of people who share a common view, which must be a familiar enough example of Aquarian thought by now, and the second is a relationship between two people with a very low emotional content. You like that sort of thing: even when you are close to somebody, you like to feel that you are still a little bit apart, still private to yourself.

*Third decanate (10–19 February)*
The last decanate has Saturn's force softened and made more flexible by Venus's influence. This isn't altogether unwelcome— the end of the sign is near, and Pisces, the next sign, is very soft indeed, so if the transition isn't to be too hard the last degrees of Aquarius will need to be a lot less strict. This is the humanitarian end of Aquarius, the part that supports every sort of good cause from animal rights to campaigning for the release of political prisoners. As usual with Aquarius, the vision is universal; you find it a lot easier to support the cause of all mistreated animals than to take a personal interest in one particular example. That doesn't mean that you don't feel involved; it means that you feel equally involved for all cases, that the principle behind the abuse is what really upsets you, and that you are naturally drawn towards any sort of organization or association which dedicates itself to these causes on a large scale. This decanate also concerns itself with the public appearance of things, and how they are seen by the world at large; if you have a job in public relations or media communications with a large corporation, then you are definitely in the right place!

# Three Phases of Life: Aquarius as Child, Adult, Parent

*The Aquarian child*
The Aquarian child shows his character rather later than some of the other signs; it is always in the nature of Saturn to be slow in its action, and it has no affinity with extreme youth and infancy. Aquarian toddlers are usually self-contained and reasonably happy little people, neither over-expressive nor over-demanding.

This is entirely to do with Saturn, of course; they will feel, even at that early age, that they are their own private people. They do have interests which are different from those of all their friends, though, and these will make themselves apparent quite early on—the Aquarian independence asserting itself. Sometimes Aquarian children seem to attract trouble to themselves at school, a process which mystifies their parents and teachers. It is actually to do with the fact that schools are hierarchical institutions, with subject teachers, house or class tutors, and senior pupils in a well-defined power structure. Aquarian children will refuse to recognize this, and will try to bypass this system wherever possible. As pupils, they are usually better at logical and scientific subjects such as maths and physics, and particularly poor at expressive Arts subjects, with the notable exception of music. Music provides expression for an Aquarian in a way nothing else can, and it is very important to him because of that. The only other way the young Aquarian shows what he feels is through his friends; his opinions are an important influence on their views, and so rather than show his feelings as an individual, he shows them by using the group. What this means to his teachers and parents is that if he changes his company he is angry about something, and is surrounding himself with the people necessary to express that feeling. When given a chance to argue, in class debate, or in an essay, he will show how clearly he thinks, and also how important the principles of things are to him—it is his understanding of the idea rather than its practical application which will develop into the political views of his adult life.

*The Aquarian adult*
The grasp of the underlying principles of things which he developed in his childhood stays with the Aquarian throughout his life. He is proud of his ability to see the thought behind the action, and proud, too, of his own capacity for logical appraisal. More than anything else, the fully-grown Aquarian is rational: to him, everything has to be there for a reason, and when he has discovered the reason he will be satisfied. Like the Sagittarian,

the Aquarian is very confident of himself, but for very different reasons. Most people are a little worried when they find themselves in a new situation, because they don't trust themselves to be able to handle anything that comes their way; the 'collecting' signs are particularly prone to this worry. Sagittarius is confident in himself because he has optimism and belief; he believes that things will work out well each time. Aquarius is confident in himself because he has logic—he is sure of what he knows, he is happy with his own opinion of himself, and he is sure that he will be able to analyse anything he meets in terms of one universal principle or another. In addition, of course, the Aquarian knows that nothing he meets will actually affect him in any way: his habit of keeping himself at a slight remove from all of his activities means that he remains constant, and unaffected by any of them. The adult Aquarian never trust his emotions, or any emotional response he may have to a given situation; emotions are far too individual and personal as far as he is concerned, completely opposed to common opinion or universal scientific principles.

It's not easy to see the impersonal Aquarian from the outside. Because they are so helpful, so friendly, so good with their advice, and so interested in the welfare of others, they appear to be radiating warmth. The logical assumption from that is that they must be in themselves warm, but it is not so—it is just that their energy is directed away from themselves. They are clever and logical, caring and inventive; but always, at the heart of things, alone.

## The Aquarian parent

Aquarian parents are models of fairness. They are never the sort who say 'Do what I say, not what I do' or 'Because I say so, that's why!' They always explain to their children the reasons and principles behind what they want them to do, and hope that the children will choose to do things their parents' way because they have seen that it is for the best reasons. Whenever a child has a grievance, it will find a sympathetic and impartial ear with an Aquarian parent. Aquarian parents are often seen as being very modern, and untroubled by the different values of the generation beneath them. The reasons are simple, and nothing to do with modernity: firstly, the Aquarian parent is quite sure of his own opinions, and those of a child are unlikely to cause him to change them; and secondly, he can see the reasons behind the apparently outrageous behaviour of his teenage children, and understand that it is essentially the same as his own behaviour was at that age.

If Aquarian parents have a fault, it is that they are not comfortable expressing themselves in an emotional way. Some children work on a very high emotional level, and demand the same in return: it is the only way that they can communicate. This is particularly true if the child is from a Water sign. In these cases there is a communication problem which the parent understands quite well, and the onus is on him to do something about it, but he will refuse. Aquarian parents don't want their children to be emotional and changeable; they want them to be self-contained and independent like themselves, and they tell them so. In creating a communications gap between themselves and their children, of course, they are well on the way to achieving their goal.

# Pisces

The sign before Pisces is Aquarius. Aquarius represents the energy present in groups of people gathered together for some common purpose. Earlier zodiac signs were concerned with the energy of the individual, first on his own, and later in contact with his immediate family and friends. By the time the zodiac has reached Aquarius, the circle of acquaintances has grown very large indeed—large enough for the energy of the sign to work best in the ideals that are held by a huge number of people. Pisces deals with a realm even bigger yet.

Imagine that. Imagine the energy that drives a single person, and keeps him alive. Extend its sphere of influence outwards, so that it becomes the energy that keeps a family together, the special warmth that makes a house a home. Extend it further, make it grow; it will go forwards in time through a person's children, and outwards in space to his circle of friends. Expand it into a whole society: now the energy is the structure of position and influence we all know so well, with the managing director at the top, and the tea-boy at the bottom. Now lift the energy above the physical level, so that it becomes the beliefs and hopes of all large groups of people, the shared enthusiasm that cuts across the structures of class and position. Where does the energy go from here? Is there anywhere further for it to expand?

Yes, there is, and that final stage is what Pisces is about. Until now the energy has been held in various forms; either the form of an individual, or within the limits of a defined group, such as a family or a nation. The final stage of the process (Pisces is the twelfth sign of the twelve) is where the energy goes beyond all forms and functions, to take in literally everything. The world of the Piscean contains everything that there has been so far, both in the real world and the world of the imagination. It contains all the feelings and ideas, all the emotions and inspiration that the universe contains. Everything is possible in the world of the Piscean, but nothing is definite. His world is without limits, but it is also without form.

Can you remember what a new packet of plasticine looked like, when you were a child? All the colours were clear and separate, but by the time you had finished playing with it, it was all the same colour, somehow. You knew that all the separate colours were in there somewhere, and that they had all contributed to what you had in front of you, but nothing was definite and identifiable any more. Pisces is like that final stage—it contains everything, but nothing is definite.

It sounds rather difficult to comprehend, doesn't it? How an individual Piscean can find some sort of reality for himself from such an impossibly vague and unformed universe is a difficult question. If you recognize the idea of the ocean of infinite possibility from your own life, as you should if you are Piscean, then you have most probably already made some sort of attempt at solving the problem.

Perhaps some sort of key can be found if we look at what

comes after Pisces. The answer is, of course, Aries again, since the zodiac is an endless circle. Aries is the point at which something definite comes into being; where something coalesces from the infinite possibilities of the Piscean stage, and becomes actual instead of theoretical. In due time, of course, whatever it was that formed in its Arian phase will develop and expand through the phases of the other signs, until it loses itself in the final dissolution of Pisces.

Now you can see that the zodiac is indeed a circle. The cycle of emergence, development and dissolution goes on and on, with each new generation made from what went before. Now you can see, too, why Pisces has to include everything: it is so that the following Aries stage can have the widest range of possibilities to choose from before one of them becomes a reality.

Being a Pisces isn't easy. The people of each sign represent their phase of the zodiacal cycle in society: the Arians are the initiators, the Capricorns are the achievers, and so on. How do you represent the dissolution of all forms and structures, the universal state of everything-and-nothing, when you are trying to be a normal human being?

To begin with, you are not going to be interested in physical things and their acquisition. Their most attractive features, solidity and permanence, are irrelevant to the Piscean mind, which deals with the possible rather than the real and practical. Similarly, since you are the final sign of the zodiac, you will not be trying to start anything or make something new from a situation. Nor will you be communicating anything new: as the final sign, you must be collecting the responses, not asking the questions for a later sign to answer. That eliminates Earth, Fire and Air, then; thankfully, Pisces is a Water sign. It is also Mutable; therefore it doesn't try to define anything, nor to strengthen it and keep going. So what does Pisces actually do?

It absorbs. Pisces is the most inward-looking of the signs and will receive, absorb, and use, any energy at all, and you will be quite unable to prevent yourself from doing it. You are sensitive to absolutely anything—to things which other people ignore completely. The atmosphere generated by the furnishings in a room is quite a powerful force, by your standards. So are the emotions and intentions of other people, as are the colours they wear, or the weather today. Like a photographic plate, a Piscean will faithfully absorb and represent anything he is exposed to, and he will then come to resemble that thing so closely that he is indistinguishable from the original.

This raises two important issues at once, and they will probably be familiar to you already. The first is that because you have the ability to absorb and reflect anything at all, you can be everything to everybody. This means that you can be commercially-minded in the company of stockbrokers and physically creative in the company of sculptors, yet still be sympathetic and caring in the company of demanding children. In doing all of these things you can forget who you are, and lose your individuality, which is sometimes a problem. At the same time, you can become so much a part of the scene that you are invisible; this may be your aim, and it brings us on to the second issue.

It is this: if you are so sensitive that you absorb the energies of anything you are exposed to, whether you want it or not, how do you stop yourself from coming into contact with something which you know will be damaging to you? The answer, which you probably use, even if you haven't realized what you are doing, is to remove yourself from the scene. You can do this in two ways: either by becoming invisible, which you do when you want to stay somewhere for a long time without it affecting you too much (an example of this is the way you behave at work), or by literally running away. Pisceans have a reputation for running away, which is looked on as a bad thing. It shouldn't be: after all, how else do fish defend themselves? You don't have the strength of the Fire signs or the endurance of the Earth signs, and you don't have the hard shells of your Water-sign colleagues the Cancerian crabs or the Scorpio scorpions, so when threatened you must simply make yourself scarce. As a further demonstration of that idea, consider this: each sign of the zodiac looks after a certain part of the body, and the natives of that sign tend to behave in the manner of that organ or limb. In the case of Pisces, it is the feet. What are feet for? Running!

There are some advantages of being a Pisces, though. The ones that everybody envies most are your imagination and your artistic taste. You are almost endlessly creative with your imagination—you can apparently make something out of nothing. The outside world is hungry for stories and entertainment; everybody loves fantasy and make-believe, but very few people have the imagination to create such worlds for themselves. You can. You can work with colours and music, too. A Libran has perfect taste, and a Taurean has the finest appreciation of materials, but neither of them can make an object produce an emotion in the onlooker the way you can. You have a talent for bringing people's emotions out of them, for catching a mood; only you can do this.

The reason that you are so good in these areas is to do with the fact that Pisces is the last of the signs, and represents energy at its finest and most tenuous. Most people don't realize it, but the reason that they like, say, a picture, is not because of the workmanship, or even what it represents, but because of the feelings it evokes in them. You realize this, because to you, their emotional response is more important than the picture. You are actually better at seeing what people feel about things than you are at seeing the things themselves. As soon as you meet anybody, you may not know much about them, but you know what they are feeling; you can pick up and read their emotional state. In fact, you can't *not* do it.

What do you do with all the sensations and feelings that you pick up? Most people shove them into a mental cupboard for a later date, and sort them out when they dream. Dreaming is a very useful process which we don't use half as much as we could; it gives us an opportunity to play with the meaning of things without their physical presence getting in the way, and it enables us to connect things at different levels. If that sounds like a Piscean process, it is: you have probably read somewhere before that Pisceans are supposed to be 'dreamy', and it's not a bad description. Piscean thought, the associative processes we noticed earlier, is very close to dreaming; you can combine the meanings of things in your mind, and live in a world where everything is symbolically true, but not necessarily physically true.

This is where your fantastic imagination comes from. What you are able to do, which the rest of us can't, is make a world in your imagination from your impressions of the outside world, and then live in it as though it were real. You can change it at will, and because you know that none of it is real, you don't get too upset by any of it. What you are doing, in fact, is watching movies on the inside of your head. The rest of us occasionally find you vague and preoccupied, but then we can't know what set of emotions you are enjoying at that instant; it's like trying to have a conversation with somebody who's listening to a Walkman.

You are imaginative, sensitive, and caring, but it may not be at all clear to you where you are supposed to be going. To some of you, it may not matter; if everything is in your imagination, and you don't like what you're feeling now, you know that you only have to wait for a few minutes and another experience will be along; perhaps that one will be more enjoyable. You are so *passive*, you see; you wait to be moved by the circumstance rather than make active moves yourself. The purpose of your existence, though, is to move round the zodiac, and that means towards Aries: somehow you have to define yourself, separate from all the roles that you play.

Thinking about the fishes of the sign is a very useful exercise. The water that they live in is the same as the sea of emotions and feelings that you live in. The water passes through them, and gives them life, and they cannot live without it. The currents of the water sweep them along, though they can swim against it too, if they try. You are exactly the same. It is worth noting that the sign of Pisces has two fishes, joined by a cord, but swimming in opposite directions; society pulls one way, you pull the other. The more definitely individual you are, the more you lean towards Aries. The more you allow yourself to be influenced by the crowd, the more you lean towards Aquarius. Pisces is somewhere in the middle.

## Early, Middle or Late? The Decanates

*First decanate (20 February–1 March)*

This is the purest form of Pisces. There is a double helping of Jupiter's energy here, and that means you are even more imaginative, even more flexible and impressionable than the other Pisceans. Early Pisceans often find that they have a hard life, full of obstacles and restrictions. It isn't really so, or no more so than anyone else's life, but when your planetary energy wants to be as mobile and as flexible as yours does, then every little obstacle seems like a major stumbling-block. In the same way, as a Mutable Water sign, you find it difficult to muster any sort of force at any one time and place; this means that you don't have the firmness of purpose to push aside things which get in your way. If your planetary energies were like a hammer, you could smash anything which obstructed you; since your energies are like running water, you have to find a way round things in your path, and you find it a bothersome business.

Early Pisceans are supposed to make good spies, and to be attracted to that kind of lifestyle. It probably has something to do with the business of being 'invisible' that we noticed earlier, as well as the fact that spies are present in all levels of society but are hidden from view. The idea of being everywhere at once but not openly so is a very Piscean one.

*Second decanate (2–11 March)*

Here the energy of Jupiter is mixed with that of the Moon. Bringing the Moon into the picture as well as a Mutable Water sign must surely make you think of the sea and the tides, and it is true that the sea and all that is associated with it is usually connected to this part of the sign. There are lots of Piscean sailors, but even if you have never been near the sea, you will probably find that you like going on voyages or journeys. Is it the idea of being on the move (Mutable Water)? Is it the idea of seeing new scenery and being open to new experiences (Jupiter's lunar sign)? Or is it that you feel there are times in life for sitting still, and times for moving on? Rhythms of time are a lunar thing, too.

The Moon also represents the general public in astrology, and your face as it is seen in public, too. If you think of how a Piscean can absorb the personality of someone else, and think of the public seeing the adopted personality instead of the real one, you can see why many Pisceans from this part of the sign want to become actors.

Finally, because moonlight is only a reflection of sunlight, a changed and paler version of the original, and in the same way that an actor's role is not the real person, this part of the sign is associated with deception and illusion. It doesn't matter whether you are the victim or the perpetrator; somehow they are part of your experience of life.

*Third decanate (12–20 March)*

Here Mars' strength and power are blended with Jupiter's optimistic imagination. The cocktail is an odd one, and it produces Pisceans with much more determination than the earlier decanates. Not that their energy and endurance is directed into making themselves famous, however; the direction of their interest, as always, lies inwards, and this end of the sign often finds itself attracted to areas of life where withdrawal from the world is a major feature. All forms of nursing, especially the care of the chronically sick or the incurable, are here, as are all forms of institutional work.

Although it is less common now, the idea of dedication to religion is one associated with the later stages of Pisces. There are two ways of doing this, both Piscean: the first is the hard and self-denying life of monastic orders, and the second involves the isolation, and the long voyaging, of being a missionary. You will see that there are a lot of Piscean ideas in both of those alternatives. If you were born with the Sun in this decanate, you will surely recognize the need to lose yourself in something which benefits others.

Here, too, at the very end of the zodiac, are the mysteries of life itself, and of the soul. Late Pisceans feel somehow at home in this sort of territory, and often develop their interest in it.

One unusual profession has associations with the end of

Pisces: prostitution. Is it an 'invisible' service for others? Is it simply a mixture of Jupiter and Mars, or is it more than that? Late Pisceans will understand.

## Three Phases of Life: Pisces as Child, Adult, Parent

*The Piscean child*
Piscean children are quite sweet. That sounds like a generalization, and it is; but it is also the impression that they give, and as with everything Piscean, the impression is the most important thing. They have the ability to be whatever anybody wants them to be, and learn at an early age to alter their behaviour to suit the parent they are with at the time. Only when they have to play multiple roles at the same time do they get confused, just like the famous example of the chameleon unable to cope with being placed on a tartan rug. Whenever an argument looms, Piscean children are nowhere to be found; they can sense the change of mood, and they know that they are better off out of it altogether.

Piscean sensitivity makes for a creative and artistic child, and one who will be very successful in his early years at school. Partly this is because of his ability to be what his teacher wants him to be; the rest of it is because early schooling tries to encourage imaginative expression, and Pisceans have a better developed imagination than anybody else in the zodiac. In contrast, secondary school is often a depressing place for the young Piscean. Here there are things to be learned in a structured and organized fashion, and some subjects which are compulsory study; the changeable mind of the Piscean sees the whole organization as impossibly restricting and obstructive. He will daydream through the subjects he dislikes, turning his mind inwards to escape into a world of imagination. Being reprimanded for this leads to a further impulse to escape; a vicious circle can easily be created. Young Pisceans need a focus for their imagination, through which they can realize some sense of their own capabilities; if this is not available, they can find themselves 'being led' by the influence of others, who may not have their best interests at heart.

## The Piscean adult

Adult Pisceans spend a lot of their time avoiding pressure. You know how sensitive you are, and you also know, by the time you reach adulthood, that the rest of the world is insensitive and brutal in comparison. Like the fishes of the sign, you are sensitive to changes of pressure in the water, and try to maintain your equilibrium at all times. Situations without an obvious way out are noted and avoided, and when suddenly plunged into unfamiliar surroundings, you will always look for the door.

You have to have a constant supply of emotional experience, just as fish need water. It doesn't have to be the emotional experience of a personal relationship; anything and everything will cause you to change the way that you feel. When you can, therefore, you try to do things which make you feel good. To some extent, so does everybody else, but in your case it is the internal response which is more important than the object which produces it. Therefore you tend to like anything which can be appreciated on more than one level; you prefer poetry to prose, and you prefer paintings to maps. In each case, the emotions produced are slightly different each time you experience the poem or the painting, and you like that. You also like being able to evoke a mood or a sentiment from an old photograph, or a favourite song; you like making associations in your memory.

Associative thought isn't logical or analytical. It's personal, individual, never the same twice. It drives other people to distraction because they can't follow it, and they tend to think of you as changeable and indecisive as a result. What they can't see is that associative thought is the whole business of life for you: the most important thing about you is your imagination, and the reality that it makes for you from collecting your emotional impressions is the one that matters for you. To the other eleven signs, it's like living in a kaleidoscope; to you, it's normal.

## The Piscean parent

The difficult thing about being a Piscean parent is that it is impossible for you to be constant or firm. Whichever face you present to your child, or whichever way you try to direct them, you are likely to change your mind before long, and this can be confusing to him. The good side of this is that he is sure to have a varied upbringing, and one which offers him a much broader range of experiences than other children of his age, but the bad side is of course that he will have difficulty in seeing his parents as constant and reliable. When you need to assert your authority you will find it difficult not to sympathize with his point of view: you are sensitive enough to your child's emotional state for it to become your own, and then you will *both* be in tears.

The good thing about being a Piscean parent is that you are always receptive to what your children are trying to tell you, so that you understand intuitively what they really mean, even if their words don't carry their meaning. This works at both ends of the age range: not only can you understand a toddler who lacks the vocabulary (but not the mentality) for complex expressions, but you can also understand a teenager, whose abrasive slang hides his real emotional state.

Most Piscean parents are artistic to some extent, and a home which already contains musical instruments and artist's materials does a lot to encourage any similar talent in their children, whether or not they are Piscean. What Piscean parents *don't* have, of course, is any sort of structure in their lives; as far as they can, they will have removed all restrictions or obstacles. Some children, especially from the Earth signs, actually need an organized life; it will be up to their Piscean parents to provide it. They will find it a very difficult thing to do.

# 3. Zodiacal Relationships
## How Zodiacal Relationships Work

You might think that relationships between two people, described in terms of their zodiac signs, might come in 144 varieties; that is, twelve possible partners for each of the twelve signs. The whole business is a lot simpler than that. There are only seven varieties of relationship, although each of those has two people in it, of course, and the role you play depends on which end of the relationship you are at.

You may well have read before about how you are supposed to be suited to one particular sign or another. The truth is usually different. Librans are supposed to get on with Geminis and Aquarians, and indeed they do, for the most part, but it is no use reading that if you have always found yourself attracted to Taurus, is it? There has to be a reason why you keep finding Taureans attractive, and it is not always to do with your Sun sign; other factors in your horoscope will have a lot to do with it. The reason you prefer people of certain signs as friends or partners is because the relationship of your sign to theirs produces the sort of qualities you are looking for, the sort of behaviour you find satisfactory. When you have identified which of the seven types of basic relationship it is, you can see which signs will produce that along with your own, and then read the motivation behind it explained later on in more detail in 'The Approach to Relationships' and the individual compatability sections.

Look at the diagram on page 16. All you have to do is see how far away from you round the zodiacal circle your partner's Sun sign is. If they are Leo and you are Pisces, they are five signs in front of you. You are also, of course, five signs behind them, which is also important, as you will see in a little while. If they are Sagittarius, they are three signs behind you, and you are three signs  in front of them. There are seven possibilities: you can be anything up to six signs apart, or you can both be of the same sign.

Here are the patterns of behaviour for the seven relationship types.


*Same sign*
Somebody who is of the same sign as you acts in the same way that you do, and is trying to achieve the same result for himself. If your goals permit two winners, this is fine, but if only one of you can be on top, you will argue. No matter how temperamental, stubborn, devious, or critical you can be, they can be just the same, and it may not be possible for you to take the same kind of punishment you hand out to others. In addition, they will display every quality which really annoys you about yourself, so that you are constantly reminded of it in yourself as well as in them. Essentially, you are fighting for the same space, and the amount of tolerance you have is the determining factor in the survival of this relationship.


*One sign apart*
Someone one sign forward from you acts as an environment for you to grow in. In time, you will take on those qualities yourself. When you have new ideas, they can often provide the encouragement to put them into practice, and seem to have all your requirements easily available. Often, it is this feeling that they already know all the pitfalls that you are struggling over which can be annoying; they always seem to be one step ahead of you, and can seemingly do without effort all the things which you

have to sweat to achieve. If the relationship works well, they are helpful to you, but there can be bitterness and jealousy if it doesn't.

Someone one sign back from you can act as a retreat from the pressures of the world. They seem to understand your particular needs for rest and recovery, whatever they may be, and can usually provide them. They can hold and understand your innermost secrets and fears; indeed, their mind works best with the things you fear most, and the fact that they can handle these so easily is a great help to you. If the relationship is going through a bad patch, their role as controller of your fears gets worrying, and you will feel unnerved in their presence, as though they were in control of you. When things are good, you feel secure with them behind you.

*Two signs apart*
Someone two signs forward from you acts like a brother or sister. They are great friends, and you feel equals in each other's company; there is no hint of the parent-child or master-servant relationship. They encourage you to talk, even if you are reticent in most other company; the most frequently heard description of these relationships is 'We make each other laugh'. Such a partner can always help you put into words the things that you want to say, and is there to help you say them. This is the relationship that teenagers enjoy with their 'best friend'. There is love, but it does not usually take sexual form, because both partners know that it would spoil the relationship by adding an element of unnecessary depth and weight.

Someone two signs behind you is a good friend and companion, but not as intimate as somebody two signs forward. They are the sort of people you love to meet socially; they are reliable and honest, but not so close that things become suffocatingly intense. They stop you getting too serious about life, and turn your thoughts outwards instead of inwards, involving you with other people. They stop you from being too selfish, and help you give the best of yourself to others. This relationship, then, has a cool and a warm end; the leading sign feels much closer to his partner than the trailing sign does, but they are both satisfied by the relationship. They particularly value its chatty quality, the fact that it works even better when in a group, and its tone of affection and endearment rather than passion and obsession.

*Three signs apart*
Someone three signs in front of you represents a challenge of some kind or another. The energies of the pair of you can never run parallel, and so must meet at some time or another. Not head on, but across each other, and out of this you can both make something strong and well established which will serve the two of you as a firm base for the future. You will be surprised to find how fiercely this person will fight on your behalf, or for your protection; you may not think you need it, and you will be surprised that anybody would think of doing it, but it is so nonetheless.

Someone three signs behind you is also a challenge, and for the same reasons as stated above; from this end of the relationship, though, they will help you achieve the very best you are capable of in a material sense. They will see to it that you receive all the credit that is due to you for your efforts, and that everyone thinks well of you. Your reputation is their business, and they will do things with it that you could never manage yourself. It's like having your own P.R. team. This relationship works hard, gets results, and makes sure the world knows it. It also looks after itself, but it needs a lot of effort putting in.

*Four signs apart*
Someone four signs forward from you is the expression of yourself. All the things you wanted to be, however daring, witty, sexy, or whatever, they already are, and you can watch them doing it. They can also help you to be these things. They do things which you think are risky, and seem to get away with them. There are things you aim towards, sometimes a way of life that you would like to have, which these people seem to be able to live all the time; it doesn't seem to worry them that things might go wrong. There are lots of things in their life which

frighten you, which you would lie awake at nights worrying about, which they accept with a child's trust, and which never go wrong for them. You wish you could be like that.

Someone four signs behind you is an inspiration to you. All the things you wish you knew, they know already. They seem so wise and experienced, and you feel such an amateur; luckily, they are kind and caring teachers. They are convincing, too. When they speak, you listen and believe. It's nice to know there's somebody there with all the answers. This extraordinary relationship often functions as a mutual admiration society, with each end wishing it could be more like the other; unfortunately, it is far less productive than the three-sign separation, and much of its promise remains unfulfilled. Laziness is one of the inherent qualities of a four-sign separation; all its energies are fulfilled, and it rarely looks outside itself for something to act upon. Perhaps this is just as well for the rest of us.

*Five signs apart*
Someone five signs ahead of you is your technique. You know what you want to do; this person knows how to do it. He can find ways and means for you to do what you want to be involved in, and he can watch you while you learn and correct your mistakes. They know the right way to go about things, and have the clarity of thought and analytical approach necessary if you are to get things clear in your mind before you get started

Someone five signs behind you is your resource. Whenever you run out of impetus or energy, they step forward and support you. When you're broke, they lend you money, and seldom want it returned. When you need a steadying hand because you think you've over-reached yourself, they provide it. All this they do because they know that it's in their best interest as well as yours, to help you do things, and to provide the material for you to work with. You can always rely on them for help, and it's nice to know they will always be there. They cannot use all their talent on their own; they need you to show them how it should be done. Between you, you will use all that you both have to offer effectively and fully, but it is a relationship of cooperation and giving; not all the zodiac signs can make it work well enough.

*Six signs apart*
Someone six signs apart from you, either forwards or backwards, is both opponent and partner at the same time. You are both essentially concerned with the same area of life, and have the same priorities. Yet you both approach your common interests from opposite directions, and hope to use them in opposite ways. Where one is private, the other is public, and where one is self-centred, the other shares himself cheerfully. The failings in your own make-up are complemented by the strengths in the other; it is as if, between you, you make one whole person with a complete set of talents and capabilities. The problem with this partnership is that your complementary talents focus the pair of you on a single area of life, and this makes for not only a narrow outlook, but also a lack of flexibility in your response to changes. If the two of you are seeing everything in terms of career, or property, or personal freedom, or whatever, then you will have no way to deal effectively with a situation which cannot be dealt with in those terms. Life becomes like a seesaw; it alternates which end it has up or down, and can sometimes stay in balance; but it cannot swing round to face another way, and it is fixed to the ground so that it does not move.

These are the only combinations available, and all partnerships between two people can be described as a version of one of the seven types. It must be remembered, though, that some of the roles engendered by these dispositions of sign to sign are almost impossible to fulfil for some of the signs, because their essential energies, and the directions they are forced to take by the planets behind them, drive them in ways which make it too difficult. To form a relationship based on sharing and acceptance is one thing: to do it when you are governed by a planet like Mars is somethings else. Even when the relationship can form, the sort of approach produced by, say, Jupiter, is a very different thing from that produced by Venus.

The next thing you must consider, then, is how you attempt

relationships as a whole, and what you try to find in them. Then you must lay the qualities and outlook of each of the twelve signs over the roles they must play in the seven relationship types, and see whether the pair of you manage to make the best of that relationship, or not.

The seven relationship types are common to all the signs, relating to all the other signs. You can use your understanding of them to analyse and understand the relationship between any pair of people that you know; but to see how the characters fit into the framework in more detail, you will need to look at the individual compatibilities, which are in the next chapter. Before you do that, though, it is worth looking at the way you approach your relationships, and noting what it is that you are trying to get from them.

# The Approach to Relationships

## Aries

An Aries is wholly motivated by his need to experience things first-hand as a result of his own actions and decisions. He is entirely self-motivating, self-sustaining, and self-centred. Most people read the word 'self-centred' as if it meant 'selfish', but that is not the case here. 'Self-centred' here means centred on the self; not centred on any ambition, possession, political persuasion, religion, friend, relative, or circumstance, just on the self.

It will seem obvious to you, as an Arian reading this, that your self matters most, and it is very difficult for you to imagine anybody thinking any other way; but the fact is, that only Arians, and people of other signs born with Mars, Aries' planet, in important places in the sky, do think this way, and that the vast majority of humanity does not.

When you enter a relationship, therefore, you are seeking to express yourself physically to the other person, and experience their response to you. You want to experience the excitement of being in love, or of having a new partner, and you want them to excite you with their response, but you do not necessarily consider them as people in themselves, and never think that you might have to put aside your own requirements to serve their needs. That's just not how you think, and it is wrong for people to criticize you for not holding an attitude which is completely alien to you.

When you do fall in love, when you have decided that projecting all your energy at an individual is so rewarding that you can think of nothing that you would rather do, you do it with all the power that your planet, Mars, gives you—and that is a great deal. Your partner is likely, whatever their sign, to be surprised at the passion you generate. Not just sexual energy, but the intensity of the emotions you can unleash. Have you ever been surprised at how strong a baby is? When they want something, they go for it with all the strength they have, whereas adults, conditioned by their ideas of polite behaviour, don't do anything with that kind of total dedication; as a result, adults find the strength, intensity, and single-minded dedication of infants surprising. Arians work in exactly the same way as babies. The energy generated by a full-grown adult, when applied with the single-minded dedication of a young child, is a little frightening; other people experience an Arian in love with them as being like this. This can be a bit much to take all at once, especially if the object of your affections is unused to such passionate displays. There is a lot of the child in your character, and you are likely to try to win people over in ways which would win *you* over. You know how quickly your mood changes, and how delighted you are with anything new and personal to you; you love getting presents, and so you give them too, in the hope that if you like them, others will. This usually works, but again it can be a bit overwhelming to be given lots of surprise gifts if you are uncertain about the relationship anyway.

Mars makes you sexually very powerful and expressive, and this has rarely caused an Arian any difficulty in relationships, provided that this power stays within the relationship and doesn't extend to other partners at the same time. Arians tend to be one-at-a-time folk, though; they focus on one person, and pursue that one person alone. Aries doesn't take the same delight in variety as, say, Sagittarius.

As a friend, it is the immediacy and open enthusiasm you generate that is attractive to other people, and you will find yourself attracted to anybody who displays those same qualities to you. No matter what their sign, if they have confidence in their actions, and they appear to be assertive and active, you will find yourself admiring them, and eventually meeting them (an Arian meets people, of course, by walking over to them and introducing himself; he never waits to be introduced). The only other sort of person you find attractive is the sort who displays qualities you can't quite fathom. This is a similar situation to the small child presented with a musical box: he likes it, but can't see how it works, and likes it the more for that. In adult life, for an Aries, this occurs most often in meetings with Pisceans; the peculiar qualities of this liaison are explained more fully later, under Aries-Pisces relationships.

Arians don't need to marry for companionship; they are quite happy on their own. They don't need to marry for security or prestige; the former is an unknown concept to them anyway, and they generate their own prestige by achieving their own targets. Besides, prestige only exists in the eyes of others, and an Arian never thinks of the others, because he is self-centred, as we have noted before. Why, then, does an Arian marry at all?

An Arian's needs are all immediate; that is, he can see what he needs for now, but cannot see what he will need for the future. Besides, he is confident that he can meet the future when it comes. He may find that he needs a parent figure to give him a framework within which to operate, and to meet his daily needs. This person is likely to be his long-term partner. Once married he will put his energy into the family unit he has formed, and the whole group becomes driven by his force and energy. He devotes his time to making sure that his family is there at the top and in front, as well as himself. What the partner does best is direct the Arian's massive energy to the best use for the family, and comfort him when things go wrong. It only takes a little while for the Arian to recover his self-confidence, just as a child does, but during that time the Arian is convinced that nothing will ever go right again, because his powers have failed him; he doesn't know what else to try, and he cannot take a view of things other than the immediate one. Consequently, the partner's job is one of comforter and supporter as well as being delighted by his energy and enthusiasm when all is well. The partner who combines all these qualities is rare, but that strange combination of co-adventurer, sparring partner, parent, and nurse is what any Arian looking for a marriage partner is trying to find.

## Taurus

A Taurean is wholly motivated by his need to give and receive physical security and reassurance. He has no real sense of his own identity, and does not spend much time thinking about who he is as an abstract idea; he only knows who he is by relating himself to his environment. Reassurance and a sense of worth are achieved by being in welcoming and satisfying surroundings.

It will seem obvious to you, as a Taurean reading this, that if you are not comfortable in your surroundings, then you are not comfortable in general, and will feel that you cannot be at your best until your surroundings are more amenable to your tastes and needs. You also know that unless there is a similar pleasantness in your emotional dealings with the people around you, then you are just as uncomfortable. You cannot imagine things being any other way, but the fact is that only Taureans, and people born with Venus, Taurus' planet, in important places in the sky, do think this way, and the rest of humanity does not.

When you enter a relationship, you want to find all that you can that is common to you and your partner, and make that the basis of your relationship. You do not form relationships by being attracted to people who are nothing like you, striking sparks off each other by parading your differences; you are not strong or secure enough in your views for that. You want them to find parts of you that they like and approve of, and for you to find parts of them that you want to care for in return. It is all to do with the way that Venus works, always finding the common ground, and promoting togetherness and unity wherever it can find a chance to do so. In your case, it is 'collecting' energy (see pp 12 and 13 if you've forgotten), so you will not be the one to make the first move. You want to take all the affection that they feel for you, and keep it for yourself, to be stored up for a rainy day perhaps. You also want to look after them, and keep them close to you, so that they will always be there for you to care for, and to give you the reassurance you need so much. This process is actually one of acquisition—you are collecting people and things you care for, and keeping them close to you. It would be uncharitable, and wrong, to say that you need them exclusively for your own security: that is only half the story. The energy flow is nonetheless going into you rather than out of you, though, and you are definitely benefiting from the affection given to you by those you love. On the other hand, they need somebody to give their affection to, and to have that affection so obviously appreciated is rewarding for them. In addition, they need security, and you are not the sort of person who is different from one day to the next; you embody reliability and security for the rest of the zodiac, and when anybody feels a need to be close to those qualities because he lacks them himself, he comes to you to supply them.

What does happen in your relationships is that you become attached to your partner, and you try to keep them close to you, as unchanged and stable as you are yourself. This is misinterpreted: to a lot of people it can seem as though you are trying to stifle them, stop them growing, and holding them against their will. I am sure that you would be horrified to think that anyone in a long-term relationship which was giving you happiness and emotional nourishment was finding that being loved by you was smothering them, but you would do well to remember the possibility of this happening, and make every effort to be flexible.

You are very sensitive about your emotional state, very easily wounded, and you carry the hurt for a long time. If it looks as though your partner wants a little more freedom, you are prone to interpret this as a criticism of your love for him, and feel wounded. At the same time, you fear that if he leaves you, you will have lost all the reassurance and nourishment you gained, and you start to fight to keep him. You are frightened to let go, and you feel that somebody is taking what's yours, so you cling on harder than before, and refuse to see reason. The situation gets worse. In fact, the situation is irretrievable from here, because you don't know how to release the pressure. Either you lose him and get hurt, or he relents a little to alleviate your worries, thus returning the situation to its pre-crisis state— which will worsen again in due time, because you will not ever see why he feels this way, and will not change your approach. if that makes you sound like a monster, it's not meant to, but it is how you work, and other people find that it needs careful handling.

A relationship which consists of two people who feel emotionally secure with each other and share the same needs and fears is what works best for you, and when you have found that, you are much better. Then you put all your energy into building a secure territory for you both, and filling this area with everything which makes your life together more comfortable. This is a long-term project, and you see all relationships this way: each new friendship is potentially a life friendship to you, and you only get into trouble when you encounter people for whom friendship is a temporary diversion, an entertaining episode with no thought of permanence.

You marry, essentially, for security. When you have a home and family around you, you feel that you have the sort of surroundings which are not likely to move around and force you to change direction too frequently. Also, you can play the role of being the centre of the family unit, which you enjoy. You don't want to be just a member of a family, you want to be the centre of the family, so that you can have it around you. As parent, householder, maître d'hôtel, and nurse you can be in control of all the material things that comprise the household. At the same time, you can gain satisfaction from caring for the rest of the family, and receive their appreciation for the way you look after the material side of their existence for them. What your partner has to do is look after you. This is an analogous job to that which the farmer does as he moves the bull from one field to another. It must be done firmly but gently, and the bull must somehow be persuaded that such a move was his intention anyway. It can be a dangerous job.

# Gemini

What a Gemini needs most is somebody to talk to. He needs to be able to form his thoughts into words, and to express them in speech, and he needs an audience for that. In return, he needs somebody to provide him with new information and a point of view different from his own, so that he can compare and contrast what he hears with what he already knows. All relationships, then, have to provide this mental stimulation and opportunity for communication.

Friendships are the easiest thing for a Gemini to form. Most of them start through speaking to a stranger, and a Gemini is always more than willing to do that, since it holds the promise of novelty and variety. In addition, friendships are usually characterized, in their early stages, by the fact that both parties are enjoying themselves. They are friends because they like being with each other, not because they have to be with each other. This light approach suits the Gemini best. The later stages of a friendship, where there is often an element of obligation, are what he dreads. Although he is unlikely to run away and find a new friend for no apparent reason, he is bothered by the thought that he might not be able to if he should want to. The idea of freedom is very important. It needs to be understood that this is not the kind of desire for freedom that needs to test itself against every known restriction for its own sake: that would be a sort of self-assertion, shown through rebellion. This is a much lighter, less considered sort of idea. It is simply that any sort of commitment or duty entails 'keeping on doing it', and it is the idea of unvarying repetition which worries the Gemini. He knows that if tomorrow is going to be the same as today, then he cannot live properly. It is as simple as that.

A friendship is ideal; it offers him the company he needs without the commitment he dreads. The Gemini can also increase his enjoyment and mental nourishment by having a great number of friends, which he does. Of course, this means that he does not have time to get too closely involved with any particular one of them, and this is entirely intentional. A process which increases the positive aspects of something while reducing the incidence of the negative aspects is bound to seem like a good idea, and so he tries to have as many friends as possible. The friends themselves are not concerned about his lack of emotional involvement. He asks no favours from them, provides very entertaining company, is pleased to see them, and never stays long enough to inconvenience them. This is why the Gemini is everybody's friend, and why nobody ever thinks to look why he does things this way. He even forgets any arguments there may have been in the past. This is because arguments are unimportant affairs to a Gemini; he enjoys them as an exercise, but since he never lets himself believe things too strongly, they are soon forgotten. Anyway, he would much rather have arguments than no communication at all. Having a different point of view is something a Gemini *likes* in other people.

Sexual relationships are a lot more demanding for the Gemini, and he is usually to be found converting them into the kind of friendship he prefers. This isn't his fault; everybody does it. It's just that the pure Gemini puts a low emphasis on physical expressions of friendship, and society teases him for it these days. A century ago nobody would have mentioned it.

Not that a Gemini doesn't like a sexual relationship at all. He is, though, primarily mental in his energies, and when he really likes somebody, he would like to express himself verbally rather than physically. Mercury's energy doesn't work through the body in the same way that Mars' or Venus' energies do. The point of a relationship to him is to provide that mental stimulation which he needs. He will see a new person as a challenge, and give all of his considerable ingenuity to thinking up ways to attract attention or delight his new love. When he has their attention, they must continue to offer him new and different ways of expressing his delight in their company. If some of these are sexual, then so much the better, but if they are always the same, no matter what form they take, then the Gemini will become bored, and lose interest. A Gemini is quite prepared to have a sexual relationship if that is the way to maintain the company of the person he finds so interesting, but he doesn't go into a relationship on his own part with physical expression as a prime requirement.

The trick to keeping a Gemini interested lies in variety and the appearance of youth. Anybody who either looks or behaves as though they were older than he is will have a hard time maintaining the relationship.

In business, the Gemini needs new things to keep his interest at a high level. Routine work, or anything that is likely to become repetitive, will quickly bore him. Again, he wants mental stimulation and a freedom from being tied to things. As a business partner, therefore, he is looking for somebody who can do the routine things for him, leaving him free to carry on with whatever takes his fancy. Since he hates responsibility, he wouldn't mind a partner who could tell him what to do, thus avoiding responsibility on his own part—but he would like to feel free to answer back or leave the job at a moment's notice if the mood took him! Where these conditions are not met, of course, he will drift from one job to another until he finds a situation which offers him most, if not all, of the environment he seeks.

In marriage, the Gemini is trying to establish a lively and lasting companionship. He is not trying to give some kind of legal basis to his personal possessiveness, nor found a dynasty to bear his name: he is trying to ensure that he is given the kind of friendship and company that he values on a long-term basis. He will do his best to make the relationship as lively as he would like it to be, and this usually brings out anything even remotely witty, whimsical or original in the partner to the full. Being married to a Gemini is a lively and colourful experience, which never becomes dull or silent. What it isn't, though, is serious, ambitious, or emotionally intense. It's not what he's in it for.

## Cancer

All relationships are personal ones to a Cancerian. This sounds obvious, I know, but not all of the other signs feel so personally involved with the people they meet as a Cancerian does. It is quite possible for a Capricorn or an Aquarian to have a working partnership with somebody that they don't really like at all. As long as the partnership serves its purpose, which may well be a commercial one, then they don't mind what the other person is actually like.

Cancerians don't think this way; in fact they can't think this way. Since they bring their emotions and intuition into play every time they meet somebody, and since their future actions are influenced by what they think of people, then every relationship, business or social, is conducted on the level of a personal friendship. Business relationships thus stand or fall on the strength of the affection the Cancerian has for his partner.

It is not possible for a Cancerian to remain cool towards another person. If he feels sympathy and affection, then he will want to share some of his feelings and care for the well-being of the other; this will show in a variety of ways, from simple sympathy in difficulties to actively helping. In a business environment this can take the form of placing orders with suppliers or contractors whom the Cancerian likes and trusts rather than new and unknown people. If the Cancerian feels antipathy and discomfort in somebody's company, then he will shield himself from that person, and appear reserved and uncommunicative. Either way, there is no middle ground; the Cancerian forms an opinion of somebody based on his personal reaction to them, and this is what guides his behaviour from then on.

What does a Cancerian want out of a relationship? The best way of finding out is probably to look at the energies of the Moon, which is the essential principle of Cancerianism. Have a look at page 21, and page 12 too.

Lunar energy needs solar energy first. What a Cancerian wants from a relationship is for somebody to offer him warmth, affection, the glow of his own personality in companionship. This is similar to the Sun pushing out light and heat to anything within range. When this flow of personal warmth is established, the Cancerian absorbs it, and generates within himself his own sort of complementary energy as a reflection of the incoming warmth. This new energy is then made available to the other person to use and enjoy. It is similar to moonlight; it is a much softer product altogether, more soothing and reassuring. It is quieter and cooler, and the great thing about it is that it can be stored, which the other sort cannot.

This caring sort of energy is not easy to see when there are a lot of people around radiating their own warmth and enthusiasm, just as you cannot see the stars in the daytime. When things go wrong, however, and the person with the ebullient energy is feeling less than radiant, the Cancerian's stored lunar energy is there to care for him, and he feels better. Cancerians need to care for people, and to have that caring recognized; they do this to express all the lunar energies formed in them by having non-lunar people radiate their own warmth towards them.

What the Cancerian looks for in a relationship, then, is to establish the circular flow of lunar energy. He needs somebody to offer him warmth and affection, and when he has that, he will reflect that warmth back as care and protection. This effect becomes more noticeable, as we have seen, when the initial source of warmth falters or fails for any reason.

As a friend, a Cancerian is constant and reliable. Once the friendship has formed, there is very little that would induce the Cancerian to break it off, because to do so would mean not caring for somebody he cared for in the past; a very un-Cancerian thing. Any variation in the level of closeness will be compensated for by the Cancerian, who will regard this as one of the little 'down' phases that all people go through, and provide more of his caring gestures to make up the difference. Even when the friendship is distant, and the friends hardly ever see each other, the Cancerian keeps his end of the bargain, so to speak, with letters and Christmas cards. Birthdays and anni-versaries will be remembered. This particular practice always astounds the distant non-Cancerian friend: it shouldn't. It arises because to the friend, the important part of a friendship is likely to be something like physical companionship or a shared goal, but to the Cancerian the important part is the sentiment. Consequently, sentimental items like birthdays are unforgettable to the Cancerian, and they are remembered accordingly.

Cancerians take friendship seriously, and are hurt when a friend is inconsiderate. They will forgive, of course, and they would never show how much they have been hurt, but they do not forget very easily, and they can suffer a long time. Friendships are important to the Cancer soul; people from the other signs have a much more flippant attitude, and may think nothing of breaking friendships when they are no longer convenient or attractive. Treating friendships so lightly is very wounding to Cancerians, and it hurts the more because they dare not show it. Of course, if they do not show it, then the rest of the world thinks no harm has been done, and a vicious circle is set up. This is why Cancer crabs have hard shells, perhaps.

Marriage is virtually a Cancerian institution. It is probably the desire to make permanent roots out of a rewarding friendship which drives Cancerians to marry; whatever it is, they suit marriage very well. It gives them a solid framework, reasonably secure against personal attack; they can build a family unit from it, and from that they can form links to other branches of their own families to provide emotional security and mutual support. Cancerians are devoted to their spouses; they are tenacious fighters for what is theirs anyway, and once married will defend mutual interests just as fiercely.

In sexual relationships Cancer is stronger than you might think: it is a cardinal sign, remember, so it defines its own territory. The relationship will be at least as intense on an emotional level as it is on a physical one, probably more so: the Moon is the great feminine principle, and is an exact match and partner for the most powerful masculine elements her partners have to offer.

# Leo

Not all Leos actually want, or need, a close one-to-one relationship which will last them all their lives. It would be a very rare person indeed who could adequately receive and reflect all the light and heat a Leo has to offer; very often that purpose is best served by a whole range of people—an audience, in fact.

Nor does a Leo ever really need a soul-mate in the same way as, for instance, a Libran does. Leos are quite capable of looking after themselves, and they don't feel left out or isolated by the feeling that nobody else is quite the same as they are; in fact, it reinforces their view that they are indeed rather special, something out of the ordinary. Many Leos are open and social on the surface, but rather withdrawn inside: it takes an unusually persistent person to attempt to look behind the brilliance and the warmth, and the Leo is not likely to thank them for doing so.

The essence of the thing is that Leos are people who exist on their own rather than in groups. There is no point in a Leo being like everybody else, or in finding somebody just like himself to be friends with: to do such a thing would destroy his sense of his own uniqueness. He needs an adoring public, and he needs friends, but he does not necessarily need a confidant or a comforter—those things he can do for himself. After all, if you are right all the time, and always get your own way, why do you need to confide in people, and when are you ever miserable?

There is a handy astrological reminder for this description of the inner Leo, and it has to do with the planetary adjectives. Jupiter's people are jovial, Saturn's people are saturnine, and so on. Leo is ruled by the Sun, and its people are . . . solitary.

When a Leo does enter a relationship with somebody, no matter how deep he intends the relationship to become, he approaches it in the same way. He has certain expectations, certain things to offer, and wants certain things in return. What he wants to do is to direct his light, warmth, love, generosity, in fact the full force of his personality radiated outwards, onto the other person. This makes them feel very special; they are made to feel as though all the good things there are in the world are happening to them at once. The Leo wants to elevate his new friend to the status of being an honorary Leo, so that they can know what fun it is to enjoy the best of life all the time.

In return he wants to be adored. Leos go through life saying, in effect, 'Look how wonderful I am to you', but a *relationship* is formed when the other person replies, 'Gosh, you're so wonderful to me'. It's not a bad way of doing things, even if it sounds a little off-putting, especially to Aquarians (who naturally represent the opposite point of view). The Leo has energy to spare, and is giving it out anyway; the partner might as well be on the receiving end of it as anyone else. This is a simple thing, which non-Fire-signs never grasp: the energy comes free—you don't have to pay for it. Water signs in particular find this impossible to understand. If the partner is then appreciative of what he gets from the Leo, the Leo's happiness is complete. He gets gratitude, in effect, just for being himself. How could anything be better?

What a Leo doesn't want out of a relationship is for his actions to be criticized. He does things in the way he thinks is best, and if the partner attempts to change or reject what he is doing, then that shows that the Leo must be, in the partner's eyes, wrong in some way. Leos are hurt by this. They do things to make people happy, and everybody has a good time whenever they are around, and then somebody dares to say that he should be doing things a different way! The Leonine display of disapproval is usually in the form of accusations of *lèse-majesté*, but beneath the regal exterior lies a deeply wounded soul. He will not forget—an attempt has been made to extinguish his light, and it will take time for him to return to his full heat and brilliance again.

In friendships, Leos are wonderfully warm. If you are appreciative of their talents, they are almost endlessly generous, and it is not necessary for the friend to attempt to reciprocate on the same scale—the Leo enjoys treating his friends. Because friendships do not necessarily have to be intimate, the Leo can remain 'solitary' within the framework of the friendship, doing what he does best and being appreciated for it. Leos have lots of friendships like this, and it is where they work best.

In love affairs, Leos are powerful and ardent lovers—what else would you expect from the heat of a Fire sign and the weight of a Fixed sign? They are constant in love—the Fixed-ness again—and are not therefore likely to change partners for its own sake. Because they are not fickle or flighty in themselves, they are easily wounded by partners who are, seeing the apparent change in affection as a criticism of themselves. It is not a situation that happens a great deal, though; few people want to trade the luxury of an affair with a Leo for anything else unless the affair is completely unworkable. And having an affair with a Leo is indeed a life of luxury; he will expect you to join him in as high a lifestyle as you can both manage. This is not a relationship where you live in romantic poverty with each other.

In marriage, Leos have to make a few compromises. In practice this means that they learn how to be themselves in ways which do not actually have their partner on the verge of tears, because they are not used to making allowances for other people. It is really a lot easier all round if the partner just agrees to do things in the Leo's way after all. Whichever partner is the Leo, then they will be the dominant force in the marriage, especially if the other partner is neither Fixed nor Fire. It is sometimes better this way, though the other partner must be prepared to take the minor role. There is no doubt that the Leo loves his partner dearly, and will show this all the time, but he will naturally expect to be the decision-maker. He does not naturally expect to be the person who does all the work which follows on from the decisions he has taken, though, and this can sometimes lead to one or two cross words. In the end, the partner will have to let him have his way, and will be rewarded with a lasting and affectionate marriage, a high standard of living, and a warm family life. It sounds like a good deal.

## Virgo

To understand how you approach other people it is first necessary to see what it is that you are trying to do with your life;

when you understand your essential motivation, you can translate that into the terms of a relationship, and you will, I hope, see that you are doing the same thing with people as you you do with everything else in your life.

The essential aim of the Virgo is to perfect things. It is as though, for you, there is only a little time left, and not much material; therefore it becomes very important to make everything as good as it can possibly be. You don't think about what will happen if you don't manage to get it all done in time, or why it is your job to see to it that each individual reaches perfection under your care, but you feel driven to do it. The answer is actually because you are at the end of the first half of the zodiacal circle; everything that was started in an individual through the energy of Aries and developed through Taurus, Gemini, and the rest must reach its perfection in Virgo. Libra is too late—the zodiacal circle is on its way back to Pisces and the end of the cycle by then.

Virgoans recognize the importance of correctness of approach; to you, it contains the ideas of efficiency and perfection at the same time, and so has considerable appeal. When you form a relationship with anyone, you want them either to respond in the correct way to your approach, or at least to appreciate the way you are going about it.

There are basically three relationships which a Virgo can have. The first, by far the commonest, is when you find somebody who you think has many admirable qualities, but could do with a little improvement here and there. You are sure that once you have been with them a few months, and shown them how to improve themselves, they will be absolutely perfect. You also think that they will be grateful to you for your efforts on their behalf. In fact, you are likely to be wrong on both counts. It never occurs to you that the reason people don't improve themselves is because those details aren't important to them; if they were, they'd have done something about it themselves by now. Secondly, you are trying to turn them into something they are not. If you succeed, you will make them ill in the long run, because you have forced them out of themselves into a role they do not fit. You are more likely to fail, because people prefer to be themselves most of the time. Your efforts are likely to be seen as an annoyance rather than anything else, however well-meaning you are. Should you find that rare person who is willing to take all your advice and be 'perfected' by you, then you enter the second Virgoan relationship.

The second Virgoan relationship is when you find somebody who is, in your eyes, perfect. This doesn't happen very often, as any of your friends will tell you. They seem to you to represent the purpose of your life fulfilled. The problem is, of course, what to do with them. You can hardly improve on perfection, nor can you criticize. It is one thing to strive constantly for perfection, quite another thing to deal with it when it occurs.

In practical terms, the relationship is distinctly one-sided. You adore them, but you have no guarantee that they will adore you. In fact, it is most likely that they won't. The best that you can hope for is that they find you useful: that sounds a terrible let-down, but being useful is more acceptable to a Virgo than to any of the other eleven signs. If you can maintain it at this level, the two of you can at least co-exist, though somebody from a Water sign would hardly call it a relationship.

The third, and probably best kind of Virgoan relationship is one with another person who has some sort of sympathy or understanding with your point of view. In this case, your energies are directed towards common goals, and you are trying to improve a *thing* rather than a person; for example, a career or ambition of some kind.

In general, Fire signs will not understand your patience and your insistence on doing things in the right way and to the letter. Air signs will not understand why you take everything so seriously: to them nothing ever really matters.

The other Earth signs will be sympathetic to parts of you, and so will the Water signs, for the most part. Taurus will appreciate your affinity and familiarity with the actual fabric of things, because that's where his heart lies; he will find you fussy, though, and you will find him slow. You won't be able to change him. Capricorn has the appreciation of the right way of doing things that you have, and he has the same liking for effective action and measurable results.

Cancer will feel the same way as you do about caring for things and being of service to others, whereas Scorpio will share your concern about looking after yourself, though in not quite the same way.

With all of these people it is important for you to see that they are doing things in the way that answers their needs, not yours. If you realize how much they can contribute, and how between you much can be achieved, then you will do well. Once you start to criticize them the relationship deteriorates, though paradoxically when they do need help you are the best-qualified person to give it. There is a fine balance to be maintained.

In all Virgoan relationships, the key seems to be to keep the degree of involvement light. When a Virgo feels very strongly for somebody else, he brings his full critical faculties to bear, and the results, at such close range, are often destructive for both partners. If the relationship is less intense and more friendly, then the Virgoan's well-meant observations are more likely to be taken as such, and his undoubted enthusiasm and eagerness to impress can be allowed to flourish. At the same time, his inability to see the whole picture at once is rendered less threatening: indeed, in a light friendship it can often prove quite amusing.

Marriage must also be approached the same way: as a friendship with common goals. Anything more intense and more enclosed will bring out the worst in the Virgo without allowing him to give of his best.

More than anything else, it pays to remember the qualities of the planet behind Virgo. Mercury is a little planet, emotionally cool, but fast-moving. So, a Mercurial person in a relationship needs to go easy on the passion, and make sure he has room to move.

## Libra

To approach a relationship in any way, no matter what sign of the zodiac you call your own, is to be Libran, because to the astrologer the meaning of the word 'Libra' and the meaning of the word 'relationship' are almost the same thing.

When anyone enters a relationship of any kind he is using the powers of Libra. Everyone has the whole zodiac in them somewhere, and when they do this or that in their lives they use this or that part of it. Wherever there is a relationship of any kind to be formed, on any level whatsoever, then Libran energies are at work.

What makes you, as a Libran person, special is that for you the Sun was in the sign Libra when you were born, and that has the effect of making that relationship-forming energy into the primary force in your existence; it runs through you, it makes you what you are, and it is as inseparable from you as your height or the colour of your eyes.

You do not, then, approach relationships in a certain manner; you approach *everything* as if it were what other people see as a relationship! For you, there is no other way to be; it is the way that Librans see things.

Personal relationships are the most important to you, in the same way as they are to everybody else. It is to do with the business of communication; you are an Air sign, and you feel you must be able to talk to your partner at all costs; speech and the exchange of ideas and feelings is more important to you than touch as a way of showing affection. If you have ever had an affair with a Taurean, you will be familiar with their preferences for touch over speech. There are other preferences too, which the other signs exhibit; but you are a talker and a sharer of ideas and feelings.

There are one or two ways in which you show your Libran need to share thoughts and feelings, which everyone else finds endearingly sentimental as well: a couple which spring to mind are Romance with a capital R, and imaginary friends. Romance with a capital R is a Libran state of mind: it consists of true love and happiness, and is usually coloured pink. It cannot be bought or sold, nor is it physical, nor does it produce anything: it is simply an idea, a feeling. As such it must be Air rather than any of the other three elements, and Librans feel happier when enjoying that particular state of mind.

Imaginary friends are really a feature of childhood, carried on into adult life. Fire sign people usually discard their teddy bears and other soft toys at an early age; some Earth and Water sign people keep them because of their memories or the comfort of their touch. Librans talk to theirs. A full personality, capable of answering back and giving advice, resides in every Libran's teddy bear, and is often consulted. All very sweet, I know, but in that very act, talking to a soft toy, lie important clues to the Libran's way of doing things.

It works as follows. Everybody needs to talk to themselves from time to time. Some people do it literally, and some just go for a walk and a think. The Libran is different. You cannot express yourself except in conversation: unless you have someone to talk to, and can listen to their responses, you don't know what to think. This is why Librans need partners and close friends, to act as confidants. In the absence of a suitable individual, a substitute is found. Pet cats and dogs are good for this, because they are alive and responsive, though they don't talk (people who insist their pets can talk back have strong Libran tendencies!). The conversation is the necessary part, more important even than the idea of having company. In the absence of a pet, the teddy bear gets pressed into service and becomes the other half of the conversation. Now you can see how everything the Libran does has to be in the form of a conversational relationship.

It should not be too difficult to understand by now that the relationship is more important than the person at the other end of it.

Incurable romantics are often accused of being in love with love; this happens when somebody prefers the delightful sensations of Romance to the reality of being somebody's close and long-term partner. Librans are like this, too.

The relationship is the vital thing. Once in a relationship, the Libran can function normally: on his own, he is lost. It doesn't have to be a personal relationship: Librans relate to everything in a personal way, be it a favourite chair or their usual route to work. There has to be some sense of being in partnership, of being tied together; what Libra likes least is not to be joined to anything, to be an outsider, or (the absolute worst) to be alone.

In a single sentence, other signs use a relationship to bring people into close contact, but Librans use people to bring a relationship into being.

If the emphasis is on the feeling of relationship, then there must be, relatively speaking, less interest in the people as individuals. Yes, Librans are to some extent vanilla-flavoured: everybody likes them, but nobody has a strong feeling about them one way or the other. There is a certain coolness, a lack of passion, which all the Air signs have. To these people nothing is ever so important that it is worth giving your all for; to them nothing is ever permanent, and there will be new things, and probably just as good, around the corner.

Is there, then, a Libran approach to relationships? Yes, but not in the way that you had perhaps expected. There is a belief that any relationship is worth having for its own sake, because to be attached to somebody or something is better than not being. Because you, Libra, are the moving force behind the formation of all these links, you have to be openly and actively welcoming, inviting the formation of friendships and a sense of togetherness, and you are all of this. You enjoy watching yourself doing it all; you get a feeling of satisfaction as people find themselves attracted to you, and the Venusian energy flows the way it should. That's the point at which somebody very sharp could spot the coolness, the slight standing back that you have to have. It's not because you are heartless or in some way being deceptive: it's the way you have to behave if your life depends on an ability to make not just a relationship with one person, but a different one with every person you ever meet.

## Scorpio

All Scorpios are sexy. Everybody knows this; in fact it's about all that anybody ever says about a Scorpio. Is it true? If so, why is it true? Does it say something about the way Scorpios approach their relationships?

The answers to those questions are yes, because of Mars; but that isn't the whole story.

The way to fathom a Scorpio's approach to relationships is firstly to determine what it is that he wants to get out of them, and then to see how he goes about making sure he does so. To start with, as in everything else in his life, the Scorpio wants to control the situation, and within that, his partner. He does this by applying his energies in a concentrated and effective way. Viewed from the other end, from the partner's point of view, this seems magnetically attractive. It is: any energy directed your way is welcome, and you tend to turn towards anyone giving out energy for free. Since Scorpio energy is an essentially emotional energy (that of the element of Water), directed and aimed in a personal and physical manner (because Mars powers the physical body), it is interpreted by the other eleven signs as the only powerful physical/emotional energy they know—sexual energy. Understand this: other signs only meet this kind of energy, or use it, in a sexual context, but Scorpios use it all the time, and not always for sex; it just happens to be the only energy they have available.

So yes, Scorpios are sexy; they radiate the energy that everybody recognizes as sexual energy. This means that everybody responds in a sexual manner to a Scorpio, which is to say in an emotionally heightened state. Scorpio loves this; it means that the whole transaction is conducted on an emotional level, which is the level on which he functions best of all. This means, of course, that he gets his own way, because he is much more familiar with manipulating emotions than anybody else, and indeed can use them as a kind of fuel. By using that kind of energy to start with, he forces his partner in the relationship to respond in the same kind, whether or not they would naturally do so. It's a similar process to the card game where the player who leads can declare the trump suit, and proceeds to win every trick in the game because every card in his hand is of that suit. This is how Scorpios get to be so successful, and so dominant. It is a self-repeating process which favours the Scorpio every time: clever, isn't it?

When it does come to sex, the Scorpio is still ahead; sexual relationships are about reproduction, basically, and that means the element of Water and the power of Mars, representing the masculine principle. Scorpio combines the two. Mars is the masculine action in sex; the feminine actions are shared between Venus and the Moon. Mars is dominant, assertive, and penetrating, and this means that Scorpio men find sexual expression quite easy. A Scorpio woman often gets a reputation as something of a man-eater, and it isn't difficult to see why; Mars' way of expressing its energies means that she has to be assertive and dominant. She can't be penetrating physically, and so has to express that trait of Mars by her behaviour in controlling the relationship. This is absolutely true to Scorpio: her reputation, if she has one, is entirely due to society's poor understanding of the way Scorpio works.

There is a part of the body assigned to each zodiac sign, too, and in Scorpio's case it is the genital organs. It is possible, as you will no doubt have realized, to have too much of a good thing. The symbolism goes further than the obvious, though: if you think how genital organs work you will have a very good idea of why a Scorpio behaves the way he does. They are usually hidden from view, for a start, and Scorpios are rather secretive people. The urges they produce are all emotional, but they are the strongest we know; people change their whole lives in response to these urges. What these organs produce is a limited resource (women have a finite number of egg cells), but it is highly concentrated, and using only a little of it has enormous results. It is also to do with the very substance of life; generation and regeneration can only occur through these organs. Scorpio is like that. Everything to him has that same sense of significance. Genital organs are serious things, concerned with life-and-death matters; using them involves the deepest parts of our being, and astrology being what it is, the deepest parts of mankind and the universe, too. Scorpios represent those energies to the rest of society in personal form—hence the intensity, the seriousness, and the sheer, concentrated power.

So now you see that Scorpios have to use sexual energy for more purposes than sex, and that the intensity of this energy and the way it is used means that they become dominant over a partner who is not as familiar with this kind of energy as they are. The question still remains, though: what is the Scorpio trying to achieve?

The answer is the same as it was on page 17: he wants to maintain and control his emotional responses. He needs to be appreciated; he wants the reassurance of a continuing flow of emotional responses from other people to comfort and sustain him. He collects, and indeed exists on, this emotional approval; unlike the Cancerian, who generates his own emotional energies in response to the actions of others, or the Piscean, who uses the emotions of others as a vehicle for his own amusement, the Scorpio needs to define and sustain himself by collecting the responses of others, and of course, he needs them to be both favourable and constant. What he is trying to do to achieve this is, firstly, to concentrate and use his energy so that his efforts always result in a response favourable to him, and secondly, somehow to keep and store his own emotional energy because it is so precious to him.

Scorpios have to keep most of their energy locked in. It is a bit like hydro-electric power: there is a great amount of water kept behind a dam, released in a controlled manner to be used profitably. If all the water is released, then disaster occurs; similarly, if all the water is used up, there is none left to meet future needs.

A Scorpio examines every relationship as it forms. 'How much will I have to give to this?' he asks himself. 'Will it mean that I have to give more than I get in return?' If so, it's a bad idea, because the net emotional balance shows a loss, and I must keep things in reserve, or augment them if possible. Will I get so carried away that I may use my energy in an uncontrolled manner, and so leave myself vulnerable when I least expect it? If so, I had better keep my involvement, or at least my commitment, under close watch, to prevent such a situation developing.' The need to conserve and control never leaves him. His greatest fear is being out of control. Quite straightforward, really: if a Scorpio is dedicated to the idea of control, then being out of that state is what he would most like to avoid.

The best way for the Scorpio to keep himself under control is to retreat a little, to bury himself under the surface out of the way of unfriendly eyes. What this means, of course, is that he never gives himself entirely to his partner, but always keeps a little in reserve. It is this hidden reserve, where his most secret self lives, that is never risked by exposing it to something as unstable as somebody else's care.

The reserved self doesn't need the stimulation or support of another person's energy, or at any rate it isn't allowed to. Consequently, Scorpios have difficulty forming deep and lasting relationships. It isn't because they aren't used to dealing with emotions, as most people seem to think; it's because they are not prepared to commit themselves entirely to another person. For this reason Scorpios form strong and successful business partnerships, but fewer good personal partnerships.

Friendships with a Scorpio form not from a desire for companionship, but because the two people are useful to each other or have a shared interest. The energy flow is inwards rather than outwards, you see. Sexual friendships are similar: the Scorpio has more than enough sexual power for anybody, but the emotional response he offers alongside the physical partnership will be very strictly controlled, and not every partner will be prepared to accept that. As for marriage, it hasn't much appeal when one partner can look after himself quite well and is unwilling to give himself fully to his partner.

The last few paragraphs paint a bleak picture. It isn't as bad as it sounds, but it does show that the popular version of the Scorpio's capabilities seldom considers the problem from both sides, as the Scorpio himself would. In those areas of a relationship where intensity of energy is a bonus, the Scorpio is unbeatable; but he suffers, or certainly seems to, as far as the rest of us are concerned, by being unable to enjoy those areas of a relationship which are light and free from care.

## Sagittarius

A relationship is usually formed when two people find that what they have to offer, and what they want in return, are mutually compatible. Sagittarians are unusual in that they have plenty to offer, and don't seem to need a lot in return. Although that isn't entirely true, as we will see in a little while, it is a good enough general rule.

Sagittarians like yourself don't need a partner as a comforter, because you seldom feel that the world is too hard on you; nor do you need one as a protector, because you don't feel threatened or oppressed. You don't want a partner to be a stabilizing influence, because you'd rather not be in a rut, and you don't need one to cheer you up and inspire you either, because you are already happy and creative. You don't need caring for, because you can get yourself out of anything you get yourself into, and you don't want anybody you have to care for, because that would limit your freedom. What you want is a playmate.

It is a difficult thing to find, and a difficult thing for other people to understand. You are more than willing to give your time and talent to anyone who will appreciate them, but at no time must you be made to feel that you *have* to give them. When that happens, you sense dependence, permanence, and commitment beginning to form, and that sets the alarm bells ringing inside your head. Time to move on, you think. As long as the other person enjoys your company, but is quite capable of pursuing his own interests in your absence, then you are happy to have him around, provided of course that you enjoy his company too.

Hierarchy is an idea which you don't much like. It is quite possible to have a hierarchy with only two people, of course: one is the dominant partner, and the other allows himself to be led. Quite a number of zodiac signs are willing to be led; it takes away the responsibility of decision-making, and gives the security of knowing that somebody is looking after your interests for you. That's not your style at all — you take your own decisions, and you don't like being told what to do by people who don't know anything like as much as you do, so therefore don't know what they're doing.

Some zodiac signs prefer to be the dominant partner, but that's not your style either. To you, that means that you have to be responsible for them, and to consider their needs as well as your own. That would stop you from chasing off after new and interesting things which cropped up during the day, wouldn't it? It would also stop you doing things which they couldn't, or would rather not, do. Altogether too much of a limitation.

You don't want to be under anyone's thumb, or walk in anyone's shadow—but nor do you want the sort of relationship where your partner follows you dutifully, ten paces behind. What you want is somebody at your side, seeing things as you see them, doing things as you do them, advancing individually but in the same direction—in fact, travelling together. Now *there's* a Sagittarian idea.

Treating everybody as a potential playmate, which you do, sounds a wonderful idea: it is open, unrestricting, and highly egalitarian. You know all this, of course; it is part of why you do it. There are problems, however, when you apply it in real life, and most of them come in one of two categories.

The first problem area is that you refuse to give some people the respect to which their position has accustomed them. Speaking to the managing directors of multinational corporations, whom you have only just met, with the same cheerful banter you use with your greengrocer sometimes causes offence. The same applies to bank managers, bishops, and royalty; as far as you're concerned, they are all the same as your greengrocer, i.e. people. You simply cannot understand how it could be any other way. Now you see why Sagittarians hate formality (they get caught up in protocol, because they can't understand it), and why all the other signs call them tactless.

The second problem area is when people simply aren't as good as you are. People come in all sizes and abilities, and for you to assume that everybody you meet shares your interests, and is as skilled in those areas as you are, is frankly naïve, but you do it nonetheless. The result is usually disappointment. Sometimes you find yourself helping them along, especially if they have the interest but not the ability, and that appeals to the teacher in you—but it also makes you feel responsible for them, and you don't like that.

Why is it that you don't want a formal relationship? What is it that makes you so dislike commitment and responsibility? Why don't you want anybody to tell you what to do?

In a word, Jupiter. Jupiter is movement, expansion, optimism. Once a thing has taken form, or become fixed, it is no longer of Jupiter—it has become limited and static, which is the province of Saturn. Sagittarius tries to avoid this wherever possible. Jupiter doesn't like being tied down, because then it cannot move or expand. A moving, expansive, un-fixed relationship without the weight of responsibility is what you're looking for, and you approach every new acquaintance with the same aim. Why have a relationship at all, you say. A good point; the answer is that you are an outgoing sign, and all outgoing signs need somebody to collect their energy, so that the flow of energy round the zodiac is maintained. In other words, you need an audience of some sort, somebody you can help, teach, and show off to as well, if we are to be honest.

Assuming that you find a playmate, somebody as talented as you are, who doesn't need you, but quite likes you, then how will you deepen the relationship without making it static?

Sexually, of course. Sagittarians, like all Fire signs, have strong sexual drives. They don't have the majesty of the Leo, nor the sheer power of the Arian, but they don't do badly (they do, after all, have the thighs, and indeed the bottom end generally, of a horse), and they are both imaginative and inventive, which the other Fire signs are not. The essential thing about a Sagittarian's sex drive, though, is that to him it is a physical thing, done for fun, a way of saying how pleased you are to be with somebody. The idea of emotional bonding and commitment has no part in it. Most of the other eleven signs are different in this respect, and are very upset by the Sagittarian's refusal to make the relationship permanent. He's honest and loyal enough while the affair's in progress, but he won't make a commitment.

Sex is a creative act to a Sagittarian; you see it as a form of giving, and you hope that something will grow from it. The procreative function of sex is never far from the Sagittarian mind; it is linked with the idea of expansion and potential for growth—not only the idea of the expanding family and the potential for the future, but the expansion of the body during pregnancy, too. Jupiter works on many levels, but always to the same ends.

Marriage isn't impossible for Sagittarians, even if it sounds unlikely. Once you have found a partner as independently-minded as you are, then there is no reason why you should not travel on, side by side, into the sunset for ever. What you don't want your marriage to be is a static arrangement, with formal routines. For you, it must stay moving, or at least make major moves every few years. It must also contain a variety of people, to maintain the movement so dear to you: either a family, or at least a large number of friends. If you can achieve this moving, expanding marriage, with your partner by your side, then all will be well; if you can't, then you feel tied down and trapped, and you will eventually be forced to break away from it to gain the refreshment you need from movement and change.

# Capricorn

Because of the influence of Saturn, the Capricorn approaches relationships in a cautious manner, carefully considering the likely outcome of things before he commits himself. He forms friendships slowly, giving time for the acquaintance to deepen and develop; he is not the sort of person to rush blindly into a long-term commitment, or to fall in love over a single glass of wine.

If all that sounds dull, it has to be said that there is a good side to the idea of a Saturnine relationship, too. The good side consists of the strength and durability of the liaison once it is formed, and its resistance to outside attack. Some friendships are light things, and when circumstances separate the partners, the friendship dissolves; with Capricorns this doesn't happen.

Once the friendship is formed, it will last for ever. Slow to form, but slow to dissolve—that's the way Saturn does things.

The essence of a relationship is its emotional content. The great love affairs, the ones which make history, are full of high passion and grand gestures, where the choices are either perfect bliss or utter destruction for both parties. Such passions appeal to Fire or Water sign people, but not to Capricorn. He doesn't really see the attraction in giving everything to an affair which distorts reality and makes impossible demands on the framework of normal life; indeed, he can see plenty of reasons why such strains and disruptions should be avoided.

For you, Capricorn, everything has to be in its place. Feelings are included in this scheme of things: you don't like your feelings to be loose, unrestrained, out of control, or public. You are a Saturnine person: you want them to be kept inside, out of public view. That doesn't mean that you are cold-hearted, but your feelings are small and tender, unlike the loud and, to you, tasteless, theatricalities indulged in by some Librans, for example. Also, unlike a Libran, whose very existence is determined by his relationships, they are not the most important thing in your life. You know this, and you are happy with the arrangement; everything in its place, according to you. Unfortunately the modern world and its media seem to place an unreasonable amount of emphasis on relationships, and they label you cold and unfeeling where you should really be termed tender and private.

You are, more than anything else, a builder. You like to build something out of your relationships, too—it would be unreasonable of you not to. When you enter a relationship with anyone, then, you are looking to see what you can build out of it, and you will do all that you can to make sure that the relationship is stable, structured, and useful. That is not to say that you spend your time cultivating useful business contacts instead of being genuinely friendly, though I dare say that some of you do exactly that, but you are well aware of how you want your friends to fit into the structure of your life nonetheless. Suppose, for example, that you have a friend who is your tennis partner. As far as you are concerned, you want to play tennis with him, and you want to chat to him about your game. You will never let him down when the pair of you have a match on, and you expect him to concentrate on his tennis as hard as you do. He isn't your business adviser, so you don't talk business to him, and he isn't somebody you share your personal worries with, so you don't confess your private fears to him. In other words, he is in a box in your life, marked 'Social: Tennis'. You will use one friend as a confidante, another as a financial adviser. It may well be that you are choosing these people for their professional skills as well as their personal qualities, but that is only because you prefer to deal with people who are recognized as being from the top of the pile—it is the Capricorn way.

Given this structured approach, a friend, in your eyes, must be somebody you can trust, somebody who is not going to change his view of you over the years, and somebody who is going to be a support to you when you need him to be. In return you will offer him similar qualities: staunch support, unwavering loyalty, reliability over a number of years. All very architectural, isn't it? That's the builder in you at work again. Other people may have friends who only last a few months, and then are never seen again, but not you. You are building a social life which will stand for a lifetime, and that needs solid foundations and good supports—not flighty friends.

Marriage is approached in a similarly architectural fashion. You are gloriously traditional about marriage—for you it lasts a lifetime. What you are looking for in a partner is somebody with whom you can build a future—that word again—and be stronger together than either of you were before. The ideal of this would be a marriage where both partners were equal in the power they held within the marriage, but this isn't often the case with you: you are too traditional for that. You prefer, in many instances, to be the senior partner, and to have your partner in a supporting role. This is because the aim of the Capricorn is to be at the top, and you reckon that if you can't achieve it on the small scale of your own home, you won't be able to manage it on the larger scale of public life. The argument is, alas, astrologically flawless.

One of the prime aims of marriage, for the Capricornian, is to extend the family hierarchy. In other words, you uphold the traditional view that marriages are for mutual support and for children. Capricorns are quite good at having children; in fact they are a lot stronger sexually than they are usually given credit for. How can anybody whose sign is an old goat not be strongly sexed? Real sexual strength is present in all of the zodiac signs where the animal has horns—Aries, Taurus, and of course, Capricorn. The sexuality of the Capricorn is kept within the structure, agreed, but that doesn't mean it isn't there; it just means that the clever chat, the flamboyant display, and the paraphernalia of The Great Romance aren't there. The power itself is directed towards the advancement of the Capricorn within the structure, as with everything else in his life. That means the production of children within a marriage, and the development of the career outside it. Capricorn women are not above having affairs with their bosses to climb the hierarchy; perhaps more than any other sign, they understand that sex, money and power are all interchangeable.

## Aquarius

An Aquarian wants a number of things from a relationship, but few of them are the same as what most other people want. What he particularly *doesn't* want is to lose himself in another person, or to lose himself in the unreal effects of being in love, or to create something better than he could be on his own from a combination of his own talents and his partner's.

He doesn't want to prove himself sexually, and he feels no need to produce children as a duty to his ancestors, in a way that, for example, a Capricorn often does. He is not trying to express his inner feelings as an attempt to communicate his existence to another person, either.

Most of these things are expressions of the energies of the inner planets, Venus and Mars; Aquarius works on a more impersonal level than that, provided by the slowest mover of them all, Saturn. Much of the business of personal expression is due to solar energy showing itself; Aquarius is on the lunar half of the horseshoe, though, and so that need, too, is absent. Whatever an Aquarian wants from a relationship must be very cool, very controlled, and very realistic. That doesn't mean unenjoyable, but it does mean that the fantasy of love has no meaning for him.

Almost everything an Aquarian does can be explained in musical terms. Why this should be so is not clear: perhaps it has something to do with the fact that music is a universal language, and that it has rhythm and measure (rhythm is a Lunar thing, measure is Saturnine). Whatever the reason, when trying to grasp the Aquarian way of doing things, a musical metaphor is often very helpful, and here is no exception. The Aquarian approach to relationships is like slow, cool jazz.

Relationships, to an Aquarian, must contain an exchange of thoughts and ideas. He is an Air sign, and so conversation and company are of much greater importance to him than physical satisfaction or any kind of possessive emotional bonding. He needs to stay circulating around society at large; to devote himself to one person and deny himself the company and stimulation he gets from everybody else he knows is something he is anxious to avoid. Love affairs are often exclusive; the two partners spend a lot of time with each other, but very little in the company of other people. Indeed, once a partnership is recognized by their friends, the couple are usually left alone. This is a serious problem for an Air sign. Earth and Water people may like to be left alone, but not Air signs. Of the Air signs, Librans like to work on a one-to-one basis, but not Aquarians. They want their social environment to stay just the way it always was; it's part of being a Fixed sign.

Friendships are the best relationships for an Aquarian, and he usually has a lot of them. A friendship is usually shared, in that the relationship is often part of a wider social group, and that suits the sign very well. Friendships are also a mutual benefit arrangement, in that friends are usually able to perform small services for each other, and being able to put energy outwards for the benefit of somebody else unable to do it for himself is a very Aquarian thing. There is also the question of status: friends are implicitly equals, which is certainly not the case in a teacher-pupil or employer-employee relationship, and often not the case in a husband-wife relationship, or that between two lovers. Remember that Aquarius is highly egalitarian; he detests any kind of relationship where one partner is in a position of power over the other. Saturn is a great leveller.

Finally, though friendships can be deep and satisfying, they don't have to be devoted: you can leave a friendship as a part-time arrangement, and pick it up again some time later if you wish. You can't do that with a love affair or a marriage. Aquarians have a need to be on their own at times, to re-order their thoughts, and to feel solitude; it is an important part of them, and if they are in a relationship which makes it difficult for them to have this time on their own then they are troubled.

All of these things make friendship the best kind of relationship for Aquarians. They know that it needn't be close or demanding, and they know that it will be flexible and communicative. It isn't as powerfully satisfying as an intimate relationship, but quantity can compensate for quality in some cases, and the Aquarian prefers to have many friends in different circles than one life partner.

Friendship usually happens on a one-to-one basis. Light though it is in comparison to marriage, it can be too intimate for Aquarians; they are happy to leave all personal involvement to their Air element colleagues the Librans, and have instead devised something unique to themselves: group friendship. There isn't a word for this process, but it is very easy to recognize. It is the relationship enjoyed by a dozen young men who go to the same pub every Friday night. It is the relationship enjoyed by all the girls in an office when they all go out together for a meal and then on to a disco. Everybody in the group contributes to the feeling of friendliness, and everybody feels that they have the support and affection of everybody else, but nobody is particularly closely tied to any other individual in the group, and so they don't feel emotionally tied or committed. Each person also feels that he is still an individual. The great feature of this sort of group relationship is that emotional support is generated without deep or personal passion. Aquarians feel very much at home in this sort of environment, as do young adults, who lack either the confidence or the inclination to form deep and lasting relationships, but who nonetheless need to feel that they are appreciated.

Aquarians are the originators of this behaviour pattern. They are an essential part of every group, and a major provider of ideas and energy within it, but they are somehow separate from it at the same time, maintaining that sense of isolation which is so characteristic of the sign.

The Saturnine part of Aquarius makes him constant and caring in all circumstances, and that includes love affairs and marriages: the problem, as far as the other partner is concerned, is to convince the Aquarian that such a personal and individual partnership is what he wants—he would rather just be friends. That is not to say that no Aquarians feel compelled to marry or fall in love, but the pure influence of the Sun in Aquarius doesn't incline them that way; the fact that they do so is because of other features of their horoscope. Aquarius itself needs variety, and mental rapport, not physical passion or personal devotion.

## Pisces

Everybody goes into a relationship for a different reason. Not everybody wants to give their all to a partner—quite a number want to get something out of the partnership without necessarily putting anything in. Pisceans aren't quite as obviously selfish as that, but it is as well to remember that Pisces is a collecting sign, and so the direction of the energies must be inwards rather than outwards.

There are two things a Pisces wants out of any relationship. The first is to generate an emotional response in himself, and on as many different levels as possible. The best kind of emotional response is that which is produced by absorbing the emotions of another person; therefore you, as a Piscean, are likely to be attracted to anybody with a strong personality, because they are emotionally 'louder', if you like, and that gives you more for your money. It doesn't really matter whether you really like your partner or not; the energy of friction and argument is just as strong, and it is the intensity of the experience that you are really after.

Another kind of emotional response is produced by being in dramatic surroundings, and you enjoy that too. Taken together, it would seem that the person who gives you most of what you want is somebody who is dramatically different, and has a lifestyle to match. This is probably the explanation for the marked tendency of Pisceans to fall for flamboyant extroverts who trample all over them.

You will have noticed that the concept of true relationship, as in friendship, rapport, and words like that, has not yet made an appearance. It isn't likely to: you're not interested in that sort of thing. If you were genuinely dependent on one other person for your emotional well-being, you would feel trapped, and would have to escape. The essential thing with a Piscean is that the experience has to keep changing—either by keeping a relationship fluid or by having a number of relationships with very different people.

You are quite capable of becoming somebody else just for the experience of it. If your partner is madly keen on sailing, you will become a weekend sailor. You will absorb his enthusiasm; you will, in fact, personify it. You will know more about sailing, in a shorter time, than you ever thought possible; you will feel perfectly at home wearing sailing clothes, whereas other people feel faintly ridiculous. Please note that none of this is permanent: what you are doing is immersing yourself in the experience of having a relationship with somebody whose passion is sailing. When, or if, the relationship comes to an end, you will step out of the role in the same way that an actor takes off his costume; and if your next intimate friend happens to be a point-to-point fanatic, you will be standing in muddy fields as though you were born to it. There is no limit to the number of times that you are prepared to perform this exercise, as long as each experience is intense enough, and different enough from the last one. You never see anything as permanent, and never hope to keep anything forever; you see people in exactly the same way. All you ask of them is that they can be intense enough to provide you with a strong emotional experience—and give you room to slip away if things look as though they are getting out of hand.

The second reason that Pisceans go into relationships of any kind is that of service to others. This quality of self-denial, the ability to lose yourself in the process of doing something on somebody else's behalf, is never far below the surface of your intentions. In relationships, it shows as the desire to befriend people who need a lot of your time and effort. These people may be ill, or unable to do things for themselves. They may be emotionally incapacitated or may have damaged themselves in some way, for instance through drink or drugs; or they may simply be demanding, selfish, and egotistical, and make large claims on your patience and time. Whatever it is, you are always ready to befriend these people. Perhaps it is because their presence draws attention away from you. It is more likely that the emotion generated by these extraordinary people is something you find interesting for its own sake. You would far rather experience anything than experience nothing.

The practicalities of a relationship are very easy for a Piscean. People find you friendly and easy to get on with; friendships form at once. There are good reasons for this, of course; what you have done is reflected back to them the friendship that they have shown you and that you have absorbed. Most people like nothing better than to be treated in the way that they would like to treat others, so the system works very well. You also know that this sort of routine generates happy emotions, and you can absorb them, too; they make you feel good.

When you fall in love, it is a full-colour experience, with stereophonic sound. What happens is that a particular person produces a response in you which you find so breathtaking that you want more of it. You know how much enjoyment you can get from your surroundings, so you alter your surroundings to produce the effects you want. By this time the affair is being conducted on the grand scale—red roses, weekends in Paris, candlelit dinners, the whole thing. As each new element is added, you get more of an emotional boost from it, until you get quite delirious from the passion of it all. By this time you are a long way from reality, but that doesn't matter—what you want is the intensity of the experience, and that's what you get.

Pisceans need variety, and they need room to move. For these reasons, marriage isn't always the success you hope it might be. That doesn't mean that all Pisceans are hopeless marriage partners by any means, but you want the imaginative fantasy to continue, and sheer familiarity often brings that to an end. As long as there is interest and variety, with new experiences and new people coming and going, then you are happy; you have your current of fresh water. Whenever dull routine and predictable practicality start to predominate in a relationship, then Pisces feels that it is time to slip away and find something new and stimulating.

# 4. Individual Compatibilities Sign by Sign

All relationships between the signs work in the ways described earlier in 'How Zodiacal Relationships Work' (p.125). In addition to that, descriptions of how someone from each of the signs attempts to form relationships with people from the other signs are given here. Remember that although each Gemini, for example, looks different, their motivation is the same, and so they will be trying to do the same things with a relationship.

You will find that there are two sections for each combination; in other words, not only can you look up Capricorn-Pisces, but Pisces-Capricorn as well. The Capricorn-Pisces section is written from the Capricorn's point of view, bearing in mind his approach to life, what he wants out of a relationship, and what he is most likely to notice about his interaction with the Piscean. What I am trying to show you is how you bargain with each other; you both have something to offer, and are looking for something in return. The Pisces-Capricorn section is written from the Piscean point of view. If you are reading about your own relationship from the opposite end, and it makes no sense to you, then think: your partner is a completely different person, and the way that they are trying to handle you is very different from what you are trying to do with them. You might find that reading the section of their sign in 'The Essence of the Signs' earlier in the book will help you understand the way that they think.

Sometimes the advice offered will appear to contradict itself. I may say that marriage is a good idea from one side of the relationship, but not from the other. It doesn't mean that marriage is impossible. What it does mean is that the qualities of one sign will benefit the other greatly in a long-term intimate relationship such as a marriage, but that the second sign will find that to fulfil his side of the bargain he has to contribute rather more than he might like. It's well worth thinking about the differences that show up this way: what is a massive problem to you hasn't even occurred to him, and probably isn't important either. Sagittarius-Capricorn is a good example.

As usual, the words *he* and *his* can be taken to mean she and her, since astrology makes no distinctions in sex here.

# Aries

*Aries-Aries*

Like most of the relationships formed by two people of the same sign, this will tend to show the pair of you, not just how similar you are, but how much of yourself you don't like. Mars is the guiding principle here, of course, and it is not in his nature to give ground or assimilate another point of view.

An Arian has to push forwards the whole time, and the problem here is going to be making sure that the two of you are in fact pushing in the same direction; otherwise there will inevitably be stresses set up, and these will lead to friction and arguments. As long as the two of you are interested in the same things, there will be no problems. Progress will in fact be much more rapid than in other partnerships, because you have twice the motive power available, and because you will fuel each other's enthusiasm for as long as your interests stay together.

The weak point in all this is that neither of you is interested in the relationship as a thing in itself; doing something for the sake of the relationship alone, when it was of no interest or profit to you personally, is something that you never do, and of course, that applies to both of you.

Another problem area is that an Arian gets frustrated at lack of progress; he has no patience at all, and is particularly annoyed when this is due to someone doing just what he wanted to do, but doing it first. When someone thwarts him by being impatient, headstrong, imprudent, or just downright selfish, then that doubles his displeasure. As you can see, another Arian displaying 'me-first' behaviour to his face does nothing for an Arian's temper. Luckily, both of you will forget the incident and move on to something else in a very short time, so you may take comfort from the thought that disagreements between Arians are of short duration, with neither side holding grudges for long.

This double helping of Martian energy, with its tendency to extremes of enthusiasm and dislike, makes for a lively friendship which is likely to be punctuated by arguments at fairly frequent intervals. As a basis for a love affair, the same thing applies: the passions will be intense, and to some extent feed off each other to give an even greater intensity; quarrels will be violent, and quick to flare, but quick to cool again also. As time progresses with such a pairing, the intensity does not diminish, but the time scale extends somewhat; arguments take longer to arrive and to fade away, but the passion and intensity of both the arguments and the good times in between remains undiminished.

As a business partnership, Aries-Aries needs careful channelling; for best effect, indeed for any progress to be made at all, you must split the tasks between you, and each devote his full attention to his own tasks. Authority within your own appointed areas must be absolute, and on no account should you attempt to interfere in any way with your partner's side of things. If this partitioning is not adhered to, your energies will hinder and oppose each other sooner or later, and the resulting arguments are wasteful of time and energy for the business (which neither of you can actually see as an entity in itself, of course).

## Aries-Taurus

On the face of it, this is probably the hardest of all the zodiacal partnerships to make work well. The intensity and eagerness of the Arian is completely at odds with the more patient qualities of the Taurean.

Venus looks after Taurus, and that means that the underlying quality is one of stability and comfort; the Arian's Mars-given qualities, demanding new experiences and sometimes danger and hardship, have nothing in common with those of Venus. This seems hard enough, but the animosity is deeper still, and the reason has to do with the fact that the signs follow on from one another in the zodiacal sequence. Aries is always striving to make something for himself; he wants to be the one to discover, develop, and use something first, so that he can truly say that it is his very own thing, and that nobody else thought of it first. What does he do when this is achieved? He fears that he might be forced to settle down and look to his responsibilities, make sure his projects become mature and established, that sort of thing. Although this is the right way for things to develop, the Arian is afraid that in settling down he would become boring, and would never know the thrill of starting something new again. Taureans show this settled state in everything they do, and because it is the natural thing for an Aries to move forwards, being the next stage in the circle, so to speak, it becomes something to fear and dislike, since it involves giving up Arian-ness. The eternally forward-looking, childlike Aries doesn't like growing up any faster than he has to, and will avoid the whole process if he possibly can.

The same process applies to Taurus in reverse. It is part of a Taurean to value the ground he stands on; think of a bull in a field, and how he continually re-defines and guards his territory. Whatever a Taurean acquires he considers his own, and it is his duty to look after it. This means that a Taurean's 'territory' keeps getting bigger throughout his life, and he becomes less and less inclined to give any of it up. The idea of an Arian trampling all over it, changing it, trying to do something new and original with it, or worst of all, throwing it away to concentrate on something completely new that hasn't been tried before, horrifies him. The Taurean has already been through the energetic process of acquisition, and he much prefers the steady state of being in possession; because Arian energies are in the past to him, he finds them irritating and clichéd, which in turn enrages the Arian, to whom they are new and vivid, and who would like them appreciated as such.

If the friendship between these two is not very intellectual, then the relationship must eventually become a series of battles, where the Aries' temper and will to win causes the Taurean to dig his hooves in even deeper, refusing to move. Eventually the Taurean's anger, slow to build but unstoppable once it has got going, will explode, and the force of it will flatten even the Arian for a while. This sort of thing is dangerous for both of them. The Taurean's flat refusal to change in any way will frustrate the Arian even more, and the partnership is unlikely to develop.

With a little thought, however, a working agreement can be found, which will work well both in business and on a personal level. What needs to be achieved first, obviously, is an understanding of each other's needs. After that, things are best arranged so that the Arian does the active work and anything new and energetic, while the Taurean does the maintenance and the support duties for the team as a unit. In this way the Arian is spared the repetition and the inactive periods he so hates, and the Taurean has plenty to look after and consider his own.

The Arian must remember that the Taurean is possessive of him too, and will be extremely jealous if the Arian shows any interest in another partner; the Taurean must remember that Arians need to move around a bit to be at their best.

### Aries-Gemini

Aries and Gemini were made for each other. The need for action in the one is matched by the need for novelty and stimulus in the other. As an Arian, you will find that the Gemini is much faster mentally than you are, and ready to move on to new challenges and new concepts almost as soon as you have arrived at them. You find all this stimulating, and relish being made to keep up, but you hope that it is all as honest as it seems to be, because you have a sneaking suspicion that the Gemini might be presenting things to you the wrong way round just for the fun of it, and you might not be quick enough to see through the deception. The trouble here is that Aries is a straightforward sort of sign, and lacks the subtlety of intellect required to play with words and ideas, to conjure fantasies from nowhere, and to make clever lies that live alongside the truth unable to be distinguished from it. Gemini, on the other hand, is almost pure intellect; everything is examined for its mental rather than physical qualities, and turned this way and that to see if it has anything interesting to offer when examined from a different point of view. Duplicity is easy for them; a Gemini is not fundamentally dishonest, but he loves arguments for their own sake, and he loves all forms of trickery.

You will not tire him out, nor he you; you have much greater physical capabilities than he does, and much more sheer strength, but his speed of reaction is phenomenal, and he uses himself much more sparingly. He does with reflexes what you do with muscle.

As a friendship, there is little to fault the pairing of these two signs; as a love match, things could turn out a little different. There is no lack of sexual compatibility; both of you enjoy any physical activity, and you will get extra pleasure from the laughter that the Gemini will bring to things. The trouble starts when the Arian falls in love; your simple and direct passion, when honestly and earnestly expressed, will amuse the Gemini, and he will turn his interest to something else. This isn't rejection; it's just that earnestness is a bit too serious for the Gemini mind, and the fun is taken out of anything for him when seriousness starts to creep in. Also, he needs variety; by the time you are getting serious about things, the relationship will have been going for some time, and he will be needing a change. If you can put up with his lightweight response and his refusal to be committed in any way, then things can continue almost indefinitely. He can provide you with a seemingly endless series of ideas and new projects, and you can explore them together. Just keep it light, and keep it moving.

In many ways, this one works best if kept at the level of two very close friends. You will never really understand or appreciate what goes on inside the Gemini's head, and how much he gets out of your adventures together; he will never believe what deep satisfaction you get out of using yourself physically, testing your own limits, doing something that nobody else has ever done, and experiencing it for yourself, first-hand. He would think such a notion absurdly over-dramatic and inflated, and prefers not to think of you, his best friend, in such terms. So you must stay side by side, moving in parallel, enjoying each other's company, and taking individual pleasures in different ways from the experiences you share. Kept like that, and kept light and active, the relationship is nearly perfect.

## Aries-Cancer

This one seems the most unlikely partnership possible, but it can be surprisingly productive if approached in the right way, and the feature that surprises most of all is its *strength*.

Both of you have the Sun in cardinal signs; this means that you are both of the belief that if you don't do things for yourself, then they won't happen. This ability, and indeed need, to get things done for yourself is something you share, and you can recognize and respect it in each other.

You realize, both of you, that you are directing your energies in very different directions, but that these directions are not necessarily opposite. The Arian is keen to find things out for himself, by direct action; the Cancerian does not feel the need for this, but is very concerned that he is in control of all the things around him. Cancerians do not just put down roots, they actively dig foundations. They want to look after things, but that means looking after them their way, and making sure that the creative and directing energy to do that comes from them and them alone. It is this directing energy, and the belief that being in control of what you do is the only way to get it done the way you want it done, that the Arian can see and appreciate in the Cancerian, and it is the personal drive, energy and confidence in his abilities that appeal to the Cancerian when shown in the Arian.

This simple mutual appreciation of forcefulness is probably enough to turn an acquaintance into an affair; after all, the Arian can only show his admiration for the other's energies by physical demonstration, because he doesn't work any other way—and the Cancerian cannot but be flattered that someone as obviously sure and certain in his opinions as an Aries is directing his energies his way in recognition of similar qualities in himself.

The problem then becomes one of timing; Cancer has a much longer view than Aries, and is likely to be considering the affair as the preliminary groundwork for a much more lasting partnership. Marriage is always a possibility, if not a necessary condition, in a Cancerian relationship of any kind. There is always the element of protection and security built in to the notion of marriage, and a Cancer feels that this will help to fight any future events involving change and the unexpected, which would of course stop things being the way he wanted them. As an Aries, you feel that this over-reliance on security is a silly idea, and fail to give it the importance which it has in the eyes of your partner; you may also feel that marriage as a goal in a relationship is not quite what you go into these things for, and you would be right. That doesn't mean that it isn't what other people go into relationships for, though.

What you will realize, Aries, is that the Cancer will look after all those areas of your life that you know you should, but can't be bothered with. They will keep you on a firm footing, and that needn't necessarily mean tied down. They will look after your home and guard your interests in exactly the manner you would like to see someone doing—that is, with energy and confidence in their approach. In return, you can give them the appreciation they deserve, and be their public representative, using your personality and flair to do the jobs that their natural reserve prevents them from doing. You can be their public face, and they will be right behind you, making sure that everything is under control and has been looked after.

The nature of this relationship is that you fight for each other, on each other's behalf, and do the work for each other that you cannot do yourselves. There are bound to be arguments, since you both like doing things in your own way, but they will pass quickly. As a marriage, it will not be easy, but it will be strong, and it will be very productive.

*Aries-Leo*

The union of two signs of similar element, such as the two fire signs in this case, is usually taken to be a good thing. This is no exception, though there are one or two problems caused by our being *too* similar.

Both of you have a need to be number one. For you as an Arian, the emphasis is on doing things for yourself, and excelling at what you do; the Leo sees things a different way. For him, the emphasis is on being seen as leader, being recognized as the natural centre of things, to whom people turn for reassurance and warmth.

As you will realize, you are not likely to give a Leo the sort of respect he thinks he deserves if you think that you can do things any better, and this will undermine his position. If, on the other hand, you can't do things any better, and should therefore look to him for advice, you will see him as a rival and be forced to compete with him until you eventually surpass him; you see yourself as a natural leader, and you think your place is in front.

If you can realize that you are essentially similar in outlook, you can get along very well indeed. You are both active, in that you prefer to do things rather than be passive and wait for things to happen. You are both essentially outward-looking and optimistic, believing that things can, and probably will, improve. You have both got a lively sense of humour, with the Arian probably the sharper of the two, and you are both capable of giving out enough energy to inspire and help others who don't seem to be able to make it on their own.

Where you differ most is that the Arian needs to make his own territory, to go where others haven't been before and claim it for himself, whereas the Leo is much happier to find himself in an existing situation and put his energies into it from the inside. Eventually he becomes the central figure wherever he is, and becomes responsible for the general morale and social life of the group. It isn't important for the Leo to be seen doing the impossible or proving that he is the best; what is important is that he be recognized as such, and given the respect due to his position.

Provided that neither of you trespass on the other's territory, your bright and radiant personalities will attract each other without much effort from either party, and an affair could easily grow. This will be conducted with all the heat that Fire signs usually generate, and the warmth of the affection will be visible to outsiders, though it will not seem especially passionate to you, since you do everything with that sort of intensity. Emotions will be easily expressed, and in a simple manner, because both of you are surprisingly unsophisticated in your emotional requirements. You are both easily hurt, and will show that you are hurt—this is usually because you both want your own way at once, and one of you has been forced to take second place.

If you can learn to take second place once in a while, perhaps in turns, then a warm and lasting marriage is possible. You can be very good for each other, with the Aries learning the pleasure of giving to others, and the Leo learning that responding to challenges doesn't necessarily mean loss of prestige.

### Aries-Virgo

In all relationships where the two Sun signs are five signs separated there is an element of adjustment to be found; that is, for the two people to work at all well together, they must be prepared to modify their usual point of view, for there is little, if any, common ground between them.

Aries is too forceful and immediate for Virgo; as an Arian, you will find that the Virgo's willingness, if not actual preference, to do the same things over and over again until familiarity is exceeded, drives you to distraction. It is enough for you to do something and get it right; it is often enough just to do it and get some sort of a successful outcome. Not so the Virgo; he likes to master the way of doing things as well as getting a result. Technique is important to him. Each time a Virgo does something it is not the same as before; he modifies his way of doing it, learns from it, understands more about the processes involved, and analyses all this in a way which is quite alien to the Arian way of thought.

If you have common interests, then you can approach them from your separate directions, and progress through each other's talents. You can be the driving force, and he can be the technique. You use his know-how and skill, but supply the enthusiasm and motivation yourself. Seen from the other point of view, the Virgo finds that he is saved from getting bogged down in small detail, and rescued from those times when he cannot provide the impetus to move forwards, by the Arian's eagerness to get things moving, and general vitality. There is always power and stamina on hand in the Aries character, and the Virgoan is grateful for it.

Because the Virgo is so careful, and needs time to analyse a new idea for a while before he commits himself to it, your way of throwing yourself into something because you feel good about it will meet with a less than equal response, and you must be ready for this if you find yourself emotionally involved with one. It's not that they don't respond, just that they need convincing that the affair is going to be the sort of thing that they'd like. They can take quite a bit of convincing at times, and are not to be won over by five minutes' impassioned protestation.

As business partners, they can be wonderful provided that both of you adapt your working style to take the other's strengths into account (the adjustment mentioned earlier). Virgoans can think of all the possibilities inherent in a business stratagem and use your energies to make them work; if you accuse him of being too picky, then you are throwing away his analytical talents, and exposing both of you to the sort of oversights that you yourself make through haste and over-eagerness. He must be prepared to make decisions in a once-and-for-all manner, and be prepared to take a few risks. If he doesn't, he loses all the advantages of your speed and talent for effective action. You must both be prepared to do things the other's way, and then things will go very well.

As marriage partners, Virgoans are very careful about the family's diet and general state of health, whereas you tend to eat anything you can find when you're hungry, because you need to provide fuel for all the energy you put out. There will be times when they seem to do things so very slowly, but you must just accept this, as they have to accept your rapid changes of mind and impassioned outbursts when things don't turn out just the way you want. To them, this looks like sheer carelessness and lack of planning, but they will forgive you.

*Aries-Libra*

This pairing is based on the attraction of opposites. In a nutshell, everything you do or feel is done in the opposite way by the Libran. That doesn't mean in terms of literally doing the opposite things, of course; but think of why you do something, the motivation behind it, and you will be able to observe the Libran doing things for the opposite reasons.

Librans are far less active than you are, and less decisive too. Where you want to do things for yourself, and rarely consider what anybody else might want to do, the Libran is always ready to listen to alternative points of view, and is quite likely to be swayed by any of them. He would much rather do something in company than on his own, which means that he is likely to find himself doing what his friends suggest, rather than be left out.

Your decisiveness will guide him easily; you decide what you want to do, and the Libran will agree. The benefit to you is that you have a companion, and the benefit to him is that somebody is taking the decisions for him, so that he doesn't have to think too hard. Librans can get very inactive and ineffective because they have an infinite capacity for putting things off until another time, and having an Arian partner will cure this. Of course, you have to be prepared to push them into action some of the time, and if you don't want any of that, then perhaps this relationship is not for you.

The problem in this particular coupling of zodiacal types is that you are both concerned with personal issues. If that sounds strange, think how much the Taurean is concerned with what he owns, or the Capricorn with his status—neither of them are bothered too much about themselves as *people*. You and the Libran are much more concerned with yourselves—you with being an individual, and the Libran with being a partner to somebody. Therefore the relationship between you has to be built on your personal relationship, and cannot rely on common interests such as your children, your careers, your shared possessions and activities, to succeed. You have to actually like each other. If the Libran feels that he isn't close enough to you, then he grows remote and dejected; if you feel that he is a weight round your neck, then you get angry and feel that you cannot be yourself on your own any more. As you can see, it is a tightrope existence, and you must both be very careful. All the 'opposite sign' relationships are like this, but yours is the only one which works at such a personal level.

In any relationship with a Libran, you are going to feel that their heart isn't in it; how else, you reason, could they account for being so slow to respond? You are seeing it from your own point of view, which is reasonable enough. The Libran wants to know how little things will be disrupted if he does something new; how much will things be the same as before? He is willing to give things a try, especially if you think it's a good idea, but he needs time to think about it, and will try to manage it so that there is very little disturbance of his usual routines. Once you realize that you are always going to be the one to make the moves, the one who wants things to happen at once, all will be well. Once the Libran realizes that being active isn't likely to throw him off balance, and that when he's finished being active he can sit down again in his favourite chair, things will be better yet.

Any long-term relationship between you, such as a marriage, or going into business together, is bound to be something of a see-saw arrangement, alternating between furious activity and periods of quiet. More than anything else, though, success in these long-term undertakings depends on your actually liking each other quite a lot.

*Aries-Scorpio*
This is the sort of relationship you always promised yourself— somebody with the strength, drive, and pure sex-appeal to give

you a run for your money, test your strength and stamina, and completely fulfil you.

The trouble is that it's not quite like that in real life. It can be, but there is always more to it than that, and it's the 'more' part that you're not too happy with. The plain truth is that a Scorpio can give you more than you wanted.

You are both ruled by the planet Mars, and that's what gives both of you the limitless reserves of energy you have. All this energy needs physical expression at least, if not sexual expression, and for the Arian it seems as though everyone else in the Zodiac is a little dull and lifeless compared to the powerful pulse of Mars he himself enjoys. Scorpio is the other, indeed the only other, zodiacal sign with Mars as the driving force. The difference between you is, quite simply, that while you are motivated by being Mars, expressing it as a physical force, the Scorpio is motivated by controlling Mars, using it as a powerful tool.

The Scorpio has none of your instinctive belief that nothing can go wrong because you will somehow be able to blaze your way through your difficulties with a touch of luck and some applied enthusiasm. For him nothing goes wrong because he stays in control, and everything runs in the paths he thought it would. The Martian energy is used to direct and control; he needs to know how things work, what goes on in the background while nobody else is looking, and how he can stay on top of it all by pulling a few strings here and there. He is very emotional, and his emotions run very deep; most of them are below the surface, but he never stops thinking, and never stops feeling things either, which most people forget. All the intensity of emotional response which in you is on the surface, in him is there but invisible. A chastening thought, isn't it?

Consequently, a love affair between you will be a very powerful thing, stronger than you can imagine. You can only imagine things on one level at a time, Aries; the Scorpio has no limits. When a little trust has grown, you will be able to see some of his depths, but nothing like all of them. You will offer him your physical self, which is all you have to offer, and is the part which means most to you, and he will match your strength. If you are very strong, he may withdraw a little, because to lose to you would entail loss of control, which he cannot risk; there must always be a little bit left in reserve in a Scorpio—only you can play all out at once. He will control you, or try to, and he will be possessive, for to be otherwise would involve losing control; you may resent this, and fight him more fiercely than is good for either of you from time to time.

A Scorpio makes an admirable business partner, but you may not like the way he withholds information when it suits him, and how things seem to be going on over your head. An open sort of business relationship, one without secrets, is easier for you to grasp, and you feel happier there too, but you are unlikely to get one with a Scorpio. Still, they are very good indeed when it comes to making money grow.

Perhaps the passions and jealousies make this one a poor idea as a marriage partnership; it will certainly be up and down for most of the time. Best as an affair, I think.

### Aries-Sagittarius

This is the last of the fire-to-fire groupings, and like the Leo partnership, you have a lot in common. This is the fire sign with the greatest mental capabilities; in fact, the greatest mental capabilities of all the twelve signs. Even brighter than the Gemini, and honest as well. The honesty of the Sagittarian, which shows itself to you, the Arian, as a bright kind of openness and optimism in speech, appeals to you. You cannot help but like a person who says what he thinks the moment he thinks it; he seems to have the same immediacy and delight in thought and speech as you have in action and movement, and he seems to get the same kind of pleasure from expressing it. All of this strikes you as very appealing, and you will be pleased to know that you are right to find it so. Sagittarians are very much a matter of 'What you see is what you get', and they are almost incapable of deception. So much so, in fact, that they are tactless in public, because they can't help telling it as they see it, and the honest truth spoken to someone's face often gives offence. Both you and the Sagittarian find this funny, and the two of you will be more convinced than ever that you are perfectly suited.

Basically, you find them inspirational. You will wish, when you have got to know them for a little while, that you could have just a little of their intellect, for which you would gladly trade some of your ease of movement and strength. This is because they dazzle you, to some extent, with their brilliant wit, their capacity for learning and remembering things, their fantastic imagination; they show you all this with such confidence and ease that you are over-impressed. Truth to tell, they show all these things to anybody, but it is the confidence and energy that appeals to you, because they seem to be speaking in your own language. They are: it is the language of the fire signs. Their tales sound terrifyingly risky to Cancerians, and woefully unplanned to Virgoans, but to you they sound like high adventure.

They find you wonderfully expressive of all their ideas. Sagittarians are changeable creatures, like their opposites, the Geminians; an idea only lasts as long as it takes for another one to replace it. Not so for you: once you have an idea, you make it work and make a success of it, and they find this very impressive. They appreciate your forcefulness, because they can never be anything for long; they love your self-assertive outlook, because it matches theirs, and they don't like dull company.

This changeable nature extends to their love affairs. It's not that they are purposefully cheating on you, but if somebody else seems attractive and available then their curiosity means that they have to give it a try. They will be genuinely apologetic afterwards, and would never willingly cause you any anguish, but they just can't resist the lure of something new, and they are going to do it next time, too, so be warned. You are likely to find this upsetting—not because you can't stand the competition, but because you can't stand the idea of being moved from the number one slot! They won't be able to see why you're so upset, which won't help at all. Whatever you do, though, don't demand loyalty: Sagittarians treat this as a serious attempt at curbing their freedom, and they will do anything to stay free. The more you insist, the more they try to escape— and probably succeed.

As a long-term proposition, this partnership is very good indeed. A business venture between the pair of you will rise quickly, but you need to employ somebody else to look after the background work which neither of you enjoy, or you will have nothing beneath you, since you are both eager to be developing new areas of business without doing much to maintain the old ones. As a marriage, provided you recognize that your partner is going to need a bit of rope from time to time, and space to feel free in, you will have a friend for life who will be almost everything you ever wanted, and who will never fail to impress and amuse you.

### Aries-Capricorn

The essential thing to remember about a Capricorn is that he is concerned first and foremost with what people think of him. If this doesn't meet with any understanding from you, then forget about any kind of relationship. Capricorns are devoted to getting on in life, so that they can be seen to be doing well. Status symbols were invented for, if not by, Capricorns. They all have high ambitions from an early age, and spend most of their lives working extremely hard so that these are achieved in one form or another. You can probably understand the idea of being number one; what you will have difficulty with is the desire to promote yourself at the expense of yourself. Think about that; a Capricorn doesn't mind hardship to himself as long as he gets what he wants, and he thinks that hard work is much too serious a thing to be enjoyed. The sheer pleasure of being you that runs through every vein of the Arian is not there in the Capricorn. This makes them, in your eyes, unimaginative, unfriendly, and dull.

If a Capricorn is interested in you, then you must ask yourself what he wants out of it, because his ambitions will still be in the forefront of his mind. He is likely to want your energy and ability to succeed first time; this last is something that he rarely accomplishes, because he just doesn't have the right way of attacking the problems, and he knows this. He recognizes your drive; it is similar to the drive of his own ambition, and he appreciates that. From your point of view, of course, you appreciate the things he has accomplished; you can admire a person who decides what he wants to do, and then goes out and does it. The pair of you, in fact, admire each other, but you can't understand why each of you does things in the manner you do. Most Aries-Capricorn relationships start off from mutual admiration.

You are likely to be the one who makes all the running in the relationship. If you are particularly wanting to find someone who cannot compete with your lively approach, then all is well, but most of you will find a Capricorn too careful, and emotionally reserved, which is not the way you work at all. In some cases, you may not be ambitious enough for them, especially if you are the sort of Arian who has a great time being himself, and doesn't really make any plans for the future. In this case the Capricorn will attempt to push you into doing things you don't much like, because if he doesn't he will feel that you are holding up his plans and not making best use of your energies for your joint future.

As a business partnership, it has much to recommend it, especially if you let the Capricorn do the organizing, and just address yourself to specific tasks one at a time. They will make sure you get the status you both deserve, and you will make sure he has the energy and drive he needs to bring his plans to fruition.

### Aries-Aquarius

This is the sort of relationship that you like. It is similar in some ways to the Gemini link, in that the rapport is light and fast-moving, and your freedom to go your own way is not hindered in any way.

An Aquarian needs to form friendships; he feels that he works best in groups of people, and would much rather give his energies to the group than concentrate on his own ambitions. When you first meet an Aquarian, it is likely to be in a group, and in those surroundings they seem to be bright and attractive, somehow representing the best qualities of all the people present. That is exactly what they are doing, because they have put themselves into the group's identity, and taken that for their own character. On their own, Aquarians are shy and rather distant, and not particularly impressive. They need the warmth of friendship to make them work properly, and when that friend is someone as naturally fiery as you, their needs are met perfectly.

You need to have a friend who is there whenever you want them ,but is never going to close you in or attempt to tell you what to do. You also need a friend who is essentially kind and honest, because your own straightforward approach to life makes you easy meat for those whose outlook is less than scrupulous. As far as you are concerned, the Aquarian is just the job. They are by nature quite straight and fair in their dealings, and are unlikely to be trying to deceive you on purpose, though genuine misunderstandings can still occur, as in all relationships. Their relatively unemotional approach to life means that you are unlikely to meet strong opposition to your own ideas, and this means that you don't have to waste time and energy convincing your partner how right you are.

On the other hand, you may find that their lack of deeply felt passion about anything is a drawback. Perhaps you would like them to be a little more forceful. Try being boorish, unrefined, rude, or cruel and see where that gets you; an Aquarian cannot stand to see any of these qualities displayed, and will make quite sure that they are not displayed again, usually by getting other friends and associates to chastise you on their behalf. You won't see at first how the Aquarian works through people he knows, rather than directly; it never occurs to you that anybody could achieve anything in any other way than by themselves, but that's exactly how the Aquarian does things. They will change your tastes, too, moderating your excesses and turning your physical grace into social grace, your childishness into charm, and your will to win into inspired leadership.

What they get out of it is your warmth; the never-failing enthusiasm and passion for things that take your fancy captivates them, and if they are the thing that you fancy, then they feel warmed, loved, and rewarded. An Aquarian cannot love himself deep down; he needs others to love him before he feels content.

As a partnership for business, it has everything to recommend it; they will be full of new schemes, and different ones, too, for they have a talent for the unusual which will surprise you. Their capacity for making contacts 'in the trade' is unparallelled. Make sure that you don't rush in and destroy the delicate networks of communication and cooperation that they set up just because you want something done immediately, and have become impatient.

Marriage could be a rarer event than you might imagine. Arians like to go their own way, and an Aquarian isn't going to try to tie you down. Aquarians are also solitary creatures from time to time, and there are times when they like their own company best, because constant emotional interchange is tiring for them. Marriage seems too restricting for the pure Arian, and too tiring for the pure Aquarian; other factors will have to make you tie the knot. Once married, though, you can be sure of a light and bright partnership, full of affection, if not very passionate; there will be plenty of variety, and challenges will be taken up and met rather than avoided. You could do worse.

### Aries-Pisces

This is an odd partnership; like the Aries-Taurus one, it brings two adjacent signs in the zodiac into confrontation, and each of them then sees what he is, what he could be, and what he fears.

This time the other sign, Pisces, is behind you in the zodiacal circle, and thus represents all the things you secretly fear. Do you want to have a relationship with somebody whose motivation is to exhibit and promote those qualities which worry you?

I know you are thinking that there is nothing which really worries you, but there is. You are quite sure that in a definite situation you can apply your directness of mind and physical approach to get things going the way you want, but what if the situation were indefinite? What if it had nothing that was certain, nothing you could be sure of, nothing static or dependable? Now you begin to see what I mean. You represent a focus of energy, a point where things happen and take form. Pisces represents defocusing, a nowhere-in-particular that is everywhere at once, where everything is possible, but nothing is definite.

Pisceans are, therefore, people of infinite flexibility, who can take up any cause or put on any appearance they wish, according to the circumstances they find themselves in. If you are playing strong and sexy, they will too. If you are playing active and sporty, they will change to suit. They will reflect and complement you, and you will find that attractive.

Pisceans long for a definite thing to be; they wish that they could be as firm and effective as you are—for a while. Consequently they see in you a desirable state, and make themselves like that to amuse themselves and to please you. You will notice the differences, though; the Piscean will never learn to concentrate on the moment, his whole being given to the immediate present; instead, he exists in a sort of no-time, where everything is immediate, but the future has the same immediacy as the past. You, of course, don't have much of a sense of future time at all. More than that, you will notice how the Piscean reacts to obstacles. Challenges are something to meet as far as you're concerned, but to him they are to be avoided. Whenever difficulties arise, the Piscean melts away, makes himself scarce, flows round them; he reappears when the problem has been removed.

As business partners, it is very difficult to make this one work, unless you are in something connected with the media or the arts, where you make the impact and the Piscean supplies the sensitivity and imagination. As a marriage, then the understanding and tolerance that comes with time is the only answer, because you are very unlike. You might learn to enjoy uncertainty of mind, and your partner might learn to appreciate the practical advantages of decisive action. As lovers, it is an interesting experience for both of you, but possibly no more than that; you will be taken on flights of fantasy where nothing seems real (and you must remember that none of it is), and they will be invited to play games where strength and passion are the preferred currency. Dungeons and Dragons, perhaps?

# Taurus

*Taurus-Aries*

All zodiacal partnerships involving adjacent signs are difficult, but this combination is possibly the most difficult of them all. The simple fact is that Arians annoy you. They are worrying to you, and they move much too quickly for you and be able to keep a proper eye on them. You like to know where things are, and where they are going to stay for some time; Arians don't stay anywhere for any length of time, and this is disturbing to you. Perhaps it was their forcefulness that attracted you; you will have discovered that it is not directed towards the defence of their position, as yours is, but towards personal movement. Their energy moves them for movement's sake; you only let yourself be moved when threatened.

They are highly active people, and need to keep busy doing things, whereas you are quite happy to keep things the way they are. This means that while you are at your best staying in one place doing one thing, they are likely to be changing from one thing to another, and you will find it disconcerting. They would like you to be active too, so that they can feel the pleasure of having a partner in action, and they will try to make you move faster than you would really like. Moving too quickly means that you cannot feel the earth under your feet, and this removes you from your element (Earth, remember? Remind yourself with the diagram on page 16). You are naturally frightened to do this, and so refuse to move as quickly as the Arian would like. He sees this as lack of spirit, but does not hold this against you in any way. He must go his own way, and has no time to spend cajoling you into joining him. The fact that you are unwilling, or unable, to join him is a great pity, but can't be helped. It is important for you to understand this—the Arian thinks no worse of you because you won't join in his activities; he simply thinks that it is your loss, and can't be helped. He doesn't feel betrayed, injured, or thwarted in any way. You feel all of these when relationships go wrong, of course; it's part of how you work. He doesn't work like you at all, and that doesn't mean that either of you are wrong, just different. Can you understand that?

Physically, you are well matched, because you both use your bodies as a prime expression of your energies. You will find Arian energy attractive, and would dearly like to be able to keep some of it for later, or to have it for your own. The Arian finds your strength an invigorating test for his sexual capabilities, and on that level at least you should have a lot of excitement and satisfaction. The problems arise when you try to convert the relationship into something steady instead of a momentary passion. The Arian gets bored, and you become possessive. The level of energy in the liaison drops, the sexual excitement fades, and you become more and more determined to hang on to what you see as yours, but which you think is mysteriously being taken away from you. The Arian senses the lack of excitement, the lack of development and novelty as the situation becomes static, and immediately looks for a more interesting project. The result is bound to be disappointment for both of you. There will inevitably be one of those thankfully rare occasions where the Taurean loses his temper in a big way, because he feels that he has somehow been deprived of what was rightfully his.

As a long-term relationship, such as a business or a marriage, this coupling can only work if roles are strictly defined and understood. If that is done, the pressure that you can both bring to bear on problems that beset you can make for a very successful team. The Aries must be allowed to do all the development work, and to do it as his own pace; everything which is untried, or has to be tackled without much preparation, must be left to the Arian. The Taurean must do all the backup work, and be allowed to make it his own territory. He must also convince the Arian that all this effort is worthwhile, by giving patience, the quality the Arian lacks above all; in return, you will be shown that new beginnings are far from impossible when your position really seems hopeless.

## Taurus-Taurus

Two bulls in the same field: quite an entertaining proposition for a spectator outside the field, but rather uncomfortable for anyone in the field, and necessarily painful for one, perhaps both, of the bulls.

The relationship is likely to start with some taste that the pair of you have in common: perhaps you like the same sort of food, and enjoy working your way round all the restaurants of that type in your area. Perhaps it is music, or some pastime. Whatever it is, you will be pleased that someone else has the same high opinion of the things that you like as you have. For a Taurean, to have someone give you credit for your tastes is an irresistible compliment to your ego. The same thing, of course is also happening to the other Taurean.

It is easy to get yourself into a sort of race in this situation, where both of you are in competition with the other to have more, or a better one, of whatever it is that you both admire and enjoy possessing. This will last until one of you runs out of money or time and is fine as far as it goes as long as neither of you take it at all seriously. Both of you will strenuously deny that it *is* at all serious, but it will be so nonetheless, because what you hate most of all is losing—and losing publicly; hence the denials that there is any kind of contest. Both of you like to have just that bit more than the other—whoever first came up with the phrase 'I'll have the big half' was undoubtedly Taurean, and most probably saw nothing funny in what he'd just said.

It is difficult for you to understand the give and take of a relationship at times, because as far as you are concerned you are right. This means that if your partner does something which you disagree with, or, far worse, tries to get you to change your ways, you feel criticized and under attack. There is no reason for you to feel this, but you do nonetheless. If the matter is a small one, you will take no notice, confident that your partner will soon see things your way, and no more need be said. If it is a request for you to do things differently, you simply take no notice, because they are wrong, and that's that. If it is something important, or the requests for unaccustomed action are persistent, then you will wait patiently, and only when the situation becomes intolerable will you move. When you move, you move to re-establish your way of doing things once and for all.

Progress and change do not come easily to a Taurean, and an easygoing, patient nature is often just a wounded Taurean hoping that the irritation will go away without having to move. Two people behaving in this way with each other is bound to be difficult. As a marriage, the best thing to do is to find an area about which you both agree very strongly, such as financial growth, or the acquisition of property, and make everything else subordinate to it. This way your personal stubbornnesses become insignificant when you both see how much you have achieved together, and your natural tendencies to keep a good things going if possible will motivate you to settle minor problems for the sake of your greater possessions.

*Taurus-Gemini*
This partnership is as difficult for you to understand as the Aries one. Fortunately for you, it is nothing like as threatening, and so you can afford to let your differences go by without worrying about being forced to make changes. You have an appreciation of peace and quiet, of letting the world go by in its own way without interference, which is simply not comprehensible to a Gemini. Their need to think, to read, to receive information and then voice an opinion on it, will occasionally make you wish you could switch them off like a radio. You can't; you will have to live with the noise.

What you find strangest of all with the Gemini is their apparent disregard for things material. If there is food in front of them, they will eat it, but it isn't anything like as important as it is to you. They like a well-appointed house—who doesn't?—but they don't see that as a reflection of themselves and their tastes as you do. What really interests them is a new idea. New information and new developments, the sort of thing you turn your back on in case it heralds change, is the stuff of life to them.

Geminis are the sort of people who think that they are always right, because they have thought about things and come to a definite conclusion. You can appreciate this, because you know that you are right, too; not from thinking about things, but from feeling them, and taking things in slowly. What will surprise and upset you is that a Gemini can change his mind completely every five minutes, and each time he is convinced that he is right. The same mental evaluation has taken place, and the same force of conviction is there, and yet he has changed viewpoint completely. This is very unsettling to you; either he is making it all up, which is potentially threatening to your stability because you may be taken in, or he is right each time, which is worrying because you can't react that fast. If you don't panic, it may dawn on you that this mental evaluation process is actually what he likes doing best, and so he does it as often as he can, continually fascinating himself with the varieties of argument he turns up. As you will realize, all this happens in the world of the imagination and does not affect your position, your territory, or your possessions one bit; you are quite safe, and can let him exercise his imagination to his heart's content. This is why he is less of a threat to your stability than the Arian. Relax, and listen to the chatter; he can be very entertaining indeed once you realize that very little of it is for real.

As lovers, you will be a strange mixture. You would like to have his lightness of touch and his way with words; he makes you feel clumsy and slow, but you find his conversation so flattering, and he makes you feel good. From the other side of the relationship, he needs your stabilizing influence when things aren't going quite the way he'd like them to, which will be a lot more frequently than you would imagine. It's because he never believes that effort is a necessary component of success. You will have to take the role of an understanding parent, while he takes that of the child.

Unless you have strong common interests, it will be difficult to make a lasting partnership from these two signs, because you are not concerned with ideas any more than he is with material things, and he will lose interest in you unless there is something you both enjoy. You must expect arguments from time to time, when he changes his ideas and denies having thought differently before; he must remember that to make his dreams come true requires patience and application, and you are his best source of both those qualities.

*Taurus-Cancer*

This is a splendid partnership. You are both concerned with the same things in life, but approach them from different, though complementary, directions. Both of you are determined to hang on to what is yours and not to lose things, but you are not in conflict with each other. The important thing from a Cancerian point of view is to have a firm base, to look after what is your own, to care about and make sure that you know about everything that goes on in your territory, and then worry about your responsibilities and your safety. The Taurean point of view is nothing like so frantic; to make sure that your territory stays yours is all; being recognized as the owner is a welcome bonus.

The Cancerian worries too much about things, whereas the Taurean trusts his own abilities and is of the opinion that if nothing is done to upset the general arrangement of things, nothing drastic will happpen. The Cancerian isn't so sure, and it is here that the relationship starts to work: the Cancerian comes to the Taurean for advice and reassurance about matters of security, knowing that he isn't going to sound silly. In return, the Taurean knows that if he wants somebody to share his possessions and his taste for the good life without getting involved in a game of one-upmanship or a situation that threatens his position, then the sensitive Cancerian is just the one. Like a younger sister, the Cancerian is mildly envious of all that the Taurean has managed to collect, and appreciates being allowed to use some of it. She may not agree completely with her big sister's taste, but she is far too reserved, and too aware of what's good for her in the long run, to voice any criticism.

Cancerians are quite capable of expanding their responsibilities and the areas under their control, and often do. They are prepared to do something completely new if they feel that it is in their best interest. It is not usual to call them adventurous, but in comparison to the Taurean, who will always take the tried and trusted method rather than risk anything unfamiliar, it can seem that way. Certainly a Cancerian is more motivated to advance his ambitions into new fields than the Taurean; but, having got there, he feels responsible for all the people under him and is unable to simply to pass over them. It's not a territorial urge so much as a caring and almost parenting feeling, but it is one which a Taurean understands at once.

Home is important to a Cancerian, because it is his personal caring environment. It needs to be secure, and it needs to be comfortable. Taureans are very fond of lavishly appointed homes, and so any home that you share together will be of great importance to you, and you will both work hard to make it as comfortable and welcoming as possible, if for slightly different reasons.

As lovers, you will be very affectionate, very caring and very understanding, through the physical electricity that the Fire signs like Aries and Sagittarius brings to a relationship will be missing. Earth and Fire are a lightning strike, after all, whereas what we have here is Earth and Water, producing a fertile environment. That works in all ways— Earth and Water people together have large and happy families.

As a marriage, the arrangement seems perfect. If there is a flaw, it may be that eventually you become so set in your ways and so home-centred that you feel a need for something else to do; but taken as a whole the marriage is unlikely to develop any more serious problems than obesity as the two of you indulge your liking for food and the security it represents.

## Taurus-Leo

This is an interesting pairing—almost interesting enough to sell tickets to watch. Two powerful animals, A Bull and a Lion, both used to being their own master, and unaccustomed to giving way on anything, attempting to make an equal relationship. If it succeeds, and there will be a few broken plates before it settles down, then it will be very strong indeed, and a union which will bring great material wealth and prestige to its partners.

The essential conflict is something similar to ignoring a 'Do Not Walk On The Grass' notice under the park-keeper's nose. A Taurean has a very acute sense of his own territory, and will have things done according to his wishes within that territory. Trespassers or people refusing to recognize his authority within that territory are seen as threats. So far, so good. A Leo, however, regards himself as the natural authority figure and centre of attention wherever he happens to be, and will behave in the firm belief that this is indeed so. He also feels free to go wherever the mood takes him, so long as he has an opportunity to display his personal warmth and radiance to a suitable audience. When he strides into the Taurean's territory he will expect appreciation and respect, and be hurt not to receive it; almost as hurt as the Taurean is by the lack of recognition he is afforded by the Leo. Neither of them is of the sort likely to smile and forget. They will insist on recognition, and because they are both Fixed signs (page 15) they will not bend an inch away from what they think is theirs. Such arguments can lead to separations lasting years; the families which don't speak to each other for generations are showing this fixed sign behaviour.

The way for a Taurean to achieve some measure of under-standing with a Leo is for the Leo to handle the theory and the Taurean to handle the practicalities. If they agree on the same goals, then the Leo can provide a way for the Taurean to display his wealth without seeming offensive (everybody likes Leos, and expects them to be rich; not everybody likes a wealthy Taurean), while the Taurean generates more wealth from the opportunities the Leo provides. If this is done, a partnership capable of generating very large amounts of money is created, provided you limit yourselves to doing what you know best, and don't branch out into the new and unfamiliar.

As lovers you will enjoy taking your territorial struggles to the bedroom; you will both be strong, but a little conventional, in your approaches to sex. As a Taurean you will have to be ready for a few tall stories from your Leo lover, and don't be surprised if this continues in the pub. Leos are the best in the world; they know it, and they tell everybody so when they get an audience. Everybody loves them for it, and nobody cares whether any of it is true or not.

As marriage partners you will be very loyal to each other, and fight on each other's behalf when necessary; you will build a home and family life which becomes richer and more plentiful as time goes on. You will have to learn that Leos are easily hurt if they think that you don't care much for some of their ideas, and you will have to develop a way of letting them down gently using that Taurean patience. You will be needlessly possessive; they are as loyal to you as you to them. They will have to learn that at home, particularly, you are the boss; you are unlikely to teach them, or spell it out for them, so they must learn it on their own. Sometimes they are as slow to accept the unpalatable as you are, so give them time to get used to the idea.

*Taurus-Virgo*
This partnership can work very well. You are both Earth signs, and so you are both interested in using your energy in the same general way. You may find the Virgoan fussy, though, and they will almost certainly find you rather hefty and careless in your approach to many things.

The essential thing about a Virgoan's approach to life is getting the details right. It matters to them that they have the right way of going about things; often they will find enjoyment and satisfaction in a repetitive job, because to them each time is different, and they are continually learning and re-learning their technique. 'Practice' is a very Virgoan word. They like things to feel good, and are much happier when they can feel and touch things for themselves. They modify whatever they own, changing little bits of it here and there to make it that little bit neater, or a closer fit, or whatever.

To you, this obsession with detail is strange. You can understand the care and attention that is lavished on belongings, because you feel strongly about that too, but the constant search for perfection baffles you. You do not like to change your way of doing something; you only learn it once, and however sloppy you become after that, you still believe that you are doing it in the same way, and will not be persuaded otherwise. The Virgoan is never sloppy; his technique is always up to the mark, and constantly in practice, because he analyses what he does as he does it. He analyses what he is about to do before he does it. He thinks about how he would analyse it before he has to. As a result, he makes the best possible use of all the material at hand, and you seem to him to be unthinking in your use of your talents. You seem not to consider how best to do something, only whether to do it. You seem not to consider how to adapt something to fit you better, only how to acquire it. Above all, you seem not to care what it is that you have, only to care that you have it, and that other people recognize this. The area in which you come closest to each other is in that of selection, where you both pick the best you can, and reject the rest—one on the grounds of flavour, the other on the grounds of excellence of function.

In many ways, you wish you could be as careful and as perceptive as the Virgo; you feel that your life could be considerably enriched by his knowledge and insight, and his knowledge of correct technique would save you from making a fool of yourself on numerous occasions. For his part, he wishes he could simply command as much as you do; what couldn't he do if he didn't have to spend his time working on such a small scale—and imagine having the confidence and wealth to be careless with it all! Your immovable presence and authority, your appreciation of material comforts, is an inspiration to a Virgo, while his skills and insight are all that you would like to be, but can't be bothered ever to strive to become.

As lovers, you will have to be gentle and easy in your approach; Virgos are delicate creatures, and are easy to trample. Try to be considerate and careful; take time over details. In return, he will have to realize that your big gestures of affection are not at all clumsy or uncaring, but genuine declarations of affection on a rather bigger scale than he thinks is proper. He must restrain himself from telling you how to do things better, which is only a mask for his insecurity (a Taurean in love is a bit too forceful for him to deal with in small sections, as he would like).

As a marriage prospect, these signs are better than most of the same-element pairings. The constantly active nature of the Virgoan will stop things from ever being too much the same, and will work hard to make all as good as it can possibly be. Let him use you as a protector and defender against his enemies and fears, whilst you use him to help you get the very best use out of whatever it is that you have achieved. Not only will you have your own bit of land, but it will have the neatest, prettiest and most fruitful garden you have ever seen!

*Taurus-Libra*

A very happy partnership, this, because both of you are motivated and directed by the planet Venus, which looks for points of common interest, and tries to promote friendship and harmony. So not only are you pleased to meet somebody else who has a similar motivation to you, but you actually like them, too; what's more, they like you in return, and that is always a good sign in a relationship.

Librans have a distinctive talent for saying the right thing at the right time, and adding little touches here and there which make things easy on the eye. They can see at once what needs doing to make a room beautiful, and will do it without fuss, just to please themselves. A Libran home is always refined and beautiful, but pleasant to be in as well, which might not always be the case were other signs to be the homebuilders. They have the same simple elegance in their clothes; whatever they wear looks just right. Even their speech is pleasant. There is always something about the way a Libran does things that makes others think 'I wish I could be like that!'

As a Taurean, you appreciate beautiful things, and you like to be near them. The attraction of a person who is in themselves beautiful and graceful is not hard to see. From the other side, they see you as offering the sort of appreciation they like, and feel that they could form a close and rewarding relationship with someone who shares their view of life. A Libran is always trying to form relationships, make friends, gather people close to him; the problem lies in the sad fact that many people do not share his aesthetic view of things, are unreliable or discourteous, disloyal even. All these things upset the exact balance of the Libran existence and cause disharmony, which he feels strongly. He knows that he can always rely on the Taurean to be constant, loyal, and unchanging; that, coupled with the Taurean sense of admiration for all things which are beautiful to look at, makes for a friendship which is especially valuable to the Libran. You restore him when the world seems to be over-demanding, harsh, and unrefined. Through you, he knows that his essential values of harmony and quiet co-existence are still worth pursuing, and are constant despite temporary indications to the contrary. He needs no training in artistic sensibilities, but he does need strength, and he has to look for it outside himself. You can offer that in abundance, and he will give you in return the grace and charm that you sometimes feel you lack.

You may feel in the initial stages of your friendship that the Libran is too cool. This is not so, but they are certainly light in their approach to things, and the airy delicacy of their way of conducting an affair may seem insubstantial to you. From their point of view, you will seem heavy and a little lacking in subtlety. They will also find you short of originality, and a slow talker. Librans are from an Air sign, remember, and they need to circulate ideas. They also need to circulate amongst people, so don't keep them indoors, and don't get upset if they like talking to everybody else at a party. They'll come back. Remember that this social circulation is as important to them as eating is to you. Do you want them to starve to death? Take things on a light level if you can, and keep the relationship mobile.

As lovers you might have to be very understanding with each other. The Libran will find your passion and strength a little overwhelming, and lacking in refinement; you will find his preference for love and romance rather than sex delightful to begin with but frustrating later. Don't get upset if he runs away, but make sure that he realizes that it is important to you just the same.

As marriage partners you should be amusing to watch. Both of you are very particular about your home environment, and you will have it beautifully furnished, but neither of you will want to do much about its upkeep, because you are both quite lazy given half a chance. You will eat the most exquisite meals in the grandest style, but neither of you will want to wash up afterwards. You will have not only to take responsibility for the house, but some of the actual work involved too, and the Libran will have to accept his share as well. 'Share' is a Libran word— the idea of equal chores and equal responsibility is one which makes a lot of sense to his Airy mind, and has enough practicality built in to keep your Taurean needs satisfied too.

*Taurus-Scorpio*

A powerful thing, the meeting of two signs opposed to each other in the circle of the zodiac, especially when they are both fixed signs. You can expect them to be just as determined to have their own way as you are, and just as hard to move in any way they feel is not quite right for them. You can expect them to be able to do all the things that you can't, but there again, you can do all the things that they can't, so you end up even. All this sounds ominous, but you have quite a lot in common, and won't find it too difficult to get on with one another provided you have enough room for the pair of you not to feel threatened by each other.

You like to be in control of your physical environment, as you know well. This means that you like to know what's yours, and what comes into, or goes on in, or goes out of, your little bit of space. It is your field, and you are the bull in that field. A Scorpio likes to be in control of his emotional environment. This means that he likes to know how he feels, and how everybody else's actions and feelings are likely to affect his own. In turn, this means that he has to look into things to see how they work and what's going on, because unless he is fully up to date with all the possibilities, he may not be able to maintain his control over how he feels. You have an easier job of it, really; possessions don't change as fast as feelings. You may feel that you have more than a little of the Scorpio in you, now that you have read about what he's trying to do; many Scorpios will feel that they have more than a little of the Taurean in them, too. They usually like having things which remind them of how in control they are, like powerful cars.

The difference between the two of you, apart from the difference between possessions and feelings, is the difference between maintenance and control. A Scorpio isn't trying to maintain his feelings in the same state; he's trying to control them, so that they do what he wants. You're not trying to control your territory; you're trying to maintain it, so that it stays more or less as it is, but improving all the while. There is quite a difference.

You will be able to see at once that if the two of you are placed too close to each other, you will both feel threatened. So powerful and strongly controlled an individual on your territory is obviously unsettling to you, especially as you seem to be unable to see what he's thinking, and are afraid that he might take something from you; on his side, he is bothered by your immovability and apparent imperturbability, which could make you difficult to control, and have a possibly upsetting influence on his feelings. Given a little distance, you will both be able to see that your areas of concern may overlap but they do not intersect, and so you need have nothing to fear from each other.

As friends and partners, you could make a great deal of money together, because you represent the signs which are concerned with the effective use of all kinds of resources, financial included. Provided you have one person to do the organizing, and one to look after the stock, you will make an effective team. You might suffer from being a little on the dull side, since neither of you are originators of new ideas, but the Scorpio's assiduous research capabilities should ensure that you keep up with new developments in business as soon as somebody else has tested them and found that they work.

As lovers, you will express yourselves very powerfully indeed, but you will find that the emotional intensity with which the Scorpio conducts his love affairs will make your Taurean head feel dizzy. You like things powerful, sure, but you like them relaxed and easy-going, too; the constant atmosphere of almost obsessive passion will leave you gasping for air. Still, if you can stand that sort of thing, you won't feel that it isn't strong enough for you, as you might have done with the Libran, for example.

As marriage partners, the same thing applies. You both want success and security, and as a couple you should have no problems in achieving these goals. When you've got all that, though, you want to sit back in relative tranquillity and enjoy it all, whereas the Scorpio is driven to do more and more. Basically, they never stop, where you feel that resting after your labours is important as the work itself. If you can live with his constant determination to achieve more, without feeling irritated or criticized yourself, then fine.

*Taurus-Sagittarius*

These two signs are very different. They seem to get in each other's way more often than not when they act together, but when they stand back and look at the other in action they can each see what the other is trying to achieve. The Fire of the Sagittarian seems to scorch and wither all that the Taurean has worked so hard to achieve, while the Taurean seems too much of a plodder to appreciate the brilliance and verve of the Archer. There are other ways to look at it, though; the Taurean can provide a solid home base for the Sagittarian to come back to when he is in one of his crestfallen phases, and the Sagittarian can provide the optimism and insight that Taurean folk often cannot find in themselves. It takes effort from both sides to achieve that, though, and there must be a strong motivation for other reasons to keep the relationship together long enough for that kind of rapport to grow.

Think of the two animals from the signs, the bull and the horse. The bull lives in his own field, and doesn't move far from it; the horse leaps over the fence, and is soon away into the far distance, running with the wind for its own sake (an important thing to understand about Sagittarians—the need to be free and the joy of doing things for their own sake out of curiosity). The horse is more beautiful when in motion, the bull more majestic when standing still. Horses are essentially a luxury item, whereas cattle are much more useful in terms of what they produce. You can perhaps begin to see that the signs do not have a great deal to offer one another.

Having a Sagittarian friend is a disturbing experience for a Taurean. They seem to move so quickly; you take life at a steadier pace where you can, and dislike being rushed. They concentrate so much on intellectual things—ideas and concepts which have no real foundation or practical application, things they read in books. One minute they are on about one thing as though it was the only thing in the world, and the next minute it's something else altogether. Never the same twice. If you thought about it for a moment, you would see that they answer the deepest questions for you—questions so deep that you might never think of asking them. You might ask yourself, as you go through life looking after and assimilating your belongings, whether there was more, and where it might come from. The Sagittarian answers you. He shows you endless realms, shows you new things coming into being as ideas, and being translated into action and form. He is a creator, and you are a collector: the relationship is a deep one, and not often questioned or examined in daily life, but there it is.

He sees you as the sort of result his ideas must eventually be seen as. After all, he is trying to make things happen; if he succeeds, then the planetary energy will be collected into one place, and become Earth where it was once Fire. Besides, without the wealth of material you offer, not only in terms of money, but also in terms of effort, loyalty, and patience, then he can achieve nothing. On a personal level, he sees you as slow and rather predictable, but he is more than a little envious of your patience and the steadiness you seem to bring to life. He would not seriously trade the roller-coaster of emotional ups and downs he lives on, but when you don't like what you have at the moment a little of the opposite always seems attractive . . .

As lovers, you would be a lot more successful physically than you might have thought, but the rest of the relationship would need a lot of work. The trouble is that you need to feel that a person belongs to you, and you to them; a Sagittarian belongs to himself and to nobody else, and if you start to get possessive, then he will gallop off and find somebody else. Even when he is pledged to you (and he is, if he says so; they never lie) he will still entertain himself with new acquaintances of the opposite sex; variety and games are very important and restorative to him.

Having the same thing all the time makes him depressed. He will choose to come back to you quite freely, but he can never be compelled to do so. Being totally loyal to him doesn't really count; he sees you as a millstone then. A Sagittarian really does need to be allowed to go his own way; trap him and his fire dies, which is useless if what you were trying to do was keep his warmth for your own private use.

As marriage partners, you will have to make allowances for their need to move around, and make sure that you give them both the space and the opportunity to use it. He will need to realize that you need a base to return to, which is permanently and unchangeably yours. If you are married to a Sagittarian, or are considering it, then you must already have found some other interest which is strong enough to hold you both together. Without that joint interest and goal, you will need to put in what is probably more effort than you would like to make the relationship really work.

### Taurus-Capricorn

This is the relationship that's built to last. Two Earth signs, one fixed and one cardinal, both interested in making things firm, secure, and unchanging, and both with a fondness for things of enduring value—here is the recipe for a life partnership. It might be a little slow to get started, because both of you will be quite secure in your own areas, and will see no reason to interrupt things to allow the entry of someone new and possibly threatening to you; when you see how similar you are to each other you will start to like each other, and things will grow from there.

This is the four-signs-apart relationship, the mutual admiration society where each partner wishes he were more like the other one. In this particular case, the Taurean is probably impressed by the way that the Capricorn seems to get recognition and respect for all that he has achieved, and is seen as a natural and obvious winner in life. Taureans would like to have acclaim and recognition for their efforts, and it is the hope of this that motivates them anew when they are despondent. They also appreciate and approve of the way a Capricorn measures his success in material terms, or in the way that the world in general thinks of as showing that he's made it in life. Sometimes Taureans get a little confused by people from the other elements who don't seem to value bricks and mortar to the same extent that they do; but then along comes a Capricorn who both reassures and encourages the Taureans, and confidence is restored. This is an important process: fixed signs do not like to feel insecure in any way, and need reassurance from time to time. For a Taurean, a Capricorn is the answer.

From the other point of view, the Capricorn finds the Taurean solidity and determination the perfect expression of the work ethic so central to his way of seeing things. In point of fact, Capricorns are just the faintest bit lazy. It is a very faint bit, agreed, but it is there, and it shows in that they will work and work to achieve something they have set their hearts on, but against determined and repeated opposition they will give up and aim themselves towards something else. If you think for a few minutes you can see why: the need of the Capricorn is to feel achievement, and if things look like being unattainable then an alternative target may give them that sense of achievement sooner. A Taurean takes opposition as a personal affront, and stays where he is until he has worn the opposition down. The Capricorn thinks this is admirable. Working hard for high rewards he can understand, but working patiently and un-ceasingly with no guarantee of having the work recognized, as the Taurean often does, strikes the Capricorn as an almost saintly devotion to the cause, and he is lost in admiration.

As a friendship or business partnership, of course, this pairing has a lot to offer; the Taurean can share in the Capricorn's achievements as reward for his efforts, and the Capricorn can aim even higher for the pair of you in the knowledge that the Taurean will never deviate from the job in hand, no matter how difficult progress becomes. You will need to have somebody else around to provide both of you with new directions and ideas from time to time, or you will become rather dull and un-imaginative, but otherwise there is a lot to recommend this as a business partnership.

As lovers, there will be many power games for the two of you to amuse yourselves with, but the cool Capricorn does not understand the nature of real passion, and his response to your Taurean physical needs may not be enough. You will have to show him that physical contact and being touched are important to you, and invite him to express himself in a similar way. He'll never quite get it right, but he can be persuaded to join in to a certain extent.

As a marriage, this partnership looks good. Your tastes are different, though; you like things soft, pretty and luxurious, with plenty of food available—the Capricorn often doesn't care what or when he eats. Some of them are very flashy dressers, though; if you can find one of these, you will have a further point of contact through your love of colour and texture, and this will help you build a comfortable home together.

### Taurus-Aquarius

This match isn't easy at all. To put it simply, they feel safest in a crowd, whereas you feel safest at home; they are better with lots of people at once, and you are better in a one-to-one relationship.

You would think that somebody who was of the opposite sign to you in the zodiac would be opposite to you in every way, but that is not in fact the case. What happens is that the two people concerned are at odds because they are in so many ways similar rather than different. It is here, where the polarity of the signs is different, where the two of you are three signs apart, that the real differences emerge. You are dedicated to the maintenance of what's yours; you have worked for it, you are going to keep it, and you want everybody to respect you for the efforts you have put into its acquisition. An Aquarian is dedicated, in just the same way, to the breakdown of all structures which imply that anybody is better than, or higher than, anybody else. Difficult to imagine, isn't it?

Why were you attracted to him in the first place? It may well have been the fact that he always has so many friends, and is so popular. You become part of the audience, find that the group is a generally happy one, and enjoy the companionship and appreciation you get from other members of the group. Then you project yourself towards the group's centre (or, as Taureans do, charge like a bull) and acquire him. Now you can become possessive with him—he is yours. Unfortunately, he is not going to see it your way. He is not going to understand the depth of your feelings, your need to hold on to what you have, your need to be appreciated. You are not going to understand why he still needs to have a hundred friends when he has you.

Aquarians like to be different. More than that, they need to be different. Whenever they see something that has been established the way it is for some considerable time and is doing quite nicely, thank you, they feel that it is time for a change, and so they disturb, rearrange, and sometimes destroy things. It is not from a sense of malice, or even one of mischievous glee: it is simply the way they are built. They represent the idea that everything has its time, and at the end of that time it must change. Change is then a natural state for them, and the movement and conversation which flows round groups of people is an environment as natural and healthy for them as your home is for you. Being static is an unhealthy thing for them; collecting things which are going to last seems absurd, because they are dedicated to the concept of change.

It would seem that there could be no contact between you, but in fact there is a genuine attraction of opposites. He is interested in the nature of constancy simply because it is alien to him, and you represent that; you are interested in the nature of change, because it shows you the world outside your own experience, and fascinates you because you know you wouldn't like to live in it for long. Perhaps you both recognize that you are different aspects of the same thing. Whatever changes is still itself, but in a different form; whatever is formed must change in time, like the seasons. You will be strong in each other's defence, and yet equally strong in maintaining your differences within the relationship.

As lovers, you are bound to have difficulties because of the differences between Taurean possessiveness and Aquarian freedom. Physically, he will be inventive and adventurous, which will excite you, yet emotionally rather uninvolved, which could make you feel betrayed. In turn, he will find your passion and devotion rewarding, though its persistence and occasionally demanding nature will make him slip out from under from time to time to see other people and feel refreshed in their company.

If a marriage is to be built out of this relationship, you will both have to compromise to a large extent; his more revolutionary and far-ranging ideas will have to be shelved, and you must offer him some sort of willingnes to adopt changes from time to time. Shared interests will help—both of you like music as a rule, though it may not be the same kind, of course.

### Taurus-Pisces

Here is the relationship you have been waiting for, where you hardly ever have to show your horns, and you can give yourself almost completely to a life of relaxation and softness, self-indulgent for both you and your partner.

You are both just what the other one needs. The softer side of you—that which, given a chance, would spend its time in pursuit of elegance, artistry, and gracious living—finds the romantic and impressionistic approach of the Piscean very easy to accommodate. They are supremely sensitive individuals, and will adapt themselves to anything which comes their way. They are refined, and fond of luxury if they can get it; your strong point of view and determined way of doing things are more than enough guidance for them, while your own tastes are much along the same lines as their own. There should be very few disagreements.

You often feel yourself to be a little dull mentally, and wish that you could be as intellectual as some of the other signs. At the same time, you are wary of the harsh brilliance of the Gemini's wit, or the simply overwhelming erudition of the Sagittarian mind. Perhaps there is a softer mind, a gentler imagination, to which you might aspire? The Piscean has exactly that, and will help you develop your own imagination in the best possible way.

The softness of the Piscean is no threat to you, and you will seldom have to fight to get your own way. Most of the time you won't notice that they have any opinion different from yours at all. You will also enjoy looking after them, and loving them, because they are so delicate where you are strong, and so very appreciative of any kindness shown to them.

From the Piscean point of view, you are the sort of firm, no-nonsense individual that he needs to put some sort of shape and organization into his life, but without being bossy. He recognizes that he is not able to take assertive action by himself and needs guidance, but he is afraid that any such guide might be insensitive to his feelings, and unappreciative of what he has to offer. In the Taurean he knows that he has the perfect answer: someone strong, determined, and purposeful, but very caring, very patient, and very sensitive at the same time. In return for having his life put into manageable order, the Piscean offers heightened sensitivity and understanding on all matters to do with the emotional response to life, and an unmatched imagination —plus the ability to escape into fantasy and self-comforting whenever life becomes too depressing!

As friends you should be constant, forgiving of each other's little excesses, and very fond of each other. It is not a relationship with which to go out and achieve things; it is much more a restorative retreat for two people who can get easily bruised in the outside world, and need a little care and attention in their private life to redress the balance.

As lovers, your relationship should be very romantic indeed, but you may be surprised and confused from time to time because they are not as direct as you, and do things in rather vague and difficult-to-grasp ways. Be patient: they are not being devious, just vague. Try not to be heavy-handed in your demands. They love you dearly, but they just don't have the physical needs that you do.

As a marriage, this pairing should work very very well, provided that somebody takes responsibility for something somewhere. It's probably best if you make the decisions and they abide by them. You're more sensible.

# Gemini

### Gemini-Aries

This is one of the best friendships in the whole zodiac; you genuinely like each other. There are lots of qualities that you both have in common, and the areas in which one of you is deficient in talent are filled by the other. There is a sort of joy in doing things together, so richly enjoyable that it is almost gleeful, except that there is no malice present, nor any sort of triumph at the expense of others. Here is the pure fun of two boys playing together—miraculously maintaining its enthusiasm and innocence right through adult life.

From your point of view, you see the Arian as the sort of friend you always wanted, and are thrilled to have found. You always want to do things at once; novelty is important to you. The Arian works on a slightly different principle, that of getting started and seeing what it turns out like, rather than waiting and thinking, but you will understand straightaway that the two approaches are closely parallel. What excites you both is the idea of immediacy. The fact that you enjoy it because you need a constant flow of new things to occupy your mind and the Arian needs a constant flow of new things to use up his physical energy doesn't make any difference.

You are faster than he is, in fact, and if the task at hand does take a little time to complete, then you will find yourself thinking of other things which seem more interesting to you, while the Arian is still enjoying himself slogging away at the current project. He is a marvel to behold, to be sure, but to you he seems to be slogging because you can never see the point of physical exertion for its own sake. You have the ability to see the thing in its finished state in your mind's eye, and that satisfies you. You do like his determination, though; you are not as good as you would like to think you are at getting things finished, and there are likely to be more than a few half-finished jobs around the house, not to mention things that you have started at work and then left pending, or handed on to somebody else when something new came along. The satisfaction of seeing a project through to its actual completion is as real to you as it is to anyone else, provided that you don't have to do too much to bring it about; this is where the Arian has the most to offer you, and you are not slow to realize this.

What he has is the power to make things take physical shape; he is an achiever in a very real sense, where you are a planner and a considerer of ideas and suggestions. He is nothing like as flexible mentally as you are, though he is quick-thinking, and decisive, both qualities which you share and like in others. The relative balance of power suits you perfectly; you appreciate his quick mind—indeed you would find him intolerable if he were not quick-witted—but you like being his mental superior, because in the area that matters to you you are on top. He feels the same way, of course; he appreciates your brilliance, because he likes any sort of confident energy, but he feels that you can't match his ability to bring things about by his own efforts. *He* needs some of your good ideas, and to be presented with the many different approaches to a problem that your imagination throws up; *you* need his energy and capacity for effective action to make your dreams come true.

Because you don't get in his way or cling to him when he needs space to work in, and because he doesn't restrict your freedom to think and talk to anyone about anything, you are never in conflict at a level deep enough to require consideration and reconciliation. Besides, you are both the sort of people who would rather get on with the next thing than examine the failure of the last one. As a friendship, the relationship is perfect.

As lovers, you will be surprised by his passion, and he will be surprised by your lightness and facility for teasing and playing. You will have to build your strength up. Neither of you have feelings which are easily crushed, so you won't have to tread carefully round each other.

As business partners, there will be no stopping you, provided you employ somebody else to do the routine work, which both of you will try to avoid if you possibly can. Somebody has to do it, you know.

As a marriage, this combination has a lot going for it. You work well with each other, you don't get in each other's way, and you keep the whole thing light and flexible, so that nothing gets on top of you. Above all, you amuse each other, and laugh in each other's company a great deal. You could hardly ask for more.

*Gemini-Taurus*

There are enormous problems built into this partnership. You are essentially as different as it is possible for two signs to be, and yet there is a sort of fascination between you. Your flexibility of attitude is the only saving grace here, because the Taurean can't change his ways, but you can—provided it amuses you to do so, and your interest is held for long enough.

There are two areas of contention—stability and reality. The Taurean is dedicated to the idea of stability. For him, the less anything changes, and the longer it stays in the same state, the better; if he can have any control over it at all, he will make sure that it is kept exactly as it is, without changing. Anything which moves or is unstable disturbs him, and he will turn away from it. Anything which puts him as an individual in a state of change or instability is very upsetting, and will be resisted to the very end. You can see how different this is from your viewpoint. If your surroundings do not change, you feel trapped. If you are not actively involved in the exchange of new ideas, making new plans and examining new problems, then you feel as though you are dying. The two of you are bound to come into conflict, and sooner rather than later. Even if you have a common interest, then the mere fact that you will want to go further and faster with that interest, while the Taurean will want to enjoy it as it is, is going to lead to arguments. Arguments to you are a part of life; you enjoy the heat, the challenge of making up counter-arguments and effective phrases on the spot. Arguments to the Taurean are a deeply wounding process, an occasional necessity from which there can be no real victory. And they are so slow! You could have written the book by the time a Taurean has read the blurb on the back, or so it seems to you. Can you slow down enough to make friends with the Taurean?

To make matters worse, there is the business of reality. For the

Taurean, a thing is good if you can touch it, and if it doesn't have a price tag on it, it isn't real. For you, a thing is good if it is a new idea, and different from others you have met; it doesn't matter whether it is real or not. As a consequence of this, the Taurean will *indulge* you—in their eyes, all your brilliance and mental agility isn't concerned with anything real, and therefore can't be important. This extraordinary response, combining head-in-the-sand ignorance with matronly condescension, will enrage you. The more you rage, of course, the more you will be ignored. You can probably appreciate that it is a defensive mechanism on the part of the Taurean, but you will never forgive it, because it appears to value your essential self at nothing, and nobody likes that.

What does the relationship offer, then? It offers you a sense of security. If it seems that your schemes are about to collapse around you, or that you will be forced to prove that your ideas actually work, then you will feel pressured, and will appreciate somebody who doesn't want you to do anything, and who will care for you anyway. The Taurean will do that. On their part, you offer them a tantalizing glimpse of a world of ideas; they don't really want to be in that world, but they would like to have a look at it now and again—it seems glamorous to them. Being able to see it, then return to their own habits and well-worn ways, is something that they like.

As lovers, you are miles apart. Taureans have a slow and possessive passion which will shock you with its intensity and stifle you with its clinging embrace; your light and flippant attitude will be seen by the Taurean as evidence of lack of commitment.

As business partners, you could do quite well provided that you looked after the sales side, while they managed the finances.

As marriage partners, if you were determined, you could make something of it; the Taurean would stay loyal to you, and if you were to appreciate the benefits of having a comfortable and secure home to return to, there would be quite a lot in it for you. But how would you occupy your mind? They are still too slow for you, and you are always going to be stifled by too stable an environment. There are better pairings than this one.

## Gemini-Gemini

As with all pairings of two people from the same sign, this friendship works quite well on the surface, but not too well lower down. The reasons for this are quite straightforward—since the planet Mercury makes the pair of you enjoy differences rather than similarities, you will find yourself disagreeing for the sake of it. In addition, neither of you brings sufficient emotional weight to your relationships to ensure that the affair will last.

Geminis love talking: the two of you will talk to each other endlessly. You never seem to run out of things to say, either; each day has more than enough in it to keep you discussing it for hours. You will both take in huge amounts of information from the television or newspapers, and then proceed to tell each other all about it, even though the other partner has already seen it! Geminis frequently alter the truth of what they say; you enjoy playing with the elements of a story in your head, and sometimes rearrange them for fun. Are you sure that you can see how another Gemini has altered his story? If it matters, this could be a major problem for you, but if you don't care anyway, then you'll both be quite happy.

A problem for the pair of you together is that you are both concerned with ideas, and explaining these ideas to other people; neither of you is very gifted at putting them into action, nor do you possess the necessary organizational talent or physical stamina to do the work yourself. This means that joint schemes could remain at the theoretical stage for a long time, and you would have to make a special effort between you to try to ensure that things actually got finished and put into action; you would feel your shortcomings particularly keenly in this respect, and would see it in the other too. Disappointment could follow.

Mercury, your ruling planet, makes you quite cool emotionally; you don't really feel at home with heavy declarations of undying love, or deeply sentimental scenes of arrival and departure. You are happy enough if somebody you like is around when you are, so that you can see them and talk to them—but if they're not, then you'll soon find something else to occupy your time. In a relationship, fo course, this means that you are both unlikely either to develop close ties to a partner or to care much if they don't feel particularly devoted to you. There probably isn't going to be enough dedication and commitment to keep the partnership going. You will both find yourselves much more interested in the next new and interesting person who happens along.

As lovers, you will spend a lot of time on the opening games. The meals out, the letters and phone calls (especially these— Geminis must communicate for its own sake) and the arrangements for meetings are all part of a very enjoyable game for both of you, and you will enjoy it immensely. When that stage is past, and it is time to build trust and friendship, you both lose interest; emotional exploration isn't as rewarding to you as the preliminary courtship. You are more than likely to start the whole game over again with somebody else. Physically, you will spend more time talking than making love.

As business partners you should be very successful provided that you don't spend all day talking to each other—if you both spend your day separately talking to non-Geminis then you will do well. It goes without saying that you should be in a job which involves words and communication—a public relations or promotional agency, perhaps.

As marriage partners you will have to learn to finish the housework more than anything else. There will be no shortage of chatter and laughter in the house, but there will also be piles of unfinished housework where the pair of you stopped to talk about something else!

### Gemini-Cancer

Another difficult match: in its way, as hard as the Taurus partnership, but considerably more fluid, so you can at least move the difficulties around a bit and put them out of your way.

Gemini is quite obviously concerned with mental output; Cancer is equally obviously concerned with emotional response. This means that the Cancerian will listen carefully and take in all that you say for as long as you care to speak—but you won't get anything like so ready a reply to your questions. You are being very open, and they are being very receptive; the reverse is not true at all.

The real difference between these two signs is that between thinking and feeling. To you, it is not important what you actually feel about anything; in fact, you would rather that you didn't get drawn into that side of things at all. As long as you can examine it, turn it this way and that, have an opinion about it, assess it, know it, then you are happy; your way of thought is rather clinical, and you don't see why you have to be affected by anything, or have feelings about it, at all. If you do have feelings about things, you look at yourself from a distance, mentally, and examine yourself having these feelings; when you have noted all there is to note, you think of something else. How different the Cancerian is! They only know something because of how they feel about it; they are more concerned about their response than the facts of the matter, and they hardly ever analyse why they feel the way they do. Imagine it—it must be like finding your way by radar: you only know where you are by the responses you receive from things you contact.

Both of you are concerned with a world of the mind rather than with physical things, and that is a point of contact worth developing. You could go to see plays together, and films and concerts; one of you would analyse the form and content of the presentation, and the other would respond to it emotionally. Two very different points of view, but you would both be enjoying yourselves. As the Gemini, you could tell the Cancerian all that you noticed or thought about it afterwards. You could probably find the very differentness of the Cancerian response interesting in itself.

Both of you like your world to be a changing world. The difference is that you don't mind which way it changes as long as it continues to do so, and offers you new things along the way; the Cancerian would like things to change to suit him, and is quite prepared to put some effort into ensuring that they do. There is a static element in Cancerian thought, one which wants to put things in order and then keep them that way, and you will not appreciate that. Look back to page 15; Cancer is Cardinal, and you are Mutable. IIf you're not careful, they will try to make you conform to their idea of how things ought to be!

There is also a need to provide a secure emotional base, like a home or family life, which the Cancer always works towards establishing; this is just the sort of thing you can't understand. It seems to embody the two things you dislike most: lack of movement, and emotional involvement. Do you dislike these things because you feel attracted to them in a peculiar sort of way? Is it that Mercury, representing the eternal young man, is unwilling to surrender his youth to become a parent (the Moon, ruling Cancer), but feels that he must eventually do it? The lure of the next sign on from your own is strangely powerful, no matter which sign you are.

Sentimental Cancerians would love you as a lover, because of all the sweet words you would say to them, and the little teasing games of courtship you are so skilled in; they would want to make you settle down, though, and you wouldn't want that. You would find their powerful emotional response fascinating, but ultimately frightening; it is so strong, so uncontrolled, so un-analytical! You would prefer to keep things at a lighter level, but this isn't going to be possible.

As business partners, you would do well if they made all the decisions (don't be hurt or insulted—they are best at looking after the company, and you are quite likely to launch off into an unconsidered project which would bankrupt you) and you handled all the creative side and the publicity, not to mention the selling, at which you are very good.

As marriage partners? You would have to be patient, and they would have to learn not to be too surprised by your bright new schemes to sell the house and buy a mobile home every summer. If they look after the house, and you look after everything else, including playing with the children, then all will be well if you really think you could handle such a long-term project.

*Gemini-Leo*

This one works very well indeed. Leos are like the Sun, warm and radiant; you behave like a planet, running rings around him, but warmed and given your motion by his energy.

What you like best about the Leo is his outgoingness. He seems to have an unending generosity of spirit, which can produce enthusiasm for anything at any time, not only in himself, but in others too. You appreciate this; not only does it give you more energy, but it puts you in contact with other enthusiastic people who surround the Leo, and this provides you with opportunities for the exchange of ideas and conversation. All your needs—variety, company, conversation, mental stimulation, enthusiasm, and outgoing energy—are met and provided for by the Leo almost as a by-product of his existence. He would do all this whether you were there or not, and therein lies another important attraction from your point of view: you are not under any sort of obligation to him for providing you with the things you need, and so you need not, it seems to you, be bound to stay with him, provide for him, or have any emotional duty to him. Paradoxically, this binds you closer to him than ever, simply because you are there through choice rather than obligation.

To say that the Leo requires nothing from you is not strictly true, but he is not likely to ask for it, and you provide what he wants as a by-product of your existence anyway, which is handy. What it means in real life is that neither of you feel that you have to put any effort into the relationship, but it is very rewarding for both of you just the same. It all looks very promising: perhaps it would spoil things if you knew the mechanics of the relationship, but to appease your enquiring mind, here they are.

Quite simply, the Leo requires an audience. He needs to feel that he is the centre of his world, that everything revolves around him, and that he is accepted as its central figure. In return, he puts out a steady flow of creative energy to influence his surroundings, and to attract the attention of those around him. The two things which a Leo can't stand are being ignored, either because he is not dominating the action or because he is seen as unimportant, and being made to look foolish. You do not threaten him with either of these things. You can hardly ignore him, because he is so central to whatever's going on, and you are never involved in status games anyway, so you are not trying to undermine him. You are an ideal audience; everything he says you will respond to, and answer him back. All this feeds his need for attention in the same way as it feeds your need for communication. In addition, your mental energies and his physical ones will complement each other; he will seize one or two of your ideas and put them into practice if they appeal to him, in much the same way as the Aries would, and that process convinces the pair of you that you are good for each other.

Sometimes the Leo just doesn't think sharply enough for you: he takes a very broad view of things, trusting in his own luck and influence to make things turn out right in the end. You would prefer it if he took a detailed look at things. The way round this is for you to do the detail work, and then advise him privately, so as not to upset his public image. Once again you are both serving your best interests in acting in this way, and the result should benefit both of you. The Leo also likes to stay with a situation he enjoys, whereas you like to move on to new things: the answer once again is for you to keep moving, but to refer back to him the things you are involved with for his support. In this relationship you can make the differences into advantages.

As lovers, you should have a great time, and an extravagant one. You will acquire a taste for *expensive* amusements.

As business partners you would have to keep an eye on the money—both of you think it is just for spending.

As a marriage, the only problem is that they are going to have their way all the time, and that's the only way they will accept. Can *you* accept it?

*Gemini-Virgo*
This is one of two relationships in the zodiac where two signs are of the same quality (mutable) but different polarity (one outgoing, the other collecting), and yet they are governed by the same planet. Here it is Mercury; Jupiter is the planet in the other

combination, which is Sagittarius-Pisces. So, a peculiar sort of relationship. In fact, you represent the different sides of Mercury at work; you will each find your astrological alter ego fascinating, and recognize much of yourself in him.

Because you are three signs separated from each other, you are each other's basis and reputation. Let me explain. From a Gemini point of view, the careful analysis of all material and all structures to see what they contain is the basis of all investigative thought: it is also the essence of Virgo, that process through which a Virgo interprets the world. From a Virgoan point of view, the ability to understand and retain new ideas instantaneously, to be able to make up any sort of argument or phrase in no time by drawing on a powerful and imaginative memory, is the height of ambition. To be recognized for that ability is real status in a Virgo's eyes: that ability is also the essence of Gemini, the sort of thing a Gemini does all the time, because he cannot imagine doing things any other way.

You both admire the other's way of working, the more so since you work in different universes. The Virgo works in a physical world; the feel of things matters to him. He is concerned with quality: whether a thing is good or not matters to him, whereas your prime concern is the concept behind it. You work in a mental world, where ideas and words are the main currency. Although Virgos are good with words, they treat them as though they were precious, and they feel that such things are not to be wasted. This makes them careful writers and speakers, and on the way they lose not only speed in communication but also that brilliance which comes from the spur-of-the-moment thought expressed in the same way.

Their careful attitude will infuriate you at times; you turn a thing this way and that in your mind, seeing if it looks as interesting another way up, while they turn a thing physically this way and that, seeing if it can be made any better, tidied up a bit, polished, improved. You may see this as a critical attitude, and it is; but remember that it is simply a physical expression of your mental curiosity. Mercury is at work behind both of you, looking for things which are different, things that can be changed.

If you let them get a word in edgeways, and you can manage not to lose your temper when they tidy everything away after you, then you can build a productive friendship between you. The rest of the world won't think so, though; two Mercury people let loose together will have great fun criticizing everything in sight, and the sharpness of your tongues will lose you a lot of friends. You will be enjoying yourselves immensely.

As lovers, you will need to work quite hard at growing any sort of emotional bond between you. Mercury is not a very emotional planet, and you are both a little cool; besides, you both enjoy pulling things apart, and any sign of un-analytical sentimentality would soon be demolished by the other with much sharp humour. You like each other, but you don't love each other much; perhaps you don't need to as much as the other signs. Virgos are perfectionists, and they can always think of something to stop you from sweeping them off their feet.

As business partners, you need to be a little more sincere and generous if you are not to lose trade; make sure the Virgo doesn't get too obsessive about things, and spend uneconomic amounts of time on small details.

There are no real objections to a marriage, but other people would find your home a little clinical, and perhaps the softer, more emotional moments of family life would be missing, too. It would suit the pair of you, though, and you would be happy enough to work together for a joint future, so why not?

### Gemini-Libra

This is a union within your own element; you feel much more at home here. The currency of the transactions between you is always going to be in ideas and words, and it is always going to be essentially light in tone; you will feel relaxed with a Libran. The heavy emotional loads that the earth and water signs can put on you are simply not present in this relationship; both of you are eager to please the other, and willing to contribute to the relationship without wanting first to get something out of it.

In many ways, the Libran is everything you ever wanted to be. He seems to embody all the best bits of you, developed into quite powerful talents; it is difficult for you not to admire him, and even harder for you to find fault at first. You like talking to people, but he seems to be friendliness personified. He seems to get the response that you always wish you would get—that is, everybody seems to like talking to him, and he seems to have the ability to make friends with everybody. He makes friends with you, too; he is a delight to talk to, and very amenable to your every suggestion. When you are with him, the world is a friendlier place, and everything seems to turn out better.

From his point of view, you are everything he needs to inspire him to better things. There are times when he can't seem to form a definite opinion about something; five minutes' consultation with you will soon have the matter analysed, stripped down to its component parts, and as like as not have fun made of its obvious faults. How decisive you are! How you seem to know what you want, and exactly what you are doing! All this is the sort of behaviour which the Libran finds exciting, and which makes him strive to keep up with you. Whenever he dithers, you have the ability to take him back to the beginnings of things, and to show him where it started; it is a most useful approach, and one which he simply cannot do for himself. The way he sees it, in fact, is as follows: if he knew more about everything, and could see what was going on, then he could make things even nicer. You can give him this insight, or, even better, show him how it's done, so that he can do it for himself. In practice, though, he gets far more out of having you around to help than he would from doing it himself, so he never quite manages to train himself this way.

It will take some time to note that there are two areas of possible disagreement between you. The first is that where you are concerned with finding out what's new and different, he is concerned with finding out what's easiest and nicest. 'Nice' is a very Libran word in all its senses: the ideas of being neat, pretty, rather bland, generally pleasant, and inoffensive are all Libran. You will see after a while that the Libran has none of your cutting edge: he would rather not criticize. You can easily assimilate this in a relationship, of course, but he is not quite the soulmate you had imagined. You will also notice after some considerable while that he is much less fond of change and novelty than you are. Though he is not greatly disturbed when it occurs, he has no need to actively seek changes, as you do. The second major area of disagreement is this: though you enjoy company, you are quite happy on your own if you have enough to occupy you— but the Libran *must* have company if he is to function properly. You could find this wearisome.

As lovers, you should have an enjoyable time. Librans are happy enough just to be liked, let alone loved; their need is for the daily reminders of fondness rather than the heavy declarations of passionate devotion that the fixed signs go for. Keep the cards and little presents coming, and your Libran will be enchanted. The word to remember is romance; Librans don't like anything too earthy or fiery—they are an Air sign, like you.

As business partners you will do well as long as your business is not concerned with anything which takes too long to produce or make: neither of you has the stamina for that. You will have to be careful that you don't spend too much time chatting to your clients or employees rather than doing hard business, and the Libran will need some help with major decision-making; apart from that, all looks well.

As marriage partners, there should be few problems. You will constantly be trying to make them more active, and they will be trying to make you less frantic, but there are no irreconcilable differences, at least not in your view.

### Gemini-Scorpio

This is an odd pairing. You are as different astrologically as it is possible to be—different element, quality, ruling planet—but you have a mental approach which is complementary. Both of you like finding things out. You are a surface reader; you take in enormous amounts of information from all sources, and use it to understand the nature of whatever it is that holds your interest. What you don't do is look for information, because it is usually there when you want it, and you don't have the sort of dedication required to do research. The Scorpio, on the other hand, does just that. He is the sort who will dig deeper and deeper until he has uncovered all there is to know about whatever it is that holds his attention. He can't use things that he reads or hears in the same way that you can, nor can he think as fast; he needs to experience things for himself, find out for himself, check things out for himself to see if all the pieces of the puzzle fit. He is never dissuaded from his goal, and always gets there in the end. What you have in common is curiosity, and an interest in seeing what there is about things that makes them how they are; you approach it from very different ends. A relationship between you will work in a similar way: you will have similar interests, but for different reasons, and will approach them in very different ways.

From your point of view, you can use the Scorpio's determination and thoroughness as a way of getting things done, where previously you would let them slide. It's quite reassuring to have somebody there to lend you firmness and muscle when you need it. In addition, you know only too well that you have a tendency to let things go half-finished, or move on to something else when you haven't thoroughly understood the first thing. Although you are a quick learner, this surface-skimming technique has its drawbacks, and you have become adept at getting round them. In a Scorpio relationship, you have the chance to explore an equally well-informed way of working, but one which offers you thoroughness and stamina above all else. It sounds attractive to you: you can imagine adding Scorpionic depth to the breadth of your knowledge, and the result seems irresistible.

From the Scorpio's point of view, you are the edge he sometimes feels he needs. For a knife to cut, you need more than pressure on the blade; you need the blade to have an edge, too. A Scorpio likes to know what's going on, but knows also that he has a rather heavy and over-serious approach to things. He needs somebody to provide him with the information he needs to stay in control (control is what he is ultimately aiming for, remember), and to show him different avenues of approach. He also needs somebody with a sense of humour to lighten things a little (your slightly waspish idea of humour appeals greatly to the hint of cruelty in the Scorpio), and to help him communicate, for he knows he can be a little reticent and unexpressive, left to himself. You are the provider of, and vehicle for, all these things.

Difficulties in the relationship will arise because he will attempt, after a while, to control you, and your mutable nature will enable you to sidestep him with ease. He is only doing it so that he can keep constant, and therefore controlled, his relationship to you, but you see this as unnecessary and undesirable. He will tire himself trying to pin you down, and you can make it very hard for him if you try, especially if he has annoyed you. The relationship may well break at this point. In addition, he will insist on everything being true and verifiable; your occasional tall tales will be examined, and you will be called to account for your deliberately misleading behaviour. You don't like this sort of thing, and it may be enough to drive you away to somewhere where life is taken less seriously.

As lovers, you are not terribly well matched; you can't tease a Scorpio very easily, and they are both passionate and possessive, while you are not. You may find that your interest wanes because there is nothing to amuse you.

As business partners, you are better suited than you might think. Scorpios are naturally successful in business, and that might keep you interested. You'll have to be the flexible one because he just can't be. A marriage will work in the same way— quite successful as long as you adapt to them, and they allow some freedom of movement.

### Gemini-Sagittarius
Like all of the pairings between two signs on opposite signs of the zodiac from each other, you represent different ends of the same stick. The name of the stick in this case is knowledge. You are both very much concerned with mental activity. The difference is that you are concerned with short-term knowledge, the here and now, what's in today's newspaper; the Sagittarian is concerned with deep knowledge, the eternal, and what's in the serious literature on the subject.

From your point of view Sagittarians are an exciting but exasperating mixture of enviable talents and irritating viewpoints.

They have the deep knowledge that comes from study, whereas you have only the immediate knowledge that comes from having seen it this morning in the paper. Somehow, no matter how hard you try, you can't seem to get your knowledge to spread out and take shape as a thing in itself that can be applied to life as a problem-solving technique. The Sagittarian can, and does. This is one of the differences between you. You are both mutable, but he is Fire and you are Air. He can apply his knowledge through his will to make things happen the way he wants them to, and you can't, because Air is to do with ideas, not reality. The Fire signs are all good at making things happen, and you find this quality fascinating and exciting in all of them. The Sagittarian is in fact the best of them all for doing this, because like you he changes this approach according to the circumstances he finds himself in; he takes other people's energy and changes it into something all his own. This is a mutable sign in action, and you have this quality in common; what exasperates you is that he can turn it into reality, and you can't. You communicate things, but you don't make them happen.

All this would be well if, you think, he used his talents properly, but he doesn't: not according to you, anyway. Sagittarians are so straight, so honest, so—well, naive, that you simply can't believe it. You can think of a million and one things that you could do if you had their vision and knowledge to add to your own opportunist talents, but the Sagittarian won't do them because some of them are a little less than legal, or are unfair to somebody else, or might inconvenience a third party. Sagittarians are so honest, it's embarrassing; you find yourself being careful in their company, because the slightest deviation from the truth on your part makes you look like a con-man. They never lie—not ever. Not even white lies. There is honesty, and there is tact; the difference lies in the choice of words used, as well you know. Sagittarians only have honesty. At the end of the day, you love Sagittarians for their wisdom, their universal knowledge, their clear insight into any situation, and their eternal optimism: but you just wish they could be a little less *noble* about things, and a little more useful in the situations of real life.

What do they see in you, you wonder? Detail, mainly. They know very well that they always see the big picture, and miss out the details. They know that they have 'what-is' knowledge, but they don't always have 'how-to' knowledge like you do. They also find your ability with words, and your conjuror's skill in story-telling and knavery, very exciting. Partly this is because they are so honest and gullible, and yet they know that they never really lose, and partly because they wish that they had your lightness of touch: Jupiter is a big planet for all his expansiveness, and they don't have your deftness.

In one sentence, you know something because you've just heard it, and they know something because they believe in it; one comes from outside, and one from inside. That's the essence of the relationship.

As lovers, you can have a lot of fun. They will teach you things, and they will enjoy your teasing them. They are a lot more physically demanding than you would think; it's because of the horse at the bottom of the sign. All animal-sign people are animals to some extent.

As business partners, you will do very well indeed when things are expanding; you both welcome challenges. The low periods would need careful management, though; neither of you is very good at maintaining what you have and staying static.

As marriage partners, you should get on very well. You will need a very big house with room for all the books, magazines, papers, TVs, and other information sources that you both love so much.

### Gemini-Capricorn

A partnership where you can use your talent for buying and selling. Capricorns think in terms of money, and you think in terms of deals; there is considerable scope here. In addition, they have a very slow, but rather sardonic sense of humour, which you find great fun. In terms of a business partnership, you could be just what the other one needs—but a personal relationship would need a lot of work.

The Capricorn is the original businessman: ambitious if

unimaginative, very hardworking, a measurable success (measurable by his bank account, that is), and a little on the serious side when it comes to having a good time with other people. Everything for him has to have weight before he can appreciate it. Something which makes an impression on its surroundings is acting in a Capricornian way, and he will try always to work this way himself. The ripple of interest and respect that runs through a factory when the Managing Director decides to pay a little visit; the way little cars give way to limousines at traffic junctions, and the effortless way limousines overtake slower traffic; the satisfying sound of expensive shoes on a wooden floor compared to the apologetic squeak of synthetic soles—all these things are Capricornian. They speak of power, authority, respect, success—and of having weight, having influence. It is difficult for you to understand this.

To you, everything is light, and constantly renewed in your imagination. Capricorn, like the other Earth signs, prefers the solidity of matter. He needs to feel that he is doing the right thing, and that he is recognized for the things that he has done. In addition, he wants to control the way things are done, and do that by his own effort. Your enthusiasm for trivia and novelty strikes him as a waste of productive time, and your constant chatter seems to have no purpose to him. Why do you need to talk, he would say, when you know what you have to do, so could be getting on with it? The idea of modifying his opinions, of exchanging ideas for their own sake, is one which he will never understand.

It so happens that you are a born salesman. All Geminis are. This is because you need the ability to tell stories to the customer in the way he wants to hear them, keep thinking of your next move, and never stop thinking in terms of money, discounts, and percentages—all at the same time. This is quite some mental exercise, and it amuses you greatly. The fact that none of it really matters to you probably has a lot to do with your success. This obvious talent will be noticed by a Capricorn, who is a litle short on the skills necessary to deal with people successfully. He will suggest that you work together, with him providing the organizational weight you lack, and you providing the communications facilities he lacks. You will see that the arrangement has much to recommend it. You will be keen to enter any kind of relationship which offers you the kind of success you seem unable to pin down on your own, and especially one which keeps your contribution flexible.

Transfer this relationship into your private life, and the problems begin at once. You enjoy varied company, but the Capricorn prefers the company of a selected group of friends. You enjoy doing several things at once (and finishing none of them), but the Capricorn can only concentrate on one thing at a time, and has to make sure that it is done properly and well. That sort of attitude seems tedious to you, and if there are a few cross words about your preference for doing things in quick bursts while the interest holds you, then you will misbehave (as the Capricorn sees it) even more. They seem to have no sense of adventure; they are always wondering if a suggested activity is worth the time or money, whether it might not be a better idea to do something else. To you, things don't need consideration: you either feel like doing them, or you don't.

If you want to become lovers, you should have no problems; Capricorns find light-hearted speech so difficult that they are entranced by your chatter. It never occurs to them that you talk to everyone this way, and that you can't really talk any other way.

As a marriage this pairing could be very productive and successful, in the same way as a business partnership would; it really depends on how much you recognize and use each other's strengths. It is unlikely to be a particularly loving or devoted match, but everybody wants that, and neither of you really wants emotional response at that level anyway.

### Gemini-Aquarius

Another pairing where the planets involved are Mercury and Saturn (Saturn looks after Capricorn as well as Aquarius, remember), but one with a very different flavour to it. This one is one of the easiest friendships for you to form, and one of the longest lasting. It isn't particularly warm or emotional as friendships go, but you both like each other a great deal, and neither of you is the sort to restrict the movements of the other. Neither of you is jealous or possessive, and both of you understand that the other, like yourself, needs the contact of a lot of other people besides just you if he is to be happy and healthy. Neither of you makes emotional demands on the other: both of you prefer to contribute to a situation rather than take from it; both of you thrive on change and novelty. It seems strange to outsiders that a friendship can be so firm when you are so cool and dispassionate towards each other, but as far as you two are concerned that's their problem. You just plain like each other, and you like things the way they are—relaxed, flexible, un-committed. You will have enormous numbers of friends whose company gives you both immense pleasure, and you may be so satisfied with the intellectual stimulation you get from each other and your friends that you may not feel the need to form a physical relationship at all.

What is the essence of this extraordinary friendship, then? It is simply this: you are both expressive of Air element energy (outgoing mental; page 13), but you each greatly admire the way the other uses this energy, and would like to copy it yourself. You are, if you like, fans of each other's technique.

To you, the Gemini, Aquarius is just what you've always thought you ought to be like. They seem to be able to bring out the best in people. They seem always to be in a crowd of the most interesting and lively company anybody could wish for. More importantly, they seem to be able to generate good ideas from inside themselves, without having to get the ideas from some-where else first, as you do. They seem to be able to work with ideas too, to make other people believe in them. You are always ready to communicate this kind of thing, but somehow it all gets carried away in the general tide of conversation, and you can't make it stick the way an Aquarian can. They seem to be different from everyone else somehow, and their difference seems to go all the way through them from head to toe. The idea of actually embodying differentness fascinates you, and you would love to share it if you could. You might not like it when you got there, of course, but from your viewpoint at the moment it seems the most tantalizing thing in the world. Essentially, you want to make things solid, to make reality out of your ideas, but not to lose your mental agility or love of variety in the process. To you, only the Aquarian seems to have managed it.

To him, you seem a brighter version of himself. He recognizes that he thinks differently from others, and that he is at his best within a group, but there is a certain seriousness he has about what he says which never goes away. It does not show itself as dullness, but rather as earnestness, as a genuine belief in his words. He would love to be able to take things less seriously, to be able to use words for their own sake and to laugh at what he says as he hears himself. That brilliant, sharp mind is what he wants, and the Gemini has it. He does not know that the brilliance comes from the reflection of incoming images from the moving surface of a shallow mentality, and that it must necessarily be so; deep thought dulls the sparkle. The Gemini's rapid wit seems to be the most entertaining thing ever created to the Aquarian, and he loves to be in the Gemini's company because of it.

As lovers? Why spoil a beautiful friendship? You probably don't need to. As a marriage, it is just an extended friendship, and should be fine; it will certainly be different, and varied too. As a business venture, you are superb together as long as you don't get bogged down in actually producing anything; stay on the consultative side, where people meet and talk to each other.

### Gemini-Pisces

This one really isn't easy. A Piscean is probably more of an opposite to you than a Sagittarian, who actually does occupy the opposite sector of the zodiac to yours. It might seem that there would be some points of contact: both of you work more with mental images than reality, both of you like change and variety, both of you are sensitive to what is going on around you. The similarities stop there, though, because you analyse and think about everything that comes your way, where the Piscean deliberately tries not to think about anything, but to let whatever it is affect them in its own way instead. At the end of the day, you are essentially unmoved by what you have seen and considered; the Piscean is overwhelmed.

The Piscean has no analytical mind at all. Turning a thing this way and that to see how it works, exercising any sort of curiosity, putting an idea into words: all of these things, so much second nature to the Gemini, are strange to the Piscean. It's not that they aren't receptive to new ideas; far from it. It's just that they prefer to be influenced by the ideas themselves. They take on the qualities of whatever it is that they're interested in, like chameleons. In the company of somebody who likes football, they like football; at the cinema they completely identify with the leading character. If they live in France, they are more French than the French; in England, they are very traditional. Small wonder that a lot of them are in the movie business—they get to be a star every day! There is never any sense of standing back from it all and assessing what there is in a given situation for a Pisces; he is completely within the situation at once, part of it rather than an onlooker.

Whilst you admire this fantastic flexibility of mental stance, you have great difficulty in understanding how they could live this way. They have no sense of differentiation—they don't sort things into categories the way you do. Even words are sometimes too precise for the Piscean mind, and they prefer to let words, sights, and sounds coalesce if possible. They prefer poetry to prose, because it has so many meanings. You prefer playing with words in the form of speech, because that way you can communicate what you think. A Piscean doesn't need to communicate, because all his responses are internal ones, and he has no desire to make a precise and individual statement about anything. You will now understand why you have a facility with numbers and figures, and why they just don't; numbers don't have much emotional content, and therefore the Piscean can't enjoy experiencing them.

You would have difficulty living in a world where everything was part of everything else, and was seen as part of an unseparated whole: you prefer to think of things as separated items arranged in sequences of space or time. Not so the Piscean.

Given these two ways of seeing things, could you ever begin to see things their way without losing your identity? You would have to forego all your love of words and wit, as well as your slightly roguish ability with money and salesmanship. You would have to accept that any reply you got to your questions would be entirely conditioned by the prevailing mood of the conversation, and all your powers of inquiry and analysis would be rendered useless when attempting to deal with such a fluid view as the Piscean's. In return you would get a glimpse of a totally internal world where everything experienced was somehow assimilated into the whole and never discarded. Psychedelia was a Piscean expression of life with the inside patterns on the outside: not really your way of thinking, is it?

The grand irony about this partnership is that you both work by being receptive to people around you, and you like that in each other. You wish he would be less emotional about things, and he wishes you would get involved for once instead of being so detached. You like each other, but never understand each other.

As business partners, you would make a poor team. As marriage partners the same applies, really: you, Gemini, would be very cruel and sharp when angered, and the sensitive Piscean would be much more deeply wounded than you had ever intended. As lovers? Not really.

Pisces needs a lot of emotional response, and it's not something you're terribly good at, nor is it important to you. You would both enjoy writing letters to each other in the early stages, but as things grew deeper you would realize that they wanted more than you could give.

# Cancer

*Cancer-Aries*
On the surface this relationship would appear to have little to recommend it: the blazing energy of Aries and the careful nature

of Cancer do not have a lot in common. In actual practice, this pairing is much more successful than it looks at first sight, and often becomes a very strong bond indeed.

In some ways, it is precisely because you are so different that this union works so well. Aries is the embodiment of Mars, the masculine sexual principle, and Cancer is the embodiment of the Moon, the feminine principle. There is thus a natural union here: the masculinity of the one is the perfect partner for the femininity of the other. It does not matter if the Arian is female and the Cancerian male, nor indeed if they are both of the same sex: the energy flow is just the same.

The Arian is very direct, very energetic, and very simple in his approach to problems. In order to achieve his purposes, he throws himself at his tasks with all his energy, and usually succeeds just by the force of his attack. He is not very sophisticated in his analysis of the situation, though, and if he is thwarted for any reason he feels confused, unable to see why things should be this way. This is a rather childlike approach, and as with children it is beneficial if someone is on hand to dry the tears. Cancerians fill this role admirably: there is something about the stunned helplessness of an Arian who has just failed to do something which appeals to the caring instinct in the Cancerian soul.

The Arian can play the role of the child to the Cancerian mother, and the arrangement is emotionally satisfying to both sides. Arians understand things best if they are direct and uncomplicated; the care and sympathy generated by a Cancerian are both of these things; what's more, they are not the sort of thing an Arian can produce on his own, and he is grateful to have his emotional needs looked after by someone who is much better at it than he is.

Both of the signs are cardinal: therefore both people are the sort who prefer to make the decisions about what form their life takes, unlike the fixed-sign people who prefer to fit into a ready-made role. One of the differences between you, though, is that the Arian really does make the decisions about the form of his life, whereas the Cancerian is often inhibited from doing so. The very effectiveness of the Arian approach thrills the Cancerian; in partnership with Aries, he gets the power he needs, and his ambitions start to become realities. It's really simple physics: water (Cancer) is a slow if steady force, but if you heat the water with fire (Aries) you get steam—and you can drive locomotives with that!

As a friendship, this is one of the most open you could wish for. Neither of you is in the slightest underhand or dishonest— Cancer because your emotions won't let you be, and Aries because he simply can't be—it wouldn't occur to him! Although you may sometimes be upset by the force of his temper when you disagree, you are grateful for his honesty, and you also know that his rage doesn't last long. You are more likely to be hurt when he asserts his independence, and rushes off in pursuit of some new adventure, leaving you behind. You have to understand that this is not deliberate cruelty, just more youthful boisterousness, and you must learn to live with that as mothers learn to live with sons who behave in a similar way.

As lovers, you have a great deal to offer one another on a very high level; it's the meeting of the masculine and feminine principles again. You will have to accept his occasional lack of tenderness, and realize, too, that you sometimes want to be with him more than he wants to be with you. Fire sign people are like that: you can't hold them down. It will break your heart before it breaks his, so accept it.

As marriage or business partners you could do very well indeed. Remember that you may share the same goals, but your methods and priorities in working will be wildly different, so allow for this. Aries will provide the drive, Cancer the care and support; but to Cancer, Aries will appear reckless, while to Aries Cancer seems a timid worrier. You appreciate each other's efforts, though: that's the key to it.

## Cancer-Taurus

One of the easiest friendships in the whole zodiac, for the Moon has a particular affinity with the sign of the Bull. The whole relationship has something of an organic quality to it, though:

intuition and the hidden pull of the tides are present in this pairing, giving almost nothing which an outsider can put his finger on, especially if he is looking for an outgoing and enterprising partnership which is visibly lively. No, this one works below the surface: this one is where you instinctively feel right with the other without knowing why, and without having to ask. You protect and nourish each other, and you never expose each other to anything which might worry or disconcert you. You feel safe in each other's presence. You don't stimulate or challenge each other: instead, you comfort and reassure each other, defending each other against anyone and everyone who is harsher and less sensitive.

What is the secret of this closeness? It is to do with something called exaltation, one of astrology's little nooks and crannies. What happens is that each planet has a sign, not usually the one it rules, where its energies are particularly well received. In the case of Cancer and the Moon, this sign is Taurus. Since the Moon is particularly happy in Taurus, then it follows that a lunar person, a Cancerian, will be particularly happy in the presence of a Taurean.

The key is in the feminine and nurturing side of both signs. The Moon is very receptive; it takes the energy of the other planets, and especially the Sun, and looks after it, modifying it and softening it as it goes. This 'looking after' process is connected with natural cycles of growth, and with natural processes of nourishment. All of this is very similar to the Taurean's emphasis on feeding and growth. Both signs are receptive and supportive: both of them give rise to a sensitive and maternal attitude in people. True, Taurus is more concerned with purely material things, and Cancer is far more able to make major changes in life, but there is much in common in their outlook. Both appreciate security, and are essentially shy in their approach to new people. As a consequence, the relationship will be very close and emotionally satisfying for both of you, but it will be very much a closed affair as far as outsiders are concerned; you see no need to share yourselves with anybody else, because you feel quite happy in each other's company.

The lunar emphasis of this relationship will mean that you don't develop anything new out of it. This isn't the kind of friendship which produces new ideas, provides mutual encouragement for pioneering achievement, or strikes sparks from the meeting of two minds which can be used to kindle bigger fires. Not at all. This is the one which works as a closed-circuit retreat for both of you. It can lead to a sort of smugness, or to fits of giggles at private jokes nobody else understands, or to a tight, defensive cliquiness, depending on other factors in the horoscopes of the two individuals.

As friends, you comfort each other and support each other: as lovers, you attempt to possess each other. The Taurean thinks that the Cancerian is his personal property, and the Cancerian feels that he has an absolute right to the Taurean's time and affections. Whilst this kind of devotion is useful in cementing a relationship, it is possible to have too much of a good thing, and there is too much of it here. Eventually you will stifle the very real joy of the early days of the affair with feelings of obligation and suspicion; neither of you is willing to let go, of course. Perhaps this friendship is best not taken to so intense a level.

As business partners, you will be industrious, but cautious; a third person is needed to give impetus and contribute fresh ideas.

As a marriage, this will definitely have the emphasis on a secure home. You will be very considerate of each other's needs, and as a safe base from which to raise a family it could hardly be bettered. It will be very static, though; you had better not have any secret desires to move around or make far-reaching changes—this isn't the sort of marriage to accommodate them.

### Cancer–Gemini

This is the most difficult friendship the Cancerian ever makes. The sign before your own is always difficult to handle; in one sense you always feel that you have grown past that sort of behaviour, but in another sense you are afraid that you find it rather appealing. A person from that sign seems to know all your weak points in advance, but despite that terrrible possibility you find them irresistible in an odd sort of way.

The essential problem is that you don't think you can actually trust a Gemini. They are never short of things to say—indeed, they think aloud at times—but what they say isn't necessarily what they believe. Belief is an emotional addition to a logical conclusion, and as such is not part of the Gemini mind. They are also likely to change their minds very quickly, as soon as another way of looking at something occurs to them, and the apparent conflict between their opinion now and their opinion yesterday does not bother them one bit.

On the other hand, you react quite strongly to what they say, and will react just as strongly to the amended version too. Constantly changing your reactions and beliefs is both wearying and worrying for you, and after a while you begin to wonder whether you can believe any of it at all. Your attempts to provide the right replies when the conversation changes will irritate both of you; Gemini will find your insistence on sticking to one thing at a time very tedious, while you find his constantly changing point of view rather devious. Neither of you are right.

You are, of course facing the world in different directions. Gemini has a very low emotional level, but a very high intellectual level, and you are just the opposite. It would be easier if you were both cardinal, or both Water, but in fact everthing about you is different. Perhaps the most difficult thing of all for you to understand is how the Gemini never takes anything at all seriously, and how the idea of putting others first never enters his head. In his turn, the most difficult thing for him to understand about you is that you feel rather than think, and place sentiment above almost all other values.

If your acquaintance is to develop into friendship, you will be need to be ready for his changes of mood and opinion. You will also need to be ready for his complete inability to understand your values—but that doesn't mean that he isn't interested in your point of view; be ready to tell him about all you feel (not easy for a Cancerian, I know) and you will maintain his interest in you. In return, you will be vastly entertained, and swept along with him as he lives his life as fast as he can; perhaps you will enjoy scandalizing yourself as you watch him get away with what you know you couldn't.

You will need the same readiness to accept his changeable nature if you are to become lovers. He will take his freedom when it suits him—not to hurt you, but because it never occurs to him that you would expect any other sort of behaviour. He is completely blind to the devotion with which you cling to him, and can have no inkling of how deeply you are wounded when he decides to try something (or somebody) else for a while. Yet you do know, don't you, deep down, that his freedom from ties, his autonomy, is just what you find so attractive?

As business partners you would do better looking after different sides of the company, and as marriage partners a similar division of labour would be the best policy. You will have to adopt his practice of logical appraisal rather than pure gut reaction to solve major problems together, but he must learn to express the emotion he secretly fears if you are to live together.

*Cancer–Cancer*
A cautious and considerate combination. You might think that having two lunar people together would make for a close and understanding realtionship, but it isn't anything like as comfortable as the Cancer–Taurus union.

Both of you go in phases, like the Moon. Sometimes you want one thing, sometimes you feel that you've seen enough of it and would like a change. You are often tired by the effort of dealing with people who are not particularly comfortable to be with, and you would like a rest, some time to yourself, some time to be private. Sometimes you want somebody to warm you and share their successes, whilst shielding you from any unpleasantness. What happens if your partner is just as changeable, but the two of you are out of phase?

The chances of you being in exactly the same phase are small, although two women living or working together will align their physical lunar cycles, as is well known; the problem doesn't get any better even if you are aligned, though. If both of you need somebody to restore your energies, you are rather stuck.

In forming this relationship, as with all relationships between two people of the same sign, you must remember that you are both motivated by the same energies, and will be trying to achieve the same result. If that result comes from a one-way transaction, so that you gain something at their expense, then obviously one of you is going to be disappointed: in fact you both are, if you think about it. On the other hand, the positive talents that you bring to the relationship are doubled since you are both contributing, but that may not necessarily redress the balance. After all, if you make cake with twice as much flour and only half as many eggs, you still get cake, but it doesn't taste quite the way you expected it to.

Both of you like to feel that you are quite sure how the other person is likely to behave. If the other person hides his feelings a little, or is uncommunicative and shy, as Cancerians often are, then you may have a little difficulty anticipating their moves. This is even more pronounced, of course, if they have changed their mood since the last time you met.

Both of you need, ideally, somebody to act as a Sun to your Moon, somebody who is going to be able to light up the partnership with his own cheerful personality and enthusiasm. If you have to play this role for each other, you are going to feel that it is something of a responsibility, and in playing that role to the best of your ability (as you will—you never give less than your best when somebody depends on you) you will feel that you are giving out more than you are getting back, which will worry you a little. Sometimes you will be unable to muster the energy and enthusiasm required to lift the pair of you because you are uncertain of what to do for the best: it is at times like this when the partnership starts to sink. The further it sinks, the more concerned you get, and the more you worry, but as I hope you can see, that's precisely the wrong sort of energy needed on these occasions.

On the positive side, you do sympathize with each other's misfortunes and cares, and can provide real support for each other in the way that only Cancerians know that they need—and that is a very big plus mark for this particular pairing. If you have mutual interests and shared goals, you can use them as an anchor point to haul yourselves out of the bad patches with, and you can make much progress together.

As lovers, you will be supremely sensitive to each other's needs, knowing as few other signs do that love exists on many levels at once, and the ones that matter most to the Cancerian are the invisible ones. You will also think that you cannot possibly have so close a relationship again. Cancerians feel this way about anybody they trust, and will hang on to people they love far longer than they should. If it really isn't working, for heaven's sake let go.

As business partners, or as marriage partners, you will never lack care and concern, though you may well lack flexibility and a sense of enterprise. Try to see the grand scheme rather than the immediate problem.

### Cancer–Leo

This partnership is almost as difficult as the Gemini one, though the difficulty is of a different kind. Here you have all the solar energy that you could want; Leo is the embodiment of solar power. You always say that you want somebody who can provide you with warmth; here he is. Why is it so difficult to form the relationship you want?

It is something to do with the fact that this is one of those pairings where both the element and the quality are different: you even represent different universes (Water and Fire: imaginary and tangible). It certainly seems as though you are a universe apart at times.

The Leo is an energy source all to himself, generating energy and radiating it outwards. He likes to feel that he is at the centre of things, and he likes things to go his way. Since he is usually the prime mover in any situation, they usually do. Thus by putting himself at the centre of a small group of people, and becoming their natural focus and source of inspiration, he achieves what he wants, and feels satisfied.

To you, this seems remarkably pompous. You feel that he does what he does not because he cares for the people who surround him, but to reassure his own vanity. You are right, of course, but are you sure that you don't care for those around you because you welcome their appreciation of your efforts, or because it enables you to keep up with what's going on? It is very difficult to assign blame in the business of planetary energies: in the end they work to everyone's benefit.

There is a mutual antipathy between you which needs to be overcome, and it springs from the fact that the two signs follow each other in the zodiacal sequence. Leo would rather enjoy the company of his friends and supporters than worry about his motives for doing so, and he sees your careful, inward-looking attitude as a criticism of his happy state. He is trying to keep things as they are, with everybody smiling: he is, after all, a fixed sign. He knows that he benefits from everyone's admiration, but they benefit from his warmth and generosity, so why not? In addition, because he believes that things can be made to happen by applying energy to them, he does so. If he stopped believing this, stopped being generous, and started to worry about whether anybody really liked him, he would be slipping back down the zodiacal scale towards Cancerianism, which he tries always to avoid.

On your part, you see him as prodigally wasteful of his energies. He also seems to have no sensitivity to the emotional climate of the moment. Nor should he, if you think about it, because he is not reacting to the thoughts of others, he is radiating energy and enthusiasm outwards from himself. Still, you see him in your terms; he seems brash and insensitive to you. He gives out personal information, which you keep very close to you indeed; how could he be so stupid? Simple: to him it isn't stupid. He is simply putting more of himself on display. You may not admit it to yourself, but you find this secretly wonderful. If only you could have the sort of confidence, that invulnerability to the opinions of others, the unshakable belief in your own capability, and not the least the sheer generosity of the Leo. All this is something you can only aim for, but never achieve: it is the exclusive preserve of the next sign from your own, and you must stay where you are in the circle of the signs.

The way to form a friendship with a Leo is to surrender to their generosity. If he wants to buy you expensive presents, accept them. There is no emotional blackmail going on—they are genuinely generous people. All you have to do is recognize them as the central figure in your life, which is the difficult bit for you. You will have to let them have their own way, and you won't like that either. Relax— there is no malice here; you are quite safe.

Whatever your relationship with a Leo, be it as lovers, business partners, or whatever, keep your worries to yourself. To express them suggests that you doubt his abilities, and annoys him. Besides, you have no need to worry—everything goes right for a Leo.

## Cancer–Virgo

This is a lovely union. You are complementary to each other; you each fill in the bits that the other hasn't got. Cancer is very emotional in its outlook, and spends most of its time dealing with the world of feelings, to which it applies care and understanding. Virgo is much more concerned with the physical world, and spends most of its time dealing with methods and materials, which it does with care and understanding. You can see at once that there is great similarity of approach.

Virgoans share your belief that little things matter. When a Virgo comes into contact with something new he spends a lot of time with it, looking at it, thinking about it, getting to know it. He spends a lot of time actually holding it, feeling it, running his hands over it—a Virgo needs to get to know the shape of things. Nor is he likely to do this just once: repeated activity is something very important to the Virgoan mind. What is happening is that the Virgo is building up a sense of how he reacts to the physical nature of something, in the same way as you work with the emotional nature of something. You understand very well the idea of doing something more than once—there is a sort of reassurance in being able to get things right again and again. 'Patience' and 'practice' are Virgoan words, and you have little difficulty in understanding the motivation behind them.Virgoans like to understand things fully, right down to the component parts. They do things in a methodical and patient way, always trying to see how the whole thing fits together, and gaining satisfaction from that understanding. In short, they handle people's external natures and movements the same way you handle their internal natures and movements, and you recognize a mind which works in a similar fashion to your own.

To the Virgoan, you seem to have the right ideas. The quality that they see as the most evident in your nature is that of caring. Not only caring for other people, which they see as an attempt to assimilate the other person into yourself (they may be right at that—had you thought of it that way?), but caring that things are done properly. Whilst this is true, it is being looked at from two very different angles: you care about details because you want the things in your care to behave in an entirely predictable way, while they care about details because they can only understand the whole by noting all the parts and then adding them up.

As friends, you should be able to appreciate both the similarities and the differences of your points of view. Remember that the Virgo's way of looking at things starts with the details and works outwards, so when they remark on some small point about you it isn't the criticism it would be coming from anybody else—it simply denotes interest and an attempt to communicate.

As lovers, you will take some time to get going. This is because of the Virgo's inability to see things on the grand scale; he is never going to be swept off his feet by mad passion, and your grand emotional overtures may not be recognized as such simply because of their scale. Affection and care, yes: helpless love, no.

As business partners you should get on very well. Virgo has the ability to make you talk, which the other signs can't do very well, and you can help him develop a feel for things which is intuitive rather than analytical. The strength of the one is the weakness of the other, and there is a genuine desire to help each other along. Both of you work hard and long when necessary, though you are both prone to overwork unless reminded that you sometimes need a holiday. You are both 'collecting' signs, and have a tendency to think that working hard solves problems, which is not always true.

As marriage partners you would be very well suited, since you can both understand and be sympathetic to the other's approach to life. Remember to look outwards and upwards from time to time, though.

## Cancer–Libra

This is an easy relationship to start. The pair of you get along passably well on the surface, and your opening behaviour, the sort you use to form an acquaintance with anybody new, suits the Libran well enough. As the relationship deepens you will see fundamental differences between you at the same time as you see how much you genuinely like each other; if you manage to accept those differences and work with them rather than against them you will make a very strong partnership indeed.

Librans are almost too nice to be true on the surface. They are ruled by Venus, which means that they will always see the best in somebody rather than criticize them. There is always something about you which the Libran can find to like, and this is very flattering to you. There is no trickery: Venus is looking for something to identify with and relate to, and it has to start on the outside, because that's what it meets first. Librans like liking things: they are an outgoing sign, remember, so they are not trying to gather things into themselves. When they say they like you, it is real. You find this captivating; you can hardly believe your ears.

Librans are very refined people. They like anything which is beautiful, symmetrical, pretty, pleasing, or harmonious. This is because Venus draws them away from anything which is unbalanced or inelegant, and as a result they are all natural aesthetes. Since your behaviour pattern on meeting somebody new is unfailingly polite (that is, you stick to the formula so that you are unlikely to find yourself in a strange situation, and so that the stranger won't try to penetrate your shell), the Libran finds you attractive. After all, to him anybody with such good manners and restraint must be a balanced and refined person, and he likes that.

The trouble with this relationship is that Librans are at their best on the surface; the murky waters of the emotions are too raw and unbalanced for him. To be fair, that's not really his fault, because he isn't a Water sign, he's an Air sign, and a cardinal one at that: he is therefore as determined to make his world work in Airy terms as you are in Watery ones. You are the different tides of mental energy—he is the outgoing, communicative tide, and you are the incoming, emotional one. Because you work in the same universe but in different directions, you find each other both amenable and infuriating at the same time.

Problems arise when you are in one of your low phases. You will be feeling very possessive of him, and you will try to tell him how much you need him and how much time you have spent with him in the past. Then you will discover the meaning of the famous Libran balance. Hit him on one side, and his other side comes round to hit you in return with an exactly equal force. He will remind you of all the things that you have done to annoy him, which he has not mentioned until now. He will remind you of how much he has given in to your selfishness in the past. All of this will hurt like hell, and you will be very shocked. Libra's picture in the heavens is not an animal, it's a machine—what else did you expect?

Realize that he deals with everybody equally, and that he dislikes anything which emphasizes one person's needs above another's, and you will do well. Show him your inner self, and let him like it. Offer him your care in return. Achieve a *balance*.

As lovers, you will emphasize the softer sides of your natures, and the union will have a romantic flavour to it. As marriage or business partners you will do well if you maintain the balance: forgive his occasional vagueness and lack of concentration and he will forgive your worries and fussiness over little things. He is really a very good partner for you.

### Cancer-Scorpio

Here the fountain meets the lake. Scorpio is the Fixed Water sign. There is a lot of you in a Scorpio, but somehow he seems to be a stronger, more powerfully developed version. You are very much in awe of Scorpios, and would dearly love to be one. You don't find them frightening, but they seem so much more effective in their dealings with people than you are, and you admire this. In fact, the relationship between you is very much one of admiration on your part.

One of the most informative ways of looking at a Scorpio and comparing him to a Cancerian is to look at the zodiacal animals. A scorpion has a hard outer shell like your crab's, and he has eight legs and a pair of claws too. In addition to all this weaponry he has a lethal sting in his tail. Like you he doesn't move from his position easily, and when in serious trouble he will sting himself rather than surrender. All of these characteristics are shown by Scorpio people: you are dealing with a creature of the same shape as yourself. Not of the same reputation, though: the biggest difference between you by far is how the world treats you, which is again just the same as the animals. The world thinks of a crab as touchy and snappy; eventually it is broken with a hammer, and the meat made into sandwiches. The world fears scorpions, and stays a respectable distance away when it finds one.

You find the Scorpio so strong and determined that you can hardly believe it. If you were so determined, you think, you would burst from the pressure. Possibly so, but not Scorpios. You take energy in and put it out again in the form of caring; your main aim is to protect—yourself mainly, but those around you too. The Scorpio is past all that. He takes energy in, and keeps it there; his main aim is to control—again mainly himself, but then those around him, and eventually everybody.

Scorpios work at a very intense level indeed. Since this is all emotional energy, you think you are familiar with it, but the sheer scale and scope of it frightens you, and you fear for your safety. That's the trouble with you, according to the Scorpio: you care for your safety, always wondering if you will get hurt. Scorpios don't care for their own safety. They know they will survive, and can take enormous risks as long as all the elements of danger are under control. Control is their motivation, and power their goal.

You will find a relationship at this level very exciting. You must not think of the risks, only of the passion. If you feel safe with them, you could find yourself sharing in their manipulations, and enjoying the sort of power you have always felt attracted towards.

From you, the Scorpio gets a reminder of the true nature of emotional energy. You generate it freely from within yourself, whereas he doesn't. You can give emotional energy out to people in the form of care and protection, knowing that there is always going to be more where that came from; your resource is infinite—after all, you are the definition of emotions, the cardinal Water sign. The Scorpio has to keep and control the emotions he has, because he feels that he has no way of making more. Your simple maternal impulses make him feel ashamed of himself; he knows he could never show that kind of devotion. You are the shy and uncertain possessor of the most powerful gift of all. The zodiac works that way, and so, of course, does life.

On all levels, this relationship is powerful and productive, good for both of you. If you can stand the pressure, you'll love the heat! When Scorpio tries to control you, you can defend yourself quite well, and in return you can protect him from having to sting himself.

### Cancer-Sagittarius

This is one of the two five-signs-apart relationships you can form. Such pairings are not at all rare, but there is a lot of work to be done by the two people concerned, because in almost every possible way you are different. A lot of patience and a willingness to adapt is required for this one to work.

You are very sensitive to what people think about you, and you are easily hurt by unkind words. Within ten minutes of meeting a Sagittarian, you will feel that you have been probed, prodded, exposed, inspected, and finally beaten up and left to die by the roadside. And yet the Sagittarian is so charming with it! How does he do it, and why is he so cruel to you?

Sagittarians are insatiably curious. They have to find out all they can about everything they meet. When they meet you, you are likely to be polite but reserved, and show a genuine concern for his welfare. How interesting, he thinks. He decides to find out more. This is not cruelty, this is the Sagittarian showing you how interested he is in you. He has an alarming talent for looking right into people and seeing their inner workings as though they were transparent. He also has a facility with words, and a desire to tell you what he has seen. They have no tact. Not one molecule. It doesn't matter where you are, or who you are with; they have to tell it as they see it, there and then. Don't even attempt to explain your embarrassment, just slip back into your shell and play with the hors d'oeuvres, for whatever else is around at the time. There is a great deal of similarity between the Sagittarian and the puppy who keeps bringing you things he has found in the garden. You don't want them, but you know that he is showing his affection. Why do you find Sagittarians so irresistible, then?

They are warm, they are open-hearted, they are free with their emotions, they are romantic, and they are always optimists. That's why. You need them to put some warmth into your world, and to show you that life isn't as hard as you make it seem. What they need in return is somebody who really does get cheered by their relentless optimism, somebody to comfort them when their schemes collapse, and somebody to look after the serious side of life for them. They know that they do have to show a sense of responsibility now and again, over such things as mortgages and taxes, but it really doesn't suit them, and they tend to shy away from it all. You can provide the home base that they need, look after the organizational side of things, and they will provide you with an exciting life in return.

You will argue over money. You are very careful with your money, and save it whenever you can because it adds to your security. Sagittarians have never understood the word 'security', and they like spending money as fast as they can. If they start to spend *your* money, there will be arguments.

If you are lovers you must try to allow for the fact that the Sagittarian is often in love with more than one person at once. You cannot expect his exclusive attention. Think of yourself as

number one wife in a harem instead. Remember that he doesn't
do any of this to hurt you, and indeed wouldn't hurt you for the
world: he just has to keep moving, and you find that upsetting.

If you want to make a marriage out of this, you will have to be
prepared to move around, and make sudden changes. It's not as
hard as it sounds—a crab, like a snail, takes his house with him
when he moves. You don't lose emotional ties just by changing
direction, you know.

### Cancer-Capricorn

As with most of the relationships formed by two people from
opposite signs of the zodiac, this one is quite easy to handle, and
in fact is concerned with the same thing, which you approach in
different ways.

In this case, the thing you both like so much is organization,
or structure. You like organized things so that you can use the
strength of the organization as a shield against your enemies:
Capricorns like structures so that they can use them as ladders to
climb to the top.

If you remember the example of the box which was mentioned
in 'The Essence of the Signs' (page 51), then you can use the same
motif to understand the Capricorn's motivation: you use the box
as a container for your private world, and he uses the box as a
platform to stand on and be noticed.

The Capricorn is concerned with material things in the same
way that you are concerned with emotional things. He uses
people's reactions to material things to define his world; in other
words, he gets his status from status symbols. That sounds a
little hollow, but a Capricorn is more than a status symbol
collector; he is the one who first decides that such things are
status symbols in the first place. He wants to be noticed and
recognized for his achievements and is prepared to work very
hard to get what he wants. He also wants that recognition to be
permanent, and to him the best way of doing that is to make it
physical. It means much more to him to have a silver trophy than
to win the race: the elation of winning only lasts for a day or two,
or until the press has forgotten about it, but the trophy stands on

his sideboard for ever. He will need to invent a whole vocabulary of success in visible form, so that people are constantly reminded of his achievements, and see him as a success. Now you see why he likes status symbols. It is expected of him. If a Capricorn chooses to display some new and expensive object, it becomes a status symbol simply because it is the sort of thing a Capricorn would have.

Given the choice, Cancer would like to be a private individual, safe with his family. Given the choice, Capricorn would like to be on public display, and known for who he is. Successful Capricorns who are millionaire recluses are only that way because it draws attention to their status; in earlier societies where there were no newspapers with gossip columns, the Capricorns were the ones with the bands of armed guards who went about reminding you how powerful they were.

What attracts you to a Capricorn? Determination, mostly; that and their withdrawn exterior. When you meet one, you will perhaps think that you are looking at a similar individual to yourself, who keeps his feelings to himself. This isn't really so: Capricorns are serious and withdrawn, true, but their emotional level is so low that you wouldn't recognize it. Emotions aren't the sort of things that you build firm reputations and business empires on, so they don't give them a lot of time. Perhaps you admire his strong determination to have things his way, no matter how long it takes him to get there; perhaps you like the self-control he shows in the face of adversity; perhaps it is simply the fact that the world looks up to him. It may even be that he recognizes the importance of the rules in life, just the same as you do. In return, you can show him that a heart of stone is capable of being warmed, and that success with people is as rewarding as success with material things.

As lovers, you will be the warmer partner, which means that the union will be a cool one—if you want love rather than sex, don't choose a Capricorn.

As business partners, you will do very well. Both of you understand the way money works, and have the knack of acquiring it. The work-place could be humourless at times though.

As a marriage, this one is very traditional, but none the worse for that. Home life will be rather formal: Capricorn is the father figure, Cancer the mother figure, and the roles will be adhered to.

*Cancer-Aquarius*
This is the second of the five-signs-apart pairings you can be involved in. Like the Sagittarian one, there are massive adjustments to be made by both of you if the relationship is to develop satisfactorily, and again the principal stumbling-block is the other person's unwillingness to stay in one place for too long.

Aquarius is the second sign to be governed by Saturn; this time, unlike Capricorn, the Saturn influence is itself of a lunar type (remind yourself by looking at the horseshoe diagram and reading page 23 again). This is a cool, low-key relationship. To extend the musical metaphor—rightly, since most of what an Aquarian does can be explained in musical terms—it is an off-beat relationship too, based on fascination and a certain quirky amusement rather than more regular forces like admiration or affection.

An Aquarian will leave you alone when you want it, and that makes him unique in the zodiac. You are very grateful for this, and a partner who does not swamp you with his presence has a lot of appeal for you. Sometimes it can be difficult to get him really involved when you do want him to be close to you, but you can't have everything.

Aquarians have a lot of compassion, and they do care; you recognize this and find it a sympathetic viewpoint to your own. Where you differ, though, is that they care on a general scale, whereas you care on an individual scale. Social injustice awakens the Aquarian spirit, where personal injustice excites yours. You will find it difficult to believe that they cannot scale down their concern to match yours, but it is so: they don't lack feeling, but they do lack involvement. You are intimately involved with every action you undertake, but they are not. It will take you some time to understand this devotion to the universal but distinct coolness towards the specific, because it isn't what you understand by compassion at all.

Aquarians have a fascination for the unusual; in fact the unusual is the usual for them. You are a very conventional soul, taking comfort in the familiarity of known and trusted things, but an Aquarian has to try the unknown just to see what it's like. You can't conventionalize an Aquarian—they need the unusual like you need affection. They also need large numbers of people, whereas you are happier with a small group. These two areas of difference, between the large-scale and the personal and between the unusual and the conventional, are going to crop up again and again in your relationship; you will have to make great efforts to get round them.

As friends you will get along easily, especially if you are part of a larger group. You both recognize that the other one doesn't like being pressed too hard to do anything, and you maintain a discreet distance. He likes your sensitivity and your quiet exterior. When you deepen the friendship and become lovers, you will find things more difficult. You require a personal devotion he just can't provide, and his affections lack the depth you seek. He will always be looking to change the relationship, and you to give it some sort of roots; it isn't easy.

Should you marry, you will have learnt that making emotional demands leads to trouble, and will have learnt to live with their flashes of independent behaviour. You will be keen to give your family the individual care you think they need, but he will say that you cosset them. Again, it isn't easy. Business partners? Yes, as long as you look after everything financial and he looks after everything else. It's a much better proposition than marrying him.

### Cancer-Pisces

The other Water-Water partnership. Again, an animal metaphor helps you to understand how you work together. Both crabs and fishes live in the sea, surrounded by the watery element that supports them in every way. The fishes move around constantly; if they don't, they sink to the bottom. Neither of them is a threat to the other, since they don't eat each other, but occasionally

the fishes get curious and come a little too close to the crab—
and then they get nipped, which they don't like at all. Life
between a Cancerian and a Piscean is remarkably similar.

The situation is quite similar to the Scorpio relationship, but
with the roles reversed; this time the Piscean is the one lost in
admiration, and you are the one who seems to have all the power
and authority. Strange, isn't it? Pisces wants to be as well-
protected as you are; he is horribly vulnerable to almost
anything you can think of, and his complete inability to do
anything assertive or decisive means that he could really do with
something like your shell. You may be reserved, but you do know
what you want: Pisces is pathologically shy, and has no real
course of action at all.

You may think you are sensitive, but your range of sensitivity
is markedly crude in comparison to the Piscean's. These people
are as sensitive as a photographic plate; they catch the mere
shadow of something and hold it for ever. They have a
remarkable chameleon quality in that they can (and do) take on
the character of their companion and his surroundings; you will
find that they share your enthusiasms with you, and even dress
in the same style, given long enough. Such fantastic sensitivity
is a revelation to you. These people can make a whole way of life
from a fleeting impression, and fashion reality from fantasy as
though it were made of bricks and mortar. You wouldn't really
like to be a Piscean: they have no control over what makes an
impression on them next, and they cannot make emotions for
themselves, only react to circumstances. No self-direction, and
no structure: not your sort of thing at all.

As friends, you have coincident views most of the time, since
your opinions are both shaped by similar reactions to external
events. The difference is that you respond to external stimuli by
deciding whether or not you need to deal with them as a threat,
while the Piscean just reacts, and has to see where that gets him.
You do not have his amazing flexibility, nor his adaptability,
but you do have some measure of control over your life, which
he doesn't. You must be careful not to defend yourself too
strongly if he threatens your privacy; just a word is enough to a

Piscean, and if you hurt them with your crab's claws you will do far more damage than you intended.

As lovers, you will surround yourselves with every emotional indulgence, and everything that produces a response from the senses. Romance is the keynote of this liaison rather than passion or power; roses and poetry are going to feature more frequently than sexual athletics. It could get a bit *too* dreamy for you, since you are cardinal in quality, and don't ever lose sight of the central objective. It will certainly be a luxurious experience.

As business partners, you really lack the edge required to make any sort of mark in the commercial world. The media loves Pisceans, though, so perhaps you could aim yourselves in that direction. You are best as employees rather than employers, though.

As a marriage partner, you could hardly do better. Most of the time they see things the same way as you do, and when they are being over-sensitive you can protect them as you so like to do. You can build a safe base for your family filled with love and understanding instead of tension and defensiveness. You will have to take the decisions, though: a Piscean just can't!

# Leo

*Leo-Aries*
This is one of the great friendships of the zodiac. You think that they are dynamic and confident, just the way you think people should be, but they change direction too much for your taste: they will no doubt settle down in a few years' time. They think that you have the right sort of enthusiasm but you are a little unadventurous, a bit of a home-lover, in their eyes; all you need is a bit of a push and you will be on the right track. How much you are going to enjoy trying to make these final adjustments in each other!

Of course, neither of you will succeed in making the other more like yourself, and it is better that you should not succeed anyway. The little differences give that extra sparkle to the relationship and stop it from becoming boring.

You do have a great amount in common. Both of you are Fire signs; both of you believe that action is better than inaction, that getting personally involved is the only way to be effective, and that your own ideas are naturally the best ones available. People who sit still, or particularly who worry about things, bore both of you very quickly—you are both optimistic and forward looking, confident that you can handle anything that comes your way.

Examine that last phrase again. Leos are not normally confident about handling new things; familiar things, yes, but not new ones. Where has the confidence come from? From Aries: to you he represents the source of all personal energy. You are always bothered that you might not have the resources to cope with anything completely new and unfamiliar, in case it requires more than you've got; Aries seems to be an inexhaustible supply of whatever it takes, and your confidence in facing the unfamiliar grows strong in his company. After all, you think, between us we must have more than enough energy for anything, and you are right.

It works the other way round, too: Aries knows that he has the raw bravery to attack anything that comes his way, but he also knows that he doesn't have the staying power of the Leo. If a problem is likely to withstand his first onslaught and require real determination to overcome, then he knows he would be better off trying something else, and changes direction accordingly. A partnership with Leo gives him the stamina he didn't have before, and he is the stronger and more capable for it.

In terms of their element, Fire, Arians always had the spark of ignition, but didn't have the heat of combustion. Together, the two signs give a steady burning fire which can be started anywhere.

In a friendship, the thing you will like about each other most is the fact that you are each as enthusiastic and energetic as the other. The Arian doesn't have to slow down and wait for the Leo, or limit his activity in any way, nor does the Leo find the Arian too cautious to share fully in his grandiose way of life. Both of you find life exciting, and you find plenty to make you smile; you are used to things going right, and used to feeling pleased with yourselves. To have a friend who feels exactly the same way is very satisfying indeed.

In love, you both bring the heat of your Fire sign energies along with you, and your physical relationship is likely to be both hot and strong. It is not that you are not romantic, but underneath the sentiment you are both essentially interested in expressing your energy through physical activity. Neither of you wants to take from the other—you are both givers, and with such generous contributions from both sides you are going to have a fine time. Enthusiasm and confidence make for more of the same: you can't lose. The only way in which you are different is that the Arian is likely to tire of the relationship before you. He is not necessarily exhausted, but he needs fresh challenges to be at his best, and too much that is too familiar makes him restless.

As a marriage or as business partners you should work very well indeed. If you try to dominate the Arian he will direct his energies elsewhere, which would be detrimental to the partnership, so try not to organize him overmuch. The only other problem is that you both like spending money more than you like saving it: somebody has got to keep an eye on the finances.

*Leo-Taurus*
This is what you could call a steady relationship. If you are the sort of Leo whose energies are best directed into material things, who dines well and has a sumptuously decorated house, then this is the relationship for you.

It is an accumulating partnership: almost from the word go you will find yourselves buying things together that somehow express the pleasure you get from each other's company. Most of these things will be expensive, luxury items that appeal to you both. Perhaps you will be surprised at how your tastes coincide: in fact they don't, but they overlap quite substantially in the realms of the opulent and ostentatious. As the relationship goes on, you will find that you have collected a large number of things together—the relationship is taking visible form as these objects.

It is a relationship where the essential principle is strength and position. The maintenance of your position is vital to both of you, and in many ways this partnership over-emphasizes the heavier facets of your personalities at the expense of the others. The Taurean's gentleness and feeling for the land will not be in evidence when in your company, and your generosity to others will be diminished in the same way.

What the Taurean is after is material security; he measures his existence by his surroundings, and the more things he can touch and keep, then the better he feels. Your way of life usually involves any number of nice objects as a matter of course, and the Taurean finds these very attractive. You are naturally generous, and will probably take your Taurean to a restaurant soon after your initial meeting, or give them a small present. They will be highly appreciative; material things are important to them, and they keep them for ever. You enjoy being appreciated, and you enjoy being generous, because it expresses your confidence and your liking for yourself. They enjoy being taken out, and love receiving presents, because it increases their liking for *them*selves. You have found the perfect receptacle for your generosity, and it will all be converted into material form.

What you want is simply someone to appreciate you, and you will certainly have that in the Taurean: the problems arise when you start to get what you *don't* want. You don't want someone who is not going to do things your way, and you don't want someone who is going to stand his ground when you are trying to move him. Taureans do exactly this. You have two alternatives: either you can both stand your ground and shout at each other, which is quite likely, and not very productive, since at the end of the day you will have to move because they will outlast you (a Taurean will stay in the same position until he dies, if need be); or you can take their point of view and bring your own special radiance to it, which is the likely result. You can now see why you are accumulating so many expensive things: they are 'Leonized' Taurean acquisitions.

As friends, you will enjoy the good things of life together. Provided that you live essentially separate lives, you are unlikely to quarrel, and the biggest problem that faces you is that of obesity, since you encourage each other's over-consumption in all senses.

As lovers you will be powerful but rather ponderous in your behaviour. Taurus gives no sparkle to the union, and it could be a bit of a wrestling match. You are both possessive, and this could slow things down further.

Provided that you don't spend too much time fighting each other from entrenched positions, both marriage or a business relationship would work well. Money is an essential lubricant in this relationship though, and if there isn't enough of it, things will stop moving very quickly.

### Leo-Gemini

There could hardly be a greater contrast between two partners than there is between the Taurean and the Gemini. The last one was a rather static and materialistic partnership, but this one is bright, alive, and fun all the way.

Gemini doesn't care how much money you have, or how generous you are. What he cares about most of all is how much joy you get out of being yourself: he has a similar feeling about himself, and he can't wait to share it with you, and to find out about your feelings at the same time.

You see him as the sort of friend you always wanted: bright, pleased to see you, actively seeking your company, and making you feel part of whatever he's doing. You love a chance to show yourself off: there is always some way to do that in a Gemini's company. You don't like dull surroundings: there is always something lively happening wherever a Gemini is, and he always regards it as a bit of a game, something diverting and not to be taken seriously. How could you not shine in an atmosphere like this? All the ponderous and static parts of your nature are miraculously converted into good-humoured boisterousness by the Mercurial talents of the Gemini. You can't stand still for too long when he's around, but he has taken away your fear of having to try unfamiliar things by doing them for you—you stay where you are in the midst of all the fun while he presents new things to you for your amusement in a constant stream. In many ways the relationship is like that between a king and his jester. He is a willing satellite, racing around you at a giddy rate while you stay beaming in the centre, and you find the arrangement very satisfying.

He sees you as somebody he can rely on. You are always going to be constant in your reactions to him, and he finds this useful. He may change his tune from one minute to the next, and he knows it full well, but to have a friend who finds him fascinating no matter which side out he is, and who will always be there, is something worth looking after. He is also well aware of the fact that he needs shelter and support from time to time when one or another of his schemes collapses; Geminis are very good talkers, but their lives seldom match their plans. In such cases it is most reassuring to have a friend who will stick up for you, not betray you, and lend you a few quid when you're broke—a sort of ersatz elder brother. Leo fulfils this role for Gemini admirably, and the Gemini loves it. It's not all take and no give, though: the Gemini can, and does, render the Leo worthwhile service. It works like this: a Leo likes to know what's going on in the world, to be up to date, so that he can stay in command. If he is overtaken by new developments, then he could be made to look silly, and this he is anxious to avoid. Finding out about things from ground level is a bit undignified for a regal Lion, so he gets his information off the Gemini, who picks up information like the rest of us breathe—regularly, without thinking about it. It looks like the king and his jester again.

As a friendship, this has everything to recommend it. You, Leo, have to accept that the Gemini will tell you different tales on different days, and you mustn't expect him to give you much in the way of respect. He does like you a lot, though: he relies on you, in fact, as much as a Gemini relies on anybody.

As lovers, you are more likely to break ribs from laughter than from the fierceness of your embrace. The light, playful, essentially un-serious way a Gemini leads his public life extends to his private life as well. The Leo must remember that the Gemini has no real notion of loyalty or commitment, but provided he can live with that, the two of you can have a wonderful time playing expensive and intimate charades with each other.

For business, the combination could hardly be bettered. Your unity of purpose but difference of approach will have your competitors absolutely baffled.

For marriage, and especially for family life, these two signs have a lot to offer each other. Leo gives the warmth to sustain a long relationship, and Gemini stops it from becoming too set in its ways.

*Leo-Cancer*
The relationships formed with the sign immediately before or after your own are the most difficult of all; to give you your due, you manage this difficult task better than the other eleven signs, but you are still unlikely to choose a partner from a sign adjacent to your own unless other factors in your horoscope predispose you to do so. The reason is simple: the sign before your own represents you looking over your own shoulder. All the things you would rather not think about, they embody.

You see a Cancerian as an impossibly worried person; how, you think, could anyone be so afraid of life as they are? How do they manage to get up in the morning? The answer is through familiar and safe routines, and with care, not at all like your confident stride through life, trusting in Fortune to smile on you. The pair of you have very, very different views on life. You give them everything, and they seem to offer you nothing in return. You wear your heart on your sleeve, but you know next to nothing about how they feel. Worse yet, they don't tell you how much they appreciate you.

It's not as bad as it seems, though you will have to try very hard to see it the way it really is. They are actually in awe of your energy and generosity. A Cancer assimilates things a bit at a time, making sure they are thoroughly familiar before moving on to the next section; the scope and power of your way of doing things, in great open gestures, is too much for them to handle all at once. You are also very loud and open when you speak; they are very shy. If they could manage to answer you in the way you expect, you would probably do something else large and dramatic by way of response, and that would be altogether too much for them to manage. Quite simply, you overwhelm them.

Cancer would like to show you how much you are appreciated, and this is done by caring for you when you are not feeling as brilliant as usual. There is no such time, you cry, and there may well not be. Even if there were, your solar, solitary nature would prevent you from either taking or seeking comfort from another, and so the Cancerian's prime function is denied. You really aren't a great deal of use to each other—one is too much for the other to handle, the other offers a response that the first one doesn't want.

There is a subtler way, too, in which the Cancerian gives you all the things you don't want. As you know, you feel confident about yourself because you have mastered your fears about yourself fairly early on in life: they only come to the surface again when you are presented with something completely new. Changing circumstances worry you, because you will have to make yourself master of them before you can settle back into the role of the relaxed, unflappable, serene, ruling figure. For this reason you are none too fond of practical jokes: you laugh because you feel you have to, but you are seething inside because somebody has tried to unsettle your confidence. Inside every Leo there is a worried person, but he is a very long way down inside, and he need not be considered most of the time. A Cancerian brings him to you in the form of another individual; just as worried, just as defensive, just as easily upset. In fact a Cancerian is much more than these, and works on a different wavelength altogether, but you don't see that—all you see is the parts of yourself you'd rather not remember.

It is difficult to make this friendship really work; you really can't function with someone who worries every time you get interested in something, and they just can't stand the tension—they think your luck's got to give out sometime.

It is unlikely that you will be lovers, at least on the level of your Sun-sign energies: if you are, though, you will find that the major stumbling block is their inability to really *give* themselves. Keep the relationship lighter if you really want to keep it going—

both of you enjoy the surface of courtship, with the flowers and the candlelit dinners, so leave it there.

As a marriage you can only make this partnership work if you adopt very traditional mother and father roles, and stick rigidly to them. The Leo is the father, the Cancer the mother, of course. A more modern or loosely structured relationship will probably not work.

## Leo-Leo

Forming a partnership of any kind with a person of the same sign as yourself is not always a good thing, but on the other hand it is nowhere near the disaster it is sometimes made out to be. At least you know what you're getting!

Here the relationship is made from two people who both like being the centre of attention, and both like having a good time. The easiest way to make this work is to avoid any sort of situation where either of you have to make a decision—each of you would like to be the one to do it, and neither of you will be particularly keen to do what the other has decided. If you are simply enjoying each other's company in an environment where the rules for behaviour are well known and familiar, then you will have no problems at all; everybody else in the immediate area will find themselves being naturally drawn to the crackle of energy between you, and before you know where you are there will be a spontaneous party.

What you like about another Leo is their openness and optimism. There is nothing secretive about a Leo, for he has no need to be. When one Leo meets another, they both feel very relaxed, because they each know that the other is not trying to manoeuvre him in some sort of personal chess game the way the Scorpio does, or use Leonine energy to meet his own needs, as the Taurean sometimes does. Openness leads to trust and confidence, and confidence to radiance as the Leonine solar energy starts to make itself felt; the situation becomes an improving circle, as each partner makes the other feel good.

A Leo puts out solar energy, and likes to see some of it reflected back to him by appreciative friends. This energy usually returns in a much weaker form than what it went out as. When the appreciative friend is another Leo, the energy comes back full strength, and the pair of them can literally bask in each other's warmth.

Similar openness; similar radiance. The combination looks very positive until you remember that only one of you can be the dominant partner, but that both of you have a real need to dominate. Once one of you is established as the dominant partner, the other one must do one of only three things: he could displace you, and be dominant himself; he could go somewhere else and become the centre of a new group; or he could stay in your shadow, which would lead to much frustration, and eventually illness. As you can see, all three lead to the dissolution of the partnership: the obvious conclusion to be drawn is that if the relationship is to survive, then neither of you must be the dominant partner. The only way to implement this is for you to take turns. Since you are Fixed signs, you have a natural reluctance to changing roles more often than you have to, and you are much better off in one position over a long period of time. The best compromise seems to be to divide your areas of responsibility between you, and for each of you to take absolute responsibility for your own areas. Stay inside your own territory for things which matter, but share the limelight for the lighter and more social side of life, where you are not so likely to be fighting for position. In some ways it is an artificial answer, but it is the only workable one. Remember that those star systems with two suns have them revolving about each other, sharing responsibility for their satellites; they cannot work any other way.

As a light friendship the Leo-Leo pairing is a lot of fun. When the friendship becomes an affair, then the gestures become even grander until one of you feels that the other is taking too much of a controlling interest. Then you will disengage with polite dignity, maintaining as much of your self-respect as possible, and quietly look for someone more suitable.

As a marriage, you should work very well provided you do not try to control each other. You both have expansive ideas and the enthusiasm to match; given time, you will be able to achieve almost everything you set out to.

*Leo-Virgo*

This is the second of the adjacent-sign relationships open to you, and it is no easier than the last one, though you may take some small comfort from the fact that from the Virgo's point of view it is even more impossible than from yours. Oddly enough, this one works very well as a business partnership, because you have all the expansive ideas and the Virgo looks for ways to put them into practice in the most effective and economical way. You provide the fuel for him to work with, and give him the enthusiasm and breadth of outlook he needs to succeed.

On a personal level, though, the partnership is not so cosy. A Virgo has a need to examine things at a very close and fine level; unless he is familiar with the detail of things he is not happy. Broad concepts have no meaning for him; he can only take things in by building a large picture from many small ones. He tends to look down rather than up or outwards, and his attention is focused on the actual workings of things rather than how they look or what they mean.

You will be able to see at once that his insistence on understanding the detail of things will lead to difficulty when he examines much of your behaviour, where the detail is missing altogether. You start at the top and often neglect the smaller details; they are not important to your scheme of things. Worse still, you are concerned with ideas and activity rather than actual material articles. How can there be any real communication between you if you deal in different universes and on a different scale?

Obviously what communication actually takes place is going to be misinterpreted, and that's what happens. To you, the Virgo is always picking holes in your arguments, pointing out inconsistencies or impracticalities, and generally acting like a wet blanket. This is not actually true, but it's how it seems to you. What is happening is that the poor Virgoan is genuinely trying to understand what you are saying, but he can only do it by building up a picture a piece at a time, like a jigsaw. If there aren't enough pieces, or if a piece is missing, or the pattern changes, he complains; and there you are trying to get him to do his own painting with a broad brush.

He appreciates your energy, the same as everybody else, but he can't get over your apparent sloppiness. I know that you're generous and expansive rather than sloppy, but to the Virgoan it seems that way. He does things again and again, building up familiarity through practice, but you prefer to let someone else do that sort of thing, and he can't understand how you could possibly think that way. It's not that you are different—it's that neither of you can see what the other is trying to do, and are thus unable to communicate.

As friends you stand no real chance unless you can find some common interest which will allow you each to see what the other is doing; as business partners, though, you would do very well, as mentioned earlier.

If you want a Virgo as a lover you will have to be very patient and try to do things on a small scale. They don't appreciate your theatrical gestures—firstly because they are rather shy and restrained emotionally, and secondly because unless the intention is matched by something material, they won't be able to understand it. They will appreciate your warmth, though, and will repay you by doing all they can to please you—a show of appreciation which will do much to win your heart.

For a marriage, there are vast differences in outlook to be overcome. You may not be able to stand the Virgo's narrow point of view, and even if your optimism cures their constant worries, they may not be able to join you in your grand schemes as you would wish.

## Leo-Libra

Librans are supposed to be the nicest people in the zodiac. To an extent it is true, but it depends an awful lot on your definition of nice. You will find them delightful company, but they are a little on the lightweight side when it comes to making firm moves. As long as you are prepared to provide the motive power for both of you, this partnership can be very rewarding.

A Libran sees you as the personification of his ambitions. Put simply, he would like to be like you. He is outgoing and sociable in the same way that you are, putting his energy out into friendly chat. He makes friends with everybody he meets; everybody likes a Libran. A lot of this is to do with the way his planet, Venus, works: Venus looks for something similar to itself all the time, and needs something to relate to. A Libran finds something to like about everybody he meets, something in the other person which is similar to something in himself. Then he talks about how similar he is to the other person, and how he has always liked being like this or like that. It's a sure-fire way of making people like you, but it's not a deliberate device, any more than you are generous for a reason: it's just the planet behind the person making all the moves in accordance with its nature. A Libran is the original source of communication between people, and of the relationship that brings into being. He is also the source of all that is harmonious, balanced or beautiful, because his insistence on drawing together those things which are similar eliminates contrast, disagreement and imbalance. It is not difficult to see why they have a reputation for being nice.

The trouble with being nice is that nobody thinks you are important or effective. We only sit up and take notice of things that stand out from, or disrupt, our previous steady state. Leos, now, they're different. When a Leo walks into a room the room sits up expectantly, and when he speaks everybody listens. A Libran would love to have that kind of effect on people. It's not the confidence he lacks, it's the effectiveness.

That's one of the things that attracts him to you: the other is that you generally get what you want, and live in a fairly wealthy way, compared to the rest of your friends. Librans would like to own all sorts of beautiful things, and live very elegant lifestyles to go with them, but they just don't have the money. Librans have impeccable taste, but they can't seem to translate it into reality like a Leo can.

What do you see them as? As charming companions who agree with your ideas, who appreciate your tastes, and who can live life on your level with no difficulty. When it comes to being decisive they are a waste of time, because they always see the other side to the argument as well, but you don't mind that. If they were at all decisive on their own, they might decide differently from you, and that would never do, would it? You see them as lazy, whereas they are simply ineffective, which is not the same thing. All in all, you like having them around. You value their opinions, but that doesn't mean you have to take their advice. They are decorative and companionable, and they don't get in the way when you're putting your foot down about something. Ideal, really.

If this relationship is limited to a light friendship, then the way to get the most value from it is to spend time doing the things where you can both contribute to the end result, such as some expensive, expansive, and artistic pursuit, where the Leo's generosity and the Libran's superlative taste can combine to produce something that could not have been achieved by either of you singly. Supper after the theatre sounds about right.

As lovers, the traditional romantic gestures will appeal to you both—the more stylish the better. You, Leo, will have difficulty convincing the Libran that you are seriously in love; they take things very lightly, and steer clear of anything resembling commitment, even though the idea of marriage appeals to them a great deal. If you want to make it permanent you will have to be very patient, and not advertise your intention. Once married, you will have no problems other than making enough money to keep up with the style of life you both enjoy so much.

### Leo-Scorpio

This is the partnership to go for if you like playing rough. Scorpios are hard fighters, and have the sort of determination which means that even when they lose they get even eventually. There is no way that you can conduct this relationship on a light and carefree level, even if you try to; it is strong and deep from the beginning. The rewards are high, and there is plenty of blazing passion on both sides: the downs are at least as deep as the ups are high, and the road is never smooth. If you fancy something you can get your teeth into, a relationship worth your time and strength, then try this one.

Scorpios do almost everything that you do in reverse. They don't put out energy as if it was free (which it is, to you, of

course)—they collect it and store it within themselves. They like
to be in control at all times, and this means that they have to
know exactly what's going on, and what everybody is likely to do.
Then they stay one jump ahead. Of course, it means that they have
to do things their way, and that's where the opposition to you
comes in. You know that you are only going to allow things to
happen the way you say, because you like organizing things, and
being at the centre, if not the front; Scorpios won't wear this at
all. Your grand schemes are improperly thought out, in their
view; there are possibilities which to you don't matter but to
them seem important, and which must be catered for. What's
more, it is obviously much better if they took over the whole
affair so that you don't miss out anything else that's important.
The arguments between you start at this point, and get worse.

You see them as unnecessarily interfering. Why can't they
trust you to get things right? Everything works fine when you are
left on your own—why do they have to try to control it? They see
you as incredibly wasteful and dangerously open in all you do—
how could you let everybody see what you are doing when they
might want to use it against you? How could you be so generous
with your time and money when it has to be so carefully
guarded? They never see that you are open because you have
nothing to hide, and generous because your energy comes for
free; it never occurs to you that they might have something to
hide, and that they might not have your facility for making things
happen.

Yet you are linked to each other, in a way. The Scorpio's real
goal is to be openly in power and publicly recognized for it, just
as you are all the time; it is this which he admires in you above all
else, and for which he forgives your excesses. You realize, of
course, that your real power comes from within yourself, and
you recognize the great store of that power inside the Scorpio,
held down by his self-restrictive control; you would like to be
able to share in, return to, and unite with, that power, and it is
this which draws you to him, and for which you suffer his
attempts to stifle your self-expression.

Any contact you make with a Scorpio turns into a power

struggle after a very short time, so you cannot hope to have a mere amicable acquaintance. Either you will dislike each other quite fiercely, as the other elements in your horoscope add to the strain felt by your two Sun positions, or you will find yourselves exploring each other at deeper and deeper levels as the great energies you represent mingle and fuse with each other. A sexual relationship is the only one capable of handling the sort of current you two generate and this will become very powerful very quickly—real life-and-death stuff, playing with the energies of life itself. Arguments will be catastrophic, reconciliations sublimely uplifting; everything about it is more intense and on a bigger scale than a relationship with one of the other eleven signs. As a marriage, the same applies: you will fight for each other in public, and with each other in private. It won't be easy, but it won't be dull either.

## Leo-Sagittarius

There is nobody on this earth you would rather waste your time with than a Sagittarian. The only person in the zodiac who makes you feel dull by comparison, and for whose place and talents you would gladly trade your own. Everything they do is a delight to you. They are lively, witty, and even more optimistic than you are; when you're together you feel you could take on the world. Fortunately for the rest of the world, you'll never get round to it because you're having too good a time imagining it all. Even if you went into business together you would need somebody to handle the actual mechanics of things, not to mention the finances. Between you, you are an ideas factory gone mad, with enough sheer ebullience to convince anybody of anything; but you're not too good on the practical side of things.

Sagittarius is confident and outgoing, as you are; but his confidence is the confidence of belief and of knowledge, whereas yours is the confidence of feeling only. Both of you are very forward-looking, far more interested in the immediate future than the past, and both absolutely sure that everything is going to turn out for the best. The difference in your attitudes is that you *feel* that things are going to be all right, and the

Sagittarian *knows* that they are.

The Sagittarian seems to know everything there is to know about everything, and to share his knowledge freely. You recognize the generosity of spirit as being similar to your own, but you find the depth of his knowledge new and exciting: you sit there and soak it up eagerly. There isn't much in the world that you feel you would like more of, that you wish someone would give you, but whatever it is that Sagittarians put out is it.

You are also fascinated by their mobility. You know that you tend to stay in the same situation if it suits you, and you know, inside yourself, that this is because you don't think that you could be so successful if you had to adapt to changing surroundings the whole time. Sagittarians seem to be able to deal with things as they come up; they can move from one situation to another and still come out ahead. Is it all that knowledge, you ask yourself, that makes them so adaptable? No, it's Jupiter. Sagittarians are governed by a big planet, so they have big ideas, the same way you do, but Jupiter moves and the Sun doesn't. They use movement to stay at their best: a static Sagittarian is a sad person indeed.

They see you as a reminder that at the end of the day it isn't the material things that make life work, but the personal energies you can put in. They know that you always believe in yourself, and they find that an inspiring thought. Sometimes they wonder, with their changeable minds, whether being a giver rather than a taker is the right way to be—but five minutes in your company reminds them that to be self-confident, generous, and optimistic is the right way for them. You *refuel* Sagittarians, and that's what they like about you.

As friends, you will get on brilliantly, but don't expect to put any of your schemes into action! You are wonderfully restorative for each other's spirits.

As lovers, your relationship should be energetic and warm (two Fire signs). He will like to keep things moving and changeable, though, where you will be happy to stay with a good thing once you get one. Your dignity might get rumpled: Sagittarians have little time for ceremony, and when impulse overrides decorum they don't mind one bit—but you do! You could find yourself feeling a little old-fashioned as your lover teases your sentimental and romantic streak, but overall it is a stimulating affair, and one which you will enjoy.

As a marriage, you should have few problems. Even if you rule your household in typical Leonine manner, the Sagittarian won't complain, provided that you don't restrict his freedom. He needs to be able to move around and feel free: give him this and all will be well.

### Leo-Capricorn

This one isn't easy. The partnership hinges on the essential difference between a person who is a success simply by existing, and a person who has made the attainment of success his life's work. On the surface and in public you can talk to each other as equals, but the approaches which led you both to the positions you occupy are very different.

Capricorn sees you as both the beginning and end of his own existence. You are successful, well liked, and have a reputation. People gather around you, listen to you, take notice of you. You are considered important. Quite often you are comfortably solvent, and when that isn't the case it doesn't seem to matter. Basically, you are a star. All that, the Capricorn wants. He wants to be seen as important, to be at the top of the pyramid. He sees you as being able to do what you do through applied self-confidence, which is quite perceptive of him, because that's more or less right. If he has confidence in himself and applies himself, he thinks, he will achieve the same result as you. As you were, he was; as you are, he will be, as the saying goes. What he doesn't see is that you have the Sun in you, radiating out through a person born when it was in its own sign. He doesn't have that. He has Saturn instead, which is cold and restrictive. when you apply yourself, you are applying warmth and sunlight to things, and who doesn't feel better when the Sun shines on them? When the Capricorn applies himself, he applies Saturn, which extinguishes warmth, adds weight, and gives a serious tone to things generally. Although the success will come in time, it will not come as easily as yours, nor can the Capricorn ever be you: the Sun does not shine out from him in the same way.

You see him differently. He gives shape to your achievements; by doing what he does without effort, you are seen as a success. A strange way of looking at things, I know, but public recognition and the acquisition of status symbols are in fact a Capricorn's definition of success, and you choose them as the means of communicating your importance to the rest of society. He works his way up the hierarchy of an organization, pointing out the shape of the hierarchy by his position; you place yourself at the top, in the ruling position, and know what it is that you are ruling because of him. Very wierd indeed.

It is very difficult for you to have any sort of a friendship. He is restrained and aloof, where you are open and generous. The Scorpio was restrained too, you may remember, but you could sense the power inside him, and that made him a challenge to you. The Capricorn isn't like that at all; inside him there is no raging passion. He is a genuinely quiet person; he has a strong sense of duty, a strong work ethic, and a low level of fun. There isn't a great deal to talk about between you.

If you are lovers, it is because the Capricorn sees you as a necessary step in his career. He is going to be cautious and rather reserved in his response to you, and you are going to be disappointed, because you would have liked some warmth and enthusiasm in return for your own, and you won't get any. A Capricorn won't move unless it is within a carefully defined framework; phrases like 'spontaneous initiative' are not part of his vocabulary. You might get to like his sense of humour as the affair develops, though, provided that you like your humour on the dry side.

As business partners you could do very well. The first thing to do is to forget your personal differences, and all about how you both got to be as good as you are; let him provide you with a framework for your creativity, and just watch your effectiveness increase. Provide him with the rewards he needs to see for his efforts in return, and you will never look back.

As a marriage, you would have to run things similarly to the business arrangement above; you would also have to provide the warmth and emotional input that a home and family require to be a success, because the cold Capricorn can't do it.

*Leo-Aquarius*
This partnership is a union of opposites in a zodiacal sense, since the two signs are exactly opposite to each other in the circle of the signs, but it is by no means a tense or argumentative relationship. Provided you stay in the public eye, and both spend time in the company of lots of other people, then you will have no problems.

To put it succinctly, Leo is concerned with an individual—himself—and Aquarius is concerned with the group, where individuality is lost in the crowd.

You are both outgoing people, who project their energies outwards from themselves rather than collect the energy that others put out, and this gets the relationship off to a good start; outgoing people find the active response of those similar to them encouraging, because it reminds them of themselves, which is good.

Aquarius is concerned with ideas and conversation, like Gemini and Libra were; like them he suffers from being rather less able to make things happen than you are, although he is the best of the Air signs in this respect. More than anything else he is an observer; he loves to be present at everything that is going on, loves the buzz of conversation and the excitement of social life, but would rather not be deeply involved. This is one of the major differences between you: you need to be at the centre of things, to be fully involved and the central source of energy for the whole situation, where he likes to be on the edge looking on, enjoying the show. Don't think he's timid—he isn't; he's just not got his heart in it the way you have. He is another Saturnine type, like the Capricorn; his interest is there, but it is cool—he doesn't radiate warmth the way you do.

He sees you as somebody who is much at home at a party or in company as he is, and as interested in life as he is, but whose personal involvement with everything is strange and mystifying.

If I was as committed to my interests as that, he thinks, I could never turn my attention to anything new, and I would be unable to see what everybody else was doing. The whole point is to see what everybody else has to offer, and see how different people interact. The Leo needs to forget himself for a while.

It is a pity that so friendly a person can't really put himself into something one hundred per cent, you think. If he was as warm underneath as he is friendly on the top, and if he stopped drifting from one interest to another, he could be really likeable. The Aquarian needs to create something from his own efforts, by himself; then he'd see how good he can be.

You can't really understand each other, though you are made of much the same stuff. What you both enjoy immensely, though, is any kind of social function. You can become the heart of it, and the Aquarian can be the circulation, moving round from one person to another, keeping the flow of ideas and contact going, which he needs to do, as an Air sign. If the two of you have just each other's company for any length of time, you find him cold and withdrawn, and he finds you domineering; in a group both of you can shine, and enjoy each other to the full. This is the way to conduct the friendship if it is intended to stay as just that: in public, and in company.

Oddly enough, you both want to be different—but in different ways. You want to be the sort of person everybody wants to be, a sort of maximum intensity version of conventional virtues, but the Aquarian wants to be genuinely different, something else. In fact, he represents all the things which the members of a group don't have in common, where you are all the things they do. Funny, isn't it?

The juxtaposition of cool difference and warm conventionality becomes more marked if you are lovers, or are married. They work at a much lower emotional level than you, which makes them intriguing and aloof when they are lovers, but seemingly less caring as spouses. You will also find that their ideas on the content and management of a household are just as cool; your ideal of the welcoming hearth with a good table will take a bit of a bashing.

*Leo-Pisces*

This is a very special relationship. On the surface, it will look very bright and glossy, but you will know that it isn't like that underneath. On some levels, this relationship will exhaust you, and on others, it will give you the answers you have always been searching for. If you are quite happy with your active life, full of friends and things to do, then don't even bother with a Piscean acquaintance—but if you can't help feeling that it's all a bit empty, and that your soul needs nourishing as well as your body, then try this one. A Piscean is the Water into which the Leo Sun sinks at the end of its day, and from which it rises again. It's not the sort of relationship you can talk about over a quick half at lunchtime, though it *is* the sort you talk about by the end of the second bottle late in the evening. Nor are the alcoholic references merely decorations; Pisces has much to do with that substance and its effects.

Pisceans are either transparent, or chameleons; I'm not sure which. They can take on the attributes, and the life-style, of the person they are with at the time. When they are with you, they are Leonine, as Leonine as you are, and for that precise reason; you project yourself onto them, and they let you see exactly that. You are both creative, and you like that in each other. The difference is that you create your own world from the real world, and live in it; they create their own world from their imagination, and live in that *as if it were real*. Read the last sentence again—it's not easy. You are successful in the real world because you make it work for you, but they are in a different universe altogether. Life to you is simple and bold, like children's building bricks; life to them is all colours at once, impossibly complex and yet undefined, like the colours you see with your eyes shut.

You see Pisceans as frail and sensitive creatures, whose talent for playing roles to suit their surroundings amuses you; you see it as a parallel skill to your own ability to impose your personality on your surroundings. They seem to be from a different reality, and that interests you, because you would like to see what this other world is like.

They see you as hefty but essentially jolly individuals, whose genuine goodness of heart and optimism shows them how they can use the strength of their own personalities to make sense of the mass of impressions and emotions which seem to flood their minds. When life seems uncertain, you remind them of the goodness, the simplicity, and the fun of just being yourself.

Pisceans respond to everything; they find it difficult to focus on any one thing to the exclusion of everything else, and you can help them do this. At the same time, you will gain from having their heightened sensitivity at your disposal, especially if the two of you have some common interest that you can spend time on together. This is how your friendship actually works, and the more of this you do, the better you will appreciate each other.

As lovers, you will have an interesting time. Pisces will not have met your sheer creative power before, whereas it is the range and intensity of his emotional response that will surprise you. It is a union of the soul as well as the body—difficult to explain unless you've tried it and made it work.

Once you have formed a relationship that works on all levels, and there are a lot of them with a Pisces, you should have the basis of a lasting marriage. They offer you the long-term sastisfaction that you could never quite define, but knew you needed, and you offer them a reliable reference-point from which to build a life in the real world.

# Virgo

### Virgo-Aries
This relationship, like many of the five-signs-apart relationships, works very well on a professional or business level, but less well on a personal or emotional level.

You see the Arian as a source of boundless energy. He always seems to be full of life, and to be eager to get things done. He seems to be much more forceful than you are, and much stronger. He has an immediacy that astonishes you: as soon as the idea is in his head, he will want to put it into action, and will not waste any time in doing so.

What you find so appealing about him is his directness and

his practicality. You, too, are usually sure about what has to be done, and see no point in wasting any time about it. It is true that the Arian wants to get things done because the actual doing of them is what interests him, whereas you are driven by rather different motives, but your approaches are parallel for the most part.

You worry about things: Arians never seem to worry about anything. The fact that they are, or at least appear to be, untroubled by second thoughts, seems wonderful to you. They are never tired out by the struggle, as you often are. People never take offence at their actions, as they frequently do at yours. All in all, they are a reliable source of strength and effectiveness, which you feel you can draw on when your own are waning.

There are one or two things that concern you about Arians, though; they are not perfect, by any means. The most important is that they appear to act before they think, and they will frequently do things the wrong way (it seems to you) because that's the way that first occurred to them. It annoys you that somebody with such an endless capacity for direct and effective action can waste so much of his effort by misapplying it. What you will never understand is the immediacy of the Arian mind; it is not his own effectiveness that interests him, it is the fact that he lives for the moment.

From his point of view, you always seem to know a better way of doing things, and that's interesting to him. You also seem to lose the spirit of the moment by considering whether now is the right time to do it, and that infuriates him.

One of the areas of your concern he simply cannot grasp is the way you need to do things for everybody's benefit. The Arian is concerned primarily with himself, and he never gives a thought to other people. It's not that he doesn't care, it's just that his energies are all used in his own interests—which is why he is as effective as you see him to be.

He also finds you pessimistic. It simply never occurs to him that things won't turn out the way he wants them to; by comparison, your consideration of the possibilities of failure is deeply pessimistic.

As friends, you will get on very well if you have some project in hand. His energy and your methodical approach should ensure a satisfactory result for both of you. If you have nothing to do, you will turn your analytical mind to him personally, and then tempers will flare.

As lovers, you are not really very well matched. What he wants is to be energetic, forceful, and passionate; you feel uneasy responding to any of these in similar fashion, and would prefer a cooler appreciation.

As a marriage, Aries is a good partner if you want the marriage to function as a team effort with set objectives, such as furthering your careers, or building a house together. If you just want a quiet and intimate environment, he isn't the ideal match for you.

As business partners, you will get on very well indeed. Do things at his speed and your way. Make sure you get somebody else to take care of forward planning and overall management, though—these areas are weak in both of you!

*Virgo-Taurus*
This is one of the more comfortable relationships open to you. There is a feeling of understanding and mutual sympathy between any two signs of the same element. It is as though you both know that the other one has the same priorities, and prefers to work in a similar way to yourself. You know that what upsets or disturbs you is likely to do the same to them; what pleases you is likely to please them too.

The element of Earth is what these two signs have in common, so life between you is very much concerned with the real and material world. No wild ideas, or fancy phrases that sound like one thing and mean another; no over-sensitive or over-secretive emotional states; no tactless and tasteless wasteful projects, just common sense and practicality. And good food, as likely as not. Taureans feel better when there's food around, and you enjoy the processes of cooking and eating too, so the two of you are likely to amuse and please each other by eating together.

Over dinner, you will have time to analyse the Taurean, and

work out why it is that you like him so much. The first thing you like about him is how much he cares for the things around him. Material objects need the proper kind of upkeep if they are to stay serviceable and presentable, and the Taurean has an intuitive grasp of this. You find it so relaxing not to have to explain this to him all the time; it is one of the essential features of your view of life, and he shares it with you. The other thing you like about him is his great steadiness, and his preference to think before he acts. In time you will realize that he may not act, having thought, and this will annoy you, but at least he isn't hasty; one thing you really don't like is people who are faster to act than you are.

The Taurean is slow to see ways in which he could do things better, but once he is convinced he will gladly accept your recommendations. This is very satisfying for you: you can be of service and you can make constructive observations both at the same time, and you are likely to be thanked for it into the bargain. Perfect, from your point of view.

Only the Taurean's refusal to make major moves, even when it is really necessary, and his unwillingness to surrender anything which was once his, ever irritate you. You are probably more than willing to trade his obstinacy for the sense of security he offers you, and the reassurance that you are doing things for the right reasons after all.

The Taurean loves you because you seem to know what to do. He has a deep appreciation of the things he knows and loves, but he doesn't know what to *do* with them; you seem to know exactly what to do with them, and in your hands they seem to improve and grow more useful still. This is true, of course: Virgoans direct their energies towards the perfection of whatever they have around them as you know, but the Taurean sees this and is appreciative of it. He would dearly love to be able to do it for himself, but at the same time is more than willing to let you do it for him. He does see you as a bit of a meddler at times; there are some things that he is content to leave as they are, which you feel compelled to do something about, and he simply shakes his head and sighs. On balance, though, the fact that you can't sit still is a small price to pay for all the wonderful things you do for him, and he knows it.

A friendship formed between you will be fond and long-lasting. It's what friendships are about, really—two people with similar views. Should the friendship deepen so that you become lovers, you will find that the Taurean is a much more powerful force than you would perhaps like. But he is gentle with it, and fairly slow in his advances, so you will neither be overwhelmed nor taken by surprise, and you will be able to adapt your responses quickly enough for you both to find the affair rewarding.

As a marriage, this pairing looks very good indeed. If you want the marriage to be active and expansive you will have to goad the Taurean into moving a little faster; otherwise you will have a static, but secure and comfortable, existence. It really depends on what you want.

*Virgo-Gemini*
This can be a rather argumentative pairing, but in many ways you are better suited to each other than most other three-signs-apart combinations. The ruling planet of both Gemini and Virgo is Mercury, so you are motivated by the same kind of energy; neither of you has anything in your character which the other cannot understand or deal with. Whether you want to put up with the way the other person insists on doing things is another matter, but essentially there are no real problems here.

Probably the most relaxing thing about this relationship, and yet one which will seldom be recognized, let alone mentioned, is that you are both rather cool emotionally. Your energies are mental rather than emotional, and both of you find it difficult to deal with things that have any kind of sentimental content. You are not at all sentimental in your approach to things, either of you, and it never occurs to you to pay much attention to your feelings when they might interfere with your analysis of the situation. Having a partner who works the same way, who prefers life without embarrassing sentimental outbursts, as you both see them, is a great help in maintaining the relationship as far as you are concerned. Even better is that you don't have to say how pleased you are that things work this way.

Because both of you have enquiring minds, you take a great interest in the way the other operates. You, Virgo, have never had a great amount of time for words and ideas, and this is fascinating to you. You have always preferred the unmistakable feel of real physical objects because they tend not to change from one moment to the next; Gemini, however, seems to have developed a whole range of techniques to allow him to use and manipulate such intangible and formless things as phrases and concepts, and you really admire this. Note what it is that you are actually doing: you are not understanding the things he holds so dear, you are appreciating the techniques he uses to work with them. You can watch him at work with interest and admiration, but you wouldn't want to do it yourself.

Gemini sees things in a similar way. He has never been much good with the real and actual detail of things as they exist; he has always been more interested in the idea of their existence. There is nothing he likes better, though, than to have something new and intricate shown or explained to him; he may well not choose to remember it or use it, but he likes it none-the-less. He has great admiration for the skill and patience you display in your dealings with the real world. Patience and skill have never been high on his list of talents, but he admires them in others, especially when they are displayed and used in a rapid and analytical manner, as they are in you.

Gemini is immune to your critical observations; he sees them as interesting points in the form of verbal communication, nothing more. Both of you like working quickly, as is always the case with the energy of Mercury, and you are both far too busy to sit and brood over the possible meanings of what one or the other of you has just said.

You live in very different worlds, but you employ the same energy to make your separate ways in them, and this gives much opportunity for discussion. Too much, in fact, since Mercury looks after communication. Gemini loves arguing for its own sake, and you think you are nearly perfect! In fact, you both think that the other is very good at what he does, and wish you could do as well. A very verbal friendship, but a very loyal one.

As lovers, you are well suited; neither of you wants to be very deeply involved. You are likely to be upset if the Gemini takes other lovers besides you at the same time: he is only indulging his love of variety, after all. Friends will try to comfort you, but they won't understand: what upsets you is the implication (in your eyes) that there must be something wrong with you.

As a marriage, this can be very good. Remember that you will have to provide all the stability and security yourself, though. It certainly won't be dull—or quiet.

*Virgo-Cancer*

This is a very easy relationship to form; both of you are very careful not to upset the other, respectful of each other's needs and preferences, and above all, not aggressive or assertive in your demands.

Like the Taurean partnership, this one is easy because you have a lot in common, it isn't the element this time, it is the concept of caring. Both of you care for others as a way of displaying your energies, because what you really need is the response from those you care for rather than to perform the activity itself.

Ideally, you see the Cancerian as a confidante and advisor. Because you are ruled by Mercury, your emotional nature is rather shallow and brittle: sometimes you don't have the capacity to deal with the emotional content of a situation. You are unsure what to do with the powerful but irrational force of sentiment, and it worries you. The power you can understand, but the irrationality you can't. What do you do? The Cancerian will comfort you. Somehow all this irrational feeling can be absorbed, re-directed, taken care of, by the Cancerian without any fuss at all. It's the sort of thing that they are good at, and you are very grateful.

When things get out of hand, you would appreciate some help in getting things back in order, but not everybody can do it in the way you would like. You want your helper to accept things your way; you want them to support and reassure you, to tell you that you were on the right track; and you want them to be discreet. Making public the fact that you are letting things get out of order is something you'd rather not do. Where do these strong but pliable, supportive but silent people come from? From Cancer.

The difference between the signs is that they work on a one-to-one basis, and you work on a one-to-many basis. You feel that you would like to be of service to a great many people; they would like to care for you on your own.

They don't have your facility with things—they often get things wrong on a practical level. They don't always think things through, because they tend to act on their hunches rather than their deductions. They are often too shy to be really effective. None of these matter to you; you can remedy most of their shortcomings, by taking those roles from them. In doing so you can be of service, which is what you want.

They see you as much more confident versions of themselves, able to put into words and actions all the things that they feel to be right, but cannot define. It is very satisfying to have a friend who does this sort of thing for you; it makes your own life more exciting, in a similar way to the plain girl who goes with the pretty girl to the party. One is the extension of the other, and the other is the support for the first.

Cancerians have a desire to change things for the better (better from their point of view, of course), but they want very much to do it with consideration and care. Only Virgoans seem to understand this need to preserve and change at the same time, and the Cancerian appreciates this. You are the vehicle for his plans.

As a friendship, this pairing works very well. You will be intuitively considerate towards each other. It may not be as verbal a relationship as you would like; you enjoy speech in a way the Cancerian doesn't, and you may find them moody.

This will certainly be the case if you become lovers: the Cancerian works at a much deeper and closer emotional level than you, and you may well find that you are out of your depth. If you keep things light so that you are working at a level you feel confident with, the Cancerian will feel undercompensated and hurt.

As a marriage, you will have to take steps to ensure that you don't take things too seriously. You have both got a strong sense of duty, and you will both be concerned to do things right for the sake of the family's future; if both of you spend too much time worrying you will forget how to enjoy the present.

### Virgo-Leo

This is a remarkable relationship. It is almost as difficult a match as it is possible to imagine for you, but then again it may be just what you want. There are a lot of things about a Leo that you hate, because you can see them in yourself—and there are a lot of things that are secretly exactly how you would like to be. The Leo can't see much in you that he feels envious of, but there are things that you do which he can't, and he thinks that it wouldn't be too bad a thing if he were more like you in certain respects— on his own terms, of course. It may well be that you don't like each other much, but that you can't live without each other.

A Leo is not subtle. You can't overlook him in a crowd. He is big, he is boisterous, he makes himself the centre of attention, and he loves it. He acts as though he owned the place, and it never crosses his mind that he doesn't. Even less does it cross his mind that his actions might inconvenience others. In a way he is right, because most people are more than happy to do whatever the Leo's doing, anyway.

It is precisely this behaviour that you find so appealing and appalling at the same time. You are proud of the fact that you consider what is best for everybody before you do what pleases you, and you tell yourself off for occasionally being selfish like the Leo. Selfishness is your pet vice; you enjoy catching yourself out being selfish, and treat it as a much more serious failing than it really is. On the other hand, you would love to be as imperial as the Leo: surely, you reason, everybody would like to do things your way too, since it is obviously the best and most efficient way of doing them. Not so, unfortunately; most people like doing things a Leo's way simply because it is more fun.

Leos are warm and kind, and they don't really care when things go wrong. For this reason, you can use them as a safety net, and probably do. When you are tired of trying to set the world to rights the Leo will cheer you up like nobody else can.

They see you like bees, buzzing here and there, eternally busy doing good things like making honey and looking after everything for the benefit of the hive. To continue the parallel, they enjoy the honey like everybody else, but they are sometimes irritated by your presence. Don't get too close.

There is nothing that you can offer in a personal sense to a Leo. There is no companionship or support that they need which you can provide. What you do offer, though, is a means of expression. Leos are full of warmth and generosity, and they like to see it put to some use. They are much too lazy to do much with it for themselves (and why should they? They don't need its benefits), but they enjoy seeing how you can put it to good use. You are the technique that refines the fire of their energy, gives it direction and purpose. Between you, you can get a lot done, but you will have to remember that you are going to do most of the actual doing; the Leo will take a much less active role. Without him, you wouldn't be able to do any of it, though, and you would probably prefer to be left to do things in your own way, so you won't be too upset.

In any relationship between you, you will have to function like the Sun and Mercury; the little planet speeds round the mighty star sitting radiantly and majestically in the centre of things. He doesn't necessarily need you to orbit him but you get a great deal more, in the form of heat and light.

A friendship between you will only work if you place him at the centre and let him radiate; there is no other way to work it. If you attempt to criticize him or change him in any way, he will move away from you, and you will lose his warmth for ever.

Should you become lovers, it will be because he wants it so, not the other way round. He will be able to offer you more energy and heat than you have ever imagined, and the best thing you can do is lie there and enjoy it.

As a marriage, this can be good provided you stay within your roles. You must let him be master of the household, and you must not attempt to change the way he likes things done. Where he invites you to suggest ways of doing things, then do so, but not otherwise, or there will be arguments. If you don't think you can stand the life of an orbiting satellite, then don't try this one.

### Virgo-Virgo

Like all relationships of the same sign, this one magnifies the faults and shortcomings of the sign as well as the virtues. The big advantage is that you know what you're letting yourself in for—another version of yourself.

This particular pairing is the easiest of the same sign matches, because Mercury is so adaptable. There are no heavy planet energies to cause imbalance, and no overabundance of emotion or sentiment to throw things out of control. Moreover, both of you pride yourselves on being reasonable and rational, so a flexible understanding or compromise of your requirements is going to be that much easier to achieve.

You have a great deal to teach each other. You are both proud of how much you know about the correct way to do things, and stress the importance of proper learning; it is unlikely that you will have had exactly identical experiences in life, and so you can teach each other what you have learnt. You will appreciate learning from another Virgo—they see things in the right way, according to you, making sure that no detail is missed out, and covering all the possibilities.

You may not appreciate their criticisms of your own ways of doing things, but you will have great fun arguing over them. Virgoans are a strange mix—unless something is theoretically impeccable, you don't want to know about it, but it has to be workable and practical as well.

There is a danger that a long-term relationship between you could become smug, self-satisfied, and rather prim. You will soon iron out all your minor differences, and then spend your days in a spotlessly clean, absolutely neat environment congratulating yourselves on how perfect you are. The way out of this is to open yourselves out so that others can enjoy your skills and expertise; on a simple level, throwing a lot of dinner parties, or at a higher level running some kind of charity or public service.

The early stages of a relationship between you will be the most enjoyable, and the easiest. Mercury is always at its best with something new—the problems come when familiarity sets in. You are both eager to please in a practical and everyday way, and you are quick to respond to new things. If you have different interests and pastimes when you meet, each will soon convert the other to his own. There is a joy both in learning a new skill, and in teaching somebody else to enjoy it; both of these give a Virgoan satisfaction. On a light and practical level, then, this friendship is easy to manage and enjoyable.

As lovers, the relationship should continue to give you what you want. It is very difficult for a non-Virgo to understand this aspect of a Virgo's life, since the Virgo most emphatically is not in it to express his emotions. More important is the need to use one's body well. You will understand each other's needs, and help meet them.

A business partnership between you would be good if both acted in an advisory capacity. Neither of you have enough of a sense of organization to take full responsibility for things, nor sufficient personal drive to make things happen for yourselves without outside help.

As a marriage, this partnership is fine provided that it looks outwards and shares its achievements with friends and relatives. Left to its own devices, a Virgo-Virgo marriage becomes cold and rather unyielding, with needless worry being more likely than laughter. Linking it into a wider community is almost essential for its health.

*Virgo-Libra*
The trouble with people one sign from your own is that they often seem not to recognize your efforts as being at all important. The things that really matter to you, that you give your full attention to, simply do not seem to feature in their lives. There is a good reason for this, of course; in terms of the

sequence of the signs, they are past all that. Nevertheless, it makes for a powerful irritant, especially when, as in your case, you want people to recognize all the things you are doing on their behalf.

Librans are almost as different from you as you could imagine; their minds work in a very different way. Where you analyse things to see how they work, trying to master the intricacies of everything so that you can use it better, they simply pick the bits that they like. It is not at all important to a Libran to know how his car works; if it goes, it's comfortable, and he likes the colour, that will do.

It never occurs to a Libran to dig beneath the surface of anything, or to try and understand anything fully. The only things he is interested in are the ones which appeal to him personally—if there is no appeal, then he has no time for it. There is a certain surface judgement in a Libran, from your point of view; a thing has to look good rather than actually be good. To be fair, that's not quite how a Libran works, but it's how you see it, and that's what matters here.

Librans are lazy. Bone idle, in fact. They inhabit a world of people and friendships rather than your round of work and duties, and this makes them do nothing all day in your eyes. Why should they, if duty isn't rewarding to them? Anyway, they are busy doing other things.

Every time you find something out of order or in need of correction, they find two things with an affinity that can work better together. Every time you upset somebody, they reassure and sooth.What Librans actually do is bring people together, and promote friendships. It's not something you can do—your job lies with organizations and objects rather than people. They look outwards where you look inwards; you are aiming for individual perfection, and they want individuals to become friends. It's another step on in the process.

You want to be of service to the community, but there wouldn't be any community to serve if Libran energy didn't create it. *That's* what they do for you.

What do you do for them? Not much, on the surface. They see

you as the dull boy who is all work and no play, and your constant frown of concern and mild irritation at the world that besets you doesn't help them at all. They like to be relaxed, surrounded by pleasant things and pleasant people. They like to take things at a leisurely pace, and most importantly to enjoy themselves while they do it. There are times, however, when they can't cope. There are too many obstacles requiring serious effort, and they can't be nice to everybody at once. The smiles fade. At these times, you are a support to them; you can help them tackle their problems in the same way that you do—one bit at a time. Your system of repeated small-scale victories leading to overall triumph is just what they need, and that's what you do for them.

As a friendship, this pairing isn't likely to last unless it has strong bonds at a deeper level. Your surface attitudes are entirely different, and you are unlikely to find each other good company unless other factors in your charts lend their energies that way.

As lovers, you will need a sense of humour. Librans are great romantics, and you see such stuff as sloppy nonsense. Or so you say: it is more likely to be an unwillingness to work with something as undefined as sentiment, because Mercury gives you no facility there. None-the-less, it is the way the Libran works, so you will have to try to accommodate each other somehow.

Marriage? This pairing makes a good team if either of you is at all ambitious, because you can support each other very well. It isn't really a love-match, though. If you want a hard-working, achieving marriage, then fine; if not, look elsewhere.

### Virgo-Scorpio

This is probably the easiest relationship of the twelve for you to form and maintain, but it isn't really much to do with hearts and flowers. When I say 'easy relationship' I mean that the planetary energies flow easily and strongly together, but the direction that they take has to do with the nature of those energies rather than the mere fact that they are united.

If the two of you ever decide to go into business, run a detective agency! Let me explain. Scorpios are strong and powerful people whose strength is not so much in their muscles as in their motivation. They need to find out exactly what's going on, think through all the possibilities, and stay in control of all of them. They are absolutely determined that everything will actually take place the way they say it will and under their control, and that way there will be no mistakes.

It all sounds good to you, I know. This is exactly the sort of person you have always appreciated and admired, and their way of working sounds like what you have been saying all along. What's more, they are brilliantly effective. Where's the catch?

The catch is a small one, and a subtle one, as befits Scorpios; it may not bother you a great deal, either. It is this: the more you do for them, the more they'll let you. Make no mistake—the Virgo works for others besides himself, but the Scorpio just works for himself.

They work with a different material from you, and one with which you are unfamiliar. You work all the time with physical, measurable things: making something out of a chunk of raw material, doing a job and getting paid for it, being helpful in a practical way and being thanked for it, and looking after the physical welfare of things, whether servicing your bicycle or giving your family healthy and nourishing food.

Scorpios don't work with any of these things. They work with the unseen powers that lie over and above all our everyday business: motives like loyalty and ambition, love and enmity, pride and fear. These motives are all products of emotional energy, and it is this that the Scorpio collects and maintains must as surely as you manipulate and work the material things you like so much.

Since you are so unfamiliar with the world of emotions, you admire his facility with them, and are quite content to leave him to it, though a little apprehensive about his motives towards you. Relax—as long as you are useful to him, the Scorpio will not abuse you, and you are very useful indeed.

Scorpios need somebody who can actually get things done for them, whose skills are firmly based in the real and tangible world. They also need this person to have the same high standards as themselves, and this is precisely where you come in. You are just the sort of friend a Scorpio is looking for: careful, controlled, dutiful, eager to please, and with high standards of performance and finish. What's more, you are no threat to him where his real concerns lie; that is, in the emotional control of his own life.

It has all the makings of a great friendship: you love finding out about things, and going into the causes and origins of things in great depth. You seem to complement each other perfectly— the Scorpio does the digging, you do the sifting, and between you, you find things. From the outside, your conspiratorial glee is rather offputting, and you are an unapproachable couple, seemingly completely occupied in yourselves and laughing at private jokes. From the inside, you are having a great time.

When the friendship grows into an affair, you must be prepared to be overwhelmed. This is the Scorpio's home territory, and you will not have met anything so intense before. The physical strength is similar to the Arian's, but the emotional strength is truly massive: you will be blown flat like a reed in a hurricane.

As a marriage, it will be fun at first, but their unrelenting emotional grip, occasionally becoming obsessive jealousy, may be too much for you to deal with.

## Virgo-Sagittarius

The last one was powerful, and so is this, but the power has mutated into speed; what this relationship is, more than anything else, is fast. In a way, it's just what you want. You are curious, and want to find things out; Sagittarius knows it all already. You want to be appreciated for what you do: Sagittarius is a born winner. You want to be able to use what you know to get results, and he already does that. You don't want anything too emotionally demanding, and Sagittarius makes no emotional demands. It sounds too good to be true, but can you stand the pace?

Sagittarians have a much better view of you than you do of them, but there again they have a fairly good view of everybody;

they are so irrepressibly confident that it unnerves you.

You understand each other pretty well. Like you, they are driven by the desire to change things from their existing state by their own efforts, and make something better and different from it all. The difference between you is that they are the originators of the ideas, and you are the means of putting them into effect. They think about changing things, and you worry about how you're going to manage it. Of course, the fact that they are involved in things at a much earlier stage of the process means that they see everything on a large scale, and everything seems possible to them; problems never cloud their vision. You have your nose much closer to the ground, making sure that the problems that arise are solved in an effective and proper fashion; you have lost sight of the original vision, and you see things on a smaller scale.

As a consequence of all this, their impractical idealism makes you angry from time to time. They never see that they will need so much time, so much money, and this and that before their wild schemes can possibly come to fruition. What you don't see, unless you are told, as you are being now, is that fruition isn't the point: the idea is the point. The idea is exciting, because it has possibilities for the imagination to play with. Once you make it real, all the fun's gone out of it. Sagittarians play in the realm of the creative imagination, and you always forget that. On the other hand, they can't understand why you can't see the whole project in a flash in your mind's eye, as they can; or why you only seem to get interested when the project's nearly finished (it's that perfection idea that you have, isn't it?). You Virgoans play in the real world at an individual component level, and Sagittarians always forget that.

Although it sounds as though you have an insuperable communications gap, it is not in fact so; you recognize that you are aiming for the same thing in different ways, and this gives you a sort of companionship. As a result, you indulge each other's excesses good-humouredly, with you muttering 'dreaming again' under your breath as you listen patiently to the latest wild idea, while they dismiss your practical objections with 'details, mere details'. One area where you will clash is in that of standards of work; Sagittarius would rather you did things quickly, while the passion of the moment is still there, and is prepared to overlook small inconsistencies, but you must attend to every little thing, and this, naturally, takes time.

As lovers, you are in for an interesting time. Sagittarius has a childlike eagerness which you will find very attractive, but he is not the slightest bit constant, or even consistent; you will have to be prepared for some ups and downs. He is at least spontaneous and sincere in his affections, and you will appreciate that.

As a marriage, this is by no means bad. He has the expansiveness, the optimism, and the energy; you can help his ideas become realities, to the benefit of both of you. You will have to be careful that his bouncy and playful manner doesn't exasperate you: try not to take things too seriously!

*Virgo-Capricorn*
With this relationship you can find yourself writ large. All your fondest ideas seem to be embodied in the person of the Capricorn. They seem, somehow, to be a fully-developed version of yourself, with all your own promise brought forth into glorious fruit. That's how you see it, anyway: Capricorns are not usually on the receiving end of such an enthusiastic press from the rest of the zodiac.

You see them this way because they are an Earth sign, like yourself. That means that they are working in essentially the same areas as yourself. Like you, they only appreciate things which are good and firm; they take reassurance from the actual presence of things. They can value themselves by reference to a physical measure, money. Emotions and words are not theirs, nor half-thought-out projects and whimsical fantasies. No, Capricorn likes things firm. If he can feel it, weigh it, or buy it, it is real to him, and not otherwise.

You can understand this. It is familiar to you, and you don't have to make any allowances for the way he thinks, because it's the way you think, too. When you are so in tune with somebody, attraction is instant, and friendship is easily brought into being.

The major difference between you is that he is at a different phase of the element Earth from you. Where you spend your time working on things to improve them, using your mind to analyse and probe, trying to find the best way of doing anything, he has it made. The achievement of the finished item is his. What you are after is the technique for improvement; what he is after is the recognition for his achievement.

You are about to protest that you would like some recognition for your efforts as well, and no doubt you would; but it is not your prime aim. If you could get the recognition without earning it, you would feel guilty, but the Capricorn wouldn't. You need to feel that you know how to do something properly before you take the applause; he simply needs to be at the top.

If you think for a minute, you can see the nature of the attraction between you. You will spend a lifetime trying to reach your own standards of perfection, and never reaching a stage where you think that you deserve the number one position. You would like a foretaste of what that position's all about, though, and in knowing a Capricorn you can have it.

From his point of view, you are something he can believe in. His view of the world states that everything is ordered and structured, and there is a hierarchy of things. Everything has its place in the structure, and everything inside that structure is doing its job in the proper way. His position in the structure is, of course, at the top. When he sees you at work, *examining and repairing the structure of things*, then he is reassured. All is well; his position is secure. If that sounded unintelligible, try it this way: imagine the world as a human pyramid, like an anthill, or a beehive. Virgos are workers, Capricorns the queen bee.

As a friendship, this one will run and run. You see eye to eye o almost everything. You both have a strong sense of duty, and of what has to be done, and you both like working hard. You are both 'no-nonsense' types, with a dry sense of humour. You have similar tastes—although for different reasons. You are both likely to like expensive and well-made things, the Capricorn because they are status symbols, communicating his position as number one, and you because of the care and skill that has gone into their manufacture. Take a Mercedes car as an example.

As lovers, you could do worse. It all depends on whether you come up to each other's expectations, since you are a perfectionist, and Capricorn only wants the best. Emotionally the Capricorn is rather cold, but that won't worry you, since Mercury is uncomfortable in scenes of either great passion or sentiment. A respectful affair, then, but satisfying to the people concerned.

As a marriage, or for business, you could hardly do better. Both of you are determined to improve yourselves, and through his determination and your application you will work wonders.

*Virgo-Aquarius*
On paper this one shouldn't work, but it does. One of the signs is oddly attractive, the other is attractively odd; work out for yourselves which is which. The attraction is probably that you are both unattractive to others; not unattractive in a visual sense, but in that you prefer situations where there is a certain emotional distance between the people involved. This distance helps you form an opinion of the other people present without feeling too tied to them. Aquarians are fond of the 'cool appraisal' method, too, and you probably recognize it in them. The pair of you probably bring it out in each other, since one of the features of any partnership is that what you have in common gets emphasized.

Aquarians, like Librans and Geminis, work in a world of speech and relationships, where people are far more important than things. That said, Aquarians are the least changeable of the three, which makes them function at about the same level of intensity as you. You are the most changeable of the Earth signs, which are usually very solid and heavy; when you and Aquarius meet you are going to be more or less at each other's level.

Aquarians like to be a face in a crowd. They are not necessarily shy, but they don't really have the force of personality required to hold the stage on their own, and they are much better in a group. Indeed, they really shine in company, becoming in some strange way the representative of the group without being part of it. They have tremendous organizational talents, in a way that you don't; not only can they see the larger picture that you have difficulty with, they see it in terms of people, which you almost never do.

If you are going to try to analyse and define an Aquarian, so that you can get to know him better, you are in for a hard time; they like to keep themselves at a little distance from everybody, so that they stand apart from the crowd. Not superior or inferior, just different, and a little distant. You will find that there isn't really a lot for you to get hold of, for you to say *that's* what makes him different. Your inability to pinpoint exactly how this strange person works will either enrage or captivate you. If he enrages you, you will obviously break off the relationship, but it is far more likely that you will rise to the challenge offered.

They will have been forming their own opinions about you while you have been busy. They see you as a friendly person with an inquisitive mind. Later on they will realize what a talent you have for seeing how things work, and how to get the best out of everything, and they will see that as an admirable thing. Like you, they are concerned to get the best out of things, but what they want to get the best out of is people, not objects. They keep thinking what a pity it is that you don't have their sense of organization and that they don't have your eye for detail or your analytical powers. They are pleased to find that you like to work in, or at least for, a group of people and not just for yourself; they are the same.

Neither of you are initiators; you both prefer to do something with what you've already got. Neither of you are comfortable being directly and personally involved with another person, but you both like company. Both of you put great store by careful appraisal. Outside that you are wildly different, but there's a fair body of similarity of approach, if not of motivation, and it may be enough to make you seek out each other's company.

As friends, you will talk non-stop, but in a rather clinical and scientific way, about everybody else you know. You seem to be on each other's wavelength, at least on the surface.

You will need a bit of pushing to become lovers, because you are both rather cool emotionally, and the enjoyment you get from talking to each other doesn't get any better for you becoming involved sexually. Mind you, if you wanted to explore this side of yourself with somebody of similar persuasion, who was unlikely to offer you more than you could comfortably deal with emotionally, and who would maintain the 'strictly experimental' pretence needed for your peace of mind, then the Aquarian would make a good partner. You would both find it greatly amusing, and that's half the pleasure.

For marriage, or business, the only obstacle would be your lack of involvement. Although you both like things cool, the bonds could do with being a little stronger if the union is to last a long time. Otherwise, you become two individuals again.

*Virgo-Pisces*
Relationships between opposite signs are never going to be as easy as some of the other pairings, obviously, but your planet, Mercury, is particularly unhappy in the waters of Pisces; this is, therefore, the most difficult of all the opposite-sign pairings. What's more, it's unbalanced: it's easier (slightly) for the Piscean to get on with you than for you to get on with him.

What you have in common is the idea of giving to others. Both of you are very good at that, and many Pisceans make their careers in the caring professions, such as medicine. What astounds you, at least until you are used to it, is that the Piscean gives to others by taking from them. He soaks up their worries, fears, and anger. He lets them unburden their guilt, share their secrets, voice their frustrations. All of these go into the Piscean, and he dissipates them.

It's difficult for you to cope with this as an idea. If everybody approached you on an intimate level you would find it very difficult to make anything useful out of it all. Perhaps the Piscean is the same with fixed procedures, rules and regulations. Had you thought of that?

Pisceans can thrive on a diet of other people's emotions. Indeed, they can't live without it. A Piscean lives in a world formed from his imagination's response to what he hears or sees, and if he doesn't like it, he moves it around a bit until it suits.

Imagine living on a giant rubbish heap, made from everybody else's belongings all piled up. Never mind the fact that you would find it unbearably scruffy; we're on about the opposite sign here, so you'd expect that, wouldn't you? Now imagine picking out a few choice items to use, and if they weren't what you wanted, or you got tired of them, you could throw them back on the pile, and choose some more. Now forget the idea of doing it with real pieces of hardware, and imagine doing it with emotions and feelings. That's Pisces.

Impossible though it must be to believe, you are both involved in the same process, and that is changing things through your own efforts to make something better. You simply use different materials, that's all. Go back a few pages and read the Virgo-Sagittarius section again. You remember how they are the original idea for something new, and you are the means of making it happen? Pisces is where it gets recycled after people have used and loved it, and worn it out.

Pisceans like you more than you would think: they are as definite as you are, and as precise, but it's all in the mind, not in reality. And, from time to time, they change their mind. You are quite certain all along about which way you are going to do things, and what has to be done, and it is all in the real world of rules and regulations, which don't change. Pisceans admire that.

As friends, you look miles apart, but you should appreciate what the other is doing, and that will lead to understanding and cooperation. Besides, the Piscean will adopt Virgoan traits when in your company, so you won't have to compromise your principles!

As lovers, you will have to be patient. You are much stronger-minded than they are, and you could become demanding; you will have to allow their sensitivity to function, and not crush it with your insistence on common sense. You could both learn a great deal.

Give them a flexible but practical framework, don't restrict their imagination, and don't tidy up after them to an obsessive extent; you could have an unusual and rewarding marriage.

# Libra

*Libra-Aries*

This partnership is formed from two people representing different sides of the zodiac, but having said that, there is a lot more going for it than you might think. People from different sides of the zodiac are not entirely opposite in their motivations, as a quick glance at the zodiac circle will remind you; you are both Cardinal signs, for a start, and you are both outgoing rather than collecting.

This means that you are both eager to make something of the relationship. Both of you approach things by giving your energy to them rather than seeing what is given to you, and both of you are of the firm opinion that your own efforts are sufficient to make the situation develop in a way satisfactory to you. Given that kind of wilingness and capacity for input on both sides, the relationship can hardly fail to work; whatever else happens to you, it cannot be said that the partnership suffers from lack of effort from either partner.

What will strike you most about the Arian is his determination and energy. He seems almost to be on fire, so keen is he to get things moving. He is involved, too, in a way that you are not; everything that he takes on is a thing of great importance to him, and it matters to him that he gets something out of it. It may seem to you that he is too intense, that his whole approach is much too urgent, and that he will surely wear himself out if he continues to live at such a pace. You are wrong on two counts: firstly, Mars drives him at that rate all the time, and gives him the strength to live at that speed, so there is no danger of him wearing himself out; and secondly, he is selective in what he does. Things that are of no interest to him he ignores completely, and things that do interest him he attacks with force and enthusiasm.

He is his own man: he does things purely to satisfy himself, without thought for others. This does not make him selfish—he simply exists through his own actions, for himself. You are at your best when in a relationship, because the relationship is what your planet moves you towards; his planet moves him towards individual and personal action. He's not really interested in what anybody else does; what matters to him is what *he* does. He will see you as somebody interesting and variable; the fact that, as an Air sign, you seem to be in changing circumstances the whole time, will appeal to him. He needs new challenges to take his interest and test his abilities; he is not really capable of sitting still. He also has no time for people who are not essentially optimists, because he would rather be up and doing than sitting and worrying. He sees you as light, changeable, and optimistic, and will be happy to stay in your company.

You find him irresistible; his confidence, outgoingness, and capacity for achievement attract you at once. Aries' planet, Mars, is associated with the metal, iron; Venus' energies are, as we have noted before, like those of a magnet. The resounding clonk as the two of you meet will be heard for miles. Once you've got him stuck to you, you'll both be completely uninterested in anyone else. That isn't a bad thing; a magnet's keeper not only preserves and maintains the magnetism, but stops the magnet making a nuisance of itself around the toolbox.

It could take as much as five minutes before the two of you will consider a sexual relationship; Arians aren't exactly romantic, but they are definitely passionate, and you will gladly settle for that.

As a marriage, this one could last. The inner secret of it is that the Arian would rather be busy and active than baring his soul, and you get more out of the relationship itself than from the person, especially if that person expects very close personal involvement. It is the very slight emotional aloofness that you both have which keeps the balance perfect. Odd, isn't it?

As a business relationship, there are no problems if you both decide to go in the Aries' direction, but let the Libran do the talking along the way.

## Libra-Taurus

This is a better relationship than it looks. In every way you are different—Cardinal and Fixed, Air and Earth, outgoing and collecting—but you have the same guiding planet, Venus. It's not a situation that happens very often, and if you want sympathy talk to your Arian friends about their Scorpio friends, because Aries and Scorpio are in the same situation.

What it boils down to is that you are both using the same energy, but using it in different directions and for a different purpose. What you can both say is 'I can see what you're doing, but I wouldn't do it that way if I were you'. It would be nice if you could both say in addition, 'I must try it your way, because it looks quite interesting', but with people being what they are, you are more likely to find yourself saying 'Why don't you do it my way? It's much better like that'.

What is it that the Taurean is trying to do? Like you, he is using Venus and its power to attract. What he is attracting are objects that he can value and cherish as his own. Sometimes he will attract people, too, but the idea is still to keep, value and cherish property. All of the magnetism is used to pull inwards, you see. As more and more things become part of the collection, the Taurean becomes more and more unwilling to make any changes, and less and less interested in anything new; what he is determined to do most of all is to hang on to everything he has, and to let none of it go.

You see him as a stick-in-the-mud, basically. You appreciate his desire to attract beautiful and satisfying things in himself, because you do the same; but then, you think, you are actually more concerned to create beautiful things, and what he wants to do is collect them. You would like to share everything you have with everybody, so that everybody gets a chance to enjoy all that you have done, but the Taurean would like it all to himself, and may not want to share any of it with anybody.

It is a very biased view, of course, and there are many good things about Taureans too: their genuine kindness to those close to them, and their steady, reliable presence in an emergency, to name but two. But despite all that, it is the differences that will be more apparent to you than the similarities. Among these you will notice particularly how personally they seem to take everything; a whimsical jibe becomes a deep wound, and they become defensive. You can restore their trust, of course, because you're good at it, but why they should be so touchy mystifies you.

They see you as ineffective and indecisive. They watch you changing your opinions, as is your habit, and mutter to themselves that others may not agree with the way they do things but at least they know where they stand, and they are consistent if nothing else. They see your obvious talent for colour and shape on display in your home and in the way you dress, and they shake their heads in despair; all that talent running to waste instead of being used to make something lasting, solid, and valuable, they think to themselves. Not that they would actually say these things, of course; Taureans think a lot to themselves, and they keep much of what they feel inside themselves; they have a capacity for endurance and putting up with discomfort which you could never understand.

This is a friendship which will centre around the things of beauty and value you both love; if this interest is maintained, the friendship will continue, and could make a good business partnership, but your personal requirements are too far apart to make much more of it on an intimate level. As lovers, one of you will have the double bass part and the other the flute's line; you're unlikely to be playing the same tune at the same time, and may not even be on the same page of the score! Marriage? Yes if the Libran has stability and material comforts high on his list of needs; otherwise, no.

## Libra-Gemini

This is one of your easier relationships. Two people from the same element, in this case Air, share a similar approach to life in general. Somehow they understand your motives without you having to explain yourself, and without you having to adjust your behaviour to compensate for their preferences and fixed ways of doing things.

Somehow a sign which is ahead of you in the circle is more exciting to be with than one behind you. In this case the Gemini finds you more appealing than you find him, but the difference isn't much. You are likely to be attracted to each other on sight anyway, and you will have lots to talk about. This is an instantaneous, perhaps even spontaneous, friendship.

Perhaps that's the level on which to keep it. What makes this relationship is the mingling of the energies of Venus and Mercury, and they are essentially light and personable planets. The weighty and serious matters usually assigned to Jupiter and Saturn are not here, nor the force of Mars, nor the vital and life-giving energies of the Sun and Moon; just bright mentality, wit, conversation, good times, small pleasures, and things like that. All in all, a brilliant recipe for a lively and hugely enjoyable friendship.

What isn't in the recipe is anything at all deep or powerfully emotional. This relationship is in the mind, not the soul. It is a relationship for sunny days and lively parties, not for long nights and heavy responsibilities. If you want the sort of partnership where you examine your motives deeply, where your innermost needs and fears are constantly in play, where obsession, worry, and tortured passion are the usual emotions, then this isn't it. Even if those things are in you, and need expression, then this relationship won't express them for you, it will skate over them. Mercury and Venus really can't handle things so big and ponderous; they concentrate instead on the lighter side of things, bringing a lively sparkle to all social activity, and making sure everybody enjoys themselves in an entertaining way.

'Entertaining'; that's exactly the word for it. Even if you deepen the friendship into a sexual one, it will still be entertaining. You will find yourselves laughing and talking as you make love, and you will have a very mobile and playful physical relationship—not at all the heavy and ponderous collisions that other combinations of signs go in for.

What you have done by choosing this relationship is to deliberately force the two lighter planets together; because of that, you will find that the relationship itself attracts you into many more social contacts than you would otherwise have had, and your circle of friends will grow and grow; at the same time, you force yourselves to deal with everything in a light-hearted and rather shallow way—it is the nature of this relationship.

How do you see each other? You see him as a dazzling wit with a silver tongue, and he sees you as charm itself. It's as easy as that.

As business partners you will do well provided your business itself can be handled in a light and fast-moving way, involving many social contacts; if it can't, then you will lack the necessary weight to make a success of it. Marriage will be similar: you will have plenty to talk about, and a very enjoyable time, but deep and heavy differences between you may not find adequate expression, and the partnership may not therefore grow very strong roots, despite its busy growth on the surface.

### Libra-Cancer

Go gently if you want this one to work. It's not impossible, but it isn't as easy as it looks, either. Once trust has been established you will have a very strong relationship indeed, as is the case with all the relationships where your signs share quality but not polarity (here you are both Cardinal, but one is outgoing and the other collecting).

You would love to make friends with the soft and fragile Cancerian; your Venusian energies would go so well with his delicate Lunar ones. The trouble is that the Cancerian is afraid that you are some kind of a threat, or that you are not serious; either way he needs time to get used to you before he makes a firm response. If you push too hard he will clam up; if you lose interest and go away, he will know that you weren't serious, and will not take you seriously in future, either. Be patient, gentle, and reassuring if you want to make a lasting relationship here.

Cancer is concerned with the emotional content of everything. You like to be in a situation where the feeling is the most important thing, or, to be a little more precise, the atmosphere; they are on the receiving end of it all, and are concerned with the way the atmosphere of a place makes them feel. Do you see the difference? A place can have a bright atmosphere, or a gloomy one; you stay if you like it, leave if you don't. You are self-sustaining, and can cheer yourself up if necessary; it's part of being an Air sign. Cancer is different; it absorbs the atmosphere of the place it is in, and develops an emotional response to it. These emotions are the normal way for Water signs to express themselves, just as speech and social contact is the normal way for you. You will see at once that a Cancer is going to be much more vulnerable to external influences than you are, and is not going to be as optimistic as you are for much of the time.

They know this too. They have developed a tough exterior to prevent themselves being damaged by contact with people whose intentions are less than kind, and it is in their own interest to maintain this, at least until they have got to know you a little. When they have accepted you, you will be thrilled to discover how sensitive and subtle a Cancerian can be. They are intensely personal, too, but not in the brash way of the Arian; they take great care of themselves, in a gentle and sustaining way that your Venusian sensibilities will admire very much. They take care of those they love, too; you will be able to enjoy the wonderful feeling of having somebody be as nice to you as you would like to appear to them. Above all, Cancerians are so soft, and so genuine, that you will feel quite ashamed of the little bit of Airy aloofness that stops you giving yourself completely to another.

They see you as a more open version of themselves. Because you are graceful and refined in manner, and perhaps a little ineffective in action, they see you as having no harshness or cruelty in you, and therefore warm towards you at once. They sense a similarity between your need to be with other people, and your willingness to do what others want, and their need to care for other people. They see your emphasis on relating as an initial stage in the process which leads to their maternal and nurturing instincts; they are reassured by the fact that your prime interest seems to lie in the other person rather than yourself. As you will realize, they are viewing the reality of the situation sideways on, but they like what they see nonetheless. The only thing which makes them shiver is the openness of your way of life; it all seems too risky for them, but they are more than ready to let you get on with it, and will be ready, too, to pick up the pieces when mishaps occur.

As a friendship, this one is happy but quiet and reflective: it smiles rather than laughs. Should the friendship develop into a sexual relationship, it will be very soft, very loving, and as romantic as you want to make it; it will lack any hard qualities, though, and if you fancy something of a challenge this isn't it. It will also become set in its ways after a while: Cancerians gain strength and reassurance from familiarity and regularity.

As a marriage, like most of the three-signs-apart matches, it will be strong but a little stormy. You both recognize that the other has qualities you would like, but seems to concentrate them in a way which is at odds with the way you would like them. The same goes for a business partnership, too.

### Libra-Leo

Almost the easiest relationship you will ever fall into (only Sagittarius is easier), provided that you can make one simple allowance. Just one.

It's ever so simple: Leo is the boss. Leos conduct life on that principle, so you will have to learn it sooner or later, and to have it in mind right from the word go saves a lot of heartache later on.

The reason is simple, and makes an easy mental picture to remember: Leo is governed by the Sun, and you are governed by Venus. The Sun stays where it is, and Venus orbits round it, shining brightly as it goes because it reflects the sunlight. Note that last phrase—the Leo is the light source.

Not too rosy a picture, but the reality is in fact hugely enjoyable. Leos are enormous optimists, and the thing they like doing best is showing off and having a good time. You are not to tell them this, of course: they prefer to see themselves as magnanimous and good-hearted philanthropists. Whatever the reality, a relationship between you will be a very warm and enjoyable thing, and well worth embarking upon should a Leo come your way. Like Aries, the Leo pushes out energy in a steady stream. He wants to make things happen the way he likes them, and he is more than ready to put in the necessary effort to achieve this. If a relationship with you is what takes his interest, then his full radiance will be turned upon you, and you will certainly feel the warmth. Lavish entertaining, beautiful presents, and all sorts of good times together will start to fill your life and you won't have to do a thing in return except appreciate his generosity. As long as the Leo is appreciated for what he does, he will continue to do it. There will be some special quality in you that he particularly admires, and it will be this that he is paying court to; he would not have chosen you if you were not, in his opinion, the most wonderfully talented person in the matter of whatever it is (Your looks? Your taste? Your grace of movement?) that he has ever met.

Isn't it a fantastic process? Mutual ego-massage, convincing each other that you are both absolutely wonderful. It is all to do with the infectious warmth and true generosity of spirit that the Leo displays: he radiates it outwards, and it reflects off everybody near him, as we noted in the astronomical parallel earlier.

You see him as a wonderful friend, and a creator of friends; you would love to be the way he is. Everybody likes him, and that is the centre of it: your planet, Venus, has much to do with the business of liking, and you feel attracted to somebody who is universally liked. Somehow nothing gets him down for long; he can always find something exciting to do, or rustle up a few friends who will come round and start a party going. A world of warmth, optimism, friendship and companionability: it sounds like everything you've ever wanted.

He sees you as Jack to his King: light, likable, and companionable, but not having anything of his regal might and power.

Are there any pitfalls? Not many: the main one is lack of movement. As an Air sign, you need variety, and movement; staying in the same place for too long does you no good. Leo is a Fixed sign, and that means that he likes to stay with an existing situation once he's got it to work the way he wants it to. You could end up finding the endless hilarity with the same old friends just a touch boring as you all grow older and fatter together. Leo won't be moved unless he says so: he is the centre, and people go round him. He won't have it any other way.

As a friendship, this one is of the best. As lovers, you may find him a bit heavy and a slow mover, but he is warm and generous, which is worth something. As a permanent relationship of any kind, this one has a lot going for it. The only thing for you to decide is whether you will trade lack of movement in return for optimism, warmth, and guaranteed success.

### Libra-Virgo

You would be forgiven for thinking that your Venusian energies enabled you to form a reasonably enjoyable relationship with absolutely anyone. It may be so, but an encounter with a really thoroughgoing Virgo will make you wonder. Of all the possible combinations of Sun signs, this one gets maximum marks for difficulty. Why? Because Virgo embodies all the qualities you'd rather forget, but know that you shouldn't really. Worse, Virgo is the sort of person who will literally tap you on the shoulder and remind you of these qualities when they feel you need it.

You work in new ideas, and hopes for the future; they work in the minor details of the here and now. You read holiday brochures and fantasize about meeting wonderful strangers on sun-kissed shores; they tell you that you can't afford it, and continue that even if you did you would have to be careful what you ate if you were not to ruin your entire holiday. They are not killjoys, at least not on purpose. They are unimaginative, though, or at least they are not imaginative in the way that you are. Grand feelings, such as optimism and Romance with a capital R (and Art with a capital A, come to that), which mean so much to you are simply beyond their grasp. How are you going to communicate, great communicator though you are, the importance to you of something whose existence they cannot even imagine?

A seemingly impossible situation. Yet for all that, there are definite points of contact between you. You know, as well as anybody ever will, that little things can cause imbalance in the whole; you see it when something is inelegantly arranged, when someone's clothes don't really go together, or when you spot clumsiness of speech or movement. The Virgo spots the detail which is out of place; you notice that the overall effect, or feeling has been ruined. Do you see the difference? You are dealing with the ideas being put forward, and the Virgo is dealing with the actual things used to do it. The difference between you is that you are capable of thinking back in the zodiacal sequence to Virgo, so that you can appreciate the small details of things, whereas he is all but incapable of thinking forwards to Libra and grasping the overall intention and effect.

Virgo, like all of the 'collecting' signs, takes things seriously. He analyses what he sees, and, most importantly, what he touches and handles. He needs to build up a physical familiarity with things, and to understand them. You haven't got time for this, of course. Things aren't people, and familiarity of the kind achieved by the sense of touch takes far too long, and is too silent anyway. Speech, dialogue, interactive thought; these are what you want. You cannot readily understand a person who would rather understand one thing fully than know about twenty to a more superficial extent.

They see you as much too hasty. Why will you not take the time to become fully familiar with things? Above all, why do you waste your obvious talents on such changeable and insubstantial things as relationships? If you could learn to appreciate the values of physical things, you could be the sort of craftsman they long to be. You wouldn't, of course: you'd be an artist, which lots of Librans are anyway. There's the difference between Art and Craft; it's the difference between Libra and Virgo.

It is not easy to make this relationship work at the level of an amicable friendship; there are too many little irritations, such as their habit of hanging your clothes up for you when you leave them on the floor as you come in from the rain. Given that friendship is unlikely, becoming lovers or getting married is rarer yet; should it happen, the relationship will work in a frenetic sort of way, caused by both of you trying to make things better for the other, but ending up in each other's way. Oddly enough, as workmates within a larger organization, you could get on quite well; problems would arise at the higher levels of management, though, if you were still supposed to work together.

*Libra-Libra*

At least you know what you're getting when you start a relationship with another Libran, or at least you should do; after all, you're one yourself.

It would actually be better if you weren't too alike, either in looks or the proximity of your birthdays; that way you would be sure that other astrological factors (see 'The Year Within Each Day', p.437) would provide differences in you, from which you could build a stronger relationship.

When you meet each other, you will be attracted to those qualities in yourselves that you find admirable. If you take pride in your appearance, you will be pleased to see that they do the same; if you are very interested in some artistic activity, or music perhaps, you will be delighted to note that their taste coincides with yours. It is enough to start a friendship on, and you will tend to concentrate on the things you have in common, because it is the Libran way.

Doing things the Libran way is all very well when relating to non-Librans, but it works against itself when used with another of the same kind. The trouble starts when you start presenting the other person with the parts of yourself that he would like to see; if you both do that for long enough, you find yourselves playing roles the whole time, and reality never enters into it. You may well be having a grand time of it, chattering away nineteen to the dozen, but it isn't productive at all because neither of you are actually communicating yourselves. So what, you say, having another person is the important thing, isn't it? Not quite. The important thing is being able to hear yourself think, and *you* do this by having proper conversations with somebody else. If both of you are saying things you don't mean, you are defeating the purpose of it all, and you will feel the strain as a result. Your answer to feeling the strain will be to start a more honest and productive relationship with somebody else, and let this one decline, but what a waste of energy it will have been—and just think how useful it could have been, to have had a friend who really understood what you were trying to do!

It will be quite easy in this relationship to produce an

atmosphere of Grand Romance, complete with pink ribbons, handmade chocolates, weekends in Paris, and all that sort of thing. Both of you will enjoy indulging yourselves, and will be even more pleased, pleased enough to feel justified, that the other person enjoys it just as much as you do. You will tell yourself that this is perfection, but—and this is important—you won't get anything from it that you couldn't have provided for yourself. Monstrously unfair of me to spoil your fun, I hear you shout, and I don't understand how lovely real romance is. Ah, but two Taureans could sit and eat cream cakes all day (and would, given half a chance); two Arians could leave their families behind, and rush off to explore the Himalayas. You would be quick to spot the disadvantages of these actions, even though they're all only doing what they like best; the same applies to you and another Libran.

The satisfaction in being Libran is in balancing your abilities against the different values of other people. If their values are the same, there's no balancing to do, is there? The whole point of a pair of scales is that they tell you when two amounts of different substances are, or are not, equal in weight. If the two items are the same, and of the same weight, there is no work for the balance to do.

This is an easy and enjoyable friendship, and will develop into an easily manageable and reasonably enjoyable sexual relationship if you so wish. It will form a fairly relaxed marriage, short of enterprise and rather untidy domestically, but good-natured and friendly; and an easy-going business partnership, ideally suited to an office environment. What it won't do is stretch you at all. If you want an easy life, no ups or downs to speak of, then this one will suit you—but if you really want to exercise your Libranness, and feel that you are getting somewhere, choose someone *different*, rather than the same.

### Libra-Scorpio

You'll love this one. It will leave you black and blue, and you will love every minute of it. You don't stand any chance at all of making it work, but you'll try and try again. This relationship, like the Virgo one, gets a maximum difficulty rating, but unlike the Virgo partnership, this one you actually enjoy all the time you're in it. As you will see by the time you have known him a while, a Scorpio is the sort of person your mother warned you about, and you didn't listen.

Scorpios are an alarming mixture of the solidity of a Taurean, and his ability to attract things to himself too, with the pure energy and force of the Arian. Librans make themselves attractive to others, and use their charm to enhance their appeal. Scorpios don't need to do that, and they are not really interested in such vague methods, either. A Scorpio is magnetically attractive to everybody anyway, it's just how he is. Note that: 'attractive', not 'attracted'. Scorpios do not do the moving. Nor do they need to be particularly charming, though that doesn't mean that they are rude. Far from it: they are accomplished manipulators of the emotions of those around them, and usually offer a very polished performance. When somebody is attracted to them, they know that they don't have to work at keeping them there; it's just a question of reeling them in, in the Scorpio's own good time.

You will be hooked, of course. If you are the sort of person who goes out looking for relationships, and you are, then you are actually going to accelerate towards him, the closer you get. It's even faster than the Libra-Aries liaison. Scorpio is governed by Mars, just as Aries is; Venus and Mars just seem unable to keep their hands off each other.

You see them as deep, mysterious, alluring, and impossibly sexy. You also see them as the sort of thing you would like to be—after all, you manage to form relationships by working at it and putting your energy into it, but he seems to do it without trying; now there's talent for you, you think. This has a lot to do with him being the next sign on, actually; everybody finds the next sign on rather enviable, because they can't get to it. Greener grass on the other side, and all that. As usual, you pick on the aspects of their character that you have in common, forming links, via Venus, between elements in both of you which are similar. What happens in this instance is that you bring out all the parts of you that are dark and exciting, and you rather enjoy playing the role. 'He's made me a more exciting person', you say to your friends. No, *you* have. What you don't notice about the whole affair is that you are turning back flips to appeal to him, and trying to get closer in to the heart of all that delicious magnetism, but he isn't changing one bit. You aren't even close to changing him. He's in control; he was at the beginning, and he is now.

He sees you as somebody light and friendly, but in no way a threat. He knows that you are about to give yourself to him body and soul, and he is looking forward to the experience not from any sense of malice, but because he is a sensualist, and he knows that he is in for a treat. Your ideas of romance, your way with words, your perfect taste and grace of movement are all exciting to him, and he can hardly wait. He is, however, determined to stay in control of everything, because you are just the sort of person he could lose his heart to, and losing control of himself is something he fears like you fear loneliness.

You have a deeper effect on him too; one which would never occur to you, but one which is instantly apparent to him, because he perceives motivations at levels deeper than you can ever imagine. You are so open, so optimistic and trusting in your approach to people, you see. On the one hand, he thinks you are naïve and foolish, whereas he has learnt to stay in control, but on the other hand he knows that he will never have the generosity of spirit to be like you. He also knows that the secret of relationships is indeed to be open and optimistic, and he feels ashamed. You will never know this. Only he knows this, and he will not even let himself realize it fully; but he will be doubly determined to stay in control of this one.

As friends or working partners, the relationship will last for as long as it takes for you to become lovers; you don't chat, you flirt. As lovers, you will be knocked flat by his power and intensity; it is likely to be more than you want over a long period of time. As a lasting partnership or a marriage, the outlook is not so good. You really represent too much of what the other would rather not think about for a deep relationship to thrive.

*Libra-Sagittarius*

Here we are at last; the easiest, friendliest, and most optimistic relationship of them all as far as you are concerned, and yet one which has more to offer than just light conversation and a pleasant time.

The reasons aren't difficult to understand. The sign that is two signs on from your own is always the one that is easiest to talk to; somehow you always have things that you want to say to them, and what interests you interests them too, but with enough of a difference in viewpoint to make an engaging conversation.

Sagittarians, on the other hand, are like Leos, but slimmer and more mobile. Not much slimmer, but a lot more mobile. What they want most of all is to see and do new things, to find out about them, and then somehow to make something useful out of them. Most of the time this takes the form of telling other people all the things that they have discovered. It never occurs to them that the rest of the world doesn't really want to know, and on the few occasions when they misjudge things, they bounce back with irrepressible optimism.

Having a relationship with a Sagittarian is an ever-changing experience. They are constantly changing their opinions as new information comes along, and they don't like to be doing the same thing for too long. A steady job with the same firm for twenty or thirty years, heaven to a Capricorn, sounds like a jail sentence to a Sagittarian. This means that there will always be something new for you to relate to in him, some new feature that you will have to match or counterbalance with something from yourself. This will do you no end of good.

They will also join in most enthusiastically with your wide social life; they are outgoing, effervescent people who, if truth be told, love showing off to an audience. It suits you perfectly: you need to keep circulating, because you are an Air sign. Put you near a moving Fire sign like Sagittarius, and there is a circulation of warm air to keep you comfortable. Great, isn't it?

They see you as the perfect friend: lively, chatty, optimistic, and interested in everything that they are themselves (your Venus at work again, picking up points of common interest).

They are more than happy to stay with you as long as you are prepared to keep moving, as they do; since you are an Air sign, there is no problem, and all goes well.

Sagittarians are capable of enormously wide-ranging and profound thought. They are the philosophers of the zodiac, and they are capable of seeing the grand view of things better than any other sign. You are also interested in the idea behind things, though you don't often stretch this part of you. Sagittarius will help you do this, and he will be thrilled to have a partner to whom he can communicate his lofty ideas; such a relationship does both of you a power of good at levels that other relationships don't touch. Communication on the surface is your stock-in-trade, but communication in depth is hard for you. Sagittarius makes it easy.

This partnership is good at every level. You are lively friends, and laughing lovers; as husband and wife you would fulfil each other's every ambition, and as business partners you would be full of enterprise and confidence. It really is a wonderful match; its only flaw is that your feet aren't always on the ground. Too many ideas, too much optimism, not enough practicality, your Virgoan friends will say. Is this really such a bad idea?

### Libra-Capricorn

The second of the three-sign relationships, and therefore similar in a way to the Cancer pairing; you are both Cardinal, so both like to start things off, make new things happen through your own efforts, but in very different spheres of influence. Like Virgo and Scorpio, your most difficult partners, Capricorn is a 'collecting' sign, and he will want to gather things in to himself rather than offer his energies to the world at large.

Capricorn is quite difficult to get to know, even for a Libran; you are not likely to run into him killing time in a bookshop, because he is far too busy; Capricorns are workaholics, every one. Assuming you do actually find him somewhere, you will get the impression at once that he isn't a great talker, and doesn't have much to say when he does speak. Not entirely correct, but not far off; Capricorns are tremendously reserved. Reserved, but not repressed; they have plenty of energy and they use it to the full, but it doesn't come out in the form of words or ideas.

What they are interested in is their standing in society. They strongly believe that the world is a well-ordered place, or at least it tries to be, and that everything in it has a position on the structure of things. They also believe that if a person puts in enough effort, then he will be able to advance himself in that structure, and be recognized for his efforts. Everybody starts out equal, and everybody has the same opportunity to advance themselves. It is the familiar work ethic of not-so-long-ago; the only thing wrong with it is its assumption that the system is indeed fair, and that work and reward are directly related.

You are wondering where your relationship with him comes into all this. It is something along these lines: you both recognize that you work in different worlds, one with material rewards and one with relationships and ideas, and even in different directions, one ready to give, and the other to receive. Yet as you pass by on different roads and in opposite directions, you notice that you have something in common: the absence of self-centredness. You have a sense of fairness in you, Libra, a sense which lets the other person have his say or his turn, a sense which accepts that things don't always stay the way you like them to be or even end up in your favour. You can live with the ups and downs, and you even welcome them, because they keep you on the move. You can usually keep your balance: it's what Librans do, after all. Capricorn recognizes this. His whole view of life depends on the balance of effort and reward, and the universal order that gives everyone a fair chance. You represent that, and he knows it. He is interested in you for that. You know that you have to think about what your partner wants if a relationship is to work, and you are quite used to going along with majority decisions for the sake of the unity of a group; you can leave your own preferences out of the reckoning when you have to. Capricorn understands that, too; he knows that there is work to be done, and that certain things are expected of him, and that he has to come up to the mark. When his reputation is at stake, he can leave aside his own preferences.

There, then, is the relationship between you: you are both prepared to put something other than yourself first. What can you build from this? A wonderful business relationship, for a start. A good marriage, one which works for the good of the team rather than the gratification of its members. A cool but affectionate friendship, spiced with his dry humour expressed in your words. You may have to work at the sexual side of things, but given time, the results may surprise you both. An off-beat relationship, yes, but by no means impossible.

## Libra-Aquarius

The last of the 'easy' relationships, and the one you see most often quoted for Librans. This is a visual relationship as much as anything, something to be seen having; sharp, cool, stylish, wryly humorous, and quite possibly platonic.

He is from your element, Air, and so like you he is concerned with words and ideas. Like you he tries not to be on his own, and loves being in a group of people. He is a stage further on in the scheme of things from you, though, and so where you are keen to make friendships and to continue doing so, he is concerned to keep groups going, and is far less keen to take the initiative. He works on a larger scale, too: the group, or large number, of people is his preferred territory, whereas yours is the intimate world of the one-to-one relationship. He finds that a bit too intense for comfort; pinned down by one person, he will find a way of bringing more people into the situation, until he has the comfort of a group once more. If you want to find an Aquarian, they are either in the pub or with their friends on holiday—in fact anywhere where large numbers of people do anything collectively.

There are other ways in which he is a larger version of you, too. Just as you can make yourself attractive to your partner by highlighting the qualities you have in common, so Aquarius can make himself represent the best of everybody in his circle of friends. In company, he is the brightest of them all, and yet without showing off; take him away so that he is on his own, and he seems much more ordinary: rather grey, even. He also has your aloofness, and to a much more obvious extent. Although he is very much *in* his group, he is not *of* it; you can see him keeping himself ever so slightly apart from them, watching what is going on with a faintly detached air.

You see him as a larger-scale version of yourself, then, but one who doesn't have the same talent for initiating things as you do. He sees you as an earlier, and slightly unreal, version of himself. If ever he doubts what he is, you will be able to remind him. In you he sees the purest form of personal interaction, and it is this that both interests and inspires him.

As friends, you will get on like a house on fire. There is something that you both find very amusing about being in a large group and yet somehow separated from it. It's like being in the film you're watching. It's not an easy thing to understand, but both of you can do it, and together you will develop it into a continuing source of amusement to you both. Aquarians like to look just a little different, if they can; you simply like to look beautiful. Between you, you develop one of the most original visual styles in the zodiac. What you manage to express is simply superior social confidence blended with a sense of humour, and the result is terrific.

Your friendship is very much a meeting of two like minds; you pride yourselves on how much you are *not* involved with each other, and you both feel that it would be rather ponderous to have a physical relationship. Consequently, this pairing is likely to remain platonic. If you do decide to become lovers, your activities will be conducted with style and wit, but without passion, because the combination of Saturn and Venus lacks that essential warmth.

As a permanent relationship, or as a business partnership, you would have to overcome the fact that you might not achieve very much in the conventional terms of success; Fire signs are the go-getters, and Earth signs end up with the rewards—Air signs have trouble converting theory into reality. You would also be rather self-satisfied and uninvolved with those around you, as Saturn got the better of Venus with the passage of time. The end result of all this, if it were a drink, might be rather thin and bitter.

*Libra-Pisces*

This is a peculiar relationship, and yet one that occurs more often than some books would have you think. It is probably the most difficult partnership in the whole zodiac to define, and that is exactly the problem: the success of this one depends on whether you can put some kind of framework into it and make it work.

The most engaging feature of this union of signs is that it is so fluid; it can be anything its participants want it to be. The problem lies entirely in finding a suitable vessel to hold the fluid, so to speak.

How are you going to begin a relationship with someone who absorbs everything you offer them, and takes the shape of everything they contact? You can't try to find a common point with somebody unless they offer you a point to have in common, can you? Perhaps you like dancing. If the Piscean is with you at the time, he will like dancing too. Not when he's with somebody who doesn't dance, though. The thing about Pisceans, as you will quickly learn, is that they are not active, but re-active. They absorb the emotional energy of other people, and make something out of it to offer in return, as a reaction. What you have to be is firm, for once; offer some firm opinions and definite preferences. It's going to be hard, isn't it. The Piscean embodies the very technique you have always used yourself, that of taking the other person's point of view as your own. What he forces you to do in this relationship is to take some of your own medicine, and analyse your own motives, which is quite hard.

He sees you as a source of ideas. He needs new ideas to react to, and he needs people too, because they generate the emotions which are where he feels most at home. What he can't do is achieve your balance, nor your sense of detachment. Emotions aren't detached things, nor are they balanced. In many ways, you are too cool for him, and you don't give him anything to get hold of. What he needs is some good old-fashioned bigotry, a point of view, or a way of doing things that he can react to. What you are offering is pure theory. You want him to respond, too; you want a dialogue. Pisceans aren't very quick with words, because they are never sure what they want to say.

It will be difficult for you to establish exactly what it is that you want to do with each other; left to your own devices, you are likely to drift apart simply because your energies cannot focus together. If you have some definite objective or shared project then everything becomes a lot easier, because within that framework you can start exploring each other's imagination, which is a very big area indeed. There is almost no limit to a Piscean's imagination; it is a tremendously receptive and sensitive tool. You enjoy ideas and moods too; between you, you can have a splendidly theatrical relationship which will fulfil every fantasy you have ever managed to think up.

Note that the real development of the relationship lies in the wealth of imaginative details and style that the pair of you can produce; if you want the sort of relationship which produces measurable results in the form of big houses and a Rolls in the drive, then this isn't it. This one is conducted on an emotional level, on an artistic level even, and the only way you will make it pay is if you both work in the film business.

Actually, as a business partnership this isn't too bad; provided you managed to be in the right business, and your roles were clear within it, you could both provide a wealth of new and creative ideas. A marriage would work in much the same fashion; you would need to be firmly committed to the partnership to supply the guiding structure, but within that you would have a very satisfying time. As lovers, you would be imaginative and expressive, but private. Perhaps the deeper levels of your friendship would be conducted the same way; you would have to get used to that, and the Piscean would have to get used to the amount of time you need to spend in social circulation. You could both adjust if you wanted to.

# Scorpio

*Scorpio-Aries*
This is a relationship which should give you plenty to think about. You live in different universes, you have different targets,

and the things you both consider vitally important don't even exist in the other one's way of thinking; you have absolutely nothing in common at all—except for the fact that you are both driven by the same planet, Mars. You will be fascinated to compare yourself with the Arian, and amazed to see how the same familiar energy works in such an unfamiliar fashion through him.

Aries lives for the moment. He never plans forwards, and he very seldom looks back to see what he has done in the past. Each moment is full of opportunity in his view, and there is an infinity of new possibilities open to him. What matters to him is not what could happen if he did *not* do something, but what he could achieve if he *did* do something. His view of things is intensely personal: it never occurs to him that other people's reactions or intentions are in any way relevant to his own existence. He exists for himself first, and makes the assumption (wrongly) that everybody else must be doing the same.

You will recognize his energy and his drive, but it will seem strange to you that he appears to use it in an unconsidered fashion. It is not really so: he lives in a world where emotions are not so important as they are to you. He only really exists when he is in action; the action itself gives him purpose and direction, and so he tries to be active all the time, because that way he stays in contact with himself, and knows who he is. It is your emotions and your mind that are the most important thing to you, but it is his body which is the most important thing to him. Where you would like to think around a problem, using your mind, and testing your emotional responses to it in various ways, he would like to use his body to attack the problem directly, by physically doing something about it.

Physical energy is powerful and immediate, but it is not subtle. You will probably find the Arian too trusting, and even rather naïve. Be careful in your analysis: Arians are not great thinkers, but they are not unintelligent, even though their mind is not their greatest asset. Carefully laid arrangements of intrigue and secrecy can be shredded by one bold stroke from the simple and honest Arian. His greatest weapon against you, but one of which he is entirely unaware, is his spontaneity; he can do anything he wants at a moment's notice, and probably will. You cannot possibly allow for that in your careful assessments, and it would be useless to try.

In many ways you admire him; he has a capacity for getting things done and converting thought into action which you don't have. It is simply a matter of your elements and qualities: Aries is Fire, and so can make the material world we live in move the way he wants it. He is also cardinal, and so can impose his will upon things to provide new beginnings at any time. You have the ability to start again, too, which you get from Mars as Aries does, but you cannot make a new situation from nothing: you are not an originator, which he is.

You see him as willpower in action, the personification of your own concentrated energy. He sees you as the master of all the things he intends to look into some day when he gets a minute, because he knows that they are somehow important.

If you want him as a friend, you will have to be more outgoing; he isn't prepared to play intricate and intimate games. If it's not easy to see at once, he isn't interested, and so you will have to arrange things so that he sees enough to catch his eye. You will be infuriated at his transparent simplicity of outlook, and he will be puzzled by how closely you examine everything. The only thing you will actually feel at home with in each other is the intensity of energy, supplied by Mars. Mars will also help you form a strong and energetic sexual relationship, one which you will enjoy very much. Aries uses his body rather than his mind in sex, and he won't notice you keeping your true, emotional, self out of the relationship. That's fine as far as you are concerned, and you need have no fear about overwhelming him with your forceful Martian energy—he's every bit as strong.

Marriage? Not really—at the end of the day he doesn't really understand you, and if he did, he wouldn't like it. Similarly, you can't live with his childish trust and simplicity on a long-term basis, either. As a business partnership, though, it's brilliant.

*Scorpio-Taurus*

Pairings of opposite signs run into difficulties more because of the similarities of the signs than because of the differences. At the same time, those similarities give the relationship a much greater chance of success than you might think. This one is no exception; you are both cautious souls, moving in a deliberate manner after due consideration, and you both feel a lot safer when you are surrounded by things which you can call your own. Novelty and instability bother you both.

Taurus is much more concerned with material things than you are, but that doesn't mean that he is insensitive to the world of the emotions. Far from it. Taurus is very sensitive indeed to what people think of him or say to him, but it is not his way to show it. You will understand this very well because you, too, keep your emotions well hidden. He will be wounded quite deeply when criticized, but because he endures the pain in silence he gets a reputation for being thick-skinned. You will know, as a representative of an animal whose insides are so sensitive that you need a shell to keep them safe, how he must feel. The great difference between you comes in what you do in response to that injury. You, Scorpio, bury yourself in a secret world of plot and counter-plot, thinking all the time about how to ensure firstly that you are never hurt again, and secondly that you are always in a position of control over your enemies. Taurus simply retreats, and comforts himself with physical pleasures. A lot of Taureans use food as a comforter, or the pleasure of having a beautiful house where they feel secure, or the enjoyment of beautiful possessions that are unchanged by unkind words. Taurus puts his trust in material things in a way that you don't.

You will find him thoughtful and reliable, but you will also find him slow. Taureans are much more willing to accept things as they are than you, and they will simply sit out difficult circumstances, waiting for better times to come along, where you would be working hard to advance yourself from that position to a better one.

They find you careful and thoughtful, which they like, but deep and unfathomable, which they don't. Rather than try to plumb the depths of your fixed Water (they would drown in the attempt), they decide that as long as you are no threat to their physical well-being they will be happy to stay with you and enjoy what bits of you they can.

A friendship between you will probably form as a sort of mutual defence arrangement—what you will like most about each other to begin with will be that you don't have to be continually on the defensive. After that, you will develop the friendship through the growing sense of reliability and support that you each find in the other.

There is a very strong sexual attraction between you, but it is a bit on the slow side, because it comes from so deep down inside you. There will be no brilliant flashes of sexual electricity; at your level the energy is more like that of a volcano, in that massive heat builds up over a long time. The union is likely to be fertile and fruitful; it's what you get if you Water your Earth!

As a marriage, this one would work well, because your energies will continue to grow towards each other over a very long period of time; some relationships are definitely short-term, but this one isn't. Once Scorpio has learned that he can trust Taurus, he need not be suspicious and can turn his energies towards making a successful life for the two of them. Taurus will provide stability, support, and warm affection for the team.

As a business partnership, this one is less good: it lacks the inventiveness and confidence necessary to make profitable progress.

*Scorpio-Gemini*
On the surface there isn't a lot of contact between these two signs. Gemini is an Air sign; to you he seems to be insubstantial, and not to take things seriously enough. He seems to have no emotions that you can gather in and work with. He is also mutable, and therefore readily accepts change for its own sake. In fact, you can't get hold of him at all, and that exasperates you.

You don't have to get hold of him, though. He will come to you of his own accord, because he is interested in the way you work.

Like the birds that follow the ploughman, he wants to see what turns up. Scorpio and Gemini share a common characteristic— curiosity.

The idea of the ploughman is worth continuing with for a few moments longer. The ploughman isn't ploughing the field to turn up the worms for the birds—he has another purpose in mind, and his ploughing is a necessary preamble to that. So, too, the Scorpio does his investigation and his analysis as necessary groundwork for his larger ambitions, but the Gemini is interested in what he turns up anyway. The larger ambitions are not of the slightest concern to him.

Gemini is the great assimilator of trivia. His energy is almost entirely mental, and is so concentrated in the rational side of his mind that he leaves almost no emotional shadows at all, which makes him almost invisible to you. Remember that you only see people through their emotional responses; Gemini responds intellectually and verbally to his circumstances, not emotionally. How you would like to have his mind! What a waste, it seems to you, to have so fine an instrument at your command and use it to collect trivia and to make witty remarks!

You are clever and devious, you know that, but Gemini makes you feel ponderous and dull. He is so much faster than you, so quick to see the different sides of things, and you wish you could match him. He even has the capability to throw away his best ideas as though they didn't matter; you keep all of yours, because they were so costly to produce. It is because he never takes anything seriously; the novelty of an idea is worth more to him than its content, and novelty cannot be kept.

He sees you as somebody with the strength to finish the job. One of his own great failings, and he knows it, is his inability to stay doing one thing for a long time. Somehow he can't raise the enthusiasm. You, however, are thoroughgoing, purposive, and successful. He can see that—and he likes it. He will never understand your need for emotional restraint, but then he doesn't deal in emotions anyway, except as an abstract concept, and he will never understand why you take things so seriously. What he does know is that his own energies are entirely mental ones, and that he lacks the forceful application that brings lasting results; your energies are primarily mental, too, and you have exactly the forceful application he needs. You are just what he needs.

A business partnership between you would be very productive indeed, because you can each contribute what the other partner particularly lacks. With your force added to his incisiveness, you could really get somewhere. Marriage would be similar, though you would have to allow for his need for movement, and realize that an attempt to dominate and dictate his behaviour would result in both of you adopting a policy of deception and subterfuge.

As lovers, you are ill matched, because his needs are for playful teasing and mental rapport, whereas yours are deeper, and both more physical and more emotional. It's like matching a rapier against a cannon—they are weapons so different that no engagement is possible. It is far better to stay as friends, and let your shared passion for finding things out amuse you both.

### Scorpio-Cancer

This is the first of the partnerships within your own element, Water. There are a great many similarities between you, just as there are between the two animals that represent you in the sky. Both of you have hard shells to symbolize how your true selves are not on show to the world at large, but must be protected against attack; and both of you have pincers with which to defend yourselves against those who get too close without being invited.

What must strike you very forcibly about a Cancerian is how very private they are. They are polite enough, but it really isn't possible to see what they are thinking from the outside. You will understand this without any trouble, but you might like to remember that this is how others see you, to a great extent. An interesting thought, isn't it?

The pair of you live in a personal and internal universe where emotions and feelings are the things that matter most. In the early stages of the relationship, you will edge round each other cautiously, trying to get some idea of how the other one works without exposing yourself to possible attack. Both of you like to be quite sure of how the other person behaves before making any kind of firm commitment.

You see the Cancerian as someone with a special talent, which you would dearly like to have: they can generate emotion. They are capable of giving themselves to, and caring for, another person without first asking themselves what they are going to get out of it, and what it will cost them in time and effort. You can't do that. On the one hand, you can dismiss it as sentimental weakness, but you know that you are lying to yourself; this is real care that we are talking about, the stuff that is like gold dust to you, and the Cancerian ability to create it from inside themselves is something you find inexpressibly moving. There are dark mysteries within you somewhere, so deep that you can only just glimpse them yourself, and they have to do with the meaning of your existence. Somehow Cancer seems to have mastered them in a way that you have not. They are clearer, softer people who can manage to exist without the strong harness of self-control that you have had to wear for as long as you can remember. You feel clever and powerful most of the time; in their presence, you feel almost ashamed of yourself.

They see you as unbelievably powerful and successful individuals whose willpower borders on the manic in comparison to their own. They know that they are not always as effective as they would like to be, and their well-known sentimental streak often prevents them from being as ruthless as is sometimes necessary. It is one thing to make a lot of emotional energy, they say, but another thing altogether to direct it and make it work for you. You can do this, and they can see that. They are in awe of your ability to direct your energies towards a specific goal with enough force to make it bend to your will. In terms of the Water element that you both represent, you are a high-pressure hose, while they merely rain softly over things. They would gladly trade some of their sensitivity for some of your intensity.

This is an easy friendship to form; you both find things in the other to admire, and in communicating that you find that you work in similar ways: what you have in common, added to what you find desirable in them, draws you together. It is a fine friendship, too; you respect each other's privacy instinctively, and so avoid the vicious circle of suspicion and withdrawal that would otherwise come into being. If the friendship develops into a sexual liaison, then you should find it deeply satisfying, with many of the needs you didn't know you had being met by the understanding of someone from the same element as yourself. It will be passionate, but it needn't necessarily be energetic.

As a business partnership this one lacks the pioneering spirit to some extent, and so might not be as successful as you would think. As a marriage, it would be a much better proposition. You would have to make sure that you developed an adequate means of expression for your differences, though; jealousies and slow rages are all too easy to generate from an overabundance of the Water element.

*Scorpio-Leo*

This one will either work or it won't, and you'll soon know which one it is. This elemental mix is Fire and Water, both of you Fixed, and therefore impossible to overcome. The result, of course, is steam, but it remains to be seen if that can be put to any useful purpose.

The essence of this is that one of you wants to be in command, and the other wants to be in control. There is a difference between the two: you get a commander's hat if you are in command, and unless the Leo gets to wear it, he won't play.

In many ways a Leo leaves you breathless with disbelief, but you cannot help but admire him, because he seems to be able to achieve without apparent effort all the things for which you work so hard. He is a natural winner; everybody looks to him as the leader of any group, and to be in his company is generally regarded as an enjoyable experience. He radiates warmth and energy without wanting anything in return; he is genuinely generous, and it is probably this, more than anything else, which makes you suspicious. Water signs never understand that warmth radiates outwards naturally, and that Fire signs have it to spare. Indeed, if they didn't do something with it, they would probably be ill. Aries and Sagittarius put that energy into movement, but Leo prefers to sit still and radiate.

He represents what you are aiming for. What you really want is to be as popular, as liked, and to have the same regal status the Leo. What you find so amazing is that he can be so open, so self-centred, and so lazy with it. Have you not spent valuable years of your time making sure that you do everything in the most effective way? How can he be so careless, so ignorant of anything except himself, and still be where he is? Because he gives energy out, and you take it in, that's why. The world loves a giver, especially when it's all for free. At the end of the day, you can find plenty about him to despise, but you love him just the same, and you'd love to be in his shoes, just like everybody else.

He sees you as somebody with the same sort of inexhaustible power as himself. He also sees that yours is restricted, and controlled, by your own effort of will. He is attracted to somebody who is as powerful as he is, and recognizes you as a sort of earlier version of himself, someone who lacks the confidence to let loose the power inside himself. He is intrigued, interested, and a little irritated by how you try to organize him, restrict him, control him. What he doesn't want is for you to be able to contain his light, to soak him up, as it were, and he will turn his light up even brighter if he thinks this is happening, while you run for cover. He needs to be the one in command, the one that people look to, and he will fight you for that role if he thinks that you are going to take it from him. What he won't do is fight you for it if he can see that it was yours in the first place; he will simply go elsewhere. If you want him, you will have to give him first place.

Really, you need him more than he needs you, and he probably knows it. Any friendship between you will develop into a power struggle in a very short time indeed, and this will still be the case if you have a sexual relationship. In fact, it will be even more so, because the two of you represent the fundamental forces of life and death in the zodiac, so your power games are played on a cosmic level as well as an individual one. If you lose, you die; if you win, you *both* die.

If there is some interest outside the pair of you that you are both keen on, then the combination of your energies will be very strong indeed. For this reason, you would do well in business together. Privately, however, you would be fighting for power in the home, which would make for a marriage lived at a fairly high volume, with flying crockery from time to time. It really depends on how much you like a good fight. You hurt yourself each time you hurt him, you know; is this what the sting in your tail is for?

*Scorpio-Virgo*
Most of the relationships between signs which are two signs apart are quite amicable, but this one is really special. There aren't many people in the zodiac whose company you really enjoy, but Virgo is one. The funny thing about it is that it's the very *un*emotional qualities of the sign that you like best; the thing that you really appreciate about the Virgoans is their no-nonsense attitudes to life.

Virgos like getting things right. They approach things in a practical way. They analyse their own approach, and decide on the best way to tackle the problem. When they get down to work, they work in a structured, methodical way, and they get things right. They waste nothing, and when it's all over, the result is neat and clean. You like this sort of thing. It's almost good enough to sit and watch, but even better is the knowledge that you can rely on them to do things properly in your absence. Somebody who does things to your standards, even when you are as obsessive as you are, Scorpio, is the sort of person you would like as your friend, and it is this shared attitude of perfectionism that attracts you to each other. It is true that you do it for slightly different reasons, but the effect is the same, and that's what you recognize in each other.

It will surprise you, when you get to know a Virgo, that they are only too willing to do things for you. It will also surprise you that they do things for the sheer pleasure of doing them and getting them right—much like a child at school who likes getting ten out of ten but doesn't care much about Mathematics itself one way or the other. This makes them undemanding friends, and good ones from your point of view, because the emotional motives that underlie all your actions are never examined by them; indeed, it seldom occurs to them that such motives even exist, which suits you admirably.

They see you as exciting larger versions of themselves, dealing with big projects with the same correct and effective procedures that they use on a smaller scale. They like your attitude: or, to be more accurate, they like your apparent attitude. Your true motives are beyond them—they live in a world of material and practical details, where the emotional content of things is almost non-existent, and where human hopes and fears are dismissed as unreliable and uninteresting.

A friendship between you is most likely to start as a working partnership, and it works brilliantly on that level. They are likely to be the most enthusiastic and reliable helpmates you will ever find, knowing instinctively how you would like to about things, and gaining as much satisfaction as you do when things go according to plan.

It is probably a mistake to attempt a sexual relationship with a Virgo. They are completely unfamiliar with your Martian energy, both in its quality and its intensity, and you will overwhelm them. At the same time, you will be irritated by their inability to respond to, or even understand, the strength of your emotional needs.

As a business partnership, things will go well. It is absolutely imperative that you are in the leading position, so that they are working for you rather than with you, in effect, but you are likely to arrange it that way anyway, so there should be no problems. A Virgoan isn't really happy leading the way, and will voice no protest if you take the driving seat.

Marriage is probably not a good idea, despite the fact that you work so well together. They will never come to terms with the intensity of your emotion, and you will wear them down after a while. They do *worry* so when they are unsure of themselves, and you will in fact make them ill after a little while. Keep them as friends and helpmates, and leave it at that.

*Scorpio-Libra*

This one gets a maximum difficulty rating, if such a thing exists for a relationship. You are different in element, quality, and just about everything else that there is; in addition, they are the sign behind you in the zodiac, and so embody all the qualities that you would rather not think about, or feel that you have outgrown. Despite all that, though, the relationship seems determined to form itself, whether you want it or not. It just happens that way—there is an attraction between you.

The attraction is the easiest thing to explain. Libra is one of Venus' signs, and you, of course, are one of Mars'. These two planets seem to have a magnetic effect on each other, or at least on the people who display their energies, such that they find themselves propelled towards each other. Librans are always looking for a partnership to form, and they have a very romantic view of life; they can be attracted to anybody, and if that person makes the right sort of response, they will form a partnership. You, of course, respond to them as you respond to everybody else, with a concentrated blast of emotional power. They read this, as everybody else does, as sexual energy, and take it as a favourable response. In this way the Libran falls victim to his own capacity for attraction; he finds himself hopelessly attracted to you. You may find this amusing, but if you are busy, you might not.

You see Librans as rather pathetic figures, but at the same time rather discomfiting. They are much less sure of their purpose than you, and you see this indecisiveness as an annoying weakness. Not only do they have no idea what they are aiming for from one week to the next, but they are likely to be holding a completely different opinion about things from one week to the next, and if you like things to stay more or less constant (as you do), that's annoying. They have a knack for saying the right thing, for putting people at their ease; they are friendly to everybody, and everybody has them as a friend. You see this as a useful talent, but when you look a little closer you are surprised at how shallow the content of their conversation really is. Why waste a talent for dealing with people so well, you think to yourself, by keeping it to so trivial a level? You can't understand that the Libran is being nice for its own sake: there is no ulterior motive.

You are actually made uneasy by their apparent happiness, the more so because you cannot understand where it comes from. Can they really have no purpose other than to make friends with everyone? Where does their energy come from? How can they afford to be so open and welcoming to everybody the whole time? The answer is actually very obvious, but you are unlikely to see it, and when you know what it is, you will be even more upset. It is simply this: they are happy to share things.

Sharing is the *last* thing you would think of. It is completely alien to the way that you work. What's worse, you know that it makes a sort of sense, but you'd rather not be reminded of that. Now you see why the relationship won't work unless you are prepared to make a special effort: how can you be happy with a person whose definition of happiness is the very thing you would **most** like to avoid?

Libra does not have this trouble. He is simply besotted with you, and you can do with him as you wish. He is helpless in your hands.

A friendship between you will last only for a few minutes before Venus and Mars, acting through you, make you decide to become lovers. In this area, the energies are most unevenly matched: Libra will be expecting something loving and romantic— your powerful passions and concentrated power will completely stagger him. From your point of view, his inability to match you with similar strength to your own will leave you unsatisfied.

As a marriage, or as business partners, this pairing would probably take more than it was worth to make it work properly. If, but only if, you were prepared to change yourself, become more flexible and less obsessive, and if the Libran were particularly strong-willed and creative, then you might make a marriage with something to it—but you might not.

*Scorpio-Scorpio*
At least you know what you're getting here. Have a look in a

mirror. Make a fist. Do you notice how the mirror image makes a fist from his other hand to oppose you exactly? That's what this relationship is going to be like.

Some signs go rather better with themselves than others, because of the accommodating nature of the signs themselves. Scorpios don't qualify on that count.

The trouble, of course, is that you both want to be in control, and neither of you is prepared to give way. You are frightened that as you find out more about him, he is busy finding out the same sort of things about you. You will attempt to find his weaknesses, and when you have done that, you will feel a lot more sure of yourself. He may also have found yours, and you may not be aware of it. He may have deceived you as to his. There are all sorts of possibilities. The pair of you may actually enjoy this game of secrets a lot more than you are prepared to admit; if so, all well and good, especially if it takes place within, say, a sexual framework. If it becomes at all serious, really seriously serious as opposed to ordinarily serious (Scorpios have a wide range of seriousness), then you will be in danger of destroying each other for ever. The venom in the scorpion's sting is not for pretend battles.

You are both very possessive. This possessiveness extends out beyond the individual to cover a vast territory of people and experience, all of whom you regard as your exclusive property. You do think that you own them in a material sense, but you are sure that you control them, and that their every movement is ultimately referred back to you. This wide sphere of influence is your own special world, and if it overlaps with that of another Scorpio, then one of you must be mistaken: if you control that bit, then they can't, can they? The idea of being mistaken is one which you do walking backwards if you are not to turn your back on your adversary, and scorpions, like crabs, walk sideways or forwards.

The way out of this constant feuding is quite simple. Go back and look in the mirror again. Now turn to face right. Take a step. You are both walking in the same direction.

You will need a common goal large enough and far enough

into the future to occupy the pair of you. If possible, it will need to have different facets, so that one of you would like to control one side of it, and the other another. You can both use your considerable organizational talents to attack this target, and you can help each other up through the structure of the thing so that eventually you both stand at the top. It is the only way; you both need a purpose, and you both like being busy, and the feeling that you are getting somewhere. You must simply ensure that in helping yourselves you are helping each other, and that you do not trespass on each other's chosen territory as you do it.

All very easy in theory, but not quite so simple in practice. As your working partnership flourishes, your day-to-day friendship will look after itself, though it may come to be inward-looking, and to discourage outsiders from joining in.

As lovers, you will have to be very sure of your own territory again. With confidence and a feeling of mutual trust will come the ability to let go some of that awesome Martian force at full strength at each other, and you will enjoy that very much; but if anything undermines that confidence and trust, then the imbalance in the relationship will have disastrous consequences. You must be particularly wary of giving any cause for jealousy. It's quite simple, really: if you are going to work with high voltage, observe the safety regulations.

As a marriage? Yes: very powerful, very private, very successful, *if* you can maintain each other's total trust and confidence.

### Scorpio-Sagittarius

Sagittarians are wonderful people. They will remind you of this fact, using those very words, whenever they feel that you need a reminder. Their arrogance makes you cringe at times, but they seem to get away with it, and you find them very attractive. They don't find you anything like so enticing though, and a lasting relationship between you is a hard thing to achieve.

You spend a lot of your time finding out about things. Background information, mainly; how things are, how they got that way, who does what, that sort of thing. You do this so that you will have an effective plan of action and a sure chance of success. Sagittarians are better than that. They know everything already; it comes built-in, somehow. They also know how people are going to move, because they are perceptive that way. And they are successful because they have energy, talent, and luck. It makes you sick.

You see them as having all the knowledge that you would ever like to have, but they appear to give it out to everybody and anybody, for free. If it were yours, your reason, you would put it to some good purpose, capitalizing on the advantage it gave you. That's fixed-sign thinking. Sagittarius is mutable; he spends his time doing things for other people, giving his talent away. He is also Fire where you are Water, so if he doesn't parade his talent and show off a little he will become ill. Energy is indeed free, to him anyway, and he does not have to collect it the way you do. He is more than happy to offload some of it in your direction, and this suits you fine for a short while, but he will begin to wonder what you do with it all.

Energy and friendliness, according to him, are for spreading around and giving out; it isn't fair for somebody to attempt to control it all. He has an almost childish sense of honesty and fair play, and he will tell you off if you attempt to take more than he thinks is your fair share. He will also resent your attempts to contain his movements; he needs to be on the move all the time, seeing new things.

He sees you as an inverted version of himself. He appreciates your inquiring mind, and admires your effective way of working; he also recognizes something similar to his own enthusiasm in your intense dedication to your own interests. What he doesn't like, though, is the way that your world is inward-facing; he is sure that you are missing the point somehow, and that knowledge and talents are to be shared. He doesn't care for money in the same way that you do, either: as far as he's concerned it is only useful when spent, whereas you can appreciate the power it has for its own sake. Power of any kind doesn't interest him— knowledge does. You can understand that, you think. Not so: you understand the power of knowledge, but he has the joy of knowledge.

Since he can offer you more than you can offer him, the friendship will be one-sided. He is quite willing to be friends with you, but only for as long as it interests him; if you are interesting, different, and communicative, then you will gain his attention, but not otherwise. You will have to work very hard indeed: how you do captivate somebody you are desperate to know, but who doesn't want what you've got? Once you get talking, you will be surprised how easy it can be: Sagittarians talk about almost anything. They will talk about grand concepts and universal deals rather than personal and individual matters, and you will find that you know more about this sort of thing than you perhaps thought. You will certainly make bright company for each other, or at least until the Sagittarian fancies a change!

As a lover, you will find him strong and imaginative, but playful in a way that upsets you; he will refuse to take the affair as seriously as you do, and you may get the feeling that he is thinking about something else some of the time. This leads to Scorpionic jealousy, and is, of course, detrimental to the situation.

As marriage partners, you would have to make some major adjustments. You would have to live with his changeability, and he would have to realize how little you like moving unless you really have to. He would accuse you of not being honest with him, and you would accuse him of not taking the situation seriously enough. It could all work out very well, but the odds are very much against it, as they are against a successful business partnership, too.

### Scorpio-Capricorn

This is the one you have been waiting for. Capricorns like Scorpios, and Scorpios like Capricorns. This is quite possibly the easiest and best suited combination of signs in the whole zodiac, and the two of you just can't help but get on with each other. What's more, you can actually do something positive for each other, which pleases you both a great deal.

Capricorn is the cardinal Earth sign. What a Capricorn likes to see is a structured approach to life; to him, everything has a framework to fit into, and a set of rules. He likes to play by the rules, and he likes to succeed. What he likes best of all is the recognition he gets for his position, and the status it brings him. A man after your own heart, as you can see.

The difference between you is that Capricorn is very unemotional. Quite cold, in fact. He is not interested in the emotional side of things, and he doesn't trust people who are; to him, such people are unreliable and ineffective, not firm enough. He likes you, though: he sees your intense Martian energy, and the way you pursue your objectives, and he is impressed. Your emotional objectives are hidden from him, and very successfully.

Because he is an Earth sign, Capricorn values material possessions. He uses these possessions and his status in his career as the yardsticks for his existence. The harder he works, the more money he has, and the higher he rises. As he goes up the ladder of success, he acquires larger cars and larger houses. Each of these represents the amount of work necessary to acquire them, in his eyes. What he is doing, in fact, is converting effort into material form, and everybody accords him respect and status according to the size and quantity of his status symbols. This is a very interesting process to you; you want to be a success too, and you want people to recognize you as somebody with obvious power. They way to do this is with material tokens, similar to the ones a Capricorn uses, but you are not really able to do this on your own, because you are a Water sign; Capricorn can help.

He sees you as a tremendous source of concentrated energy. He is a hard worker himself, but he has to do it with patient toil over many years, because his ruling planet, Saturn, has none of the immediate heat and force that your planet, Mars, has. Quite often he gets very tired; he knows that he has to press on, and he knows where he wants to be at the end of it all, but it takes a lot out of him, and it takes a long time. When he sees your talent for concentrated activity and organized control he sighs with envy. It's exactly the sort of thing he would wish for if he had three wishes (except that he's too down-to-earth to believe in fairies).

What makes you such firm friends so quickly is mutual approval. You are both likely to find the other visually attractive, since you both dress in a way that suggests a businesslike approach. As you get to know each other, you encourage each other to talk about plans and projects, and voice your approval of the other's approach. With the Capricorn's perception of structures, and capacity for long-term effort linked to your sense of purpose and ability to discern motives, you will make a formidable business partnership which will bring you greater rewards than either of you could achieve on your own.

As an intimate relationship this combination suffers a little from being too regimented and goal-oriented. As a marriage it would be very successful in terms of your careers and material success, but it lacks warmth and the ability to comfort itself in times of trouble. Sexually, you find the Capricorn a bit of a puzzle; they are strong and potent like the goats of their sign, but they don't have *passion*; depth of feeling just isn't in them.

### Scorpio-Aquarius

The last of the Fixed signs. There is a lot that you two have in common; or, to be more accurate, you indulge in similar behaviour for different reasons, and you can recognize it in each other. The essential idea is one of remoteness, of keeping yourself to yourself.

Aquarians are funny creatures. You will not be able to notice anything unusual about them at first, because they don't do anything that sticks in your memory. Your particular memory, remember, works with the emotional responses and motivations of those around you, and an Aquarian is an Air sign, so he is emotionally rather cool. He is also ruled by Saturn, the coldest planet astrologically, so you can't expect him to generate a lot of emotional heat for you to pick up.

Aquarians are sociable. So sociable, in fact, that you will seldom find one on his own. In a group of people he really comes to life, somehow taking on all the characteristics of the group as a whole. What he likes doing is meeting lots of new people, and being in company. He's not too keen on personal and intimate relationships, because in them the emotional temperature tends to rise, and he'd rather be cool; larger groups are where he's at home.

The interesting thing about all this socializing is that although he is very much part of the group, he keeps himself aloof within it, as though he was watching a play unfold around him. He is interested and amused, but he is not really committed to the hopes and fears of any of the individuals in his group. He is polite and friendly, and he likes his surroundings to be full of friendly people, but his best friend is still himself. The thing he feels most strongly for, actually, are ideas which affect a whole group of people, such as a political opinion, or a protest movement. He is dedicated to being friends with everyone, and that means that everyone has to be on the same level as he is; he is firmly opposed to all kinds of hierarchy, and any system which gives one person more power than another. Nobody has power over him, he thinks; he is unique, special, independent, and his own man.

You can recognize in him the idea of keeping your own thoughts to yourself while appearing to be an active member of a group—it's the sort of thing you do all the time. You're not so keen on his egalitarian ideals, though; to you, power is one of your main aims. He is, of course, the outgoing part of the cycle of which you are the incoming: what he is doing is putting his energies out into a large group of people, and you collect it back in again. Both of you need large numbers of people to function effectively, and you both keep yourselves effectively one step back from the people you spend your time with.

In you he sees the principle of emotional control taken to its highest form. He doesn't like your love of power, but he likes your ability to analyse and gauge any situation, because it is a similar process to the one he uses. What he would perhaps like to have is your passionate belief in yourself and your own purpose; Saturn doesn't give him as much heat as other people have, and he finds that attractive.

It is surprising that the two of you talk to each other at all; you may just be too remote ever to risk communicating. Assuming you do, the friendship will be firm but cool; you realize how necessary the other is to your own activities in the long run, you appreciate your similarities, but you don't feel the necessity to talk about it all the time. It's an instinctive thing.

As business partners you are too far apart in your basic principles to make much progress, but as marriage partners you could suit him better than he would have you believe: you wouldn't get in each other's way, but the Aquarian would appreciate some of your Martian heat. Sexually you will find him cool, but strong and inventive; from time to time he will really surprise you.

### Scorpio-Pisces

Some of these relationships are good for your career, and some have been good for your physical well-being; this one is good for your soul. Pisces is the last of the Water signs, and the most fluid of them all. Completely unstructured and infinitely flexible, he represents the ultimate challenge to your ideas about yourself.

Pisces lives entirely in his imagination. Like the two fishes of his symbol, he lives in the emotional world of the Water element, and often seems to swim in two directions at once. Self control isn't important to him, as it is to you; instead, he lets his emotions flow wherever he wants, and forms his reality out of them. He is completely caught up in whatever he is feeling at the time, and his version of the truth is formed from the feelings he is experiencing at any given moment.

The randomness of this horrifies you. You want to tell them to get hold of some sort of plan, some set of rules, so that they can at least be consistent in themselves, and then to impose some sort of order on their surroundings. Their whole existence seems so disturbingly loose.

They are not likely to be impressed by the argument. For a Piscean, the essence of life is to feel the force of emotion, to be carried along by the experience. Even if the emotion is a bad one, there's no need to worry, another one will be along in a minute. There is, of course, the awful thought that the world might run out of emotional energy, but luckily there are people like you around to store it up and keep the flow going with your intensity and passion.

You are, of course, worrying for nothing; if you let your emotions go, as they do, you would soon find that the tremendous pressure subsided almost as soon as it was released, giving a gentle flow for you to swim around in. The Piscean is the next stage in your emotional development—after you have learned self-control, and have gained the confidence never to doubt your own identity, you can allow yourself to let go a little, and see where it gets you. Your problem is that you don't actually have that confidence.

As you can see, on a day-to-day level the Piscean is so different from you that you can have hardly anything in common; it is only on a life-long level that you can see how they are one step ahead of you. Still, life is lived on a day-to-day level, and that's where relationships are formed. As a friendship, these two signs get on very well—rather better than you would like. Let me explain. Pisces will take the form of anything which his companion wants him to be, so if you are going to be forceful and dominant, they will respond in a similar manner, which you will find most encouraging. What you won't find encouraging is that they will instinctively know what you *really* mean, because they are almost psychically sensitive; it is no use at all being devious with them, because they can perceive your real meaning at once. It is no use trying to control them, either; water runs through your fingers, you know.

If you want to extend this shadow-boxing into your love life, you will find that they are a lot more subtle and sensitive than you had at first supposed; they are capable of matching your emotional strength when it suits them, but you can't match their changes of temperament.

You would find them difficult business partners, unless you defined the rules very closely indeed; their mutability means that they will frequently modify their way of working as it suits them, and that would infuriate you. Marriage would be rather better; there the private side of your life needs to be developed as well as the public side, and what they have to teach you about the development of your Watery energies would be beneficial in the long run.

# Sagittarius

### Sagittarius-Aries

This is a very good relationship. They think you are bright and interesting, and you think they are dashing and sexy. Both true, of course: you are both Fire signs, and so you see each other in your true colours.

Arians are very active people; they don't function properly unless they are actually doing something. An idea isn't enough for them—it's only the beginning. They are impatient to see what happens to the idea when it is put into action, and so they do exactly that. Only in the performance of the action can they understand the idea, which you ought to think about.

You see them as fantastically energetic, and you are envious of their ability to turn ideas into actions. Because you are a Mutable sign, you are very good at breaking things down to see what can be extracted from them, but you are much less effective in getting things going, especially when you have to start from scratch. You need something to work with. Aries doesn't—all he needs is a direction to go in, and he's away. Where you will turn an idea around in your head for some time, comparing it to other, similar thoughts you might have had, Aries takes the first idea he comes across and races off to put it into action. What's more, he gets it right first time. Whatever an Aries does is active and effective: in other words, it works. A lot of this is to do with his being a Cardinal sign, but whatever it is, you wish that you could do it.

He has his faults, of course. He won't think before he acts, for instance. It may well be that this is because unless he acts he can't think, but it does have a few drawbacks. He also has no sense of time: everything for him has to happen right now, this minute, just as it does for a young child.

He is very self-sustaining, and he is self-centred, too. This means that he is very happy on his own; he doesn't need a partner for support or protection, and he doesn't really think of sharing his time with somebody else. If somebody else wants to be there while he's being active, then that's fine, as long as they don't get in the way, and don't expect him to stop what he's doing to attend to them. This sounds rather selfish, but it is actually self-*centred*. No matter: it appeals very strongly to you, because you know how he feels. It has all the action, freedom, and movement you could wish for, and none of the commitment you are so keen to avoid.

Is it the perfect partnership? No, not quite. It has all the rugby-team mateyness that you could wish for, and you could hardly get a better companion for an adventure, but the Arian can't offer you intellectual stimulation. He knows it, too: that's what he comes to you for.

He sees you as a great source of inspiration. You can see and understand all the things which he can't quite grasp, and you can tell him what they are like. As a young child will bring a book to its grandfather, and ask him what's in it, so the Arian wants the Sagittarian to show him the inner meanings of things, to tell him how things work, and to fire his imagination. He wants to act on every idea you tell him; everything you say gives him something new to do. Between you, you can create real achievements out of your slightest whim, and the idea of that attracts you enormously— but you would also like him to be able to converse and argue with you at your own level, and he just can't do that, no matter how much he would like to.

As friends, you are ideally suited. You will keep each other amused and cheerful, and you will be able to laugh together at a world which seems altogether too set in its ways to go off and try new things, as you both like to do. As lovers, you are equally well aligned—Aries is more physical than you are, and stronger too, but neither of you use sex as a symbol of personal commitment, so you are unlikely to misconstrue each other's intentions. They are simple souls, though, and will not understand your liking for changing partners every so often.

As business partners you will be unbeatable, provided that you have somebody else on hand to take care of the routine work, and to tie up all the details while the pair of you launch yourselves off into yet another new venture.

As a marriage, this pairing will work very well, provided that you realize that you will eventually have to do things their way; that said, you would rather do things in an Arian way than in the way of some of the other signs.

### Sagittarius-Taurus

This relationship is very difficult, and yet in real life it seems to struggle along somehow. It may be that the best thing about this relationship is that the ruling planets of the pair of you—Jupiter and Venus respectively—are essentially kind and well meaning in their nature. If they were not, you would end up throwing plates at each other.

Taureans are essentially static people. The very idea of movement bothers them. They are equally disconcerted by the idea of novelty, since that threatens them with the dissolution of their existing way of life. Difficult for you to imagine, isn't it? You couldn't exists without movement and novelty, and the idea of forming a relationship with somebody so opposed to your own way of life seems difficult to comprehend, even for you.

What they are trying to achieve is a stable way of life, where everything is secure, and where every physical need is met. Taureans are very much lovers of home comforts—they measure themselves by the size and comfort of their homes, and by the amount they have in their larders, just as you measure yourself by how clever you are, and how much you know. They are physical where you are intellectual, and they want comfort where you want excitement.

They are very slow to anger, and will endure a great deal of strain and stress before they eventually take steps to rectify the situation.

Their stability and reliability can have a sort of appeal to you; you wouldn't like to be that way yourself, but somebody who represents constant values in a changing world isn't hard to appreciate. At the end of it all, you realize that what they have is what you are trying to achieve; you want things to take shape as a result of your ideas, for your Fire sign energy to become established in the world as Earth sign energy, such as Taurus. You also know that when you shoot one of your Sagittarian archer's arrows into the air, it will eventually fall to Earth. Although Taurus is the end product, by the time you get there, you will no longer be Sagittarian, and that's why you fight shy of it. You appreciate their stability, and you admire the care that they have lavished on their home and possessions, because you know that you just couldn't give that much time to that sort of thing; but you don't want to be part of it.

They see you as somebody who changes their opinions from one moment to the next, and who seems determined to undermine all that they hold dear. Their eventual reaction to you is to ignore you: they see that you are not concerned with the material world in the same way as they are, and so you do not threaten their possessions. You are also not important, for the same reasons; ideas can safely be ignored by Taureans, because what matters to them is material wealth. This infuriates you: you don't mind them not accepting your ideas, but not to be recognized for having ideas of importance in the first place really drives you wild.

Friendship depends to some extent on having parallel, if not identical, viewpoints. Since you have to struggle even to recognize the existence of each other's way of thinking, you are unlikely to be close friends. Should you be lovers, you will find that the Taurean is capable of a tremendous passion, but you will find it more than you want to deal with, because the emotional content is at least as much as the physical; you would like things a little lighter in tone.

If you marry, it is obviously because you want a secure home base, which the Taurean will gladly provide for you. Don't complain if they are unwilling to change as quickly as you would like them to, or if they place constraints on your personal freedom.

As business partners, you are a lot better than you might think: you do the selling, and let them do the buying.

*Sagittarius-Gemini*

Gemini is the sign opposite to you in the zodiac, and that means that they have all of your talents, but displayed in the opposite way, which you find irritating. They are so like you, but so different—they seem to be interested in the same things and for the same reasons, but they use them in very different ways, and you find yourself wondering why they won't do things the right (i.e. your) way when it would be so easy for them to do so.

They wonder about you in the same way, of course. Had you thought of that?

A Gemini is the only person in the zodiac who could find you dull. While you are reeling from the shock and the insult to your intelligence, think about how much smaller and faster Mercury is than Jupiter. They are quicker on the uptake than you are, and cleverer in their manipulation of words and ideas. They are also faster movers physically, and their hands can do quick little tricks that yours couldn't begin to.

The idea of little tricks is one of the things that bothers you about Geminis. There is always the suspicion that they are somehow less than honest; you, of course, are absolutely straight, so the slightest deviation from that will show in comparison. You are right: Geminis aren't always honest. They're not consciously dishonest, either; the idea of honesty just doesn't apply to them, because their energies are directed towards their own amusement, and not towards public duty. If it amuses them to twist an argument a little for a better effect, then they will do it; similarly, if there is some fun to be had from a little sleight-of-hand, then they will do that, too.

Geminis seem to spend their time accumulating surface knowledge; it annoys you to see them wasting their talent this way, when they could be investigating the higher intellectual pursuits. It does not occur to you, though, that they like doing things their way, that they don't really have your capacity for pure knowledge, and that they can't see why you spend your time with worthy causes when you could make an absolute fortune using your perception commercially.

Essentially, they use their powerful mentality to amuse

themselves, while you feel obliged to use yours for the benefit of everyone. Your attitude seems pompous to him; his seems selfish to you.

It must have struck you by now that there is more to forming a relationship than matching mentalities. There is, but in this case it is the area you keep returning to again and again, because it is the single thing which, more than anything else, you pick up on in each other; everything else gets pushed aside.

As friends, you will get along wonderfully; you will be eager to tell each other new things that you have noticed, and your love of news and gossip generally will keep you chatting away for ever. Gemini will have a little fun at your expense from time to time when he thinks that you are being dull, but you will forgive him; in your opinion, being dull is a punishable offence anyway, and you are grateful for his reminders.

As your lover, Gemini will surprise you: he is even lighter in his affections than you are. Not only does he not want to be involved, he doesn't really want things to be excessively physical anyway—he doesn't have half an animal for his sign the way you do. Sometimes you will be left thinking that you could really do with somebody a little more basic in his tastes.

As business partners you will do very well, but neither of you have any time for boring routine work; this could be a problem, as could the fact that neither of you have much tolerance of things going wrong—you would rather be off starting something new than helping an ailing project through a sticky patch.

These two signs work very well when married to each other. It's not a relationship which values stability and wealth, but it will give you what you want: bright conversation, plenty of variety, and a not-too-serious outlook.

*Sagittarius-Cancer*
This one is as difficult as the Taurean relationship, but in different ways. In the final analysis, it is probably easier, because the Cancerian will change his position more easily than the Taurean; in fact, he is quite keen to make progress, because he is a Cardinal sign. The problem with the Taurean was how to

match your desire for movement to somebody who was determined to stay static; the problem here is how to match your openness and love of company to somebody who is very shy and reserved.

Cancerians do not live their life on the outside in the way that you do. They are extremely sensitive, and they respond very quickly to the emotional needs of others; understandably, they have to have a mechanism for shutting off this response, or they would become exhausted just by walking down a crowded street. Remember, Sagittarius, that these people absorb energy from others; they don't pump it out like you do. If, then, they absorb, they don't have much of a choice in what they take in; they will have to take what comes. This makes life a much riskier business than it is for a Fire sign like yourself, and they will make very sure that they trust a person first, before they allow themselves to absorb his influence.

When they find that somebody is in need of their care and protection, they respond at once with love and care. You probably wouldn't notice that anybody needed help—it's not easy to feel a lack of energy in somebody when you are youself an energy source. This is how Sagittarians get their reputation for being unsubtle and insensitive; it's not that you don't care, it's that you can't see when care is needed, or how much.

A Cancerian shields and protects—himself, his family, his friends. He responds, too: it's how he acts. Look at that again— Fire signs act of their own accord, but Water signs react to the actions of others. Cancer, because it is governed by the Moon, reacts by reflecting the kind of light you shine at it. Treat a Cancerian harshly, and see how the crab's pincers nip; treat them with kindness, and they will respond with kindness.

A Cancerian will treat you very warily at first. Your ever-changing point of view means that he has continually to re-evaluate you, and see whether he needs to change his responses, or perhaps retreat into his shell: his own security comes first, remember. This process takes time. When you have a new enthusiasm which completely captures your imagination and makes you want to devote the rest of your life to it, as is usual for Sagittarians at weekly intervals, the Cancerian is rather slower to

react than you would like. He is also decidedly short on
enthusiasm, by your standards; he just doesn't have the energy
to throw away in the way that you do. He also worries: what is he
to do if things don't quite work out? He doesn't have your ability
to recover from setbacks in a matter of minutes, you see.

He gasps at your openness, and closes his eyes in fright at the
risks you take; on the other hand, he loves your warmth and
genuineness, and he finds your eternal optimism very cheering.
You tease them for being so cautious, but you appreciate their
selfless devotion to the care of their families and friends—
higher motives are something you are very aware of, and anyone
who displays them, in whatever form, gets your approval. On a
selfish level, there is something that they do for you which no
other sign can: when one of your imaginative schemes has
collapsed, leaving you temporarily floored, they will care for
you, and you appreciate that. A friend whose life you brighten
when you are up, and who comforts you when you are down,
isn't a bad thing at all, and you know that.

As friends, you are an odd couple, but you like each other's
company. It's not easy to see why; perhaps it is because they
reflect a little of yourself back at you, and that's the kind of
audience you like. As lovers, you are a long way apart. They are
very emotionally involved, whereas you are not; their enthusiasm
also goes in phases, like lunar phases, which will surprise you at
first.

Marriage will take some working at for this pair of signs.
Cancer is very home-loving, and seeks always to make a safe
retreat for himself and his family; Sagittarius wonders what all
the fuss is about. You will have to adjust to each other. The same
goes for a business partnership; if you handle the marketing, and
they handle the financial side, you won't have any problems—
but don't try to tell each other how to do the job!

### Sagittarius-Leo

This is the other partnership possible within your own element.
Theoretically it should be as much fun as the Aries pairing, but it
isn't. It isn't at all bad, and you enjoy each other's company, but

the Leo doesn't bring a smile to your face the way an Arian does. He's a bit static, to your way of thinking. He's bright and warm, generous and friendly; but he isn't keen on seeing new things in the same way that you are, and when he travels, he does it surrounded by familiar things, so that he isn't really changing his surroundings at all. He's not a mover like the Arian, and he hasn't got anything like your intellect; what he's got is warmth and generosity, but you have enough of that yourself, and so you don't find his all that remarkable.

The truth of the matter is that he likes you a lot more than you like him. Not that you dislike him particularly; he's optimistic, open, and lively just like you are, and that's more than can be said for most of the other signs, but he doesn't have anything that would make you want to trade places with him. He adores you, though.

What you have that he wants is wisdom. Look at it this way: Aries has physical confidence, an implicit belief in his own body and its capabilities. Leo has enough of that to be going on with, but more importantly he has social confidence—the stuff that makes everybody cluster round him and want to be his friend. Sagittarius has spiritual confidence: it is his soul that is bright and strong, and the Leo finds that desperately desirable. An Arian wants simply to do things; a Leo wants to be recognized for what he is doing. In the Sagittarian's high principles he sees the perfection of his endeavours: action accumulated into experience, wisdom distilled from that experience, then handed on to influence others, and gratefully acknowledged.

Leo is fine as long as he stays where he is, and he knows that. If anything displaces him from the centre of the action, or something new comes along and changes the order of things, he is troubled. How envious he is of your confidence and mobility! He is confident enough on his own, of course, but only as long as he has people around him; he can't take his achievements along with him the way you can. Leo is expansive and generous, and Aries is mobile, but only Sagittarius is both; Leo would love to be like that.

What he enjoys that you wish you did (but this he can't give you) is everybody's approval and friendship. Everybody loves a Leo, and he loves being generous to his friends in response to that. The process is self-sustaining, and everyone benefits. Not everybody loves a Sagittarian, as you will have learned by now, though they work in the same way; possibly it is because Leos tend to hand out material comforts, whereas Sagittarians hand out truth and knowledge, which don't always go down so well.

As friends, you get along very well, provided that you can slip into the subordinate role necessary for the friendship to continue. Leos like their friends to treat them as important figures; your dislike of pomp and ceremony could be a hindrance here.

As lovers, you will have a lot of fun; Leos are pretty conventional in their tastes, but they are strong, and they like a good time. There will probably be quite a bit of rolling around on the floor—both of your signs are animals, remember.

The drawback about going into business together is that you won't be able to work for somebody who knows less than you do, whereas the Leo won't play if he can't be boss. The same applies to marriage—he has to be the master of the house, and if you don't want that, then don't marry a Leo. He won't want you to go wandering off on your own, either, as you will inevitably feel drawn to do.

### Sagittarius-Virgo

Three-signs-apart relationships aren't usually a good idea; not unless you like having rows, anyway. This one is less of a strain than most, because both of you are pretty flexible in your approach to things, and because both of you have a strong sense of doing things for other people's benefit. All this helps the pair of you make the compromises necessary to form a relationship.

The essential problem is one of scale. You have a boundless imagination which needs to roam free, forming great universal concepts and apply them to the whole of mankind; they have very little imagination, and even less time for hypothetical concepts, preferring to concentrate their energies on the actual job in hand and to make sure that every detail of it is attended to.

You see things through a telescope, and they see things through a microscope. Quite some problem, as you will appreciate.

What you have in common, and it is worth building on, is an interest in how things work, and how to do things for the best. In their case, the emphasis is on the actual mechanics of the process; to them 'How does it work?' means taking it apart with a screwdriver; to you, it means 'What do people do with it? How does that help them? Why do they want to do that?

It is important that you should not cross over into each other's territory. As partners, you can accomplish a great deal together, with one of you looking after theory and application, and the other one giving time to technique and efficiency. If you start to apply your generalized grasp of things to specific tasks, you will make errors of detail. Similarly, he lacks both the facility to deal with the theoretical instead of the actual, and the scope to handle things on your scale. Don't criticize him for being fussy over details: somebody has to be, and he has a talent for it. It's not your field, so leave him to it. In the same way, you can cheerfully ignore him when he criticizes you for having your head in the clouds.

After a while you will recognize each other for what you are—experts in parallel fields that do not touch or overlap in any way.

Mentally, you are quite different. Both of you like to see the inner states of things, but the Virgo analyses carefully, bit by bit, whereas you grasp the whole thing at once, and perceive its meaning in one go. You are similar but different emotionally, too. Neither of you wants to feel tied down, but in your case that is because of a love of freedom, whereas for the Virgo it is simply that he feels lost with irrational things like emotions, and so tries not to have much to do with them.

As friends, you should be able to understand each other, at least. You have similar views, but for different reasons, as we have just seen; if you come to an understanding about the difference of scale in your views of life, then you will probably enjoy comparing your experiences. As lovers, you are not really suited. Virgos are too careful altogether; you prefer things to be a bit more boisterous. In any case, the Virgoan doesn't have the energy of the Fire signs, nor any of your sense of exuberant fun.

As business partners, you need a third person. You work on a large and impractical scale, Sagittarius, and Virgo's scale is too small; most things happen in the middle, and who will look after that?

You *can* work together as a marriage, though you will find their small-scale view very frustrating. The necessary technique is for you to attack common problems from different ends in your own ways.

### Sagittarius-Libra

The best of the lot, as far as these relationships go. There's more to matching people astrologically than just comparing Sun signs: but having said that, you won't get far if the Sun signs *don't* match, and as far as you're concerned, this is the one to go for.

You like Librans. It's as simple as that. When you have one of your great ideas in your head, they are interested; when you tell them about it, they like listening. They talk back, too, in just the way you would like them to—brightly, with interest and humour. Their attitude is one of optimism, like your own, and they are quite sure that the next thing is going to be even better than the current one, just as you are. They are friendly, too; they positively adore company, and don't like being on their own any more than you do. When you decide that it's time you got up and did something, they ask to come along for the ride, but they don't get in the way; that's just how you like it. They will fall in love with you, which flatters you enormously, but they don't get emotionally dependent on you, and they don't cling. Nor do they get moody or temperamental—in fact they will do almost anything to avoid an argument, and would much rather think about something else instead, preferably something new and entertaining. Just the same as you, in fact. If you were to sit down with pencil and paper, and make a list of all that you wanted in a partner, you wouldn't come up with anything better than a Libran.

You can't find anything wrong with them at all; in fact they are suspiciously well suited to you, and you may wonder why.

To be fair, they are just as pleasant to everybody, because

that's how they are; you may have suspected this. On the other hand, not everybody finds their light and friendly outlook on life to their taste; it happens to suit you very well, so you might as well make the most of it.

Librans are Air sign people. They live in a world of thought, speech, and ideas, where what you say is more interesting than what you do, and where nothing lasts for very long. They are also the Cardinal Air sign, so they are the most active and assertive of their element. You, on the other hand, are a Fire sign, which is to do with creative physical activity; but because you are the Mutable Fire sign, your activity tends to have mental rather than a physical emphasis. So you are the sign of mental activity, and they are the sign of active mentality, which is pretty much the same thing. Now you see why you like each other.

They see you as being much more assertive and effective versions of themselves. That same envy you have of the Arian's energy, they have of yours. They also see you as the ideal conversational partner: they love talking, and you never seem to run out of things to say. They like being entertained, and you seem to know so much (their own minds don't hold deep knowledge like yours does).

As friends, you are perfect. You lead your own lives, but in parallel, and you love to tell each other everything that has happened to you. Your conversations can never become heavy: there is always laughter and entertainment in them somewhere. Even after many years, you should be able to note how genuinely *pleased* you are to see each other, and how much you have to say to each other. Arguments just never seem to surface; you are completely sympathetic to each other's point of view.

As lovers, you should be almost ideal. Librans are a bit on the cool side sexually, but they are very friendly, and being a cardinal sign will give them enough strength to match your Fiery power. Neither of you take it too seriously, and both of you like the affair to be flexible and full of variety; these two things alone make it more enjoyable for you both than your other relationships, even if they have more passion.

As business partners, you will dominate. They are your

partner, not you theirs, and that means that if you have some areas where you are lazy, they won't fill in the gaps for you: not necessarily a good thing.

If you marry, you should be very content. The Libran will make your day-to-day existence very pleasant indeed, through his talent for making things relaxed and graceful. Neither of you are much good at fighting your way out of tight corners, though, and you may need some of that quality at some stage.

*Sagittarius-Scorpio*
There are quite a lot of Sagittarians who have relationships with Scorpios. Like everybody else in the zodiac, they are attracted to the intense energy that the Scorpio puts out. With this particular pairing, the Sagittarian finds that the Scorpio is nothing like as much fun as he had hoped, and the Scorpio finds that holding the Sagittarius in check is more trouble than it's worth. Eventually the Centaur, tired of being made to rear up by having the Scorpion under his hooves, takes his quiver and brains the little beast; then he gallops off into the sunset wishing he hadn't been so hasty.

Scorpios are all the things that you hate most, and what makes it worse is that you can see what they're doing it for. They are secretive where you are frank, underhand where you are honest, and manipulative where you are generous. What they are trying to do is stay in control of everything. To them, it is important that the result of every action is known; if it is not, a situation leading to possible loss of control could result, leaving the Scorpio vulnerable to attack. They take great pains to assess the motivation of everybody they come into contact with, and are masters of interpersonal politics. If there is any plotting going on, then the Scorpio either knows about it, is doing it, or—very Scorpio, this—suggested it. The amazing thing to you is that nobody can see this process going on; Scorpios take great care to keep their actions and feelings well hidden, and for the most part it works. It doesn't work with you, though; you can see into the situation without trying, and the devices of the Scorpio are quite visible to you. How angry this makes the Scorpio! How stupid he is made to feel, too, when you open a conversation by referring to some of his scheming, as in 'What are you doing hiding under the desk with a tape recorder, Scorpio?'

The fact that you seem not to care for your own safety, and are absurdly honest in your speech, makes him cringe in embarrassment; but the fact that you seem not only to get away with it but to benefit from it makes him grind his teeth with rage.

He sees you as a holy fool, protected by angels from the consequences of your naïvety. You see him as raging at his own insecurity, somebody who would be a lot better off if he could have the confidence to trust other people with himself. It's not really a good basis for a relationship.

For you to be good friends is unlikely. When you do have conversations, you will be aware of how much the Scorpio is trying to take off you, and how little he is willing to give in return. You would welcome his views on things, even if they were different to yours, but you know that he isn't going to let you know what he really thinks, and that annoys you. When you lose your temper, of course, he just smiles; other people's emotional outbursts are like food to him, because it puts him firmly in control of the situation.

A much likelier reason for you to be together is sexual attraction. Your ruling planets have much to do with it: Scorpio's Mars is a power for containment from outside, and your Jupiter is an irresistible expansion from within. Both of you enjoy the way the pressure rises when you are together. Scorpio is actually stronger than you are sexually, Sagittarius, but it won't be exhaustion that will make you decide you've had enough—his obsessive and possessive emotional energies will get to you first.

You don't like each other's methods enough to be reasonable business partners. As marriage partners, you would have to accept that the Scorpio will want to contain your energy, and that you would be unable to roam lest his awesome jealousy erupt. You would, of course, attempt to influence him for the better (as you would see it), but he will find it difficult to be as open or as flexible about things as you are. Present him with a variety of things and he simply tries to control all of them at the same time—he just can't let go. Eventually you would just get up and leave for good.

*Sagittarius-Sagittarius*

As with all the pairings between identical signs, this one has plenty to recommend it, and a few drawbacks as well. At least you are both Mutable signs, which means that you are both interested in examining a different point of view; if you were both dogmatic and unwilling to change your views at all, you would be in trouble from the start. You are both outgoing signs, too, which again brings benefits, because you are both willing to contribute to the situation; if you were both collecting signs, you would sit there each waiting for the other person to put something into the relationship.

So much for the good side of things. The trouble with this relationship is that you are both right. You both know all that there is to know about everything, and you both know it. You are therefore both right all the time; the trouble is that you are likely to be different. It is a difficult thing for a Sagittarian to understand that truth is essentially a personal concept, and that what seems true to one person may not be acceptable, or even credible, to another. If the other person is a Sagittarian like yourself you are doubly confused. You had thought that somebody like yourself would be able to see things the right way (i.e. your way), but it turns out not to be like that. You are also bothered because they are just as persuasive as you are, and their arguments are as clear and convincing as your own: it is all most unsettling.

Not that you spend much of your time deep in philosophical discussion, even though it does interest you greatly; you have other things to show each other. One of the great things about being a Sagittarius is your capacity to be inspired and excited by somebody else's interest, especially if it is new to you, and if they can communicate their own enthusiasm for it. Other signs retreat into themselves when faced with something unfamiliar, but you welcome it cheerfully. Obviously, another Sagittarian will have much to show you, and indeed much that he wants to show you; you welcome all of it. When you have a shared interest, you go off and do it together, but you don't get under each other's feet and you are not dependent on each other: these are the qualities you expect to find in others (because you have them in yourself) and you are delighted to find them in another Sagittarian.

A friendship between you may well be episodic in nature. Both of you have other things to do, and will go off and do them; when you both have time, perhaps you will see each other again, and talk about what you have been doing. Your friendship doesn't need to be regular to be enjoyable; it isn't formed from emotional dependency, but from a shared love of action and excitement. Something to look out for in a Sagittarian friendship is a tendency to talk about what you are hoping to do, rather than what you have already done; Sagittarian thought looks ever forward and upwards, and the future is more exciting to you than the past.

As lovers you will be evenly matched in terms of energy and inclinations, of course. You will be able to indulge in as much horseplay (don't ever forget the animal that forms your bottom half) as you want, and you gain much enjoyment from the knowledge that for both of you it is the spirit of the moment that counts. Love may well be for ever, but for you it must be right now as well.

As business partners you are hopeless: you both want to do the interesting bits, and neither of you can be bothered to stay up late doing the accounts. The same goes for a marriage: you are going to have to make sure that somebody does the household chores sometime. Not that either of you are great home-builders; as long as you have books to read, maps to plan your next journey together, and somewhere to sleep, you're quite happy.

### Sagittarius-Capricorn

This is the most difficult of all the Sun-sign relationships for you to handle. It isn't that the Capricorn has any real trouble dealing with you, though he could think of other people he would rather be friends with, but that your planet, Jupiter, has a particular dislike for the sign of Capricorn. Capricorn is one of Saturn's two signs, of course, and Jupiter has never been too keen on Saturn; one planet tries to break out of all restraints, and the other tries to form closed frameworks. Read pages 22 and 23 again to remind yourself of what we are dealing with here.

You dislike Capricorn quite strongly. He seems on the one hand to have all the qualities you are trying to gain for yourself, which makes you envious, but he also seems to deserve them less, which offends your high principles.

If you remember the sequence of the zodiac signs you will get a better idea of what I mean. Sagittarius, as you know, is proud of his knowledge and perception. What he wants to do is to distribute this knowledge for the benefit of everybody, and to gain recognition and reputation as his reward. Capricorn, the next sign on, represents that reputation and recognition. Capricorn is what everybody sees as a man of reputation: the head of the company, the managing director, the big landowner, the plutocrat. You will notice at once that all these definitions contain images of money. That's what makes you mad: why is it, you ask, that the only reputation that seems to have any weight attached to it is a financial one? Why can't you be recognized for your ideas, in a Sagittarian way? The answer to that is that Capricorn is an Earth sign, and weight is of course a physical property, so therefore connected to physical matter, and hence to the element of Earth. Anything which has weight and importance on this planet is of the Earth; how do you think the planet got its name? (No, I'm not joking!)

Anyway, at the end of it all, the Capricorn has the money, the power, and the reputation, and you don't. You could live with this if it weren't for the fact that he hasn't got a fraction of your knowledge. Nor has he your warmth, your compassion, your imagination, your willingness to help, your spiritual depth, the nobility of your soul, or any of your optimism. In fact, he strikes you as a thoroughly uninspiring individual, and yet he has all the rewards this life can offer. Few things make you really angry, but this does.

He is quiet, methodical, and a really hard worker. He likes

things ordered, and regular. He likes things to be in their places, and for there to be well-defined links between these places. He fits brilliantly into any corporate structure, and rises through it by regular hard work, and identification with the corporation. In other words, he's a company man.

You couldn't imagine anything worse, could you? No imagination, no freedom, no impulsiveness. No far horizons, no knowledge, no vision.

He sees you in an equally unflattering light. You have no organization, no structure. You won't wait for anything; you have no sense of time. You have no reserve, no tact; you also pay no respect to your superiors. Worst of all, you give things away—knowledge, warmth, companionship. Why can't you see that if you have things that other people want, then you should sell them, not give them away? No wonder you have no money.

From this you will understand that a friendship between you will be almost impossible in your terms. If you tell a Capricorn anything, he will use it to advance his own reputation, not yours. In addition, if you refuse to recognize him as the successful person he is, he will end the friendship—to the Capricorn if there is no reward then it is not worthwhile.

As lovers, your motives are somewhat different. Physically, everything will be fine—Capricorns have a goat for their animal, so you know what to expect—but deep down, you make love for fun, and they make love as part of a career plan.

As business partners, you can do very well, *if* you are prepared to take it as seriously as they do. Capricorns are wonderful businessmen anyway, but they lack your entrepreneurial spirit. If you provide that, and direct your energies firmly to the job in hand, then Capricorn will see to it that you both become very wealthy.

Marriage? Possibly—but it isn't a love match, it's an arrangement, a private deal. You give all your warmth and knowledge to them, and they give all their practical management skills to you. The result is that your ideas and personality get converted into money, and they have the pleasure of your company and talent as an exclusive right, which appeals to the snob in them. Not a bad arrangement—but short on romance, so be warned.

*Sagittarius-Aquarius*
It is difficult to comprehend how two signs, ruled by the same planet, could be so different in their attitude towards you, but there it is: Capricorn and Aquarius are both Saturn's signs, but where the Capricorn pairing is almost impossibly hard, this one is delightfully easy. It is similar, in many ways, to the Libra partnership.

Aquarius is a bit of a paradox, but since both sides of it appeal to you, there are no problems. On the one hand, an Aquarian loves company, and is always involved with some social group or other, but on the other hand, he feels that he is different from everybody else, and is attracted to anything unusual, or which makes him stand apart from the crowd. All of this is fine by you—you like a varied social life too, and anything which is different you find interesting.

Aquarius is an Air sign, as Libra and Gemini are, and as in those relationships, this is one where you seem to have a lot to talk about. Aquarians don't have your depth of insight, but they have a refreshingly wide range of interests, and they get quite passionate when talking about issues which arouse their concern. This means that you can have a good argument with an Aquarian, pulling at the subject between you like two dogs with a stick, and both enjoying the affair enormously. Only the two of you will realize that you *like* this process; other signs will be horrified at what they see as bitter feuding, though Gemini will appreciate what you are up to, and probably join in for the hell of it. The difference between Aquarius and Gemini, as far as you're concerned, is that you really disagree quite fundamentally with what the Gemini is doing, whereas most of the time you are in agreement with the Aquarian's principles, and that makes your arguments much more playful affairs.

Principles are funny things; to have them, you have to be able to look outside yourself, and think of the wider implications of things. Both you and Aquarius have high principles, and you appreciate this in each other. In the Aquarius, it often shows as a particular political persuasion, or a devotion to humanitarian causes. Another thing you might notice is how determinedly egalitarian they are. In an Aquarian's world, everybody is equal, and all hierarchies or master-and-servant relationships are seen as a bad thing. This isn't so far removed from your own view that respect is given rather than demanded, and that everybody should be free to do what they please.

You see them as talkative and sociable people, who believe in good causes and are prepared to argue their case. They see you as refreshingly enthusiastic friends, honest and loyal, not afraid to speak your mind, and with the right sort of ideas about most things.

A friendship between you is a very easy thing to produce. You find a great deal of comfort in knowing somebody who is likely to understand what you are trying to say, but is not necessarily going to agree with your opinion in every case. It is also good, in your eyes at least, to have a friend who doesn't want to be too closely tied to you emotionally; Aquarians are quite cool in that respect, and they understand your need for freedom very well, since it is similar to their own need to be independent.

As lovers, you are very well suited. They have plenty of physical stamina, and they like playing, but they don't need deep emotional commitment. That's just how you like it.

Business partners? Maybe, if you can find something which maintains your interest and doesn't offend your principles. You're good as a team, but are you really businessmen at heart? Marriage would be a much better bet—a lively, open partnership, looking forwards to a better future. You might find that it lacked a sense of traditional family values, but you could supply that.

### Sagittarius-Pisces

A very interesting partnership, as indeed all relationships involving Pisces are. It is a sign containing every possibility, but often it doesn't know which one to choose. Nothing about the Piscean is clear-cut; when you try to pin them down, they run through your fingers. It's what you would expect from Mutable Water, if you think about it.

The zodiac comes up with some strange combinations, and this is one of the strangest. Although you are of different elements, representing different directions (they are incoming, you are outgoing) in different universes (they are imaginary, you are real), you are ruled to the same planet—Jupiter. All that expansion and growth, all that energy for increase, is *inverted* in the Piscean. Where you radiate energy and enthusiasm outwards, exploring distant lands, and gathering experience and knowledge, they are expanding inwards, discovering new and more fantastic realms of experience and sensation inside themselves, painting ever more complex patterns on the *insides* of their heads. Fascinating idea, isn't it?

They are sensitive and imaginative like nobody else in the zodiac. These people can think in terms of colour and music, drama and poetry, and sometimes all of them at once, in a way which you find compelling. They can be anything they want; they take their cues from the situation they find themselves in, and somehow manage to be all things to all men. The whole business fascinates you; your curiosity wants to know what the real nature of the Piscean is, under all the disguises.

There isn't one. They really are who they say they are at the time. There is a fundamental difference between you, which, although it sounds far removed from daily life, actually underlies everything you do together, and it is this:

You think that once you know something, it is an unalterable fact for ever. The truth never changes, in your view. The Piscean knows that today's answer may not be quite so true tomorrow. In his view, truth is defined by the person to whom it seems true, and that person is constantly changing.

So the Piscean is as keen to know things as you are, but he enjoys the way that what he knows changes as time goes by. You can sense this somehow, and you are very curious to experience it for yourself.

You see them as fascinating creatures, so sensitive that the slightest stimulus will set their imaginations off into flights of creative fantasy. You can't quite see all this as being useful, though, and you have the sneaky feeling that a lot of your own knowledge may be similarly viewed by others.

They see you as great sources of creative energy, enough for you to wear your ideas on the outside, which they find very impressive. They see your clarity of thought as particularly desirable, because in your case you do appear to have compromised your imagination to obtain your logical approach. Because you are so much more confident and expressive than they are, they see you as an admirable blend of creative imagination and worldly success. This isn't quite right, as you will no doubt tell them, because you are honest that way, but you must admit that it's very flattering of them to see you in those terms.

Friendship between you is formed out of mutual curiosity and admiration rather than what you have in common. You have conversations like magicians practising their art on each other; you give them ideas to see what the Piscean does with them, and they give you impressions of things from which you try to guess the original stimulus. Like Art, these encounters work on more than one level at once; you find it exacting but satisfying, and although you think you know what you get out of it, you probably couldn't explain it to anybody else.

Should you become lovers, you will find yourselves communicating on two more levels simultaneously—the animal and the spiritual. You will have to be a little less robust in your approach than is usual for you, but when it all works you will discover dimensions of yourself you never knew you had.

As business partners you would only do really well if you were in a media-related business. You are both too good with ideas and not good enough with routines, finances and organization to feel at home in a traditional business structure.

If you married, you would be happy enough, but unless one of you has a practical streak somewhere, you would need all sorts of help to manage your finances and do things like fix the plumbing. Not that you'd care: in this marriage, material things are definitely a low priority.

# Capricorn

### Capricorn-Aries

In the long run this relationship needs a fair bit of work if it is to be successful, though initially there are a lot of things you appear to have in common, and you will find that attractive. Both of you like to be effective in your actions, and you like to see things getting done rather than sit around thinking about them, but the motivation behind your preferences are very, very different.

The major difference between you is your idea of time. Aries lives for the instant: it is pretty difficult for him to imagine tomorrow with any degree of seriousness, let alone next year, and extreme cases may have difficulty with this afternoon, especially before lunch. You, on the other hand, can see next year as though it were today, and have no problems laying plans for five or even ten years hence. What you are doing is building for the future, while what he is doing is living for today. If you go into partnership with an Arian, you cannot expect him really to understand how important it is to you that things be done at the proper place and time; to them, if they want to do it, they will do it at once. Neither the future nor the past has any bearing on what an Arian does at this moment; only what he feels at this moment is of any importance. As you can see, his capacity for immediate action can be very useful for getting things started, but he needs (in your view, at any rate) careful guidance if his talents are not to be wasted, and if he is to help you realize your plans.

There is something very simple about an Arian, and it is rather noble at the same time: quite simply, he does things for the joy of doing them, not for the reward at the end. You know very well what makes you such a hard and willing worker is the recognition you hope to enjoy at the end of it all: in your world, the harder you work, the higher you rise.

Aries is simpler than that. He doesn't care what people think of his efforts. It never occurs to him to do something purely to enhance his reputation. He only knows whether the task at hand appeals to him—if it does, he will do it, and if it doesn't, he won't. What he actually works for is the pleasure of being at work; for him, the enjoyment he gets from experiencing action is as important as the pleasure you get when you are promoted to a new position. His whole existence is centred around the physical sensations of being in action. What he does something *for* doesn't matter—what matters is that he does it, and that he does it now. Aries is a pure physical force.

You appreciate his direct approach to things, his energy, and the fact that everything he attempts, he completes. You like his confidence, and his capacity for effort. If you had that kind of strength, you think, you could do anything. But there again, you remind yourself, that kind of explosive energy can only last a short time, and what you would really like is sustained energy over a longer period. What you want is steady heat, whereas the Arian provides ignition or explosion.

He sees you as a father figure. You have a longer view of events, and you are more sensible, in his eyes. You are surrounded by all the material tokens of seniority, and he sees you as older than you are because of them, and because it is obvious that you think and move much more slowly than he does. One day he would like to be like you—but not yet!

As friends, you will be pleased to find that you are aiming for the same goals. You will share a dislike for indecisive people, and an appreciation of anything that gives quick results from firm action. You will probably approve of each other's taste in cars and clothes, but for different reasons.

As lovers, you should be evenly matched. Capricorn has the stamina, while Aries has the strength; both of you come from the sign of an animal with horns, so you are both strongly sexed. Capricorns aren't usually very keen on experimental sex; strong but conventional is how you like it. As it happens, Arians are similar, because for them the body is more important than the mind, and so their imaginations aren't put to work thinking up variations; there will be few complaints from either of you.

As business partners, you could do very well provided that you channel his energy effectively; you will have to do the organizing for the two of you.

You would make a better marriage than many would think. Be prepared for the Arian's temper, and try at least sometimes to do things on the spur of the moment for his sake if nothing else. Essentially, you both appreciate each other's capabilities, and are willing to share your own in return for some of your partner's.

*Capricorn-Taurus*

This is a much easier relationship—one of your best. If stability and the enjoyment of your hard-earned high standard of living is what you want, then the Taurean is just the person to share it with you. They are an Earth sign, as you are, and so they understand instinctively the importance you place on what you have to show for your efforts. They appreciate beautiful things, too, and have similar tastes to yours.

Taureans are dedicated to steadiness, and the pursuit of a life without disturbance and change. When they are in a situation which seems both comfortable and manageable for them, they do all that they can to keep it as it is; they regard it as their particular territory, and will resist any attempts to dislodge them from it, defending it to the death, if need be.

What you like about Taureans is that they are the originators of the good life: sumptuously decorated houses, fine foods and wines, cars with leather seats and soft suspension are all Taurean. What a Taurean needs most of all is physical security, and by that he means surrounding himself with objects which he can touch and be comforted by. He needs to know where his next meal is coming from, and he needs that meal not only to nourish him, but to reassure him that he is as fine a person as he thinks he is, by its physical qualities. If you think about that for a moment, you will realize that not only must the Taurean have a very full freezer at all times, but it must be full of luxury food as well. If all he has to eat is basic foodstuffs, then he doesn't feel reassured. The same sort of ideas apply to his clothes and house as well.

To you, work is energy being converted into money; in the Taurean, you have a person whose existence is devoted to the appreciation of what that money will buy. You find that in itself reassuring, and when you wonder what you are working so hard for, five minutes with a Taurean will remind you.

The only problem with Taureans is that they are so static. You appreciate stability as much as anyone else, but you do like to feel yourself making progress and moving along through life; Taureans aren't interested in moving, only in making where they are more comfortable. There is a puritanical streak in you, which comes, unsurprisingly, from Saturn, and which enables you to do without life's little luxuries on the way to better things; Taurus won't do without *anything*.

They see you as exactly what they would like to be— financially successful. They miss the point to some extent, in that you are financially successful as a sort of side effect of being at the top of the pile, but that is entirely understandable because the idea of position doesn't have a lot of meaning for them. What they would like is to be able to afford all the lovely things they are so fond of—and it seems that you have the ability to turn time into money, which is true.

As friends, you will enjoy each other's company immensely, and will particularly enjoy spending money together; they will find your sense of the status of objects as interesting as you find their sense of texture and colour. You could both end up extremely fat, of course; food is a major pleasure with Taureans. When matters get serious, though, and you need to discuss your next move, you will seek advice from elsewhere; their defensive approach to business isn't always what you want to hear. Should you go into business together, they make wonderful partners, because they will always be supportive and reliable; the initiative, however, has to come from you.

Although having a lover of the same element as yourself is usually a good thing, you might find that they are more sensitive emotionally than you had realized, and you could be out of your depth a little. On a sexual level you may be surprised by their strength and possessiveness.

This pairing makes for a good marriage provided that your main aim is to have a secure and enjoyable home life; if you are more interested in achieving than enjoying you will find the Taurean more of a hindrance than a help.

### Capricorn-Gemini

This is a very dry and crackly sort of pairing: there are plenty of things to produce sparks between you, but almost no heat. Emotionally, this one is conducted at a very low level, and because of that it may be the sort of thing you are looking for.

Gemini has the fastest thinking brain in the whole zodiac. He is able to see the point of a sentence before the speaker has finished. He also likes re-telling stories, with slightly altered details, just for fun. He can play with words and ideas like nobody else, and he doesn't really believe any one of them. This isn't surprising: Nature makes ducks waterproof because they spend a lot of time in the water, and it makes Geminis immune to persuasion by the words they use so much.

What a Gemini needs more than anything else is to be amused, and he does this by absorbing huge amounts of new information. He doesn't remember it all, and he doesn't want to: he just wants to read it or hear it, and for it to keep him amused for a few minutes.

He is not working to a plan in the same way that you are, though he does have a better sense of time than, say, an Arian. He isn't part of a structure, either; he doesn't feel that everything is best if it stays in its appointed place. There is a strong streak of the anarchist in a Gemini, which rises to the surface every so often when he feels that things aren't changing fast enough to keep him amused, and that he had better do something about it.

Geminis don't share your belief that hard work is the only way to achieve your goals, either. They are, given half a chance, extremely lazy. It's not really their fault—they are an Air sign, which isn't at all practical or down-to-earth, and they are governed by Mercury, which doesn't have the weight or driving force of, say, Saturn or Mars.

So far, it seems you are trying to form a relationship with an idle, fork-tongued anarchist; what is it about them that captivates you? Firstly, his sense of humour. Geminian humour is all verbal and cerebral; there is very little of the simple clown in it. Your own sense of humour is wry and dry, and his sharp wit appeals to you a great deal. Because of the Saturnine influence you bring with you, in your presence his humour becomes even more piercing and sardonic, and in return your own becomes more verbal and better expressed. The pity about this process is that the lighter side of the Gemini's humour, the awful schoolboy jape side, gets lost; you have no time for that sort of thing, and so your Saturn influence crushes it out of the Gemini before it gets a chance to show itself.

The other thing you like about Geminians is their ability to analyse situations at work. They are fast, accurate, and dispassionate, and you admire them for it. If you were like that, you think,you could really make some progress. It never occurs to you that Gemini isn't interested in that sort of progress, does it?

They see you as rather slow, and too careful by half, but they like your black humour, and they would like to enjoy the capacity for self-indulgence that your financial success brings with it. As long as you continue to move up, and to be with powerful people, the Gemini will stay around to be entertained.

As friends, the main attraction is that you are both unemotional; neither of you is likely to get sentimental about the other, and you are both thankful for that. You are much stronger sexually than the Gemini, so if you should become lovers you will be the dominant partner. If you keep things varied, the Gemini will perform well enough; become serious or obsessive, though, and he will quickly lose interest.

As business partners you are wonderful together, provided that your ambition is strong enough to override any twinges of conscience arising from the Gemini's *very* sharp deals.

Marriage? Yes, if you make a few allowances for each other. The flavour of the marriage is hard, though, like bare furniture: fine if you like that sort of thing, but most people like cushions now and again.

## Capricorn-Cancer

This is the union of opposites, and as is always the case in astrology (and real life too), you have a lot more in common than you would think.

Cancer, like you, is concerned with the structure of things. He is reserved, polite, and proper in his dealings, as you are, and mindful of the rights and requirements of others, as you are also. He is a collecting sign, as you are, and is therefore concerned with taking in energy from others so that he can strengthen his own position. Finally, he is a Cardinal sign, as you are, and so he thinks that he won't get anywhere unless he does something about it personally.

Familiar, isn't it? The difference is that his world is internal where yours is external. His purpose and aim is to protect what is his from the attentions of the world, whereas yours is to have the world applaud you for what you have achieved.

Imagine that everyone was given a large box to help them live their life. You, Capricorn, would have the outside of the box painted in fashionable colours, and decked out in fabrics which would show off your status to everybody. This done, you would climb on top of the box so that everybody could see that you were higher up than they were. Now consider Cancer.

Cancer would live inside the box. The outside would be completely plain and featureless; unremarkable and uninviting. Not hostile, not rude, but private nonetheless. Inside would be the most comfortable and cosy home you could imagine, where the whole family would live their lives with much love and affection. The purpose of it all would be emotional nourishment, support, and protection.

The box represents the structure of your life and your career, of course. To you, it exists for you to be able to get to the top; for the Cancer, it exists for his reassurance.

Neither of you can live without that structure. Both of you find it the essential feature of your lives, and if it is ever dissolved, you will build another one at once, in much the same way as spiders with webs.

Cancer has the same sense of time as you do, and is interested in working towards the far future in a patient fashion. You are both builders: he is interested in laying the foundations, and you are interested in the topping-off, but you are both builders at heart, and you can appreciate it in each other.

He sees you as rather too public in your tastes, and uncomfortably spartan and self-denying in your personal life, but he welcomes your serious approach to getting on in life.

You see him as a bit of a worrier, and a little too sentimental about things to be a really effective decision-maker, but you appreciate his determination to succeed. You also welcome his belief that the traditional way of things is probably the best.

As friends, you will take time to get to know one another; once you have each other's trust, the friendship will last for ever.

As lovers, you will find that the Cancerian is as strong as you are, but in different ways; you will find his emotional needs difficult to respond to at first.

In business, you should do well, though you are both better suited to rising through a big organization than to starting up on your own.

Marriage between you is a good idea, because it is a long-term thing, and both of you work better over a longer period. You must appreciate how vital the Cancerian's home life is to him, though.

### Capricorn-Leo

You don't find Fire signs enjoyable: this partnership, along with the Sagittarian one, is easily the most difficult of the twelve for you. Put quite simply, Leos make you spit.

They are lazy, good-natured souls, and they seem to be well-liked for it. You can understand being liked for working, but not for being idle; the fact that they seem to be able to do exactly that annoys you. It never occurs to you that you can't buy affection, that being pleasant isn't to do with being rich, or that hard work won't necessarily make you popular, but that's just how you are—that's the disadvantage of being an Earth sign, and you knew that there had to be one somewhere.

You know what confidence is; it's that inner warmth that comes from being in control, being right, and being able to afford to do what you like. You have it, in some measure, and the harder you work, the more of it you hope to get. It's expensive stuff, as far as you're concerned, because it is only achieved in return for much labour; but there again, if it didn't cost you a lot to get it, you wouldn't feel that it was valuable, would you?

from being in control, being right, and being able to afford to do what you like. You have it, in some measure, and the harder you work, the more of it you hope to get. It's expensive stuff, as far as you're concerned, because it is only achieved in return for much labour; but there again, if it didn't cost you a lot to get it, you wouldn't feel that it was valuable, would you?

Leos were born with it. They have warmth, confidence, and affability enough to throw away—and they do. The sheer waste of it all offends you. How can they be like that, you cry—though what you really mean is why can't I be like that?

The truth of the matter is that you are jealous of Leos. Leo represents the Sun, the source of light and heat, the centre of the solar system. Against their light, you are thrown into shadow. Saturn's weight, the source of your power, is made to seem what it is in the Leo's sunshine—small, cold, grey, and dull. Your achievements are all external: inside you are still the same as you were when you started. What you have managed to do is to compel admiration and respect for your position, but that can't compete with somebody who gives out warmth and light for free. Basically, Leos make you look like Scrooge, and you don't like it.

They see you as somebody out to usurp their position as the natural centre of the group. They see your structured approach to life as being rather unimaginative and cold, and they would rather not give time to it. Life is one big party to a Leo, but they have to have an audience, and they have to be the star of the of the show; if you look as though you will threaten that then they will be most displeased. There is a sense of nobility about Leos: they show royal displeasure if they feel that they are not given due recognition.

A friendship between you is going to be something of a power struggle: both of you want the other to admit that you are the prominent partner. The way round it is to give the Leo preference in a social and personal context, and to concentrate your own power in the world of finance and business. The only trouble here is that neither of you will pay much attention to the other's sphere of influence, since you both rate the other's as un-important and trivial. The power struggle continues on a physical level if you become lovers.

As business partners you could do a lot for each other. Leo has the confidence, and the capacity to inspire confidence, that you often lack. Leo doesn't have your capacity for hard work, or anything like it, but he has an organizational ability which will surprise you when you first meet it. After a while you will recognize that it is as effective and reliable as your own—and considerably more flexible! He hasn't your touch with money, though, so you'll have to look after that for him.

Your marriage would certainly be fun to watch. You would live in the finest style, and have some memorable rows when you felt that your partner was being too selfish. It would need a lot of adjustment from both of you to be really successful, though it would be strengthened by children. Leos love children generally, and are natural parents. Both of you have dynastic ambitions, and see children as extensions of your own excellence going on to the next generation; your own children would give you a common goal.

### Capricorn-Virgo

Here is the second pairing from within your own element. It is much lighter in tone than the Taurean one, and less of its energy is converted into physical objects. From your point of view, it is quite a thought-provoking relationship, and one in which you feel quite comfortable.

The emotional force of Taurus is absent here; Venus' romantic energies are replaced by the altogether cooler ones of Mercury, and you are probably happier with the swap.

Virgo, like Gemini, is a clever and analytical thinker. In this case the mental talents are directed to practical ends, as you would expect for an Earth sign, and the result is an analysis of processes and techniques rather than words and ideas. Virgos are experts on how to do things; they know what to do, how to do it, what skills and tools are needed, and how to add extra little touches to get the result they want. When they meet something new they will take it to pieces to see how it works—sometimes literally! They are thoughtful and methodical in their approach; they like to understand a thing fully and thoroughly, right down to the level of its components, before they feel at home with it.

You will appreciate all this, and feel reassured by the Virgoan approach. There are times when you are working so hard that you don't have time to think, or when you know what has to be done but you aren't sure why it has to be done that way; Virgo tells you the reasons why, and it all makes sense to you.

You have to believe in the order of things: if they are not in their places, if there is no structure and pattern, then you are lost. Virgo reminds you that the order of things carries on down to the smallest level, right down to molecular level, if need be, and you find that very comforting.

On a personal level, you are one of the few people who find Virgo's methodical approach praiseworthy, and his obsession with getting things exactly right admirable. Most people find him picky and over-critical.

He finds your success an inspiring thought. He can see that you work in a similar way, but on a larger scale to himself, and if he had the time and energy he would be just like you, he feels sure. Whenever he has doubts about the correctness of his approach, he looks at what hard work has brought you and feels pleased.

Given that you find each other mutually admirable, a friendship is likely to form very quickly. You fit together very well indeed: he will try constantly to do things for you, and you will be proud of him for it. It is, in fact, his way of showing his affection. He cannot express himself with soft sentiment; instead he shows his affection by being useful. Being useful is the finest thing he can imagine, just as being successful is your fondest dream; if he is useful to you, and you are made more successful because of it, then you have the makings of a fulfilling relationship, though not all of the signs would recognize it as such.

As lovers, you will find that the absence of any sense of the romantic produces a rather dry and dutiful relationship. Virgos are critical of any process which they think could be done better—mind your self-esteem as you get into bed!

You would make a good partnership in business. Virgos can't always see the whole situation at once, but you can; there again, you sometimes can't see the details of things, but that's just what they're best at. You compensate for each other's deficiencies beautifully, and you both enjoy the actual process of working. A really winning combination.

The same sense of industry and purpose would go into a marriage between you, and that would make it a success in material terms. The relationship would lack emotional warmth, though, and it could be seriously short of laughter. You both take life too seriously at times.

### Capricorn-Libra

A very interesting combination. You are two very different people, but each of you has a major talent that the other finds highly desirable, and that's what gives the relationship its initial impetus.

Librans are not practical people like Virgoans. They deal in words and ideas, like all the Air signs; they don't care how a thing gets done so long as they like it when it is finished. In fact, Librans care a great deal about how a thing looks, and they care even more that it should look attractive.

This is the thing that captivates you about a Libran: they have *taste*. They have other qualities, too, but you react most strongly to the ones which apply to your world, and you understand material things much more easily than you understand ideas and feelings. Librans have the ability to choose the most graceful, the most elegant, the most pleasing to the eye, time and time again; you, on the other hand, can't seem to get a lot further than deciding what you want and how much you are going to pay for it. Once your life has been touched by a Libran, compliments start to come rolling in, and you are very keen for that to start happening, very keen indeed.

Librans are professionally nice people: there isn't anyone

who doesn't like them. This quality, instant likability, as you see it, is very attractive to you; it makes you rather ashamed of your own rather low social profile, and your own reputation for being too serious.

There are disadvantages to being everything to everybody, though, and one of them is that you have to keep changing your mind. Indecisiveness isn't something that ever troubles you, and it is that very thing which makes the Libran so eager to make your acquaintance. If some of your firmness of purpose, sense of organization or simply hardness of exterior could be transferred to the Libran, he would be delighted. He is never certain which course to take, never able to decide what to do next for the best, and never able to say no to anybody if he thinks that they might be upset. All of these weaknesses are very apparent to him, as is the fact that you have none of them, and he would love to change places with you.

There are drawbacks to the partnership: just because you admire certain qualities in each other doesn't mean that everything else slips into place, you know. Libra is likely to find you rather serious; he would like you better if you laughed more often, and if you shared his pleasure in going out and being among friends. You would like him to be firmer in his approach to things which demand it; at times he can be impossibly lightweight, and it just makes you sigh with frustration.

A friendship between you is going to be either on or off. In many cases your interests won't coincide to a great enough extent for you even to think about seeing any more of each other than you have to; but on other occasions you will feel that you get enough out of each other for you to ignore your differences. In the best instances you will admire what the other one is trying to do: Capricorn will understand the importance of the intimate personal relationship to the Libran, and the Libran will understand the Capricorn's need to be seen as the best.

A sexual relationship between you would be a lot more successful than you might think, given that friendship itself is so difficult to achieve. Librans have just a hint of coolness somewhere in that impeccable style, a suggestion of vanity which means that they are always making sure that they are looking good rather than giving themselves totally to the experience. Capricorns understand this; it is part of their nature too. You can build a very exciting sexual partnership out of that, provided that you don't do things *too* publicly and get yourselves arrested, of course.

A business partnership isn't really Libra's sort of thing, or at least not in the same way that it is for the Capricorn. Marriage, on the other hand, is a very Libran thing. Try this one, Capricorn, and you will have a stylish home but a lazy partner—because once the relationship is permanent the Libran's purpose is complete!

### Capricorn-Scorpio

This is the easiest of them all, from your point of view. There are some pairings in the zodiac which fit together so closely that the joins are invisible, and the combined strength of the two is more than twice their single strength. One of the partnerships (there are only two) is Taurus and Cancer, and the other one is this. It isn't a comfortable partnership, either to be in or to handle from the outside, but it certainly achieves its aims. It is ruthless, dominant, and wonderfully effective.

Scorpio is interested in the maintenance of power and control. To him, knowing how people are likely to react is essential intelligence; when he has this intelligence he can control the entire situation. Everything that a Scorpio attempts is done with tremendous power, directed in precisely the right way to ensure the desired result. They are secretive people, and they go to great lengths to keep their own movements hidden; they also go to great lengths to determine and discover the hidden movements of everybody else.

As you can see, they are very powerful, yet very private; you are different in that you want to be in power and publicly recognized for it. Different aims, but not all that far apart; certainly there is much that you have in common, and you are close enough in outlook to enjoy each other's company.

Scorpio is trying to be powerful, and you are trying to be in a position of power: one is a condition of potential, the other an established state. You represent what happens when the Scorpio's power is converted into material wealth, and he represents the invisible network of influence which later becomes crystallized into the organizational structure you love so much.

He sees you as being the steady state of permanent control, very much the sort of thing that he admires. He is seeing the weight of Saturn, in fact, which restricts and encloses. He himself works through Mars, that irresistible force applied suddenly and to one point, and so he hasn't got your stamina or your patience; you haven't got his immediate power, though, so it balances out.

You are not likely to be friends so much as co-conspirators: you will have a special vocabulary of codewords and symbols, each of which refers to people in positions of power and their position in your schemes. From the outside, it seems impenetrable, untrustworthy, and generally hostile; inside the partnership, though, you are having a glorious time. This is the only relationship which has what you would no doubt describe as a properly professional and serious outlook on life. It is also the only one where the other partner is at least as ambitious as you are.

You don't generally mix business and your emotions; be doubly careful with the Scorpio, whose business is emotions. He will be as cool and businesslike as you are, but he will be playing with your emotions the whole while. You will see just how important they are to him if you develop your friendship into an affair, and you will also be introduced to the full force of Mars. Scorpio will knock you flat, sexually, though it is comforting to know that eventually, after a very long time, you will prove to be the stronger of the two, simply because of your greater capacity for endurance. It will take too much out of you to find out, though; don't try to match him if you argue on this subject.

As business partners, you were made for each other. There ought to be a law against business partnerships of this sort, to give the others a chance.

As marriage partners, you should be reasonably suited. You

will need to be in the seat at the head of the table, but he will actually be in control, because marriages are emotional things, and that's where he is stronger. If he gets obsessive about something, you will have to let him win, because he will break up all that you have built together rather than lose, and you wouldn't want that.

*Capricorn-Sagittarius*
After the pairing which is closest to yourself comes the one which is the furthest away. Like Leos, Sagittarians seem to embody all the things you would rather not come into contact with, and being with them just brings out the worst in you. And yet they are irresistible: there is something engaging about them which you feel drawn to, and wish that you weren't.

Sagittarians are open and optimistic people; to them everything is full of life and interest, and they like nothing better than to have something new and untried to look into. They are insatiably curious, and childishly trusting; in their world there are no hidden pitfalls, and even if there are they know that they will come to no harm.

All of this you can tolerate quite easily; to you it seems simply that they are rather young in their outlook, and you find yourself adopting a parental role with them. You indulge their enthusiasm with an avuncular twinkle in your eye, and they play up to it.

What is less easy for you to tolerate is their knowledge. Sagittarians seem to have been born wise beyond their years, and they already know all that there is to know about everything before you even open a conversation with them. Once you do, they assume that you would like to know what they know, and they tell you. They are bubbling over with knowledge; they simply can't keep it all to themselves. This is a bit hard for you to take: you have fairly traditional views on education, and it goes against the grain to be told where you are going wrong by somebody who behaves like a five-year old with a new toy the whole time. What makes things worse is they're usually right.

The most incomprehensible thing of all about Sagittarians is their insistence on freedom and movement. They won't let themselves settle down and put down roots the way you think that they should. The very idea of staying in the same job, or doing the same thing, for years on end, the way you do, makes them feel faint, and quite often they will change jobs, or even careers, for no other reason than that they have been doing the same thing for over three years, and it bothers them.

You know how fond you are of a structured and ordered existence, and how you see the rules and regulations of a formal lifestyle as a solid framework on which to build? Sagittarians are just the opposite. They are frightened of frameworks, because to their eyes every framework looks like a cage. Being trapped is their greatest fear: they are never afraid of anything new, but the thought of never changing from something that they don't like terrifies them. You, of course, would always prefer an eternity of something that you knew, no matter how bad it was, to the possibility of the unknown and untried.

You see them as childish, charming, infuriatingly clever, and short of staying-power; they see you as successful and powerful, but lacking in sparkle, and far too hardworking for your own health.

Any friendship between you is likely to be built on a sense of mutual fascination: most probably the Sagittarian will take you on as a project, attempting to inject what he sees as necessary gaiety into your life, while you will feel that he needs calming down and directing, and will attempt to do that for him. If you succeed, you will quench the fire in him completely; it is actually a better thing if you allow yourself to be taken along with him on some of his adventures—as long as you stay close to him you will come to no harm.

A Sagittarian lover will be everything you could want for as long as he retains his interest in you; they get bored after a while and start looking around for somebody new. Not better, just new—there's no question of not making the grade, it's just that novelty is a big factor in attracting a Sagittarian.

Pick somebody else as a business partner: Sagittarians are rarely interested in high finance. Money doesn't seem as real to them as it does to you, and the work required to make a lot of it simply isn't worth it to them.

Marrying a Sagittarian is actually a very smart move from your point of view, provided that you don't stifle them. They are always warm and forward-looking, which is a big bonus in a life-long relationship, but for them to maintain this outlook you must be flexible, and not try to tie them down too much.

### Capricorn-Capricorn

Forming a relationship with somebody of your own sign is easy on the surface, because you should know what you're getting. There are a few of the same-sign combinations, though, which don't work as well as they should because it is part of the nature of the sign to resent competition, and that can happen here.

The only drawback to this relationship is that both of you are striving to get to the top; if the relationship is the most important thing in your lives, then one of you has to lose somewhere, and that will cause resentment. There is an easy way round the problem, though, and it is one which most Capricorn partners employ without even thinking about it.

It is simply not to let the relationship be the most important thing in your life. Most Capricorns are far more interested in their work than they are in their private lives anyway, and rightly so, since public success rather than private happiness is your eventual goal. Besides, you can always pack your private affairs into a separate compartment of your life, and give them some time and attention when you get a spare minute; they needn't interfere with your career at all.

Your only problem in the past has been to find somebody who understands all this, somebody who will give you support when you need it, somebody who is as keen to succeed as you are, and who will understand if you are too busy to give them any time when they may need it. This person will have to be at least as tough as you are, at least as able to endure emotional hardship, and at least as able to sacrifice the comforts and pleasures of the present for the rewards of the future. What they will have to be is another Capricorn.

Having another Capricorn as a partner in any sense means that they understand your motivation, and will make allowances automatically for those times when you are too busy to be sociable, and when other signs would say you were being miserable or rude.

It sounds a good idea on the surface, but it means that the relationship will have a very low emotional content; how could it be otherwise? If you want warmth, love, and affection in your life, to compensate for those qualities which you know that you are short of, then don't choose another version of yourself to supply them. On the other hand, if you really are dedicated to getting on in life, and you don't feel comfortable with intangible things like sentiment and affection, then this will no doubt suit you. If you do choose this partnership, then you will both be supporting each other in your struggles, and indeed as the years pass the relationship will become a sort of achievement factory. Both of you will rise higher and higher in your chosen professions, gaining more and more of that Capricornian product, money.

As a light friendship, this pairing has little time to say more than a few words as they pass in the lift at the office, but as a life partnership, either in business or as a marriage, it is much more productive, as we have already seen. The key element is, of course, time: Capricorn does everything best over the long period, and relationships are just the same.

Sexually, the success of the relationship depends on how much time you are prepared to give to this side of it. Sex, power, money, and status are interchangeable to you, and it will be very satisfying to you to have a partner who understands this without being told. This could be the only sexual pairing where you can really express your understanding of sex and power, and where you won't be putting your partner off.

### Capricorn-Aquarius

The sign which is one stage further on in the zodiacal cycle from your own is always enticing but elusive. Usually it represents some sort of idea which is beyond your capabilities, and is governed by a planet whose energies are very different from your own. In this case the difference between you is considerably lessened by the fact that you are both looked after by the same planet, Saturn.

You know what you are going to find in another Saturnine individual, and that familiarity before the event, so to speak, gives you confidence. They are going to be reserved, unemotional, a bit cool. Yes, they are, but in every other respect they are vastly different from you. The things which will hit you hardest are firstly that they are very friendly and sociable, which you are not, on the whole, and secondly, that they are very firmly opposed to the idea of anybody being in a position of power over anybody else.

This will confuse you. Surely Saturn will give them some sense of structure, you think. Indeed it does: but in the opposite direction to yours. You are concerned with vertical structures, where every person is at a different height from everybody else, and the direction of movement is up or down. Aquarius is concerned with horizontal structures, where everybody is at the same level, and connected in a network of friendship and shared interests. The direction of movement is out, through, or along.

Aquarius is an Air sign, which means that they are working with words and ideas, a realm in which you are not at home. You can understand the Aquarian's version of the Air element better than you could with Gemini and Libra, though, because it is Fixed here, and therefore less likely to slip through your fingers. If you watch an Aquarian in action in any social gathering, you will be able to see how similar he is to you. The only reason you have not seen it before is that you are so much at sea in any sort of personal or emotional situation that you think them all to be the same. In fact, each group and each party is different, and if you watch the Aquarian you will be able to see how he handles people with the same practised ease that you handle money.

He is always at the centre of the discussion, but he is never attached to one particular person. The party seems to flow round him, but he is never moved along by it. Although he is very much part of the crowd, he is not of the same stuff as the crowd; he is just a little bit different, separate, distanced almost.

That same distance is there in his eyes, if you look: he knows what he's doing the whole time. He's not heartless, and he's not calculating or manipulative as a Scorpio is, but he doesn't let himself get carried away unless he wants it to be that way. It's as though he's ballasted, so that he always floats and always stays upright. In fact, he *is* ballasted—by Saturn.

Once you have seen how cool he is, and how he keeps himself separate and different from all his friends, whilst being a good friend to all of them, you will be hooked. Here is somebody, you will say to yourself, who is as professional in his social life as I am in my business life.

There's more to him than that, actually; he has high principles, humanitarian politics, and a determinedly modernist outlook on life which doesn't fit at all with your cherished ideals of tradition and privilege. You will fight over these things as your friendship deepens. You may see him as cool and stylish, but he sees you as self-centred, over-conventional, and an opponent of progress. It is always much more difficult to think kindly of the sign behind you than the one in front of you, mainly because the sign behind you shows you your own bad side in some respects—some Aquarians are mercenary enough to trade their principles for hard cash, which is very Capricornian!

Because he is cool, and you are often too busy to give the time to such things, you may not develop a sexual relationship at all; even if you do, it will be characterized by its cool, almost 'blue' (in a jazz sense) flavour rather than by intense passions.

Aquarius isn't likely to be quite the business partner of your dreams, though his social skills could undoubtedly be put to good use; like all the Air signs, he isn't really at home in fixed routines where the product is more important than the people— he prefers it the other way round.

As a marriage partner he is a much better bet. He is cool enough not to make emotional demands upon you, and independent enough to have things to do when you are working late; the question is, though, are you really interested enough in each other to marry in the first place?

*Capricorn-Pisces*

This is as unlikely a combination as you could ever imagine, and yet it works surprisingly well; you couldn't wish for a less structured and less ambitious person than a Piscean, yet they seem to welcome you, and you seem to enjoy their very changeability. How does this come about?

Partly it is because of their extreme sensitivity. You are not very good at expressing yourself, and you only give the merest hints when you think that you are opening your heart to the world. Pisceans are sensitive enough to pick up the little that you offer, and respond to it in a big enough way for you to gain emotional satisfaction from it. Their response, though genuine, is in no way forceful or enveloping, however, and it will break over you like a wave on the shore, leaving you unchanged—and that's just how you want it. What you want is somebody who can respond to your needs, but whose response doesn't throw you off course in any way, or stop you from doing what you see as your work. Pisceans fit the bill. There is a lot of emotion in a Capricorn, but it is slow and deep, like the ocean—the Capricorn animal has the tail of a fish, remember—and Pisces is the only Water sign further on in the zodiac than Capricorn; therefore it is the only one through which the Capricorn can express that energy.

On any other level than the emotional, Pisceans are just the same as you are. To be fair, they are just the same as anybody else in the zodiac, because they are able to take on the qualities of the person they are with at the time, through a process of absorption and reflection. This means that while they are involved with you, they are just as ambitious and hard-headed.

Most of the time Pisceans are unsure of which direction to take. The fact that you are very sure of where you are going is attractive to them; while they are with you they can become part of your life and take your firmness of direction on themselves. It means, of course, that they are then heading in the same direction as you are, but they don't care too much about where they are going, as long as they are going somewhere.

You mustn't expect them to be able to be firm on their own

account; what happens is that you take the decisions, and they mimic you. Left to their own devices, they probably won't do things forcefully enough, and you will find that some of your schemes are starting to come loose at the edges; only you have the power and the authority necessary to hold things the way you want them. At the same time, if you control their actions too closely, they will be unhappy and try to escape—Piscean fish are very sensitive to any sort of pressure, and it causes them a lot of pain.

Friendship between you is likely to be formed from a basis of mutual emotional sympathy: if you keep it at that level, without trying to control or restrict them, then the friendship should prove satisfying to you both. If you become lovers, then you will have to make allowances for their changeable moods, and they will have to allow for your lack of imagination (by their standards)!

You could do wonders in business with a Piscean if you are in any kind of media business; they just slip right in. Marriage probably isn't such a good idea for you, though; they will want more of your time than you are prepared to spare them.

# Aquarius

## Aquarius-Aries
On the surface, this relationship has a lot to recommend it. Arians are strong and active, and they like to be where the action is; they're not the sort to stay at home and read a book. They are also highly independent and self-motivating; they don't need somebody else to help them get the best out of their life. You may thing that because you, too, are of an independent turn of mind, and enjoy the social scene, that you would be ideally suited. Not so: you are indeed both independent, and the result is that you don't really need each other.

Arians are very active, but also very physical. They are at their best when they are actually doing something, and using their muscles to do it—their particular kind of planetary energy needs to be expressed through the functioning of their bodies. When they are not physically active, they don't know what to do with themselves. Not surprizingly, they try to spend as much time as they can in action.

Their universe is physical; they like real problems which they can overcome through hard work and sweat. Yours is the world of ideas—the principles of the matter are more important to you than how they are put into action, and you will have a great deal of difficulty understanding the Arian's insistence on doing it himself. He likes to be personally involved; only if he actually does things for himself can he get anything out of the experience. In this respect he is very different from you, because you don't mind at all if somebody else does the deed.

He is independent, like you are, but more than that he is individual. He is concerned entirely for, and with, his own existence. It isn't that he is selfish; it is simply that other people are outside his comprehension. All of his values come from what he feels as he does things, and he can't understand anything that is not in his own direct experience. He can't understand why other people aren't the same as he is either. Such a sense of being alone and individual, the centre of existence, is very alien to you. You are the representative of the idea of doing things in groups; you see everything as part of a larger society, whose members share the same hopes and ambitions. You like to think yourself independent and aloof, but only within the framework of a larger group. Aries doesn't have to recognize the existence of any group, or even of society; he is independent, full stop.

You see him as a tremendously energetic person, full of confidence, and eager to get stuck in to whatever there is to be done. You are slightly in awe of his keenness for getting his hands dirty; somehow you can't bring yourself to get so involved with anything. He seems childishly naïve, in some respects; his opinions seem to be formed instantaneously, without any thought for what other people might say, and he seems never to consider what might lie behind some of the things he gets involved in.

He sees you as lively and sociable, but oddly unwilling to say what you really mean. What he likes about you is that you can always see the reasons behind things, and the helpful way you explain these to him makes him feel that you have his interests at heart. For somebody as helpful and as friendly as you, he will do anything he can, like a child who is eager to please.

You like being useful to Arians—it's part of how you work. In return, they give you their enthusiasm and energy, and the warmth your cold Saturnine heart needs.

You may not make the best of lovers, because you just can't muster enough heat to match the Arian's fiery Mars. You have strength and stamina of your own, and a cool sense of the erotic and the tantalizing, but Aries isn't subtle enough to appreciate you on that level. He likes it hot, physical, and right now, please.

As business partners you should be very successful. You can do the thinking, and he can do the work—between you, you should go a long way.

Marriage is a difficult subject for either of you to think about. It stops the Arian from rushing off and doing things on his own, and it means that you have to commit yourself to one person. You both need movement, though of different kinds, and marriage may not suit either of you. Even if you're sure that it's what you want, you may have to wait a very long time before you find an Arian who feels the same way.

## Aquarius-Taurus

This pairing isn't very easy, at least not in its initial stages. You are so very different in almost every way. You would like to be out with your friends, but the Taurean would rather stay at home. You welcome new ideas, because they exercise your mind, but the Taurean hates them, because he likes things to be predictably constant. Above all, your definition of wealth is in ideas, but theirs is in possessions.

The thing that will strike you most strongly about Taureans is their insistence on familiarity and security. They like to be in familiar surroundings, doing things the way that they have always done them; anything which takes them into unfamiliar territory is quite frightening to them. If they can't avoid being away from home, they will try to impose their own routines on their new surroundings; the best example is the Taurean on a package holiday who tries to get a cup of tea wherever he goes.

Security is a physical thing to a Taurean; he gets real comfort from his possessions. He is also comforted by what he wears, and particularly by what he eats; the idea that mere possessions could improve your opinion of yourself is likely to fascinate you, but you won't really understand it. They seem to be so easily satisfied, in your eyes; you wish they had a broader outlook, one which took in the needs of more people than just themselves, and which saw beyond the simple acquisition of material security.

From the other point of view, they see you as kind and fair, but cold and distant. You don't seem to *enjoy* yourself enough, in their opinion. You are as comfortable in the company of your friends as they are in the company of their favourite possessions, and they can appreciate that, but you don't seem to get any real enjoyment from the things you have, and they think that's rather sad. Still, as long as you don't interfere with what they have, and don't threaten their territory, then they won't mind too much.

There is one area in which you have a common interest: music. Not all Taureans are musical, nor all Aquarians for that matter, but most of you are. The reasons for this are, as usual, linked to the planets which govern your signs. Taurus is looking for the comfort of a pleasant environment for all of his senses. This includes his hearing; he will be very fond of tunes he knows well. He is fonder of pure melody than you are, though you probably have a better understanding of rhythm and time. Together, Venus and Saturn produce harmony (in a musical sense); a shared interest in music may well help form a friendship between you.

A friendship between you works best if you let yourself become an addition to his group of friends; that way, you get a wider circle of acquaintance, and he doesn't lose anything with which he was familiar before, which is the best arrangement for both of you.

An affair between you could be better than you might think;

you are both strong, and both have stamina. Your emotional coolness will hurt him, though, as his passion will surprise you. His possessiveness will bother you, too—you like, and indeed need, variety. You will both need to compromise; you are more flexible than he is, though, so it's really up to you, if you think it's worth it.

The same problems occur in a marriage. They will want to do things their way or not at all, and you will have to be very persistent if you are to get them to make any major changes. Lack of commitment isn't the problem—it's a simple unwillingness to change, and you will find that quite wearing.

As business partners you will be very supportive to each other, but the partnership will lack the spirit of enterprise necessary to make new projects successful. Why? Because the Taurean is wary of anything new, and because you won't let yourself get involved in them to the extent necessary to ensure success.

### Aquarius-Gemini

This is a very comfortable and entertaining relationship for you to be in. The two of you are both Air signs, and that means that you are both more concerned with words and ideas than with the actions they imply, and neither of you like getting bogged down in the emotional side of things. Gemini is, in fact, very dry indeed emotionally: almost without deep feelings at all. As far as you are concerned, this isn't a problem, and anyway you are both so busy talking to each other and laughing at each other's jokes that the subject hardly ever crops up.

When it does, you will notice something about the Gemini that you find a little distasteful: he is unprincipled. Or, as he would no doubt put it, he is more flexible in his thinking. To him, an idea is something to play with; he likes to turn it around in his mind, see if he can get it to mean something else, see if he can make new things from it. To experiment in this way with words themselves is part of the Gemini way of life—a thing has only the meaning that you give it for that instant, and nothing is ever the same for all time. Such an approach is a little shocking to you—

ideas are almost sacred things to you, to be strengthened rather than dismantled, and to be used for the guidance of mankind generally rather than for the amusement of an individual. Ah, well, that's the difference between the Mutable Air sign and the Fixed Air sign. It would probably do you good to be able to take your beliefs less dogmatically, and to be able to play with them in the Gemini's fashion; after all, everything must go from the Fixed phase of its existence to the Mutable eventually, as we noted on page 15.

For his part, Gemini sees you as just a little bit dull. Don't be upset: he just likes his people lively and quick-witted, that's all, with an eye for a bargain and a bit of a game on the side. Your big talent, that of being friendly to everybody, and being the driving force behind any group you care to join, is not important to him. He can talk to anybody he likes, and be friendly, too, if it suits him; all the Air signs can, and so it's not an impressive thing, in his view. Groups of people, and particularly the beliefs and opinions they all share, don't matter to him one way or the other; Geminis prefer to work on an individual basis anyway, and have little time for fixed opinions. He is willing to listen to what you have to say, though, particularly if he hasn't heard it before—his appetite for novelty is even greater than yours. He uses you as a source of new ideas, which he then plays with and disassembles to see if there is anything else interesting contained in them. This is a one-way process—don't expect him to contribute anything in return. If he did, would you listen? If you listened, would you trust what he had to say?

The friendship between you is based largely on the fact that you both enjoy talking; you enjoy talking to each other, and you enjoy talking to other people, too, which means that you can keep up the social circulation that you both need without threatening the relationship between you. Obviously, this is a good thing. The other good thing about this pairing is that neither of you expects, or offers, any sort of deep emotional attachment; you are 'just good friends'—literally! The disadvantage of this is that you don't support each other much, but then neither of you expects it, so that isn't so bad.

As lovers, you are quite well matched. Neither of you likes things too intense, and both of you like a sense of humour in your sex life. Gemini is likely, if anything, to be too lightweight even for Aquarius, in the final analysis: he would probably rather talk and play games than get serious about anything.

In marriage, as in business, the big question is whether you would ever get anything done. You like each other well enough, and you can keep each other amused for ever, but he is so easily sidetracked by anything new; you will have to allow for this.

### Aquarius-Cancer

This, along with the Pisces pairing, is probably the most difficult relationship of all from your point of view. Almost everything there is about a Cancerian is exactly opposed to your own point of view, and you will find it very difficult to get to know them thoroughly enough for you to understand why they feel the way they do. This is a great pity in many ways; both of you would like to care for the other very much, since caring is what you both do best—but in very different ways.

You are, as you know, most comfortable in a crowd of people, and especially if they are your friends. People expect to bump into you socially; they know that if they go to a party the chances are that you will be there, chattering away to all and sundry. You also know that you have a private, interior personality, which is known only to you, and never communicated to anyone else at all—not ever. The public face is friendly and helpful; the private person may not be. Whatever he is, he has a very serious view of himself, and he likes his own company and his own thoughts best. When his own thoughts look likely to take up too much of his time, the private person puts on a public face, and goes out with his friends, or does something which helps other people; anything to turn his attention away from himself.

Can you imagine a person whose interior is all that they have? Can you imagine a person as private as you are inside, but who has no public personality to hide behind, and whose sense of insecurity makes them shy and nervous when they have to deal with more than a few people at once? Cancer is like that.

You are similar in many respects. Both of you, for instance, need other people to bring out the best in you, to allow you to communicate your planetary energies fully. You like to think that you can be of use to society as a whole; Cancer likes to think that he can be of use to his immediate family and friends. You work on a much larger scale, of course—and in time as well as space, because you are often thinking about the far future when you adopt a course of action—but you are both trying to do the same thing: that is, to benefit other people, and to be appreciated for that.

Cancer's urge is to protect and nourish, whereas yours is more impersonal, and in that you can see the biggest difference between you: the difference between the emotional response and the logical response. Aquarians have a distrust of emotional responses; they are random things, and they can appear to distort the truth from time to time. You are always concerned that things should be fair and true, without bias of any kind, and you will suppress your own emotional responses to eliminate any possible bias in your own judgements. Not that you could do otherwise, of course: the suppression of emotion is as good a description of the action of Saturn on the Lunar side of a person as you could ever devise.

Cancer is all emotion, no logic. Emotional security is all he is interested in. He will do anything to protect himself and his family against what he sees as a hostile world, and he values the affection they give in return.

You will see them as defensive shy worriers; they see you as friendly but impersonal. A friendship between you will take some time to get going—first you have to gain their confidence, and then you have to trust them with your internal emotions. It may not be possible for you to do this; if you manage it, you can be sure that Cancer will look after you with a devotion you could not have imagined. What you can offer them is an example of caring on a bigger scale; if they can understand it, they will take it as seriously as you do. It may not be possible for them to widen their viewpoint sufficiently to take in your ideas; though they will appreciate the ideals behind your opinions, they are likely to find them too cold emotionally.

As business partners, on the other hand, you could do very well indeed; each of you supplies what the other one lacks. Of course, being business partners keeps things on the unemotional basis which you like best; as lovers, things would be the other way round. You would be completely unable to reply to the Cancerian's emotional demands, and quite unused to the intensity at which they would conduct the affair anyway. You would feel not only lost, but trapped as well—a most uncomfortable situation for you, and one perhaps best avoided.

If in time, you learned how to trust and respond to each other, you might consider marriage. It wouldn't be easy: you need to be on your own, and they need to cling. A lot of adjustments would have to be made.

## Aquarius-Leo

Leo is the sign of the zodiac you find it easiest to dislike. The feeling is entirely mutual, but provided that neither of you take yourselves too seriously you can be quite good friends—something that isn't at all unknown with signs opposite each other.

The reason for your antipathy is actually political. Not party political—though it could be—but to do with your principles of equality. Leos have an inbuilt feeling of superiority. It seems to them that they are somehow better than the rest of us—grander, larger than life, more important altogether. As a result they often lead extravagant and flamboyant lifestyles, surrounding themselves with lots of friends, and admirers. It often seems as though a Leo's life is one long party, and that his social life is similar to that of a king and his court.

It is this that irritates you. In your view, everybody should be the same. When you see the Leo being the centre of attention, you want to give somebody else a turn. You want to see him made to look silly, or somehow humbled; anything to stop him being so self-important. Note that you don't want a chance to wear the crown yourself—you just don't want him to either.

What you haven't seen is that although you may not need the

Leo to put some light into your life, *other people do*. His energy and warmth are given out for free; he is an essential part of any group of people—he is its centre. A great many people like being around Leos, and to bring him down to the same level as the rest of us would not only harm him, it would deprive us of the good he does.

Leo is, if nothing else, personal. He is very fond of simply being himself. You, of course, are impersonal: what you do, or what you represent, is far more important to you than who you are. You therefore see him as selfish and opinionated, without much care for the future or for that of anyone else; he sees you as another face in the crowd, but one whose high principles mean that he has forgotten how to enjoy himself. You will see, I hope, that you are both wrong; you are trying to define the other person's existence in terms of what has value for you but not for him.

If you are prepared to let him be at the centre of things, and take the leading role, then things will be better automatically, because he will be in his natural place. Your place is around him and by him, but not at the centre. You can still enjoy the company of the rest of your friends; indeed, the group will be brighter for having the Leo at its centre. All you have to do is accept his version of himself, and not try to limit him. You are both very sociable people, and have plenty to contribute to any group in your own ways; if you spend your time at war with each other nobody will benefit.

Whether or not you succeed as lovers depends on whether you let yourself accept what he has to offer. Leos are genuinely warm and generous people; you are unused to such open affection, and may not allow yourself to be warmed by him. If you do, you may feel that you have to offer something in return. Not so: Leos are content if you enjoy what they offer. All you have to do is tell him how much you enjoy it.

As business partners you will do best if Leo is seen as the boss. He may not be the boss, but he must be seen that way. He does do things in an expansive way, but he's no fool: Leos are much better organized than most people expect, and are quite capable of looking after a number of things at once. He will appreciate, in private at any rate, your cool appraisals of the situations you face.

For a marriage partner, you could do a lot worse: Leo will have to be lord in his own home, but he will provide a feeling of well-being and warmth which you could never produce on your own.

*Aquarius-Virgo*
This is another difficult one, though less so than the Cancer pairing. At least there are no emotional problems here; Virgo usually keeps his feelings to himself unless he is very angry, and even then it will be due to some rule being broken rather than an irrational outburst of feelings. You feel at home with his kind of mentality.

You are both very reasonable people: you both have a fondness for reasoned scientific thought. Virgo likes to know what the correct way of doing anything is supposed to be, and you like to do things for the right reasons; there are plenty of similarities there.

Virgo is wonderfully practical, in your eyes. You have always been better at handling ideas than the practicalities of their application, but Virgo is one step further down yet—he is the sort of person who understands the machines that do the work. To you, this interest and knowledge about things at their smallest and most basic level is as fascinating, and as remote, as molecular biology. You are full of interest and admiration, but you know that you could never do this sort of thing for yourself.

In Virgo, you see your own idealism translated to the material world. Virgos think things through first. They decide what has to be done, and then do it in the best way possible, making the best use of the tools and time they have available. Nothing is done haphazardly, and everything is to the highest possible standard, no matter what it costs in effort. Virgoans are not lazy, and they are not selfish either: they seem to exist to do things for other people, and in the best possible way.

You like all this. You like his ability to see into things—it matches your own. The problems start when you realize that looking into things is the end of the matter as far as he is concerned. His close-up view of the details of things never takes in the whole picture. What really matters to you, the universal application of ideas, has little interest for him. Ideas aren't practical things, as far as he's concerned, and his view of things doesn't really lend itself to considering more than one person at a time. The problem is one of incompatibility, but with an interesting twist. You have similar approaches to things, but you work in different worlds, and on different scales: there is almost no common ground.

A friendship between you isn't impossible, by any means. You are capable of being friendly to anyone, because you are an Air sign, and although he is an Earth sign, he is Mutable, which speeds him up to somewhere near your pace. In addition, he is ruled by Mercury, the planet of words; he doesn't talk like a Gemini, but he's chatty enough. You seem to want to talk to each other—your aims and methods interest each other, and your analytical approaches do too.

Though you are suited to each other, you are not really suited to being lovers. Both of you are cool emotionally, and neither of you can generate the heat and passion necessary for an affair to be self-sustaining; obviously it just isn't that important to you. It isn't really the right situation for your talents: Aquarius does better being publicly rather than privately appreciated, while Virgo's often critical comments can destroy a relationship before it has had time to establish itself.

As with the Cancer partnership, this one is good from a business point of view, and for the same reasons: you each provide what the other lacks. Add your talents for seeing the larger situation to the Virgo's capacity for hard work and you have a very productive combination.

A marriage between you would be as productive as a business partnership, but you might have some trouble generating enough emotional warmth; you could grow apart from each other.

*Aquarius-Libra*

This is probably the easiest of your relationships. Libra is interested in the same sort of thing as you are—that is, talking to people—and he goes about it in a similar sort of way. He is as friendly and as outgoing as you are, and as much at home in a social setting. If anything, you are too much like one another!

What first attracts you to a Libran is his lightness and pleasantness. He seems to have a knack of putting you at your ease, and of saying things which you want to listen to. What he says isn't necessarily new or different, but he seems to say it in a way that you find agreeable, and you are left with the impression that he is a very nice person to know. He is genuinely interested in being your friend, but he never makes any demands on you.

This is exactly the sort of thing you want. What you are reacting to here is Air sign energy, the same stuff as you yourself are made of. The great thing about it, as far as you are concerned, is that it is light, bright, and flexible, and never gets bogged down in the dark waters of emotional demands and expectations. It is essentially a surface thing, and doesn't touch the inner layers of the person at all. Some people (Cancerians, for instance) would find this a major drawback—they would want the relationship to come from the core of the person, not the surface—but it suits you well, and the Libran too.

A relationship between you, then, is bright and friendly, and full of new ideas. Neither of you gives yourself completely to the other, but that doesn't matter at all; the relationship wouldn't be able to stand the extra weight if you did, and neither of you would want the responsibility of the other one's inner self anyway.

What you have that the Libran doesn't is the ability to work on the grand scale. As you get to know a Libran, and watch him in company, you will see that he is dedicated to forming personal relationships on a one-to-one level. He has lots of individual friends, and he treats each one separately as though he were the only other person in the world. You have lots of friends together; you see them together, you have fun with them together, and you prefer to see them all at once; individual, one-to-one relationships are sometimes more intense than you would like.

What he has that you don't is charm. That doesn't mean that you're tongue-tied and clumsy, but Libra's charm is so strong that it becomes a physical force, shown as grace and style. He doesn't seem to be able to make a clumsy move; he always looks attractive, whatever he wears; his sense of colour and style is perfect. Librans can make wherever they are a nicer place to be, just by being there; you can't do that, and if you tried, it would come out as a better way of life instead of a more enjoyable one. They're not the same thing.

If your friendship develops into an affair, you need have no fear; it will be every bit as enjoyable as your original relationship. Most affairs have a heavy emotional ingredient, and you are rightly wary of that, but Libra is different. For him, an affair is a thing of Romance with a capital R; it becomes a game where roles are played and enjoyed in place of real feelings and commitment, and you can enjoy that as much as he does. Sexually you are both playful, and not too demanding: you are a good match for each other.

In business together you are not quite such a good idea, unless you are in some kind of public relations or personnel business. You would both rather sit and talk to people than get on with the serious business of working, and since neither of you are Earth signs you will lack the ability to convert work into money the way they do.

Marriage would be a good thing, from your point of view. Your Libran will make sure you have an attractive life together and a beautiful home, but they need your sense of organization to stop them being lazy.

### Aquarius-Scorpio

You may be attracted to a Scorpio. There is nothing to be worried about: everybody is attracted to a Scorpio. They are that sort of person. If you decide to form some sort of a relationship with them, though, you would be well advized to think about what you are taking on: they work in a very different way from you. They see everything in terms of emotions, like Cancerians and

Pisceans. They will rearrange the rules of the game to suit themselves, something you would never do. Finally, they will never, ever, lose or let go. They may be a lot more than you want.

It would be a reasonable thing to assume that, since you are both Fixed signs, you would both be trying to do the same sort of thing. It is true, to a certain extent, but the difference in the elements you represent does its best to disguise the fact. You are both trying to keep things going—but there the similarity ends. For your part, you would like to understand and be part of the common interest that makes different people become friends and associates. The Scorpio, however, would like to understand and control the desires and concerns that make different people become friends and associates. Try it this way: if all of society were a forest, and all the people trees, then the Aquarian would want to see the topmost leaves waving as the wind blew over them, and the Scorpio would want to control the underground river that their roots all drank from.

In your view, people act the way they do because they all have a shared belief; they act for the best motives, and so things will get better in the end for us all. In the Scorpionic view, people act the way they do because they all have desires and fears; if these are understood, they can be controlled by the Scorpio, and he need fear nothing from any of them.

Your view is upwards and outwards; his is inwards and downwards. He is at least as penetrating and analytical as you are, but he is looking for different things. Universal principles and humanitarian ideas don't interest him; he is working to provide extra information for himself. He is envious of your understanding of society as a whole—he has to spend too much time with individuals, he thinks, and he would like to develop your talent for seeing the larger scene. He could do with some of your social skills, too, or so he thinks: he has a reputation for being either secretive or irresistibly sexy, and he would actually like to be anonymously pleasant on the surface whilst remaining secretly powerful underneath. I know that your social skills don't actually work that way, but that's how he sees you.

You see him as magnetically attractive, and very powerful. He seems to have the same sort of mental control that you have, and the same cold logic; he also seems to have the physical power that you lack, but held in check, controlled, in the way you are sure that you would if you had that power. It's just how you see him, in fact, because he isn't really like that. He doesn't have your cold logic at all; he has a hot, irrational temper, held down and controlled by cold logic, and he daren't let it go. It is a much more explosive situation than yours; he certainly can't allow himself the luxury of being kind to others in the way you can— he needs all his energy to look after himself.

A friendship between you is bound to be something of a battle. It will only take you a few minutes to realize that they are interested primarily in themselves, in a way that you are not, and that they will happily use whatever you have to offer them for their own profit, without offering anything in return. You need exchange of ideas and friendship, and this isn't it: as soon as you are able to free yourself from the scorpion's claws you will be off. The best way to do it is to be even cooler than usual; Scorpio reacts to your emotional heat, and if there isn't any you are invisible to him.

You are most unsuited as lovers, unless you are specifically trying to experience passion, possessiveness, jealousy, obsession, and all the other high emotions which usually have so little meaning to you. Scorpios take sex very seriously—much too seriously to talk about it, as you would like to do.

The major obstacle to your business success is that Scorpio won't trust you not to betray him unless he feels that he controls you. You are above that sort of thing, and the suggestion that you are unprincipled annoys you. In any case, you would rather not be in business with him than be controlled by him.

Marriage would be another battleground. Eventually you might understand him, and make allowances for him; in return you will have a partner whose drive and sensuality will really fire your imagination. You would stay with each other—Fixed signs do—but he will always be suspicious of anything new or different. Can you live with that?

### Aquarius-Sagittarius

The last of the Fire signs is likely to make your best friend. The partnership forms very easily; only Libra is easier, and this one is probably better for you in the long run.

It must have seemed up to now that there is no other sign of the zodiac where the mind is interested in ideas for their own sake in the way that yours is. You must also have been disappointed to find that almost everybody else is concerned either with themselves and their own welfare, and in the odd instances where this is not so (Libra) attention seems to be focused on two or three people at the most.

Sagittarius can change all that. Sagittarians are so confident about themselves, and their ability to cope with anything that Life can throw at them, that they give almost none of their attention to their own well-being. Instead, they direct their energy upwards and outwards, and give themselves entirely to the quest for, and the spreading of, knowledge. Sagittarians, like you, are interested in the truth that lies behind everything.

It all sounds too good to be true; here at last is the partner with whom you can swap ideas and experiences all day long! It is true, and it is even better than you had dared hope: Sagittarius thinks in a different way from you, but a way which is complementary to your own. You can take a positive interest in the difference in your approaches, even!

The difference is a simple one. You work from the outside inwards, defining a general principle in a logical manner, and applying it to everybody equally. The approach is very scientific. Sagittarius works from the inside outwards, from an unshakeable *belief* in what must be right. You will be tempted to label this sort of knowledge, probably saying that it is 'intuitive'. You are wrong: Sagittarians are *inspired*. They look for knowledge in everything, and they find it. What's more, when they find it, it is pretty much as they knew it would be—as though they knew it all already. This process is endlessly absorbing to you: you could sit and watch it for hours. Sagittarians like to have somebody to talk to, to share their discoveries with them, but that person has to be used to big ideas, and they have to be able to think clearly. You are exactly the right person for the job.

Friendship between you is almost instantaneous. You have so much that you want to tell each other! They are more emotional than you are, but because the dominant emotion is happy enthusiasm, you enjoy them being that way. They see you as a bit on the reserved side, but they are determined to make you laugh if they can: they feel sure that you are capable of it!

As lovers, you will probably laugh a lot. Sagittarians have a silly and boisterous side to them, but it is so obvious they don't take things seriously that you don't feel trapped by becoming involved. They also like to stay fancy-free, if they can; since you like to be independent too, you are unlikely to complain.

In business you could be unstoppable. Sagittarius has the drive you sometimes lack, and you have the overall sense of organization that gets lost in his enthusiasm. You make a great team. The same holds true for marriage; the only question there is whether you can both sacrifice your independence to the extent of actually getting married! If you do, you won't regret it, but it will be a difficult thing for either of you to do. You may well decide that you are happy enough with each other as you are— and not bother.

### Aquarius-Capricorn

This is a very difficult one from your point of view, much more difficult than the other way round. The sign that is behind you in the zodiacal sequence usually represents all the things that you have left behind, so to speak: people from that sign are living examples of the sort of qualities you would like to think that you have grown out of.

The problem is similar to the one you have with Leos—it is to do with status and position. Capricorns take their station in life very seriously. They work very hard and for a very long time, denying themselves all the comforts that the other signs find so enjoyable, but keeping their sights fixed the whole time on the position they want to be in, at the top of the tree. When they have made it to the top, they want the world to see where they are, and to be impressed by it. At any stage in their career they would like you to notice how much better off they are than you, and to admire the things that show you their status: their fine house, the BMW in the drive, and so on. They never give anything away; every ounce of their energy is devoted to furthering their career, making a life of lasting quality and material comfort for themselves and their families.

You are strongly opposed to almost everything the Capricorn does, and particularly for the reasons that he does it. You know that you could do all of that if you tried—all you have to do is use your Saturnine energy the way he does—but you also know that if you did, you would be slipping backwards. The only thing that you agree with in his methods is the fact that he is prepared to push himself very hard and to work long hours for what he really believes in; you are like that too.

Everything the Capricorn wants out of life has a price tag on it. His goals are all material; he doesn't give himself a lot of time to ponder on ideas and principles. This isn't surprising; he is an Earth sign, after all. All the things you want out of life are without price, and most of them are not physical at all; they are qualities or beliefs, like friendship, truth, and justice.

He can see your talent for analysis, and your ability to lead and motivate large numbers of people. He is sure that he could make a lot of money with that sort of ability, and he can't see why you don't. He can see that you have a large number of friends, but he can't see why you don't use them as business contacts. Above all, he can't see why you don't want to be better than the next man, or to have a bigger car.

You are going to have a lot of trouble trying to explain yourself to him. He isn't very receptive to ideas; he prefers practical examples. He's no good at catching nuances from your speech, either, or at being imaginative. Most difficult of all, perhaps, is his highly traditional point of view; the sort of things that you consider logical, effective, and innovative are to him 'simply unthinkable—just not done'.

You are only going to be friends if one of you is crossing over into the other's territory (that is, if you are relapsing into material comfort, or if he is being unusually progressive), or if you are working together for the same organization, such as a political party. Without shared goals, you will fight. All business partnerships between you will have to be that way, too. You will both be able to work long and hard if you have a common target, but if that isn't the case you will criticize him for his mercenary motives and his lack of imagination, and he will feel resentful.

Marriage, because it often has shared goals, isn't a bad idea. Both of you prefer to work over a long period of time, and neither of you expects instant results. Your personal relationship could be a bit cold and dry, though—two Saturn people don't generate much heat.

As lovers? Well, you like things lighter and more playful than Capricorn, but he is stronger than you. He has a better-developed sense of humour, too, even if it is something of an acquired taste. You like things cool and off-beat, though, so once you are used to each other it would probably work very well.

### Aquarius-Aquarius

Forming a relationship with somebody from your own sign is both a good and bad thing. You know more or less what you're getting, which is a good thing, but you are not getting anything fundamentally different from yourself, which means that you don't have to stretch your capabilities to accommodate them, and so you don't make as much progress as you might.

In this case, the union is by no means as bad as it might be: in fact, it is one of the best of the same-sign pairings. The odd thing about it is that although it is rather slow to get going, it improves as time goes on. If it survives the initial stages and becomes something with a long-term element in it, such as a marriage, then it may turn out to be the most satisfying relationship of the twelve.

The reasons for that are, of course, entirely to do with Saturn, lord of Time; only another Saturnine person can provide support and companionship at the level you want it (that is, not very intense) for the length of time that you want it (for years). Aquarian and Capricorn are the only choices for that kind of long duration, and Capricorn doesn't always see things your way, as we have noted.

To begin with, your relationship will be very friendly and sociable. This is hardly surprising; both of you are virtually professional socializers, and if you can't function on a social basis then you can't function anywhere. You can, in fact, go quite a long way on just that level: you needn't offer or demand each other's trust or affection—you could keep things light and sociable, chatting away whenever you saw each other, going to the cinema together, or things like that.

When you deepen the relationship you will find that you have a deeper understanding than you had perhaps supposed. Each of you will need some time away from the other, some time when you can be alone with yourself and your thoughts. You need frequent changes of scene and company, and you don't like being in the company of any one person for too long. Who else would ever understand that but another Aquarian? Anyone from the other eleven signs would take it as a signal to end the relationship if you wanted a few days on your own, but you don't have to explain it to another Aquarian. Better still, you will understand the same behaviour in them.

You make some strange demands on a close relationship. The partner must be similar to you, but different. You must both enjoy the company of others, and be part of the crowd, but at the same time you must feel that you are both separate and different from the crowd in some way. Your partner must be close to you, and take the relationship seriously, but not be attached to you. Above all, he must let you go your own way, and alone if that's the way you want it from time to time. Only another Aquarian can do all that.

Friendship is no problem: what about an affair? It is likely to be very enjoyable for both of you. If you let your imaginations get to work you can have a wonderful time, similar to the sort of affair you would have with a Libran. There is the merest hint of wistful sentiment in the Aquarian soul, which could be persuaded, in circumstances such as these, to blossom into a pale and delicate romance. There is also a dry sort of electricity in you, the same power which makes you so zealous in support of your egalitarian ideals. If this power can be expressed sexually, then the two of you could make a crackling, sparky, free-form relationship, something very different from the sort of stuff the rest of the zodiac gets up to. What you have to guard against is taking your relationship too seriously: then Saturn makes your loving dull and earnest, and you lose all the fun from it.

In business together you become an extension of each other, but that doesn't mean that you are any more successful than you were separately. You will still need somebody practical and somebody creative: somebody non-Aquarian, in other words.

In a marriage, you will get better as time goes on. Your differences, and your efforts to remain different from and independent of each other will keep you from becoming dull and inflexible. That way, the essential Aquarian spirit, which needs to stay mentally active, keeps going, and keeps you going, too.

### Aquarius-Pisces

The relationship you have with the sign which is the next one on from you is always rather strange. You want so much to be part of their world, to progress to their stage in the cycle, but somehow it always seems to be unattainable. They know you very well, of course; they have already been where you are, so to speak, and they know that they can sink back into you when things get tough.

Pisces seems impossible for you to understand. You pride yourself on being able to handle ideas, and being an Air sign ought to give you a certain adaptability, but Pisceans are something else altogether. Whenever you try to pin them down, they slip away. Whenever you think that you understand what they mean, you find they meant something else. There doesn't seem to be anything constant about them; your attempts to define the principle on which they work get you nowhere.

The truth of the matter is that they don't work on any principle at all; they take on the behaviour of what surrounds them. These people react emotionally to everything and everybody they meet, and form a pattern of behaviour from those responses.

To be so open to external influence is staggering to you; you are the complete opposite. Though you take in all that you see and hear, very little of it has any real effect on you; you analyse it, examine it, and remain unaffected by it for the most part. Pisceans are not nearly so controlled. They positively enjoy being swept away by an intensity of feeling or experience—they live life in Technicolour, digital stereo sound, and probably a number of other processes yet to be invented.

It is difficult for the two of you to form a relationship that satisfies you both at once: if things are light and cool enough for you then they are unlikely to be intense enough for the Piscean. Your social life could be the answer; Pisceans get as much enjoyment from their friends as you do, though in a different fashion. Another good idea is probably music, that key to your own emotions; if you have a shared interest in that, it will serve as a starting point.

A deep relationship between you is bound to have its problems. Remember that the Piscean will pick up and reflect whatever you project; if you want to be on your own for a while, then the Piscean will feel completely isolated and abandoned, because he will have absorbed your emotional state. You will have to be careful. Episodes like this will enable you to see, perhaps, why he is so difficult to pin down; if he absorbs the emotions of wherever he is, then he must have some means of distancing himself from those he doesn't want to be near. It is his self-regulation mechanism, in the same way as being cool and logical is yours.

As lovers, you could have a wonderful time, or not: it is really up to you. He will be able to recognize and reflect the slightest emotion from you, so it all depends on how much you want to put into it. The softer and more romantic you are, the warmer a response you will produce in the Piscean. Sexually, Pisceans are capable of making any fantasy into reality—how imaginative are you between you?

In business you would be better than you might think. Let the Piscean absorb some of your logical approach; in return, pay attention to the way he absorbs the feeling of what's going on.

When he says that the time is right for a product or a service, it usually is.

If you were married, the Piscean would keep things from becoming too static. They may be emotional, but they're not obsessive, so any rows would soon be over.

# Pisces

*Pisces-Aries*

This is one of the most difficult relationships for you to form, although it is probably a little easier for you than it is for the Arian. It represents, in many ways, the unattainable ideal as far as you are concerned, in that all the things that you would like to be, the Arian already is. By being close to him you can have a taste of what it's like to be further round the zodiac than you are.

Aries is definite. He may not be much else, but he is certainly definite. He knows where he is going, and he knows how he is going to do things; what's more, he actually goes out and does them, without wasting any more time in thinking about them. His whole existence is centred around effective action; he is useless unless he is actually doing something, and he knows it. Consequently he keeps himself as busy as he possibly can, and that way he stays happy.

Being in action the whole time means that he is seldom at rest, and that he never has time to think. What's more, he never has time to consider the subtle qualities of things, and for that reason a lot of what you have to offer is lost on him. He simply isn't sensitive to the meaning of things the way you are; as far as he's concerned what you see is what you get, and the physical qualities of anything are all that matter.

From your point of view, he is everything you find appealing, and everything you are trying to avoid, all in the same package. He is simple and straightforward in his approach to life, so much so that he seems naïve at times. His physical strength and power are enormous, and yet you know that he wouldn't use them against you on purpose, because he has no malice in him. He is incapable of being devious or cruel, and you feel safe in his company. His emotions may be strong, but they are easy for you to read, and he isn't trying to trap you. You are reassured by that thought.

One of the unexpected ways in which you suit each other is that you don't crowd each other's space. When an Arian has something to do, he concentrates on doing it, which means that he ignores other people. If the truth be told, he likes his own company best, because he doesn't like wasting time talking to people when he could be active. If you are in the way when he is busy, you will sense it, and melt away in the usual Piscean fashion. He won't mind in the least; in fact he will rather appreciate it. On those occasions when you want to slip off and do something without him, he can usually find something else to do, and he won't be bothered. You can see that your preference for mobility and his preference for getting on with the job are quite compatible, though not in the way that you would immediately think.

He sees you as something almost akin to a fairy creature, a wonderful and fascinating being who vanishes when he tries to pin it down. He never understands the range of your imagination, or your emotional sensitivity, but he remains endlessly fascinated by it. He can see that you have none of his physical capabilities, and that you simply can't meet a problem head on and deal with it, and he feels that he ought to do this sort of thing for you. It is a very good arrangement, though you will have to do something in return.

What you will have to do will become apparent quite early on in the friendship. Arians have no sense of time; to them, everything happens in an eternal present. Consequently, on the odd occasions when they fail at something, they are terribly upset; like toddlers, they cannot imagine how they fell over, and how the pavement bit their knee, and how they are ever going to recover. Your job is to comfort them, and it is something you are very good at, especially as they only need it for a few minutes; you can melt away again afterwards.

You won't be able to complain about the intensity of the experience if you become lovers. Arians are all strength and drive, and you will love it—provided that you can respond strongly enough in return.

You could succeed in business together, but probably only in the media, where your imagination would be useful. He has enough drive for both of you, but he needs directing over the long term, and you may not have the firmness of purpose for that.

As marriage partners, you could make a lot of progress in the early years, but after that it looks less promising. You would eventually find him too simple and straightforward, unless he could adapt to your way of thinking.

*Pisces-Taurus*
This is a very easy relationship to form, and a most relaxing one to be in, for both of you. It moves extremely slowly, though, and there are no sudden moves. A friendship between you would have rhythms which would be noticeable over years, not weeks, so if you want something snappy and rapidly-changing, this isn't it.

What you will notice first about a Taurean is how steady they are. They are always going to do things their way, and in their own time, and they don't let anything put them off. This can be very reassuring. It can also be very exasperating, because when you lose your temper with them, you are not going to have the slightest effect. You could beat your tiny fists on their chest with rage all day, and they wouldn't take any notice. This is Fixed Earth, remember, and Mutable Water just runs off it like the rain from the hills. Yes, I admit that the rain eventually erodes the hills, but it does take several lifetimes.

What you have in common with a Taurean is an appreciation of the emotional qualities of material. This sounds impenetrable, I know, but there are some things which make you feel good just to be with them. Some houses are like this, and some rooms. Favourite old pullovers are like this, and so is a bowl of soup on a cold day. Pisceans appreciate the mood that these things generate, and feel reassured by it, while Taureans get to the same result from the opposite direction: they have an appreciation for the substances in themselves, and feel reassured by their warmth, familiarity, and 'rightness'.

You will realize at once that there are a lot of things you could do together which you can both enjoy in your own ways. You would probably enjoy going to the opera, for instance: the Taurean enjoys the lavish sets, the sumptuous surroundings, and the familiarity of a plot that he already knows, while you enjoy the fantasy and the drama of it all. Staying at home and entertaining is another example. Taureans are famous cooks; they have an almost magical affinity with food. From your point of view, there are the evocative smells of the kitchen, the almost invisible feeling of satisfaction radiating from a Taurean as he does the cooking, the chatter of everybody at table, and all sorts of things like that. Both of you can enjoy the atmosphere of an event, and that forms a strong bond between you.

The problems arise when the Taurean refuses to change or try anything new. No matter how much you enjoy something, you get bored with it after a while, and you long for something else. Taureans simply don't; what's more, they won't change under any circumstances. The way out, of course, is just that: it is time for you to slip away as you always do. Unfortunately, Taureans are very possessive, and they will be forced to act rather than lose you. When this happens, the outcome is very upsetting for everybody concerned.

You appreciate their stability, reliability, and appreciation of your sensitivity. They appreciate your softness and imagination, your recognition of the importance of the emotional side of things, and, though it sounds rather harsh, the fact that you are no threat to their security.

If you like your quiet life together, it can go on for years, with the friendship slipping easily into marriage. You stop them getting too dull, by providing variety; they stop you from floating away, by providing an anchor. This can be very useful if the two of you are business partners, and is of course a sure recipe for a stable marriage. Only as lovers will your differences show. He will appreciate your sense of romance, but you are likely to be bowled over by the strength of his passion. Taureans have deep and powerful passions—they just take a while to get going.

## Pisces-Gemini

This one probably isn't such a good idea. It is like a knife in the water: it glitters and flashes with a wicked attractiveness, but it is sharp and deceptive to touch.

Gemini is Mutable, like you are, and his greatest assets, like yours, are his mind and his imagination; however, any similarities end there.

A Gemini analyses his surroundings, in a way that you do not. To him, every new thing is a puzzle, something that he can apply his mind to and solve. He takes situations and people apart, probing here and there, seeing what there is to see, looking at them from all possible angles; he *examines* them. When he has understood something, he plays with it if he can, to see if it does anything different, or interesting, if approached in another way.

To you this process seems horribly clinical. He seems to lose completely the essence of the experience by dissecting it. You don't work like that; you let the experience wash over you, feeling its qualities as you absorb them.

The major difference in your approach is that you are quite willing to be changed by the experience, and even to become part of it, while he is determined that he will not be affected by it in any way. He is trying to understand things from an intellectual viewpoint, and as far as possible to leave emotional responses out of it. Geminis don't have the same facility with their emotions that you do, and they tend not to enjoy them.

Because he stands apart from the things he deals with, and doesn't feel personally involved in the way that you do, he can be rather cruel; anything is reasonable, according to him, if it helps him understand what is going on. The result of this is a curiously amoral viewpoint, which shows itself from time to time in his actions and, more frequently, in what he says.

Geminis have a lot to say for themselves. They are the great talkers of the zodiac; everything they experience is converted into words and re-broadcast, in a similar process to the way you convert everything you experience into images which are stored inside your dream-memory for creative re-cycling later. The only difference between you is that the products of his experience are put out again for public consumption, whereas yours are kept for internal use only.

If you remember the similarities between what the Gemini does and what you do, then you will be able to handle him very well; you may even be able to enjoy a lot of what he comes up with. What you won't enjoy, though, is the way that he sometimes changes the truth of things. All he is doing is playing with the words, changing the order, or making adjustments to the story from time to time. It amuses him to do so, just as it amuses you to fetch images from your imagination and replay them when you are bored. The only difference is that his games come out as speech, and a lot of people don't realize that they are games. He attaches no emotional weight to what he says, of course, and doesn't expect anyone else to either.

A friendship between you can be very bright and bubbly on the surface; after all, if you mix Air and Water you can usually make foam. He will love analysing your imaginative ideas, and you will probably enjoy absorbing his observations. If the pair of you work together in any sort of business where communication is involved, you could do very well indeed. It probably isn't such a good idea to be your own bosses, though, because you are both too changeable.

Being lovers will have its problems. Geminis have no sense of romance, because to their way of thinking it is all sentimental nonsense; nor are they happy with the emotional demands of an intimate relationship. They are not particularly physical, either; you would be much better off staying as friends.

Marriage will be difficult. He will dismiss your impressionability as woolly-headedness, and you will come to dislike his sharp intellect. Besides, neither of you like things to be too stable for too long.

*Pisces-Cancer*
This is the first of the pairings within your element; here you find yourself in the company of somebody else whose view of life has

the emotional side of things at the top. Cancer is Cardinal, though, and you are not; you will find to your surprise that these people are very determined to have things their way, and you will have no alternative but to do as they tell you.

It won't take you very long to feel familiar with the Cancerian point of view. They are careful, self-preserving individuals, and they make sure that any threats to their security are adequately dealt with in advance wherever possible. Cancerians work on the principle of defence rather than avoidance, though they have been known to dodge the issue at times; their attitude is certainly one that you understand, anyhow.

They are very protective of those they care for; if you are part of a Cancerian's 'inner circle' you know that they are doing everything they can to shield you from any harm from outside, and to give you any emotional reassurance you may need on the inside.

If you look at how they go about caring for their friends and family, you will be struck by something which is only visible to Pisceans and Scorpios, and which you would both dearly like to be able to do. Cancerians can generate emotional energy. Scorpios collect it, and Pisceans absorb and reflect it, but Cancerians actually generate it. Theirs is the original maternal instinct. The fact that they have an apparently endless source of inner strength is something you find quite wonderful, and you admire them very much. It seems so much better a thing to be than what you are at the moment; they seem to be able to do without effort all the things you have to work at.

It may help you to get your relationship into perspective if you consider that the two of you are separated by the scale on which you work. To be sure, the Cancerian seems to be so much more intense, to care so deeply for others—but then Cancer works on the level of a parent to a child, on an individual basis. Pisces is a much more widely-dispersed form of the same energy; Pisces can care for everybody, not just your immediate friends and relatives. What is concentrated in one place can't be everywhere at once, and vice versa.

A friendship between you will be very easily formed; you

instinctively understand, and identify with, each other's likes and dislikes. Once you have got to know each other a little better, you will find that you allow yourself to be led by the Cancerian. He will do things in the way that is best for him, and you will align yourself, Mutable as always, so that you are both facing the same way. The odd thing about this is that although he is leading, he isn't leading you anywhere new or interesting, and you will get bored. Your need for security doesn't work in the same way as his—you know that you can vanish when things get tight, and he knows that he can't. Therefore you don't mind seeking out new experiences just to see what they're like, but they are sure to worry your Cancerian. You may be timid in comparison with an Arian, but against a Cancerian you are positively rash.

Being lovers is likely to be a very rewarding experience for you both. Cancerians are stronger physically than you might imagine, but their true interest lies in the emotional relationship behind the sexual one. They are as sensitive to the little details of romance as you are, but they have a stronger passion, which you will enjoy. The only trouble is that they are possessive. Not quite to the extent that Taureans are, but more than you would like them to be, all the same.

As long-terms partners, both in business and in marriage, there is the problem of restricted progress to be dealt with. He is effective, but not adventurous; you are the other way round. One of you, at least, has to have both qualities if you are to do more than merely stay your ground.

## Pisces-Leo

Here you meet somebody who is different from you in every way, and yet who seems to have a great affinity with you. They don't have your love of variety, and they are completely insensitive to the feelings of others at times, and yet you can't help liking them.

The most useful way of comparing you is by looking at actors and the way they perform. It's not a bad analogy, because you both feel very much at home in the theatre, and you may well meet your Leo in a theatrical setting. If a Piscean actor works through reflection, then the Leonine one works through projection. You are well aware of the way you allow yourself to absorb and represent what people want you to be; when your audience looks at you they see in you what they want to see, and you are happy to reflect their expectations back at them. Leos don't work that way at all. They project themselves through the role they are playing, so that their own energy shines out from behind the costume. Nobody in the audience is in the slightest doubt who it is that they are watching. They know that they are seeing the actor rather than the character, but they don't mind. Leos are the stars of the show; the audience would rather see them being themselves than see them in character.

From your point of view, being close to a Leo can be a very good idea. They simply radiate warmth and fun: wherever they are is the place to be. If you can absorb this from them, and it isn't hard for somebody like you, then you can have as good a time as they do. The clever part comes in being not quite as Leonine as they are, because there is only room for one of them in their world, and they resent competition quite strongly, but you are more than sensitive enough to spot that situation in its early stages, and melt back into the background for a while.

Together you will have a very good time indeed. Everybody loves a Leo, and they have lots of friends. For somebody like you, who likes dramatic and interesting people, and plenty of variety, their social circle should provide you with more than enough emotional energy for your needs. There are odd occasions when a Leo feels unloved and unsure of himself, and he is difficult to comfort then; still, your ability to be there when you're needed and not when you're not is most likely to give the Leo what he needs.

He sees you as somebody who seems to sparkle all the more brightly as he puts more energy into you, and he likes to see that. He also sees you as an imaginative source of new ideas, which he can put into practice. He doesn't feel that he's stealing your ideas, because he knows that you probably don't have the capacity to make your dreams real in the way that he does—and he's right. It is a mutually beneficial arrangement for both of you;

your imagination is tied to his ability to organize and make things happen. Without your ideas, it must be said, he would run out of things to do.

Friendship between you looks like the attraction of opposites, and on the surface it probably is. To begin with, you will play roles with each other, preferring to stay behind your masks until you get to know each other better. Even when you have been together a long time, there will be little routines that you will perform with each other for fun. At a deeper level (which the outside world does not see) you will realize that you are both very useful to each other over the long term, too, and that you probably need each other to get the best from yourselves.

As lovers, the only problem you should have is whether you can afford it all; once Leo has shown you how to turn your fantasies into extravagant realities it's difficult to stop.

As business partners, provided that the business itself isn't too dull, you will be wonderful together. Similarly, marriage is a good idea too, as long as you don't let it become all work and no play. Keep things bright and the marriage will last forever.

## Pisces-Virgo

You probably expect things to be difficult with a person who represents the opposite sign to your own, and you won't be disappointed. What is likely to annoy you more than anything else about him is his ability to pin you down and hurt you; the fact that he doesn't really mean to hurt you only makes it worse.

Virgo is Mutable, just like you are; that means that he is at least as quick on the uptake as you are, and he doesn't mind if things keep changing, either. He is an Earth sign, though, and that gives him patience and endurance in a way that your Water sign doesn't. In addition, he deals with the real world—feelings are very low on his list of priorities.

Like the Gemini, his mind is sharp and penetrating, but it has a disconcerting 'dryness' to it; emotion and sentiment aren't there at all, and you will find it difficult to come to terms with that. What he does have, though, is a talent for analysis and understanding, and it frightens you.

The overall feeling, as far as you are concerned, is one of precision. You are interested only in how your car feels, and whether a different one would make you feel any better. Virgos are interested in how their car works and whether they can do anything to make it any more efficient. In the same way, you eat the food you like, but Virgos eat the food that does them good. Whether they like it doesn't come into the argument—but if it wasn't good for them they wouldn't eat it, no matter how good it tasted.

Virgo understands everything in a very precise way. He will be able to say exactly what it is that you are doing, and why. He will also be able to tell you how to do it better. This is a very painful process for you: you are used to being able to please yourself, with nobody able to define you precisely. Your vagueness and constant mobility is both your greatest defence and your greatest pride—but Virgo can pin you down and tell you what you're doing. Speared fish tend to writhe a bit, and you are no exception. The reason the Virgo does it, though, is because he wants to help. Impossible to believe? Not if you think about it for a minute. He is Mutable, remember, as Gemini is, and as you are. His way of reacting to outside influences is to break them down and analyse them, until he understands what makes them the way they are. Then he tries to make a better world by putting things back together in a better order. In other words, he tries to improve things where he can, for everybody's benefit.

You see him as short-sighted, over-critical, and unfeeling. What you should see him as is somebody who is as familiar with the workings of material things as you are with the workings of emotion and sentiment, but whose special interest leads him to examine smaller and smaller details, while yours leads you to deal with larger and more universal feelings and ideas. His energies are focused and concentrated; you are unfocused and diffuse. You are simply at opposite ends of the zodiac, and that's all there is to it.

He sees you as disordered, vague, and something of a victim of circumstance. He can just about believe that such a person as you, completely unfamiliar with the details of the real world, could exist, but he is sure that you need his help. What he should see, but probably can't or won't, is that the world of the imagination is just as real as any other, and that being receptive to it opens up huge realms of experience which are otherwise inaccessible. His security comes from knowing what's going on; yours comes from knowing that you can run away from trouble if things get difficult. He threatens your mobility, and you threaten his understanding of the world: no wonder you feel that you are attracting each other.

Friendship will only grow if you each trust the other not to invade your own world. As lovers, you will find Virgo's range of response rather limited, while his unintentional criticisms may wound you at vulnerable moments.

As business partners, as with a marriage, you will really need a third element (a common project or another person) to help bridge the gap between the areas  in which you function best.

### Pisces-Libra

Although this one ought to be similar to the Leo relationship, and although it is true that it does work best on an artistic, or at least a personal, level, the fact remains that it is less satisfying in many respects than the Leo one is. Why?

The probable answer is that this relationship is too soft. Both of you are known for your affability, for your willingness to fit in with other people's wishes and preferences. The trouble is that neither of you like being the one to make the decisions, and if you are both looking for a lead from the other then you may not get anywhere at all.

You will get a better idea of what is actually happening if you look more closely at what the Libran is trying to do. He's not somebody who absorbs energy from others; that's your territory, and yours alone. What he's trying to do is to promote agreement and balance. He wants to find points of contact, and if possible points of agreement, between himself and anybody else he meets. He starts on a fairly simple level, by enthusing about the same things that you do, but it soon extends to all sorts of other areas. The point of it all, as far as he's concerned, is to link himself to you as a balanced partner, perfectly matching or counterbalancing all the quirks in your character with all of the quirks in his. The problem is that he can only do this on a one-to-one basis, but feels a need to do it with everybody he knows. What he ends up with is a series of intimate friends, all of whom are convinced that they are his special partner.

From your point of view there is a good side and a bad side to this. The good side is that he usually has a varied and active social life, so that he can build as many friendships as he can. He needs to stay in circulation; he is an Air sign, and they need to keep moving. You are a fish who likes to swim in running water, too, so the two of you will enjoy being in company as much as you enjoy being together.

The bad side is that you may feel tied by his idea of relationship. Librans aren't jealous, but relationships are the only things that really matter to them; they can't function unless they have somebody by their side. While you may be quite happy, and indeed flattered, to play that role for a while, there will come a time when you feel like slipping away for a bit. Without a partner they are lost—how can you do it? And how can you be the partner they need, who must counterbalance what they have to offer, when you can only absorb and reflect what you receive? The fact is that they need somebody firm and active to take the decisions for them, and preferably somebody with some sort of talent in the real world. Your world of moods and impressions is no place for a Libran; he can only relate to one thing at a time.

Friendship between you is best if it centres around a shared interest. He would dearly love to add your sensitivity to his own artistic tastes, while your rather uncontrolled emotional whirl could benefit from some of his balance and order. Libran order isn't restricting in any way, it simply makes things nicer and puts them into a better relationship to each other, to create more pleasant effect. You could probably do with some of that. As you can see, you have a lot that you can give to each other, and a lot that you can take. What you have to do is give and take freely, but with both of you standing up, unsupported. The moment you start to lean on one another, you'll fall over.

Should you fall in love, which is all too easy for you both, the affair may well resemble something from a Mills and Boon romance. Remember that such a relationship is a sort of ideal for a Libran, and he will enjoy the relationship far more than he enjoys the person he shares it with. You are similar; your imagination goes into overdrive when you are given a chance to surround yourself with the paraphernalia of romantic love. In a way, then, neither of you are *really* in love with the other person, which is possibly just as well.

In a long-term relationship, either in business or as a married couple, the problem of decision-making will recur. One of you has got to be realistic, and it will probably be the Libran at the end of the day; he is a Cardinal sign, after all. You could be dithering for a long time, though, while he makes up his mind.

## Pisces-Scorpio

This is the sort of thing you have been promising yourself. Like a diet of chocolate cake, it will do you no good, and you know it, but you don't care a bit. Scorpio is a Water sign, like yourself, but with the kind of force and intensity you can only dream about. He will chew you up and spit you out, of course. You know that you can escape in the usual way, but you also know that he can probably find you, wherever you hide, and you're not at all sure that you want to escape anyway. Scorpio is a very dangerous drug, but if addiction is the price of ecstasy, then you're prepared to pay.

Scorpio seems to have all that you've ever wanted, in many respects. He is so sure of what he wants, for a start. When he has decided on something, he will go straight for it; it may take him a while to get it, because there will inevitably be people in the way, but he will get it in the end, and he won't take as long over it as many would have done. Like you, he is sensitive to the feelings of those around him, and he lives in a world where hopes and fears are much more important than bricks and mortar. He is not afloat or adrift in this world, though, as you are; he knows exactly where he is going, and he doesn't allow himself to be influenced by what's around him. His confidence in himself, and his sense of purpose, are much too sure for that. He is a predator in your home waters.

What you want from him is to be able to bask in the power he puts out. He is so emotionally powerful that being near him is like getting a mild electric shock—he makes you tingle. We have mentioned before that you want the intensity of the experience more than you want it to be good or bad, and you will find this person's company simply irresistible. Most people think that Scorpios are very sexy: they are, but only because sexual energy, that is the energy of Mars, is the only sort that they have to play with. What it works out as in real life is that Scorpios do everything with the intensity that other people reserve for sex only. You don't really care: it is simply the most intense energy you have ever experienced, and you want to be near the source of it.

What could he ever want from you? He has most of your sensitivity, and he is far more effective and controlled, you think: as far as you can see, you have nothing that he could possibly want. He wants two things, one on the surface and one from very deep down in your soul. Firstly, he wants to be invisible, and secondly, he wants your confidence. The first part, being invisible, is relatively easy to understand. Scorpio needs to know all that he can about everybody who is around him. and for that reason he has developed the habit of digging deeply into people's past history so that he has all the information he needs. He is rather obvious while he does so, though, or so he thinks; nobody could miss that intensity of energy when it is put to work (in fact, most people miss it completely, because they just don't have the sensitivity of the Water signs; but that doesn't stop the Scorpio from feeling obvious as he does his researches). Being able to disguise himself by fading into the background is something he would love to be able to do. He wouldn't become part of the background, as you do, he would just like it: his sense of identity and purpose would still be there. Devious, yes?

The second part, about wanting your confidence, is more difficult. It is simply that the reason that a Scorpio is so powerful and so secretive is that he is protecting himself. He doesn't trust himself, and that's the truth. You have the confidence to cast yourself upon the waters and see what comes along: he daren't do that, not ever, and he thinks that your habit of doing so is truly wondrous. Perhaps, over a very long time, you could teach him how to relax, to be trusting, and not to worry.

Having a friendship, an affair, a marriage, or going into business with a Scorpio all boil down to the same thing from your point of view. You are so helplessly drunk on his sheer magnetism that you are of almost no practical use to him anyway, but ask yourself this: do you want a relationship that leaves you as limp as a wet rag from the intensity of it all the whole time? Have you the strength for it?

*Pisces-Sagittarius*
This is a lot better than you would think. Not only do you have the same quality—you are both Mutable signs—but you share a planet too: Jupiter. Not many pairings work in this way; Gemini and Virgo is the only other one.

What you have in common is your optimism, your imagination, and your sense of fantasy. Both of you have the geniune ability to greet the future with enthusiasm, because you are sure that it will be interesting and worthwhile. None of the other signs can do this. Partly it comes from your belief that no serious harm will come to you, and partly because you both get bored easily, and welcome anything by way of a change or novelty.

Sagittarius isn't living in a dream world in the same way that you are. He's in the real world, making huge progress and bounding along from one adventure to the next; his humour and optimism never let him down, and he gets out of trouble time and time again by an almost uncanny blend of sheer talent and the most sublime good luck.

He has the warmth of Leo and the adventurous dash of Aries too, but he has something over and above them both: he has imagination, and he has knowledge. Sagittarius' mental capacities are the most highly developed of all of the Fire signs, and may even exceed those of Gemini. He can think logically and clearly, sure, but what characterizes his thought is that his heart is in it:

in other words, he believes in what he says, and it is the emotion behind the thought that makes him so much more attractive to you than Gemini or Virgo.

He doesn't have your sensitivity, and he would rather live in the real world than your world of moods and feelings, but he knows that your world exists, and he is curious to find out more. His interest helps you warm to him; he is sure enough of his own position not to feel the need to challenge you, or frighten you away. In addition, his enthusiasm and genuine good humour are there for you to absorb and enjoy.

He doesn't cling, because he values his freedom, and assumes that you do the same. He is loyal and trustworthy, though, because he is already so secure that there is no advantage for him in being dishonest. Besides, his principles are higher than that.

You see him as a sort of labrador retriever: friendly, bouncy, and loyal, always ready for a new adventure, and sure that it will be fun. When you look at the real world, and the people in it, it always seems to you that they are having such a dull time; a Sagittarian is the only person, you think, who seems to have struck the right balance between responsibility and enjoyment, and who hasn't let the search for material security close the doors of his imagination.

He sees you as representing the finer things in life, and its subtler values, too. Whenever daily life gets too dull for him, a few minutes with you will re-awaken his imagination and let him see the meanings behind the things he does. This in turn re-awakens his intellect, his knowledge, and his wisdom. He needs you as a sort of pure source, to which from time to time he returns for refreshment.

You wouldn't want to be each other, but you like and admire each other a great deal; for this reason any friendship between you will be close and loyal. You might not want to become lovers, but if you do, you will find that his bounciness extends to all areas of his life, often at the expense of subtlety. There are better business partnerships than this one, because you would both sooner change directions than stick at something if it doesn't work at the first attempt, but it's not at all bad as a marriage. You have the humour and the imagination to see past your immediate problems to a brighter future ahead.

### Pisces-Capricorn

There can be no more unlikely pairing, on the surface, than the soft and sensitive Piscean and the hard-headed, taciturn Capricorn. Yet this is a useful and satisfying pairing; it is based on alliance and help rather than power and passion, but it is none the worse for being gentle, and none the less deep either.

Capricorns are not the world's great communicators. They have a fairly fixed view of the world, and they work long hours to fulfil what they see as their duty to those both above and below them in the order of things. They are well-regulated people, who keep their feelings to themselves, for the most part, and devote any spare energy that they may have to bettering themselves.

They are not dumb, but they take a while to get talking, and they are not very expressive. You are the ideal person to listen to them: they express their feelings as strongly as they can, but it takes somebody as sensitive as you to realize that they are in fact shouting. Capricorns are very grateful for the attention that you give them, and particularly for the way that you get the message the first time, so that they don't have to go through the agony of trying to express themselves twice. They don't like being told what to do, and they don't like people who pull them away from the things that they have to get done. Luckily, you don't do either of those things. Your energies are too slight to move the Earth of a Capricorn, and anyway you don't have enough push to change the direction of a Cardinal sign. Nor do you stay when they don't want you; you know when they are busy, and you fade away.

Like elephants, they don't forget. If there's anything that you would like them to do, they will do it for you, because you have been kind enough to listen to them from time to time, and they are therefore in your debt (as they will no doubt see it). As it happens, there is a great deal that they can do for you, and they don't have to move a muscle to do it—they have only to be themselves. It is simply this: your own life can get a bit hectic from time to time, and you often allow yourself to get swept away by something that takes your fancy. It is very reassuring to have some kind of constant, something unchanging to which you can relate, and to which you can compare your experiences—a sort of anchor and yardstick in one. It is, of course, much nicer if that constant can be a person, and in the Capricorn you have exactly that.

Capricorn will enjoy listening to your experiences. They will sound very outlandish to him, and he will be very thankful that he doesn't live in your world, but he will enjoy hearing them nonetheless. You keep him up to date; the Earth doesn't feel quite so dry and dull when the flowing Water of Pisces has washed over it.

Friendship between you, then, is a quiet and fond affair, often conducted over long periods of time. Neither of you needs frequency of contact to intensify the experience: it isn't going to get any more exciting, and anyway that isn't the point here. Besides, you both have plenty of other things to do, and if the other one were around more he'd only be in the way.

As a lover, you might like his slow and traditional approach, but there again you might not. He will be constant, but that isn't always important to you; will you be faithful to him, or will you let yourself be swept away by newer and stronger passions?

A Capricorn as a business partner is always a good idea: business is his home ground. He will probably do more for you than you for him in this respect; the best thing for you to do would be to reflect his energies, and do things the way he does them.

Marriage could be a good idea—perhaps better than most people would imagine. Everything with a Capricorn gets better over the long term, and you could benefit from his steadiness, provided that he doesn't expect you to be like him all the time. He will be very successful, given time; if you'd like to share in his success in return for being his companion and confidant, then stay with him.

*Pisces-Aquarius*

A relationship between yourself and the sign which is behind you in the zodiacal sequence is always difficult. The people of that sign always seem to be particularly hostile to your way of thought, and yet they can be a great support to you, if you would let them be so.

Aquarians are too cool for you. They are analytical, like Virgos, but on a scale similar to your own. At least you could retreat from a Virgo's nitpicking by thinking of finer and higher things, but the Aquarian can follow you into your imagination, and shoot you down from there. You can speak to him of passion and beauty, and of Art with a capital A, and he will speak to you of the spirit of the times, the pleasing optical effect of regular and proportional shapes, and of the Expressionist movement. What to you seems achingly personal is to him highly impersonal, and can be explained and analysed away. He will not allow you to think that what you feel is in any way individual and unique; to do so, for him, would be to suggest that collective thought, where everybody shares the same opinion, is in some way not possible.

He will encourage you to think, and especially to speak, to express your thoughts, because he is an Air sign; what he doesn't hold with is the business of feeling, which to you is the most important part of expression, and more important than thinking.

Perhaps it is because they can see the meanings that lie beyond our normal actions that the Aquarian upsets you so. Only he and Sagittarius can appreciate your world, and you feel that Sagittarius is on your side because his brain and his heart work side by side; for cool Aquarians, though, the brain is definitely the senior partner. It may also be the fact that he is indeed so cool emotionally which upsets you; he will cast a very faint shadow indeed in your world of feelings, and so it will be difficult for you to see him properly.

You can get very angry with him, if you try. The thing that really makes you mad is how, for all his wide ranging interests and his willingness to get involved with political or humanitarian causes, he never really seems to get *involved*—or at least not by your standards. If he got carried away by his arguments or his beliefs, or if he cared enough for something to give his all for it— just *once*—then you'd forgive him. What you want is for his confounded know-it-all smartness to be completely submerged in the passion of the event, but you know it won't happen.

Do you know why you do this? Because you fear that you might be just like that. You have this nagging doubt in the back of your mind that you might be as cool and unmoved as he is, watching life's experiences float by you like so many video films. You're not like that, of course, you're much, much more involved; but because you are concerned to experience things as intensely as possible, to really *become* each new thing as it passes, you worry that you might not be using yourself as well as you might. That's what you don't like about Aquarians; they are what you see if you look over your own shoulder to see where you came from.

If you don't let him worry you, and you don't get angry, the two of you can have a very pleasant time. Aquarians are accomplished socializers: in fact, they are at their very best in company, more so even than the rest of the Air signs. They are bright conversationalists, too, so things need never be dull; just don't look for the personal intensity of experience that is so important to you. They're not you, remember.

It's probably not such a good idea to become lovers; they are much less successful on a one-to-one basis, and they don't have the emotional range that you find so desirable.

There are worse people to go into business with, but you won't enjoy their way of working.

Marriage is possible, but not necessarily a good thing, unless you are both prepared to try and see things from the other's point of view. You could do each other a lot of good, but you may not choose to see it that way.

*Pisces-Pisces*

A partnership with somebody from your own sign emphasizes the mutual talents and shortcomings of the pair of you. In the case of two Pisceans, it is almost impossible to say which way it will turn out; you can take your pick from hundreds of roles, and can play any one of them.

Pisces, perhaps more than the other signs, works on more than one level at once. At the very least, there is an outward appearance and an inner meaning; often there are quite a number of stages in between as well, as well as a few further on and further out, if you see what I mean.

Consequently, the union between two Pisceans can take almost any form. At the very highest level, it may be an almost telepathic rapport between two musicians or dancers, who seem to know in advance what the other is about to do. It may be a long and caring friendship, where each intuitively knows what the other would or wouldn't like, without having to ask. Then again, it may be two people from widely different lives, who trust each other and enjoy getting very drunk in each other's company every Thursday night.

You won't be able to give each other encouragement but you will be able to give each other *dis*couragement, in that you will be able to suggest escape routes to each other, so that you can avoid being decisive or, even worse, definite about things.

You can have no secrets from each other; each of you is sensitive enough to be able to read the other quite easily. After a few futile exercises in one-upmanship, you should come to trust one another, simply because you have no alternative, and because you have more to offer each other by being constructive and helpful than not. Eventually you will begin to use your relationship as somewhere to offload emotional rubbish which you have picked up recently; you can have a great deal of fun sorting through each other's experiences. It's a bit like living in a scrapyard; after a while you get quite good at spotting the useable items from the junk.

You can stop each other getting lonely, in a very specialized way. Only another Piscean can appreciate things on the sort of levels of meaning that are important to you, and therefore only another Piscean can help if you want to talk about those levels of experience, or to offload them onto somebody else. The other signs can usually find somebody from elsewhere in the zodiac besides their own sign who will understand what they are trying to say, but for a Piscean only another one will do.

This isn't the sort of relationship you get into because you want it to go somewhere; this is the one you choose precisely because you know that it won't. This is the sloppy armchair of friendships: it's no good for your back, and it doesn't look very smart, but you can come home, kick off your shoes, and fall into it with a sigh. You know who your friends are.

For exactly the same reasons it makes a very poor business partnership. Neither of you is assertive enough, and to focus your energies in the commercial world you need somebody other than another Piscean.

As lovers, you are likely to encourage each other's worst habits. It will be a very private relationship, because you know that no outsider will be able to appreciate what is going on. At its highest level, it will be sublime, almost spiritual; at its lower levels, you will simply indulge each other's sloppiness.

If you choose this pairing for marriage, it is because you definitely want it to be a retreat from the world, somewhere you can stop acting for a while. Perhaps you have a strenuous public life. It's not a marriage which in itself is ambitious or progressive, but it could be just what you are looking for—the one place where you don't have to be invisible.

# 5. The Year within Each Day

You have probably wondered, in odd moments, why there are more than twelve varieties of people. You know more than twelve people who look completely different. You also know more than one person with the same Sun sign as yourself who doesn't look anything like you. You also know two people who look quite like each other, but who are not related, and do not have birthdays near each other, so can't be of the same Sun sign. You will have come to the conclusion that Sun signs and astrology don't work too well, because anyone can see that there are more than twelve sorts of people.

You will also have wondered, as you finished reading a newspaper or magazine horoscope, how those few sentences manage to apply to a twelfth of the nation, and why it is that they are sometimes very close to your true circumstances, and yet at other times miles off. You will have come to the conclusion that astrology isn't all that it might be, but some of it is, and that you like it enough to buy magazines for the horoscopes, and little books like this one.

It might be that there is some other astrological factor, or factors, which account for all the different faces that people have, the similarities between people of different Sun signs, and the apparent inconsistencies in magazine horoscopes. There are, indeed, lots of other astrological factors we could consider, but one in particular will answer most of the inconsistencies we have noticed so far.

It is the Ascendant, or rising sign. Once you know your Ascendant, you will see how you get your appearance, your way of working, your tastes, your preferences and dislikes, and your state of health (or not, as the case may be). It is perhaps of more use to you to consider yourself as belonging to your Ascendant sign, than your Sun sign. You have been reading the wrong newspaper horoscopes for years; you are not who you thought you were!

You are about to protest that you know when your birthday is. I'm sure you do. This system is not primarily linked to your birthday, though. It is a smaller cogwheel in the clockwork of the heavens, and we must come down one level from where we have been standing to see its movements. Since astrology is basically the large patterns of the sky made small in an individual, there are a number of 'step-down' processes where the celestial machinery adjusts itself to the smaller scale of mankind; this is one of them.

Here's the theory:

Your birthday pinpoints a particular time during the year. The Sun appears to move round the strip of sky known as the zodiac during the course of the year. In reality, of course, our planet, Earth, moves round the Sun once a year, but the great friendly feature of astrology is that it always looks at things from our point of view; so, we think we stand still, and the Sun appears to move through the zodiac. On a particular day of importance, such as your birthday, you can see which of the zodiac signs the Sun is in, pinpoint how far it has gone in its annual trip round the sky, and then say 'This day is important to me, because it is my birthday; therefore this part of the sky is important to me because the Sun is there on my special day. What are the qualities of that part of the Sun's journey through the zodiac, and what are they when related to me?' The answer is what you usually get in a horoscope book describing your Sun sign.

Fine. Now let's go down one level, and get some more detail. The Earth rotates on its own axis every day. This means that, from our point of view, we stand still and the sky goes round us once a day. Perhaps you hadn't thought of it before, but that's how the Sun appears to move up and across the sky from sunrise to sunset. It's actually us who are moving, but we see it the other way round. During any day, then, your birthday included, the whole of the sky goes past you at some time or another; but at a particular moment of importance, such as the time that you were born, you can see where the Sun is, see which way up the sky is, and say, 'This moment is important to me, because I was born at this time; therefore the layout of the sky has the same qualities as I do. What are the qualities of the sky at this time of day, and what are they when related to me?'

You can see how you are asking the same questions one level lower down. The problem is that you don't know which bit of the sky is significant. Which bit do you look at? All you can see? All that you can't (it's spherical from your point of view, and has no joins; half of it is below the horizon, remember)?

How about directly overhead? A very good try; the point in the zodiac you would arrive at is indeed significant, and is used a lot by astrologers, but there is another one which is more useful still. The eastern horizon is the point used most. Why? Because it fulfils more functions than any other point. It gives a starting point which is easily measurable, and is even visible (remember, all astrology started from observations made before mathematics or telescopes). It is also the contact point between the sky and the earth, from our point of view, and thus symbolizes the relationship between the sky and mankind on the earth. Finally, it links the smaller cycle of the day to the larger one of the year, because the Sun starts its journey on the eastern horizon each day as it rises; and, if we are concerned with a special moment, such as the time of your birth, then the start of the day, or the place that it started, at any rate, is analogous to the start of your life. Remember that you live the qualities of the moment you were born for all of your life; you are that moment made animate.

The point in the zodiac, then, which was crossing the eastern horizon at the time you were born, is called the Ascendant. If this happened to be somewhere in the middle of Gemini, then you have a Gemini Ascendant, or Gemini rising, whichever phrase you prefer. You will see that this has nothing to do with the time

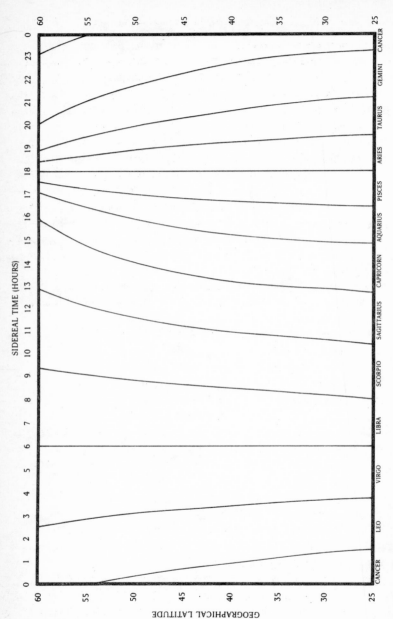

SIDEREAL TIME (HOURS)

GEOGRAPHICAL LATITUDE

Different signs are on the horizon at different times according to where you live. This is because of the difference in latitude. (See page 442.)

of year that you were born, only with the time of day.

Have a look at the diagram opposite, which should help explain things. If two people are born on the same day, but at different times, then the Ascendant will be different, and the Sun and all the other planets will be occupying differentparts of the sky. It makes sense to assume, then, that they will be different in a number of ways. Their lives will be different, and they will look different. What they will have in common is the force of the Sun in the same sign, but it will show itself in different ways because of the difference in time and position in the sky.

How do you know which sign was rising over the eastern horizon when you were born? You will have to work it out. In the past, the calculation of the Ascendant has been the subject of much fuss and secrecy, which astrologers exploit to the full, claiming that only they can calculate such things. It does take some doing, it is true, but with a few short cuts and a calculator it need only take five minutes.

Here is the simplest routine ever devised for you to calculate your own Ascendant, provided that you know your time of birth. Pencil your answers alongside the stages as you go, so you know where you are.

1. Count forwards from the start of your sign to your birthday: e.g. for Pisces, 20 February is 1, 21 February is 2, and so on.
   Total days: . . . . . . . . . . . . . . . . . . . . . . . . . . . . . . . . (max. 31)

2. Add to this the number by your sign:

   | Aries | 183 | Leo | 304 | Sagittarius | 61 |
   |---|---|---|---|---|---|
   | Taurus | 213 | Virgo | 334 | Capricorn | 92 |
   | Gemini | 243 | Libra | 1 | Aquarius | 122 |
   | Cancer | 273 | Scorpio | 31 | Pisces | 152 |

   New total is: . . . . . . . . . . . . . . (max. 365)

3. Divide by 365, and then

4. Multiply by 24. Answer is now: . . . . . . . . . . . . . . . . . . . . . .
   (Your answer by now is between 0 and 24. If it isn't, you have made a mistake somewhere. Go back and try again).

5. Add your time of birth, in 24-hour clock time. If you were

born at 3 p.m., that means 15. If you were born in Daylight Saving/ Summer Time, make the necessary correction to give the true time. If there are some spare minutes, your calculator would probably like them in decimals, so it's 0.1 of an hour for each six minutes. 5.36 p.m. is 17.6, for example. Try to be as close as you can. New total is ....................................

6. Astrologers always work in Greenwich Mean Time, so if you live outside the UK you probably need to add some more hours to your total. The correction for the USA, for example, is as follows:
     If you were born in PST, add 8 hours to your total;
     if you were born in MST, add 7 hours to your total;
     if you were born in CST, add 6 hours to your total;
     if you were born in EST, add 5 hours to your total.

7. Nearly finished now. Outside Britain you will need to subtract four minutes for each degree of longitude West of Greenwich. For example, if you were born in New York, which is 74°W, then you subtract 74 x 4 minutes, which is 296 minutes, or 4 hours and 56 minutes (4.93 hours if you're doing it all in decimals).

8. If your total exceeds 24, subtract 24. Your answer must now be between 0 and 24. Answer is ...........................

9. You have now got the time of your birth not in clock time, but in sidereal (or star) time, which is what astrologers work in. Page 440 has a diagram with the signs of the zodiac plotted against latitude. Along the horizontal axis are the values 0 to 24 in Sidereal Time. Look against the time you have just calculated, and against the latitudes of the place where you were born, and you will see which sign was rising at the time and place you were born. For example, if your calculated answer is 13.6 or there-abouts, and you were born in Florida, then you have Capricorn rising, but if you were born further North, in New England, then you have the late degrees of Sagittarius rising instead. Latitude can make quite a difference, as you can see.

# What Does the Ascendant Do?

Broadly speaking, the Ascendant does two things. Firstly, it gives you a handle on the sky, so that you know which way up it was at the time you entered the game, so to speak; this has great significance later on in the book, when we look at the way you handle large areas of activity in your life such as your career, finances, and ambitions. Secondly, it describes your body. If you see your Sun sign as your mentality and way of thinking, then your Ascendant sign is your body and your way of doing things. Think of your Sun sign as the true you, but the Ascendant as the vehicle you have to drive through life. It is the only one you have, so you can only do with it the things of which it is capable, and there may be times when you would like to do things in a different way, but it 'just isn't you'. What happens over your life is that your Sun sign energies become adapted to specifically express themselves to their best via your Ascendant sign, and you become an amalgam of the two. If you didn't, you would soon become very ill. As a Cancer with, say, a Virgoan Ascendant, you do things from a Cancer motivation, but in a Virgoan way, using a Virgoan set of talents and abilities, and a Virgoan body. The next few sections of the book explain what this means for each of the Sun/Ascendant combinations.

Some note ought to be made of the correspondence between the Ascendant and the actual condition of the body. Since the Ascendant sign represents your physical frame rather than the personality inside it, then the appearance and well-being of that frame is also determined by the Ascendant sign. In other words, if you have a Libra Ascendant, then you should look like a Libran, and you should be subject to illnesses in the parts of the body with a special affinity to that sign.

# The Astrology of Illness

This is worth a book in itself, but it is quite important to say that the astrological view of illness is that the correlation between the individual and the larger universe is maintained. In other words, if you continue over a long period of time with a way of behaviour that denies the proper and necessary expression of your planetary energies, then the organ of your body which normally handles that kind of activity for your body systems will start to show the stresses to you. A simple example: Gemini looks after the lungs, which circulate air, and from which oxygen is taken all over the body. Gemini people need to circulate among a lot of people, talking and exchanging information. They act as the lungs of society, taking news and information everywhere. They need to do this to express their planetary energies, and society needs them to do this or it is not refreshed, and does not communicate. You need your lungs to do this, too. Lungs within people, Geminis within society: same job, different levels. If you keep a Gemini, or he keeps himself, through circumstance or ignorance, in a situation where he cannot talk or circulate, or where he feels that his normal status is denied, then he is likely to develop lung trouble. This need not be anything to do with a dusty atmosphere, or whether he smokes, although obviously neither of those will help; they are external irritants, and this is an internal problem caused by imbalance in the expression of the energies built into him since birth. In the sections which follow, all the observations on health are to do with how the body shows you that certain behaviour is unbalancing you and causing unnecessary stress; problems from these causes are alleviated by listening to yourself and changing your behaviour.

# Your Ascendant

### Aries Ascendant
If you have Aries rising, you are an uncommon individual, because Aries only rises for about fifty minutes out of the twenty-four hour day.

What you are trying to do with yourself is project your personality through an Arian vehicle. You will always be trying to do things faster than anybody else, and this can lead to hastiness and a certain degree of accident-proneness. What you see as the correct way to do things involves immediate action by the most direct method, to secure instant, and measurable, results. You feel that unless you are directly and personally responsible for doing things, then they cannot be done, not only because you believe that only you can do them properly, but because you get no satisfaction from letting anybody else do anything. Personal experience of everything is the only way you learn; reading about it, or watching it, does nothing for you.

You are likely to have headaches as a recurring problem if you push yourself too hard, and you should watch your blood pressure too. Mars, ruling Aries, is a strong and forceful planet, and it is bound to get you a little over-stressed at times. You are also likely to have problems digesting things properly. Astrologically, all illnesses apply to your external condition as well as your internal condition, so think carefully; when your head aches you are banging it too hard against a problem which cannot be overcome that way, and when you are not digesting properly, you have not understood the implications of what you have taken on. In both cases, allow time to think and consider.

## Taurus Ascendant

If you have Taurus rising, you should have all the Taurean physical characteristics: quite thick-set, big around the neck and shoulders sometimes, and with large hands. You should have a broad mouth, and large eyes, which are very attractive. You should also have a good voice—not only as a singing voice, but one which is pleasant to listen to in conversation too.

The Taurean method for getting things done is to look forward to, and then enjoy, the material reward for one's efforts. It is part of Taurean thinking that if you can't touch it, buy it, own it or eat it, it isn't real and it isn't worth much. You will also be concerned to keep what is yours, not to waste your energies on what won't gain you anything or increase your possessions, and not to attempt anything which you don't think you have more than a chance of achieving.

Taureans do have taste; not only taste for food, which they love, but artistic taste, which they develop as a means of distinguishing things of value which they would then like to acquire and gain pleasure from owning. Unlike the Capricorn way of doing things, which values quality because it is valued by others, Taureans enjoy their possessions for themselves. The drawback to the Taurean approach is the lack of enterprise, and the unwillingness to try things just for the fun of it.

Taurean Ascendant people have throat and glandular problems, and all problems associated with being overweight. They can also have back and kidney problems caused as a result of an unwillingness to let things go in their external life. A lighter touch is needed in the approach to problems of possession; shedding unwanted or outworn things in a desirable process.

## Gemini Ascendant

If you have a Gemini Ascendant you should have expressive hands and a wide range of gestures which you use as you speak (ask your friends!) and you are perhaps a little taller than average, or than other members of your family. Gemini Ascendant people also have dark hair, if there is any possibility of it in their parents' colouring, and quick, penetrating eyes which flash with amusement and mischief; Gemini Ascendant women have very fine eyes indeed.

The Gemini approach to things, which you find yourself using, is one in which the idea of a thing is seen as being the most useful, and in which no time must be lost in telling it to other people so that they can contribute their own ideas and responses to the discussion. The performance of the deed is of no real importance in the Gemini view; somebody else can do that. Ideas and their development are what you like to spend time on, and finding more people to talk to, whose ideas can be matched to your own, seems to you to offer the most satisfaction.

There are two snags to the Gemini approach. The first is that there is a surface quality to it all, in which the rough outline suffices, but no time is spent in development or long-term experience. It may seem insignificant, but there is some value in seeing a project through to the end. The second snag is similar, but is concerned with time. The Gemini approach is immediate, in that it is concerned with the present or the near future. It is difficult for a Gemini Ascendant person to see farther than a few months into the future, if that; it is even more difficult for him to extend his view sideways in time to see the impact of his actions on a wider scene. Both of these things he will dismiss as unimportant.

Gemini Ascendant people suffer from chest and lung maladies, especially when they cannot communicate what they want to or need to, or when they cannot circulate socially in the way that they would like. They also have problems eliminating wastes from their bodies, through not realizing the importance of ending things as well as beginning them. In both cases, thinking and planning on a broader scale than usual, and examination of the past to help make better use of the future, is beneficial.

## Cancer Ascendant

The Cancerian frame, through which you project your energies, may mean that you appear rounder and a little fatter than others of your sign. Your energies are in no way diminished; in fact, you are likely to be even more determined to have things your own way. Your face could be almost cherubic, and you could have small features in a pale complexion with grey eyes and brown hair. The key to the Cancer frame is that it is paler than usual, less well defined than usual, and has no strong colouring. Strong noses and red hair do not come from a Cancerian ascendant.

The Cancerian approach to things is highly personal. All general criticisms are taken personally, and all problems in any procedure for which they have responsibility is seen as a personal failing. You will be concerned to use your energies for the safe and secure establishment of things from the foundations up, so that you know that whatever you have been involved in has been done properly, and is unlikely to let you down in any way; you are concerned for your own safety and reputation. The other side of this approach is that you can be a little too concerned to make sure everything is done personally, and be unwilling to entrust things to other people. Not only does this overwork you, it seems obsessive and uncooperative to others.

The Cancer Ascendant person has health problems with the maintenance of the flow of fluids in his body, and a tendency to stomach ulcers caused by worry. Cancer Ascendant women should pay special attention to their breasts, since the affinity between the sign, the Moon as ruler of all things feminine, and that particular body system means that major imbalances in the life are likely to show there first. There could also be some problems with the liver and the circulation of the legs; the answer is to think that, metaphorically, you do not have to support everybody you know: they can use their own legs to stand on, and you do not have to feed them either.

### Leo Ascendant

Leo as the determinant of the physical characteristics makes itself known by the Lion of the sign—you can always spot the deep chest, proud and slightly pompous way of walking, and more often than not, the hair arranged in some sort of mane, either full, taken back off the face, and golden if possible. Leo ascendant people have strong voices and a definite presence to them. A Leo ascendant will bring to the fore any hereditary tendency to golden colouring, so reddish or golden hair, or a rosy complexion, may be in evidence, as will a heavy build in the upper half of the body.

The Leonine way of doing things is to put yourself in the centre and work from the centre outwards, making sure that everybody knows where the commands are coming from. It is quite a tiring way of working; you need to put a lot of energy into it, because you are acting as the driving force for everybody else. Preferred situations for this technique are those where you already know, more or less, what's going to happen; this way you are unlikely to be thrown off balance by unexpected developments. The grand gesture belongs to the Leo method; it works best if all process are converted into theatrical scenes, with roles acted rather than lived. Over-reaction, over-dramatization, and over-indulgence are common, but the approach is in essence kind-hearted and well-meant. Children enjoy being with Leo Ascendant people, and they enjoy having children around them. The flaws in the approach are only that little gets done in difficult circumstances where applause and appreciation are scarce commodities, and that little is attempted that is really new and innovatory.

The health problems of the Leo Ascendant person come from the heart, and also from the joints, which suffer from mobility problems. These both come from a lifetime of being at the centre of things and working for everybody's good, and from being too stiff and unwilling to try and change in position. The remedy, of course, is to be more flexible, and to allow your friends to repay the favours they owe you.

### Virgo Ascendant

A Virgo Ascendant should make you slim and rather long, especially in the body; even if you have broad shoulders you will still have a long waist. There is a neatness to the features, but nothing notable; hair is brown, but again nothing notable. The nose and chin are often well-defined, and the forehead is often tall and broad; the voice can be a little shrill and lacks penetration.

The Virgoan Ascendant person does not have an approach to life; he has a *system*. He analyses everything and pays a lot of attention to the way in which he works. It is important to the person with Virgo rising not only to be effective, but to be efficient; you can always interest them in a new or better technique. They watch themselves work, as if from a distance, all the while wondering if they can do it better. They never mind repetition; in fact they quite enjoy it, because as they get more practiced and more proficient they feel better about things. To you, being able to do things is everything, and unless you are given a practical outlet for your energies, you are completely ineffective. There is a willingness to help others, to be of service through being able to offer a superior technique, inherent in the Virgo way of doing things, which prevents Virgo rising people from being seen as cold and unfriendly. The problems in the Virgo attitude are a tendency to go into things in more detail than is necessary, and to be too much concerned with the 'proper' way to do things.

People with a Virgo Ascendant are susceptible to intestinal problems and may be prone to circulatory problems, and poor sight. All of these are ways in which the body registers the stresses of being too concerned with digesting the minutiae of things which are meant to be passed through anyway, and by not getting enough social contact. The remedy is to lift your head from your workbench sometimes, admit that the act is sometimes more important than the manner of its performance, and not to take things too seriously.

### Libra Ascendant

Libra rising will give you a pleasant and approachable manner which will do a great deal to hide your anxieties and prevent people thinking anything but the best of you. You should be tallish, and graceful, as all Libra Ascendant people tend to be; they have a clear complexion, and blue eyes if possible, set in an oval face with finely formed features.

The Libra Ascendant person has to go through life at a fairly relaxed pace. The sign that controls his body won't let him feel ᵗrushed or anxious; if that sort of thing looks likely, then he will slow down a little until the panic's over. There is a need to see yourself reflected in the eyes of others, and so you will form a large circle of friends. You define your own opinion of yourself through their responses to you, rather than being sure what you want, and not caring what they think.

The drawback to the Libran approach is that unless you have approval from others, you are unlikely to do anything on your own initiative, or at least you find it hard to decide on a course of action. You always want to do things in the way which will cause the least bother to anyone, and to produce an acceptable overall result; sometimes this isn't definite enough, and you need to know what you do want as well as what you don't.

The Libran Ascendant makes the body susceptible to all ailments of the kidneys and of the skin; there may also be trouble in the feet. The kidney ailments are from trying to take all the problems out of life as you go along. Sometimes it's better to simply attack a few of the obstacles and knock them flat in pure rage—and in doing so you will develop adrenaline from the adrenal glands, on top of the kidneys!

## Scorpio Ascendant

A Scorpio Ascendant should give you a dark and powerful look, with a solid build, though not necessarily over-muscled. Scorpio Ascendant people tend to have a very penetrating and level way of looking at others, which is often disconcerting. Any possible darkness in the colouring is usually displayed, with dark complexions and dark hair, often thick and curly, never fine.

The Scorpio Ascendant person usually does things in a controlled manner. He is not given to explosive releases of energy unless they are absolutely necessary; even then, not often. He knows, or feels (a better word, since the Scorpionic mind makes decisions as a result of knowledge gained by feeling rather than thinking), that he has plenty of energy to spare, but uses it in small and effective doses, each one suited to the requirements of the task at hand. It does not seem useful to him to put in more effort than is strictly necessary for any one activity; that extra energy could be used somewhere else. The idea that overdoing things for their own sakes is sometimes fun because of the sheer exhilaration of the release of energy does not strike a responsive chord in the Scorpio body, nor even much understanding. There is, however, understanding and perception of a situation which exists at more than one level. If anything is complicated, involving many activities and many people, with much interaction and many side issues which must be considered, then the Scorpio Ascendant person sees it all and understands all of it, in its minutest detail. They feel, and understand, the responses from all of their surroundings at once, but do not necessarily feel involved with them unless they choose to make a move. When they do move, they will have the intention of transforming things, making them different to conform to their ideas of how things need to be arranged.

Scorpio Ascendant people are unable simply to possess and look after anything; they must change it and direct it their way, and this can be a disadvantage.

Scorpio illnesses are usually to do with the genital and excretory systems; problems here relate to a lifestyle in which things are thrown away when used, or sometimes rejected when there is still use in them. It may be that there is too much stress on being the founder of the new, and on organizing others; this will bring head pains, and illnesses of that order. The solution is to take on the existing situation as it is, and look after it without changing any of it.

### Sagittarius Ascendant

If you have a Sagittarius Ascendant you should be taller than average, with a sort of sporty, leggy look to you; you should have a long face with pronounced temples (you may be balding there if you are male), a well-coloured complexion, clear eyes, and brown hair. A Grecian nose is sometimes a feature of this physique.

The Sagittarian Ascendant gives a way of working that is based on mobility and change. This particular frame can't keep still and is much more comfortable walking than standing, more comfortable lounging or leaning than sitting formally. You tend to be in a bit of a hurry; travelling takes up a lot of your time, because you enjoy it so. It is probably true to say that you enjoy the process of driving more than whatever it is that you have to do when you get there. You probably think a lot of your car, and you are likely to have one which is more than just a machine for transport—you see it as an extension, a representation even, of yourself. People will notice how outgoing and friendly you seem to be, but they will need to know you for some time before they realize that you enjoy meeting people than almost anything else, and you dislike being with the same companions all the time. There is a constant restlessness in you; you will feel that being static is somehow unnatural, and it worries you. You are an optimist, but can also be an opportunist, in that you see no reason to stay doing one thing for a moment longer than it interests you. The inability to stay and develop a situation or give long-term commitment to anything is the biggest failing of this sign's influence.

A person with Sagittarius rising can expect to have problems with his hips and thighs, and possibly in his arterial system; this is to do with trying to leap too far at once, in all senses. You may also have liver and digestive problems, again caused by haste on a long-term scale. The remedy is to shorten your horizons and concentrate on things nearer home.

## Capricorn Ascendant

This sign often gives a small frame, quite compact and built to last a long time, the sort that doesn't need a lot of feeding and isn't big enough or heavy enough to break when it falls over. The face can be narrow and the features small; often the mouth points downwards at the corners, and this doesn't change even when the person smiles or laughs.

The Capricorn sees life as an ordered, dutiful struggle. There is a great deal of emphasis placed on projecting and maintaining appearances, both in the professional and the personal life; the idea of 'good reputation' is one which everybody with Capricorn rising, whatever their sun sign, recognizes at once. There is a sense of duty and commitment which the Sagittarian Ascendant simply cannot understand; here the feeling is that there are things which need doing, so you just have to set to and get them done. Capricorn Ascendant people see far forwards in time, anticipating their responsibilities for years to come, even if their Sun sign does not normally function this way; in such cases they apply themselves to one problem at a time, but can envisage a succession of such problems, one after another, going on for years.

The disadvantages of this outlook are to do with its static nature. There is often a sense of caution that borders on the paranoid, and while this is often well disguised in affluent middle-class middle age, it seems a little odd in the young. This tends to make for a critical assessment of all aspects of a new venture before embarking on it, and as a result a lot of the original impetus is lost. This makes the result less than was originally hoped in many cases, and so a cycle of disappointment and unadventurousness sets in, which is difficult to break. The Capricorn Ascendant person is often humourless, and can seem determined to remain so.

These people have trouble in their joints, and break bones from time to time, entirely as a result of being inflexible. On a small scale this can be from landing badly in an accident because the Capricorn Ascendant keeps up appearances to the very end, refusing to believe that an accident could be happening to him: on a large scale, a refusal to move with the times can lead to the collapse of an outmoded set of values when they are swept away by progress, and this breaking up of an old structure can also cripple. They can get lung troubles, too, as a result of not taking enough fresh air, or fresh ideas. The best treatment is to look after their families rather than their reputation, and to think about the difference between stability and stagnation.

*Aquarius Ascendant*
Having an Aquarius Ascendant will make you more sociable than you would otherwise have been, with a strong interest in verbal communication. There is a certain clarity, not to say transparency, about the Aquarian physique. It is usually tall, fair, and well shaped, almost never small and dark. There is nothing about the face which is particularly distinctive; no noticeable colouring, shape of nose, brows, or any other feature. It is an average sort of face, cleanly formed and clear.

The person with an Aquarian Ascendant wants to be independent. Not violently so, not the sort of independence tht fights its way out of wherever it feels it's been put, just different from everybody else. Aquarius gives your body the ability to do things in ways perhaps not done before; you can discover new techniques and practices for yourself, and don't need to stay in the ways you were taught. There is a willingness to branch out, to try new things; not a Scorpionic wish to make things happen the way you want, but an amused curiosity which would just like to see if things are any better done a different way. There is no need for you to convince the world that your way is best: it only needs to suit you.

Of course, an Aquarian needs to measure his difference against others, and therefore you feel better when you have a few friends around you to bounce ideas off, as well as showing them how you're doing things in a slightly different way. You function best in groups, and feel physically at ease when you're not the only person in the room. You are not necessarily the leader of the group; just a group member. Group leaders put their energy into the group, and you draw strength and support from it, so you are unlikely to be the leader, though paradoxically all groups work better for having you in them.

A handicap arising from an Aquarian Ascendant is that you are unlikely to really feel passionately involved with anything, and this may mean that unless you have support from your friends and colleagues you will be unable to muster the determination necessary to overcome really sizeable obstacles in your chosen career.

You are likely to suffer from diseases of the circulation and in your lower legs and ankles; these may reflect a life where too much time is spent trying to be independent, and not enough support is sought from others. You may also get stomach disorders and colds because you are not generating enough heat: get more involved in things and angrier about them!

## Pisces Ascendant

Like Aries rising, Pisces is only possible as an Ascendant for about fifty minutes, so there aren't many of you around.

Pisces Ascendant people are on the small side, with a tendency to be a bit pale and fleshy. They are not very well co-ordinated and so walk rather clumsily, despite the fact that their feet are often large. They have large, expressive, but rather sleepy-looking eyes.

You will prefer to let things come to you rather than go out and look for them; you are likely to be unsure of your ability to cope with being yourself. Birth time is likely to be crucial; if you were born just after sunrise, you may find that you have no desire to live any kind of public life at all, and as a consequence you may be attracted to any sort of activity where you are either on your own or at least protected from the jostle of everyday living.

The major problem with a Pisces Ascendant is the inability to be active rather than reactive; you would rather be reacting to outside influences than generating your own movements from within yourself.

A Piscean Ascendant gives problems with the feet and the lymphatic system; this has connections with the way you move in response to external pressures, and how you deal with things which invade your system from outside. You may also suffer from faint-heartedness—literally as well as metaphorically. The remedy is to be more definite and less influenced by opinions other than your own.

# 6. Three Crosses: Areas of Life that Affect Each Other

If you have already determined your Ascendant sign from page 441, and you have read 'The Meaning Of The Zodiac' on page 11, you can apply that knowledge to every area of your life with revealing results. Instead of just looking at yourself, you can see how things like your career and your finances work from the unique point of view of your birth moment.

You will remember how the Ascendant defined which way up the sky was. Once you have it the right way up, then you can divide it into sectors for different areas of life, and see which zodiac signs occupy them. After that, you can interpret each sector of sky in the light of what you know about the zodiac sign which fell in it at the time that you were born.

Below there is a circular diagram of the sky, with horizon splitting it across the middle. This is the way real horoscopes are usually drawn. In the outer circle, in the space indicated, write the name of your Ascendant sign, not your Sun sign (unless they are the same, of course. If you don't know your time of birth, and so can't work out an Ascendant, use your Sun sign). Make it overlap sectors 12 and 1, so that the degree of your Ascendant within that sign is on the eastern horizon. Now fill in the rest of the zodiac around the circle in sequence, one across each sector boundary. If you've forgotten the sequence, look at the diagram on page 16. When you've done that, draw a symbol for the sun (☉—a circle with a point at its centre) in one of the sectors which has your Sun sign at its edge. Think about how far through the sign your Sun is; make sure that you have put it in the right sector. Whichever sector this is will be very important to you; having the Sun there gives a bias to the whole chart, like the weight on one side of a locomotive wheel. You will feel that the activities of that sector (or house, as they are usually called) are most in keeping with your character, and you feel comfortable doing that sort of thing.

Make sure you have got your sums right. As a Capricorn born in the afternoon, you might well have Gemini rising, and the Sun in the eighth house, for example.

Now is the time to examine the twelve numbered sections of your own sky, and see what there is to be found.

# The Angular Houses: 1, 4, 7, 10

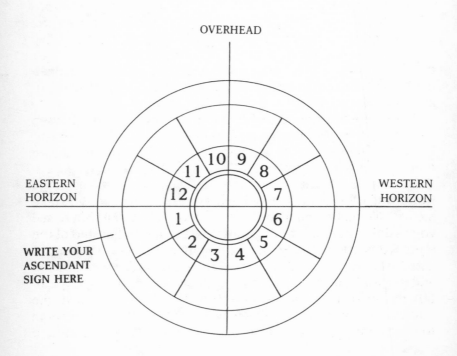

These are the houses closest to the horizon and the vertical, reading round in zodiacal sequence. The first house is concerned with you yourself as a physical entity, your appearance, and your health. Most of this has been dealt with in the section on Ascendants. If you have the Sun here, it simply doubles the impact of your Sun sign energies.

Opposite to you is the seventh house, which concerns itself with everybody who is not you. Partners in a business sense, husbands, wives, enemies you are actually aware of (and who therefore stand opposed to you in plain sight) and any other unclassified strangers all belong in the seventh house. You see their motivation as being of the opposite sign to your Ascendant sign, as being something you are not. If you have Capricorn rising, you see them as behaving, and needing to be treated, which is perhaps more accurate, in a Cancerian manner. This is how you approach seventh-house things. Use the keywords from 'The Meaning of the Zodiac' (p. 17) to remind yourself what this is. If you have the Sun in the seventh house you are your own best partner: you may marry late in life, or not at all. Perhaps your marriage will be unsuccessful. It is not a failure; it is simply that you are to a very great extent self-supporting, and have neither the ability nor the need to share yourself completely with another.

The whole business of the first and the seventh is to do with 'me and not-me'. For the personal energies of this relationship to be shown in tangible form, it is necessary to look at the pair of houses whose axis most squarely crosses the first/seventh axis. This is the fourth/tenth. The tenth is your received status in the world, and is the actual answer to the question 'What do you take me for?' No matter what you do, the world will find it best to see you as doing the sort of thing shown by the sign at the start of the tenth house. Eventually, you will start to pursue that kind of activity anyway, because in doing so you get more appreciation and reward from the rest of society. Your efforts in dealing with others, which is a first/seventh thing, have their result in the tenth, and their origins in the fourth. Expect to find clues there to your family, your home, the beliefs you hold most dear, and the eventual conclusion to your life (not your death, which is a different matter). If you have the Sun in the tenth, you will achieve some measure of prominence or fame; if your sun is in the fourth, you will do well in property, and your family will be of greater importance to you than is usual.

There is, of course, some give and take between the paired houses. Giving more time to yourself in the first house means that you are denying attention to the seventh, your partner; the reverse also applies. Giving a lot of attention to your career, in the tenth house, stops you from spending quite so much time as you might like with your family or at home. Spending too much time at home means that you are out of the public eye. There is only so much time in a day; what you give to one must be denied to the other.

This cross of four houses defines most people's lives: self, partner, home, and career. An over-emphasis on any of these is to the detriment of the other three, and all the arms of the cross feel and react to any event affecting any single member.

If these four houses have cardinal signs on them in your chart, then you are very much the sort of person who feels that he is in control of his own life, and that it is his duty to shape it into something new, personal, and original. You feel that by making decisive moves with your own circumstances you can actually change the way your life unfolds, and enjoy steering it the way you want it to go.

If these four houses have Fixed signs on them in your chart, then you are the sort of person who sees the essential shape of your life as being one of looking after what you were given, continuing in the tradition, and ending up with a profit at the end of it all. Like a farmer, you see yourself as a tenant of the land you inherited, with a responsibility to hand it on in at least as good a condition as it was when you took it over. You are likely to see the main goal in all life's ups and downs as the maintenance of stability and enrichment of what you possess.

If these four houses have mutable signs on them in your chart, then you are much more willing to change yourself to suit circumstances than the other two. Rather than seeing yourself as the captain of your ship, or the trustee of the family firm, you see yourself as free to adapt to challenges as they arise, and if necessary to make fundamental changes in your life, home and career to suit the needs of the moment. You are the sort to welcome change and novelty, and you don't expect to have anything to show for it at the end of the day except experience. There is a strong sense of service in the mutable signs, and if you spend your life working for the welfare of others, then they will have something to show for it while you will not. Not in physical terms, anyway; you will have had your reward by seeing your own energies transformed into their success.

# The Succedent Houses: 2, 5, 8, 11

These houses are called succedent because they succeed, or follow on from, the previous four. Where the angular houses define the framework of the life, the succedent ones give substance, and help develop it to its fullest and richest extent, in exactly the same way as fixed signs show the development and maintenance of the elemental energies defined by the cardinal signs.

The second house and the eighth define your resources; how much you have to play with, so to speak. The fifth and eleventh show what you do with it, and how much you achieve. Your immediate environment is the business of the second house. Your tastes in furniture and clothes are here (all part of your immediate environment, if you think about it) as well as your immediate resources, food and cash. Food is a resource because without it you are short of energy, and cash is a resource for obvious reasons. If you have the Sun here you are likely to be fond of spending money, and fond of eating too! You are likely to place value on things that you can buy or possess, and judge your success by your bank balance.

Opposed to it, and therefore dealing with the opposite viewpoint, is the eighth house, where you will find stored money. Savings, bank accounts, mortgages, and all kinds of non-immediate money come under this house. So do major and irreversible changes in your life, because they are the larger environment rather than the immediate one. Surgical operations and death are both in the eighth, because you are not the same person afterwards, and that is an irreversible change. If you have the Sun in the eighth you are likely to be very careful with yourself, and not the sort to expose yourself to any risk; you are also not likely to be short of a few thousand when life gets tight, because eighth house people always have some extra resource tucked away somewhere. You are also likely to benefit from legacies, which are another form of long-term wealth.

To turn all this money into some form of visible wealth you must obviously do something with it, and all forms of self-expression and ambition are found in the fifth and the eleventh houses. The fifth is where you have fun, basically; all that you like to do, all that amuses you, all your hobbies are found there, and a look at the zodiac sign falling in that house in your chart will show you what it is that you like so much. Your children are a fifth-house phenomenon, too; they are an expression of yourself made physical, made from the substance of your body and existence, and given their own. If you have the Sun in the fifth house you are likely to be of a generally happy disposition, confident that life is there to be enjoyed, and sure that something good will turn up.

The eleventh house, in contrast, is not so much what you like doing as what you would like to be doing: it deals with hopes, wishes, and ambitions. It also deals with friends and all social gatherings, because in a similar manner to the Aries/Libra axis, anybody who is 'not-you' and enjoying themselves must be opposed to you enjoying yourself in the fifth house. If you have the Sun in the eleventh house, you are at your best in a group. You would do well in large organizations, possibly political ones, and will find that you can organize well. You have well-defined ambitions, and know how to realize them, using other people as supporters of your cause.

The oppositions in this cross work just as effectively as the previous set did: cash is either used or stored, and to convert it from one to the other diminishes the first. Similarly, time spent enjoying yourself does nothing for your ambitions and aims, nor does it help you maintain relationships with all the groups of people you know; there again, all work and no play . . .

If you have Cardinal signs on these four houses in your chart, then you think that using all the resources available to you at any one time is important. Although what you do isn't necessarily important, or even stable, you want to have something to show for it, and enjoying yourself as you go along is important to you. To you, money is for spending, and how your friends see you is possibly more important to you than how you see yourself.

Fixed signs on these four houses will make you reticent, and careful of how you express yourself. You are possibly too busy with the important things of life as you see them, such as your career and long-term prospects, to give much attention to the way you live. You feel it is important to have things of quality, because you have a long-term view of life, and you feel secure when you have some money in the bank, but you don't enjoy your possessions and friends for your own sake. You have them because you feel that you should, not because they are reason enough in themselves.

Mutable signs on these four houses show a flexible attitude to the use of a resource, possibly because the angular houses show that you already have plenty of it, and it is your duty to use it well. You don't mind spending time and money on projects which to you are necessary, and which will have a measurable end result. You see that you need to spend time and effort to bring projects into a completed reality, and you are willing to do that as long as the final product is yours and worth having. You are likely to change your style of living quite frequently during your life, and there may be ambitions which, when fulfilled, fade from life completely.

# The Cadent Houses: 3, 6, 9, 12

The final four houses are called cadent either because they fall away from the angles (horizon and vertical axes), or because they fall towards them, giving their energy towards the formation of

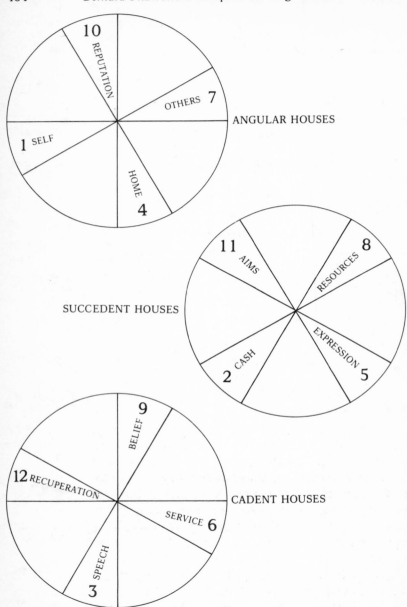

ANGULAR HOUSES

SUCCEDENT HOUSES

CADENT HOUSES

the next phase in their existence. Either way, affairs in these houses are nothing like as firm and active as those in the other two sets of four. It may be useful to think of them as being given to mental rather than physical or material activities.

The third and ninth houses are given to thought and speech, with the ninth specializing in incoming thoughts, such as reading, learning and belief (religions of all kinds are ninth-house things), while the third limits itself to speaking and writing, daily chat, and the sort of conversations you have every day. If you have the sun in the third house, you will be a chatterbox. Talking is something you could do all day, and you love reading. Anything will do—papers, magazines, novels; as long as it has words in it you will like it. You will have the sort of mind that loves accumulating trivia, but you may find that serious study or hard learning is something that you cannot do.

The third house concerns itself with daily conversation, but the ninth is more withdrawn. Study is easy for a ninth-house person, but since all ideal and theoretical thought belongs here, the down-to-earth street-corner reality of the third house doesn't, and so the higher knowledge of the ninth finds no application in daily life. The third-ninth axis is the difference between practical street experience and the refined learning of a university. To give time to one must mean taking time from the other. If you have the Sun in the ninth, you are likely to hve a very sure grasp of the theory of things, and could well be an instigator or director of large projects; but you are unable to actually do the things yourself. Knowledge is yours, but practicality is not.

How this knowledge gets applied in the production of something new is a matter of technique, and technique is the business of the sixth house. The way things get done, both for yourself and for other people's benefit, is all in the sixth. Everything you do on someone else's behalf is there, too. If you have the Sun in the sixth house, you are careful and considerate by nature, much concerned to make the best use of things and to do things in the best way possible. Pride of work and craftsman-ship are guiding words to you; any kind of sloppiness is upsetting. You look after yourself, too; health is a sixth-house thing, and the Sun in the sixth sometimes makes you something of a hypochondriac.

Opposed to the sixth, and therefore opposed to the ideas of doing things for others, mastering the proper technique, and looking after your physical health, is the twelfth house. This is concerned with withdrawing yourself from the world, being on your own, having time to think. Energy is applied to the job in hand in the sixth house, and here it is allowed to grow again without being applied to anything. Recuperation is a good word to remember. All forms of rest are twelfth-house concepts. If you have the Sun in the twelfth house you are an essentially private individual, and there will be times when you need to be on your own to think about things and recover your strength and balance. You will keep your opinions to yourself, and share very little of your emotional troubles with anyone. Yours is most definitely not a life lived out in the open.

These houses live in the shadow of the houses which follow them. Each of them is a preparation for the next phase. If your Sun is in any of these houses, your life is much more one of giving away than of accumulation. You already have the experience and the knowledge, and you will be trying to hand it on before you go, so to speak. Acquisition is something you will never manage on a permanent basis.

If these houses have Cardinal signs on them in your chart, then preparation for things to come is important to you, and you think in straight lines towards a recognized goal. You will have firm and rather simplistic views and beliefs about matters which are not usually described in such terms, such as morality and politics, and you will be used to saying things simply and with meaning. Deception and half-truths, even mild exaggeration, confuse you, because you do not think in that sort of way.

If fixed signs occupy these houses in your horoscope, your thinking is conservative, and your mind, though rich and varied in its imagination, is not truly original. You like to collect ideas from elsewhere and tell yourself that they are your own. You rely on changing circumstances to bring you variety, and your own beliefs and opinions stay fixed to anchor you in a changing world; unfortunately, this can mean a refusal to take in new ideas, shown in your behaviour as a rather appealing old-fashionedness.

Having mutable signs on these houses in your horoscope shows a flexible imagination, though often not a very practical one. Speech and ideas flow freely from you, and you are quick to adapt your ideas to suit the occasion, performing complete changes of viewpoint without effort if required. You seem to have grasped the instinctive truth that mental images and words are not real, and can be changed or erased at will; you are far less inhibited in their use than the other two groups, who regard words as something at least as heavy as cement, and nearly as difficult to dissolve. Periods in the public eye and periods of isolation are of equal value to you; you can use them each for their best purpose, and have no dislike of either. This great flexibility of mind does mean, though, that you lack seriousness of approach at times, and have a happy-go-lucky view of the future, and of things spiritual, which may lead to eventual disappointments and regrets.

Houses are important in a horoscope. The twelve sectors of the sky correspond to the twelve signs of the zodiac, the difference being that the zodiac is a product of the Sun's annual revolution, and the houses are a product (via the Ascendant) of the Earth's daily revolution. They bring the symbolism down one level from the sky to the individual, and they answer the questions which arise when people of the same Sun sign have different lives and different preferences. The house in which the Sun falls, and the qualities of the signs in the houses, show each person's approach to those areas of his life, and the one which will be the most important to him.

# 7. Sun Sign Trivia

## Tastes and Preferences

### Aries

*Clothes*

Arians are active people, and so have an instinctive dislike of formal clothes; besides, formal clothes usually inhibit rapid movement, and an Arian tries never to allow that to happen. You will be much happier in anything red; it is Mars' colour, and the more you wear of it, the more in tune with yourself you will feel. If you are depressed or out of sorts, and you are not wearing red, then change clothes at once; you will feel much better in your own colour. You don't look too bad in patterns involving straight lines or solid areas of colour, because you match the incisive and bold visual statement thus produced, but you look rather disconcerting in anything with a small or busy pattern, because onlookers see the neatness and fussiness of the small pattern, sense the powerful energies from you, and become confused. You will look good in any kind of sportswear, because the way your planetary energy makes you move your body will always give you an athletic stride; this, when matched to sportswear, gives an overall impression of fitness and readiness for action which suits your character down to the ground. Don't become lazy and wear a tracksuit and trainers the whole time, though; the temptation is enormous, because as an Arian you are lazy about things which don't concern you overmuch, like appearance, and you have a tendency to dress as a child on occasions. Is this because wearing adult clothing suggests a seriousness you try to avoid? Your favourite clothes are probably old ones, and the reasons for this are many. Firstly, they are probably a bit loose, and that helps you move in them. They are comfortable, and that stops you feeling trapped. They served their purpose once, and were fashionable then, so you don't have to think any more about them (the phrase here is likely to be 'I've got a jacket; what do I need another one for?'). Lastly, nobody will complain too much if you go off and do something mildly adventurous in them, so you can get them as dirty as you like. The mind of the child in his muddy jeans who dislikes his restricting Sunday School suit is always there in the Arian, who would rather his clothes allowed for his behaviour than the other way round.

*Food and Furnishings*

Arians like eating, which is just as well, because they need to if their phenomenal energy output is to be maintained. But notice that they eat because they are hungry, not because they enjoy food as such. Left to themselves, they eat anything which is available at the time, because they don't usually think too hard about what they're going to eat. If you are trying to give a dinner party for an Arian, though, there are one or two preferences you might like to note. Firstly, they usually eat meat. It may be the association with strength and muscle, or it may be the colour (they like red meat). Secondly, they are traditionally supposed to like all sharp, acid, or hot flavours, so a curry will never fail. If you remember the child inside every Arian, and make it easy to eat, your efforts will be appreciated. For a dessert, remember the Arian child again, and serve anything which you know is popular with children.

In their homes, Arians like the furniture plain and strong, perhaps because they tend to bump into it a fair bit. Don't expect fussy furnishings, just solid, much used, much loved pieces which probably don't match, because they were bought individually as the mood took the owner. Ornaments are rare in the Arian environment, because they serve no immediate purpose and the Arian has no sense of nostalgia. The favourite colour will be red again, but there may be some cooler blues to provide contrast. Arians like their music loud, and their toys where they can find and play with them, so the video/stereo systems will be very obvious. Machinery is another Arian pleasure, so the kitchen should be full of tools, especially knives, and there may be machines as ornaments, such as model cars.

### Hobbies

Real cars are a source of great joy to Arians, and the quintessential Arian vehicle is the Ferrari. It has every Arian feature: it is bright red (usually), single-minded in its design, highly expressive of its purpose, and blindingly fast. It has no room for any luggage, not much room for any passengers, and is at its best when taking one person a long way at high speed. It is also selfish, self-indulgent, and slightly childish. It is impossible to think of a car which sums up the spirit of Arian energy better. Not every Arian can afford one of course, but wherever possible the Arian will choose the coupé or better still the open-top version of whatever he can afford rather than the saloon, and that rather than the estate. Given a choice of colours he will choose red, and given a choice of engines he will choose the one with either the most power or the most noise. As long as there are sports cars, there will be Arians to buy them, take them to pieces, love them, drive them too fast for their own good, and generally make the rest of us smile indulgently and shake our heads, professing to know better. We are missing out on the pure joy of headlong speed, which is the Arian's birthright.

Other things which Arians enjoy are all mechanized sports, including things like shooting; all combat sports; and all pastimes which include metals or metal tools. This takes some surprising forms—artistic Arians sculpt with metal chisels, or make wrought iron work; musical Arians play in brass bands.

## Taurus

### Clothes

Taureans are very fond of their clothes; they like them to reflect their own idea of themselves, and to show everyone else how nice they are. Since you like to touch things, you will like to touch your clothes too, and that means that you will not like clothes which have a disagreeable feel to them. Synthetics are not a large part of your wardrobe; natural fabrics are much nicer to the touch, and because they come from the land rather than the laboratory you will prefer them. You have a marked preference for silk—I don't know whether it is because of its extreme softness to the touch, or because it is expensive, and is therefore something you can treat yourself to as a declaration of wealth and security, or whether it is simply that silk tends to be made into more elegant clothes because of its rarity, and it is the quality of the cut and colour that attract you. Whatever it is, silk attracts you, as does any other soft luxury fabric, such as cashmere.

You don't like your clothes too tight because the build of a Taurean looks a little, well, trussed up in tight clothes. Because you move slowly and sometimes a little heavily, you have learned to let the cut of the clothes do all the work for you, so that you look well-dressed when standing still. Taureans look quite majestic when stationary, and you will obviously capitalize on this. Male Taureans look good in well-made suits with plenty of room in them to give an impression of wealth and comfort, and female Taureans look good in anything which isn't too closely cut and which gives an impression of womanliness without girlishness.

Favourite colours are green and pink—Venus's colours—and there is often a link to the element of Earth in that floral designs seem to be eternally popular with the sign. Taurean men often affect 'farmer's fashion', whereby they wear green and brown a lot, with tweed jackets and comfortable brogues. Such clothes are usually comfortable and soft to the touch, and have a reassuring 'countryside' feeling to them, suggesting a placid and timeless existence of rural contentment which appeals very much to the Taurean psyche. Taurean women have wonderful colour sense, and an unerring eye for the best made dress on the rail, which usually turns out to be the most expensive. This discovery serves to reassure her that her taste is indeed as fine as she knew it to be, and the purchase is made without delay.

Whenever you see someone whose clothes are well-made, well-fitting, not particularly avant-garde or up-to-the-minute, but which do a lot for their wearer without the wearer needing to do much with them, then you are looking at Taurean taste.

*Food and Furnishings*

Taureans love food. It's as simple as that. They also like the process of eating, and they like the food to be as substantial as they are, so they are not the sort of people to pick daintily at the hors d'oeuvres and then declare that they are full. As cooks, they put a great deal of effort into the preparation of food, and particularly its tasting and testing; their most sensitive sense is that of taste, and they like to do more with that than with any other. They are not particularly innovative cooks; they have a feeling for traditional recipes, and enjoy maintaining that tradition.

A Taurean likes to eat meat, and to eat plenty of it. A good roast is the heart of a satisfying meal for a Taurean, and he will take as much of it as he thinks he can manage, then eat it in a steady manner at his own pace until finished, enjoying every mouthful. It is difficult for other people to understand the satisfaction that a Taurean gets out of food. Other people eat to keep going, or to be sociable, or for something to do: but food is a spiritual thing for a Taurean. It nourishes every part of him, both body and soul, and must not be rushed or ignored. Show this book to your friends so that they will believe it at last.

Apart from meat, Taureans eat everything else in season, although they are not great fish eaters. They like all luxury foods—caviare, asparagus—and all rich foods, especially those which have been enriched by that archetypical Taurean product, cream. They also like heavy desserts; cream and chocolate: anything will be fine as long as there is a lot of it. Their sweet tooth is legendary.

A Taurean house is a very comfortable place. It is always very well furnished, but the prime purpose of all the money that has gone into it is to make it very comfortable, rather than be something with which to impress one's friends. Of course, if you do find it impressive, and point this out to your Taurean host, it will be much appreciated, because the secondary aim *is* to impress—but the primary aim is comfort.

There will be soft furnishings throughout; velvet curtains, deep carpets, and cushions on all the chairs. Colours will be green and pink again, and floral designs, especially chintz, will be much in evidence. Even if there are no floral designs, there will be flowers around, usually in pleasing arrangements. Taureans like flowers, and they like exercising their sense of colour and balance, so they buy (or grow) large amounts of flowers and spend happy hours arranging them. There is usually other evidence of artistic thought, too; pictures on the walls rather than objects, and usually something musical, such as a piano, or at the least a record player.

## Hobbies

For hobbies and leisure activity, the Taurean has two areas of talent which he can easily develop. The first is his sense of colour and sound; almost any musical activity from singing to conducting will give him satisfaction, and almost any activity in the Fine Arts will do the same. Painting, sculpting (so strongly material and permanent! Ideal for the Taurean mind), or any handicraft will appeal, and can be done well. Some Taureans, in fact quite a lot of them, have become interior designers and decorators because these careers combine a sense of colour with a physical activity where you work at your own pace. Many Taurean women find themselves in the beauty or fashion business where their feel for colour and fabric finds expression. The second area is the Taurean's affinity with the earth itself. Gardening, long country walks, and any rural pursuit are all very relaxing to Taureans. Again, many have become farmers because the career can offer so much of what they really like and need. Taureans must not feel in any way ashamed of their liking for quiet and the country; the closer they are to the land, the better they are in every way.

# Gemini

*Clothes*

Geminis aren't as interested in clothes as some of the other signs; probably this is to do with the fact that they are busy thinking about other things. Then again, a Gemini loves change in all its forms, so is unlikely to have a particular style of dressing by which he can be identified; he is far likelier to prefer to change his appearance to suit his mood. Since Geminis are usually tall, with long faces and limbs, they sometimes find it difficult to find anything which fits or suits all of them at once; the result is usually that they dress in separates rather than suits or dresses. Mercury, the ruling planet of the sign, is traditionally associated with the colours yellow and grey; not many people wear yellow all of the time, and anyone wearing grey is unlikely to be remembered for that. How does the Gemini's particular energy show itself in his clothes, then?

The key is in the principle of variety, which the Gemini loves so much. Mercury, and therefore the Gemini mind, has an affinity with small patterns, and the Gemini's clothes will often reflect this. Nothing florid or discordant, but a sense of busyness in the design which parallels the constant activity of the Gemini mind. Colours will be varied, too; often two or more different colours will be worn at once, just as the Gemini mind usually handles two or three tasks at the same time. Moreover, the colours will be lively, the sort that provoke admiring comment. Again, the intent, possibly subconscious, is to display the lively interest that the Gemini has in everything he meets. Colours of power and assertiveness, such as red and black, are too heavy for Mercury's child, while muddy greens and dark blues are too static and unmoving. This leaves yellow, and the livelier hues of the blue and brown family. It also leaves grey, especially light grey, which is neither imposing nor too conservative.

Geminis like dashes of colour here and there; they think it adds interest and novelty. Expect to see bright accessories with a neutral main colour. The clothes themselves must not be too constricting or too formal; Geminis like to move, and they like to move their shoulders and arms a lot. A jacket which prevents this will never be taken out of the wardrobe. Pockets are essential too—Geminis have a lot of things to carry, like keys and money, and something to write with. There is no such animal as a Gemini who does not have a writing instrument to hand—just in case he needs to communicate!

*Food and Furnishings*

Geminis are nothing like as keen on food as their predecessors in the zodiacal cycle, the Taureans. If a Gemini is fully absorbed in what he is doing, he is quite likely to lose his appetite altogether. The reason for this, of course, is that his real nutritional needs, his mental ones, are being met.

When they do eat, though, Geminis like the food to be entertaining in itself. Anything that is enticing to look at, or colourfully presented, will please them; so will unusual flavours or combinations of flavours. Anything that is a mixture of two things at once, such as sweet and sour sauce, or paella with its unique fish and fowl blend, will appeal to the duality of their nature. Nothing should be too much of an effort to eat if a Gemini is to be pleased: he likes to talk and eat at the same time, and having to concentrate on what he is eating will strike him as far too much like hard work. For this reason they avoid heavy meats and luxury foods; the physical security they represent is unnecessary for a Gemini. A Gemini is not at the dinner table to show off his status, or to soothe himself with lots of food; he is there to entertain and amuse himself, and his choice of both dishes and dinner companions are to that end.

The Gemini home is a light and airy place, with room for movement. Heavy drapery and dark furniture are not usually to be found here. Light chairs, usually with slatted or otherwise open backs, are often the rule. Windows are large, and chairs are often by windows and doors so that the sitter can feel that he is looking outwards ready for movement and interest from outside rather than looking inwards to the hearth or centre of the room. Ornamentation is light in feeling; actual ornaments are usually delicate and pretty, but not sentimental in tone. They are often collected in pairs, which is to do with the 'twins' of the sign again.

Geminis like toys: their houses are full of the latest electronic devices. If it aids communication, saves time, or both, there is at least one of it in a Gemini home, whatever it is. They could always do with at least one more telephone, for example.

*Hobbies*

Whatever a Gemini tries as a pastime must be mentally stimulating for it to hold his interest; it must also be quite light and mobile in a physical sense, too. Geminis like dancing, for instance: it has a lightness and speed of movement which they find most appealing and expressive of Mercury's energies, while the choreography is enough to keep them thinking for a while. Among the ball sports, tennis is the best, but badminton is possibly better yet—the competitiveness isn't the thing, it's the lightness and the movement.

Many Geminis are musical, and again they are attracted to the lighter sounding instruments: violins and flutes are common choices, cellos and tubas most unusual.

Many Geminis write, of course, and then their hobby turns into a career; the same happens to those who are skilled in some fine craft, such as the repair of watches or jewellery. In all these activities, the physical effort is quite light, but the mental involvement is much greater; this typifies the Gemini energy in action.

# Cancer

*Clothes*

Whatever Cancerians wear, you can be sure that the emotional and sentimental content of the garments is far more important than the colour, or whether they are currently fashionable.

Cancerians wear clothes so that they feel good. 'Good' in this context means that the wearer has happy associations with the particular garments or that they make the wearer feel a certain way. A favourite jacket, for example, may be the one which you wore all the time during a certain holiday, and so wearing it puts you in a holiday mood. Or a certain pair of shoes may make you feel like dancing, and wearing them puts you in a party mood all day. You may have a sweater or something which actually belongs to a friend of yours, but you keep it, and wear it, because it reminds you of them.

Cancerians, like the Moon, go in phases. At the beginning of a phase, you will feel that it is time for you to buy some new clothes, and so you will go out and choose some up-to-the-minute styles. Since these please you, and you feel smart in them, they soon become favourite clothes; each time you wear them you feel smart and up-to-date, even though fashions change during the time you do this. At the end of the phase, you are still very attached to your favourite clothes, although you are likely to be the only person you know still wearing that particular style. When you go browsing in the shops you find yourself looking for more clothes in the same style, because you like things with which you are familiar. After a while the shops don't seem to have any clothes like that any more, and you wonder why. When you realize what has happened, you start a new phase, and the cycle repeats. How fashionable a Cancerian looks depends on which stage of the phase they're at.

Cancerian women often go for blues and greens, though the more extroverted ones look better in white and silver, the colours of the sign. Pearlescent and iridescent finishes are lunar too, and younger Cancerians may find themselves interested in these.

Male Cancerians are conservative in dress. They are also prone to mismatching things, though this is not because they are colour-blind, or anything like that; it is because they are mindful of the sentimental association of each garment, and tend to dress in a range of pleasant thoughts without paying much attention to the overall effect!

*Food and Furnishings*
The Cancerian is a better host than guest, although that doesn't

mean that they are ungrateful guests: far from it. As hosts, they are concerned to see that everybody has a pleasant evening, that social niceties are observed, and that nobody has to deal with anything they would choose not to. When you have them as guests, the process must be reversed.

Since Cancer is the first Water sign, it follows that the people of the sign like food that either contains a lot of liquid, or originally came in liquid, like fish. Since they are also associated with early nutrition and especially milk, then it also follows that they would like foods which are milky or creamy both in content and texture. Mousses, both sweet and savoury, will go down well, as will any form of dairy produce. Fish is the essential Water sign main course, but the Cancerian will be dismayed if there are a lot of bones to extract; it's the sort of thing that leads to mess and embarrassment, which the Cancerian will be afraid of; certainly a Cancerian host would never offer guests anything which might lead to any embarrassment in actually eating it.

Salads contain a lot of water, and a lot of salad vegetables are specifically associated with the sign. Fluid flow is vital to the Cancerian metabolism, and foods with a high water content are beneficial here. The best drink for the sign is pure water; spring water in particular has a direct connection with the sign.

The Cancerian home is exactly that. It is a home rather than a house, because it is primarily there for the Cancerian to live in and feel safe in, rather than be some sort of glossy advertisement for its owner that visitors can come and marvel at.

Because of its purpose, it is likely to be a little untidy. Cancerians put things where they would like to put them at the time, depending on their mood; when the rest of the world is looking they will mind what they are doing, but in their own homes they don't care because they don't have to.

Families are important to Cancerians, so expect the whole family to live in the whole house all of the time. Expect toys and books all over the place, and expect the furniture to be an odd mixture of the past and the present. Some of this is due to 'phases' in furniture-buying, but some of it is due to the sentimental value of the pieces themselves. Much of the furniture will be well-worn: it is important to note that it is also well-used and well-loved.

The colours will be relaxing, and usually on the pale side; nothing too strong where lunar energies are concerned. There may be one or two glass ornaments; glass is a Cancerian material, and so holds more appeal than, say, brass.

*Hobbies*

The pastimes and hobbies the Cancerian finds himself attracted to all have Cancerian qualities in common, which is not surprising. To be a Cancerian pastime a thing should contain as many of the following as possible: water, quietness, patience, determined strength, and sensitivity.

Sports connected with boats and the water are obviously candidates here. Water skiing will satisfy those Cancerians with Fire signs on their Ascendants, while the less energetic sorts will enjoy fishing. Cancerian fishermen enjoy spending quiet days by the river more than actually catching anything. Wrestling is Cancerian, where boxing is Arian; it may be to do with defence rather than attack. If so, it is easy to see why chess appeals to Cancerians too.

Silversmithing is an obvious Cancerian craft, but there are less expensive ones where patience and care are the required virtues, like photography; knitting is a Cancerian craft too, with obvious links to the family and home life that are so important to the sign's way of thought.

# Leo

*Clothes*

It doesn't really matter what sort of clothes a Leo wears; the important thing, and the noticeable one, is the way he wears them. Leos have the uncanny ability to look good in anything at all—this is because they are expressing their own warmth, creativity, and confidence through the clothes they happen to have on at the time, and anything, worn well, looks good.

Given some sort of a choice, the Leo tries to wear things that suit him, and takes care to show off his physique. The Leo physique includes a prominent chest (it's where the heart, the Leo organ, lives) which always gives them a powerful and well-built look, especially given that they walk very upright and hold their heads high.

A few years ago, male Leos could be found literally showing their chests, usually with a gold medallion to draw attention to it. That fashion has now passed, but the taste for self-decoration is still there in every Leo, waiting for a chance to show itself. Recently the TV series 'Dynasty' has provided female Leos with an example of the style of their sign: the enlarged shoulders, making the upper half of the body more prominent, and the open display of wealth and decoration, are very Leonine indeed.

Male Leos are usually conservative in their dress sense, waiting until a style has become well established in public taste before adopting it for themselves. When they buy clothes, they always buy the most expensive available, and make sure it fits well; the idea is firstly to express the Leo's idea of his own quality, and secondly to provoke the admiration he so enjoys. His favourite colours are actually those of the Sun, such as gold, but it is outside conservative taste at the moment for men to dress in yellow and gold, so the Leo compromises with rich and royal colours instead, like maroon and deep blue. The love of gold is transferred to his jewellery. It is most unusual for a mature Leo male not to have at least a gold watch and a gold ring, and he often has much more.

Female Leos work along the same lines. They like their clothes to be flamboyant and obviously wealthy—and they show this by using real materials rather than synthetics whenever they can, including fur, of which they are very fond.

*Food and Furnishings*

Leos make wonderful hosts, and sometimes less than wonderful guests if you are trying to feed one. If they are giving the party, they are eager to show you that their parties are bigger, better, and more lavish than anything else you have ever seen, so you just go along and enjoy it. If they are a guest at a party, they have a tendency to tell everybody what they would have done if it were their party, which can be difficult.

Leos like eating large amounts of luxury foods; it is a way of showing their taste for the best in life, and their determination to enjoy it. Of course, a diet consisting entirely of rich delicacies brings its own problems, but that is another story. If you are trying to feed a Leo, a large and impressive piece of meat is the obvious choice, as is anything which contains oranges or lemons as a decoration or flavouring. This is because citrus fruits are solar fruit in astrological thought, and so will appeal to the solar sign, Leo.

Leos like their drinks to be big in flavour, so strong red wines are favourites. They also like to show exclusivity and opulence, so champagne is popular too. Even the beer has to be a luxury brew—Leos don't drink 'ordinary' beers. Unlike Taureans, who have a similar liking for good food, Leos don't like things too sweet.

A Leo's home is a luxurious place. Everything about it is there to remind both its owner and his guests that the owner is a very special individual. All the furnishings and fabrics will be on a grand scale, and very rich and heavy materials will have been used. In small rooms this can have an overpowering effect, and there is more than a slight possibility that the decoration will have been taken to the ridiculous. Leos are the sort of people whose taste runs to tiger-skin bathmats and gold-plated ashtrays.

The colours will be warm, and the central heating will have been turned up to match; solar people like solar warmth, and Leos are irritable and withdrawn when they feel cold. Naturally they will ensure that this doesn't happen to them in their own house.

Leos want their guests to feel comfortable, and to be impressed; there will be one or two large pictures on the walls, generally of a big subject grandly treated. Overall, the place is a palace; it is both a demonstration and a reminder of the standard of living a Leo expects.

*Hobbies*

Leonine hobbies are no mere pastimes or things dabbled in; if a Leo takes something up, he does it well enough to pursue it professionally. Leonine photographers do not take holiday snaps, they compose landscapes, they do their own processing and enlarging, and they exhibit the results. Leo sportsmen are professional sportsmen; the emphasis is on the individual disciplines, because Leos don't really fit into teams very well.

The great Leo interest is the theatre; it is the perfect vehicle for Leonine energy, since it enables you to express yourself to an audience, to be up in a place of prominence with the spotlight on you. There are, and have always been, many great Leo actors.

Leos are essentially creators; they paint, they make things in wood and metal—especially gold, their own planetary metal, if they can afford it—but it is the act of creation which is the important thing.

# Virgo

*Clothes*

Virgoans don't have a particular style in clothes. They are not particularly dressy, nor do they have some sort of colour or preferred fabric by which you can recognize them. What they do have, though, is neatness. Virgoan clothes are always well cared for, and are never found with hanging threads or missing buttons. At home, the shoes all have shoe trees, and every shirt has a hanger of its own.

Virgoan women like clothes which are styled in a classic way, and unlikely to go out of fashion overnight. What appeals to them about their clothes is not actually the style so much as the quality of workmanship; if they buy the clothes whose standards of production are pleasing to them, that usually means expensive clothes, and a lot of these are in classic or at least well-established styles. Neat stitching appeals to the Virgoan mind, and straight seams. When possible, they choose clothes with little details—tucks, pleats, seam and cuff details—which show off the skill of the person who made the garment. Favourite colours are usually subdued; navy is the preferred shade, but some dark browns and greens are favoured too. To stop the whole effect being too dull, Virgoans choose white for contrast; then they infuriate all the other eleven signs by keeping the white bits absolutely spotless the whole time, no matter what they have been doing.

Virgoan men look best in business clothes, and they enjoy wearing them; the feeling is that it is the right outfit for the job in hand. Small patterns are favoured over plain fabrics—the busyness appeals to the busy Mercurial mind.

Virgos of both sexes have one big problem with clothes. Since their sign governs the intestinal system, they tend to be long in the body to emphasize this. There is nothing wrong with this, but clothing manufacturers have some strange ideas about where your waist ought to be, and Virgos are always finding that their clothes assume a waist some inches away from its true position. Needless to say, this is a great annoyance.

*Food and Furnishings*
Having a Virgoan to dinner requires a little thought. As you know, Virgo, you are quite clear in your own mind about what you like, and how you like to see it. You may well be a careful eater, and if you are served something which in your view contains too much fat, or too much white sugar, for example, then you are upset. After all, you say to yourself, if I was entertaining them, I wouldn't serve them anything they didn't like; I would have made sure first. You are also slightly put out if the presentation is inelegant, or, worse, careless. Foods which require inelegant eating techniques—such as some pastas, or some Chinese foods—meet with your disapproval, especially if you know that you are not very skilled with chopsticks, or whatever. Having to display your clumsiness in public is very embarrassing.

When you give a dinner party, things are different. Neat settings, linen and china to complement each other, and dishes which are chosen to suit the guests, cooked as well as you know how, which is very well indeed.

Your own choice of food reflects your inquisitive nature. Any dish with many flavours, subtly mixed, will interest you, as will any dish which 'takes a bit of understanding' because it is not obvious at first sight or taste how the effects were achieved. Straightforward meat and two veg is not your style; the meat is too much of a muchness for you, and indeed many Virgoans are vegetarians anyway.

Your taste in furnishings is actually quite easy to define, in contrast to your taste in clothes. Once again, the first thing an outsider notices is how clean and tidy everything is, but it doesn't take him long to notice afterwards that everything contains small patterns. Bathroom walls and floors are done in small tiles, sometimes with a simple geometric mosaic pattern, and often in blue and white, the Virgo's favourite combination. Living room floors are parqueted, and the wallpaper has a small pattern, sometimes floral. Always there is a small pattern, something to divert the eye initially, and then reassure it with the regularity of the pattern.

There will be small ornaments and interesting objects to look at; each of them has been chosen because it can hold your interest and fascinate you with its complexities for about ten minutes, which is about as long as you want.

The absence of strong colours and large objects, and the preponderance of white in some rooms, will give a clinical or scientific impression to some. They misunderstand. Your house is not meant to create or reinforce any emotional response; it is a light and clean environment for doing interesting things in, and where everything has its place.

*Hobbies*
What sort of interesting things? Anything which keeps you busy Virgos have more hobbies and pastimes than any other sign except possibly Gemini, and it is Mercury's restless energy which drives both signs. Never one to sit still for long, Virgos like to keep busy. A lot of you are interested in keeping your bodies in order, and so are attracted to solo sports where the idea is not to win but to take exercise: walking, golf, and cycling spring to

mind. If ever there was a Virgoan machine, the bicycle is surely it—it is light, mobile, efficient, and good for you.

You will probably spend a great deal of time working on your home; Virgos are the real craftsmen among DIY enthusiasts. Female Virgos are traditionally associated with dressmaking and all needlecraft, but that doesn't mean that you can't do the bricklaying as well, nor that Virgoan men can't make curtains. Whatever it is that claims your interest, you can be sure that it will be a practical pursuit, aimed at improving what you've got.

# Libra

*Clothes*

Librans are wonderful dressers. It doesn't matter what they wear, it looks wonderful. There are two reasons for this, and both of them are to do with Venus: the first is that whatever they wear is instinctively balanced—a colour here is balanced by another colour there, or a shape here is complemented by a shape there. The sort of mistakes the rest of us make, wearing a favourite jacket with a pair of trousers that really don't go with it at all, are unknown to Librans.

The second is that Venus gives you such grace of movement that you can make anything look good, and usually do. Style is a cross between confidence and movement, and you have both; the clothes don't have to do it all for you. For this reason you usually avoid very heavy clothes, because they won't allow you to move, and also constricting clothes, for the same reason. The Libran woman prefers dresses to separates, and full skirts to straight ones, because it lets Venus express itself through her movement.

Librans are soft people, or at least give that impression; consequently they choose soft materials; wool is a favourite, especially in the form of jersey, which allows movement, of course. As for colours, Venus' own colour is green, but just about every colour in the rainbow has been advanced as the colour for Libra, short of black. In fact, Librans are partial to *light* colours: light blue, light green, light tan, anything at all provided that it isn't too intense a hue. Libran women wear pastel colours all the time, and Libran men have a collection of golf sweaters in bright mixtures of pale colours. The overall impression is one of cleanness and attractiveness—a bit like a soap powder advertisement!

Neither sex will ever wear red as a main colour—it is far too Martian. They are quite partial to pink, though; the archetypical Libran garment, if there is such a thing, must be a fluffy pink sweater.

Decoration is another Libran touch. Embroidery and other fancy work on clothes, such as lace, really annoys some signs, but it seems to attract Librans. Libran men are currently mourning the passing of the frilled dress shirt, it seems.

*Food and Furnishings*
Libran taste in these areas is again dominated by the requirements of looking attractive to the eye, not being too heavy, and being balanced. Being ruled by Venus means that Librans have a sweet tooth, but that sweetness will have to be balanced. Sweet and sour sauce sounds like a good idea, but it isn't very attractive visually. Chinese and Japanese food is generally a good idea with Librans, though, because of the emphasis on presentation and on the balancing of one flavour and texture with another. What Librans really don't like eating is anything very heavy and meaty, where the sheer amount of food is supposed to be impressive in itself; the whole roast ox you would offer a Leo isn't really to a Libran's taste.

Libran homes are simply beautiful, with emphasis on both words. What makes them so is the precise balance achieved by placing the furniture in such a way that the shapes and masses are in harmony. No room looks cluttered, and none look bare; all look attractive, welcoming, and somehow artistic. What they are not, though, is cosy; comfortable, yes, but not cosy, in much the same way as the rooms laid out in a furniture showroom. You, of course, find it exactly to your taste, because you arranged it; other signs wish their own homes were like yours—but when they get home, they're somehow glad they're not. They love to come visiting, though, and that's just what you like best.

*Hobbies*
Librans spend their spare time in artistic pursuits. If your pastime doesn't seem terribly artistic, then consider this: is it an activity which exactly balances the deficiencies of your working activities? Is it quiet because your work is noisy, or vice versa? I expect so. What you are doing is redressing the balance, of course; very Libran. As well as artistic pursuits, Librans read a lot. It is false etymology to connect Libra and library as words, but they do seem to have an affinity with the printed word. Perhaps this accounts for the huge sales of romantic fiction— they are all bought by romantic Librans!

# Scorpio

*Clothes*
Scorpios are usually very noticeable for their style of dress. It is often very luxurious, and sometimes a little theatrical in the case of women; in all cases, though, it gives the impression of power.

A Scorpio's favourite colours are red and black. Red shows the energy of Mars, and the intensity of energy which the Scorpio brings to every aspect of his life, while black shows the power of restraint and denial with which he masters his emotional forces. Red and black are also the colours of blood and death, of course; in other words, they are the colours of our most deep and vital fears and feelings. Scorpios are well-versed in these; they conduct every moment of their life at that level of intensity, and the colours they choose reflect this. To the onlooker, though, the combination of such strong colours and the powerful, almost sexual nature of Scorpionic energy is a little hard to take all at once; it certainly can't be ignored.

Restraint is usually seen as a good thing in a man's way of dressing, and so male Scorpios are usually to be found in business suits during the day. They are noticeable because the quality of the cloth is usually higher than one might expect, and the colour is just a shade darker. In a society where most businessmen look the same, the Scorpio is concerned to show that he has something deeper, more mysterious, and of a different quality.

In their spare time, Scorpio men like to show strength and purpose through their clothes. The colours are still on the dark side, and the shapes a little formal by comparison with some other signs, but the fabrics are much more varied. There is almost never any decoration, nor is anything worn too loose; such things show a changeable and a lightweight mind, and the Scorpio won't allow that.

Both sexes are widely supposed to be fond of leather. It is true to a certain extent, though to be accurate it is Capricorn's material; a little thought, though, will help you see why Scorpios should find it so attractive. It is an extra skin; it is hard, impenetrable, and protects the wearer. Scorpios like the idea of protecting themselves from the outside world. It is also a sensual material, because of its animal qualities, and its smell. This causes an emotional, and sometimes sexual response, in both the onlooker and the wearer, and it is this kind of energy with which the Scorpio is most familiar. If his clothes produce this kind of emotion by themselves, then he is bound to like them, isn't he? Besides, leather is a power symbol because of its relative expense, which is another Scorpio plus point; and last but not least it is often black.

Scorpio women often dress in dramatic styles to express, and receive, that strong emotional response they need so much. They are equally at home in both the 'little black dress' or something far more dazzling, but they will never wear anything which has weak colours or a soft outline. Romantic frills and pastels can't communicate the power of a Scorpio, so she will choose something with direct and uninterrupted lines, and clear colours. They like showing and hiding the body at the same time; whenever tight or revealing clothes are fashionable, Scorpio women are pleased. Loose or floaty fashions are generally ignored—Scorpios know what they have to do to express that Martian energy, and will do it regardless of fashion if necessary.

## Food and Furnishings

Scorpio food is easy to understand—it needs to be strong and powerful in flavour, and provoke a response. If it is in some way associated with sex, so much the better. That gives quite a range to choose from. Highly spiced or hot food (such as chili) is usually to their taste, because of the Martian heat of the peppers and spices, and all kinds of seafood go down well because of the Water sign association. Scorpio is the fixed Water sign, and so prefers the larger sea animals; how about crab or lobster instead of prawns? Most shellfish are supposed to be aphrodisiacs, and even if they are not, Scorpios enjoy the emotion generated by the idea. Failing that, he likes rich flavours associated with power and position, so all red meats and classic wines will attract him too. Like their other Water sign friends Pisces, Scorpios enjoy alcohol; you may need brandy in this instance, to adequately express the heat of Mars.

Scorpio homes are places of the senses. Everything in them is calculated to produce a strong emotional reaction. This means that the decoration will be in strong colours, and the furniture will be chosen for effect rather than because it is cheap and cheerful, or because it has nostalgic associations. It sounds a bit obvious to say that there will be a leather sofa, but it is surprising how many Scorpios do like leather furniture. Often considerable time and money have been lavished on the bedroom and bathroom; they are private places for sensual activities, and the Scorpio values the time he spends in them.

## Hobbies

Scorpios don't have a great deal of spare time—at least, not time where they lie about not doing a great deal. Mars keeps them active the whole time, and the sort of sporting activities which appeal to them are the ones where self-control is needed in dangerous circumstances. Motorized sports are a good example, especially motorcycling; so are things like potholing and mountaineering, where concentration and self-discipline are part of the adventure. Being a Water sign, they like active water sports, and particularly *under*water sports, which offer the right combination of physical activity, exploration, and risk.

When they can't go out, they read. Anything which offers the ideas of secrecy and finding out appeals, so favourite novels are usually spy stories or whodunnits.

# Sagittarius

## Clothes

Sagittarian taste in clothes is virtually non-existent—they are often the scruffiest people in the whole zodiac. The reason isn't hard to fathom—it is all to do with the need for movement, and the dislike of anything formal or restricting, that characterizes everything else about the sign.

It's not that the Sagittarian intends to be under-dressed for the occasion; it's just that none of the reasons for dressing up have any meaning for him. For example, people often dress smartly when they are in a formal situation, such as going to a wedding, or to a job interview. This is done to show a form of respect to the social position of the other person present, or in the hope that they might think well of you. Sagittarius is interested in neither of these ideas: he only shows respect when he thinks people merit it (and sees no reason why he should do it among friends at a wedding), and he is confident enough in himself not to care whether people think well of him or not. If they don't, that's their loss. Some people also dress up to make themselves feel better—but Sagittarius feels fine anyway, because he always has Jupiter to cheer him up. Finally, many formal clothes, being Saturnine in nature and purpose, are physically restricting—ties and suits for men, suits and court shoes for women—which Sagittarians see as an uncomfortable restriction on their movements, and so to be avoided if at all possible.

Whatever they wear, Sagittarians are fond of blue. It is used to show how relaxed they are about things, and how easy of access, unlike the intense and slightly hostile effect of the bright red favoured by Arians and some Scorpios. Apart from this preference for blue, Sagittarians have no other particular favourite colours, but will wear anything which strikes them as likeable and fun.

There is an element of the outdoors in Sagittarian clothes. Even in the most restricted situation, they will find a way of putting in some reference to travelling, foreign lands, or horses. Their clothes are always chosen with outdoor use in mind; where another sign might look at a jacket and ask himself whether it was in this year's style, a Sagittarian looks at it and wonders how it will stand up to pouring rain, and how useful the pockets are.

Jeans are the great Sagittarian garment. They are informal, they are tough, they have an image associated with travel and adventure, they emphasize the thighs, the Sagittarian part of the body, and they are blue.

Sagittarian style, if there is such a thing, takes clothes from anything associated with travelling or horses. Riding boots, hacking jackets, cravats; jumpsuits and flying jackets from the pioneer aviator days; leather jackets from motorcycling; jeans from the American West; big sweaters and anoraks from mountaineers and polar explorers. In addition, anything that is recognizably from distant lands, such as India or China, finds a home in the Sagittarian wardrobe.

## Food and Furnishings

Sagittarian taste in food is simple—you like everything. Endlessly energetic, and so perpetually hungry, you will eat whatever is put in front of you. With this sign, the countries or lifestyles associated with the food are as interesting as the food itself: hence a love of fast food, because of its association with the open spaces and the automobile-based culture of the United States. You love Indian food too, because of its associations with distant places. Lastly, Sagittarians are fond of all sorts of game; perhaps the connection is with the Archer who is the top half of the sign. Anything that is usually shot before it is eaten, from hare to venison, you will find to your taste.

A Sagittarian house is a glorious cross between a junk shop, a sports shop, and a library. Wherever you go, there are books, usually supplemented by piles of magazines on every possible subject. There are also various 'interesting things', which

Sagittarians acquire on their travels, and never throw away.

Sagittarian rooms are seldom blue, despite the preferences of the sign: warm reds and browns are much more common, because, more than anything else, a Sagittarian home is warm and welcoming, for friends and visitors as well as the owner. Furniture is comfortable first, stylish later in these places; the essential idea is to provide somewhere for people to sit, talk, read, and play. In a Sagittarian house, maps and magazines are laid out on the floor as travel plans are discussed; there is a smell of coffee and toast as Sagittarian appetites are catered for in an informal way; and large dogs, Sagittarian favourites, wander in and out begging titbits from visitors in an appealing fashion.

*Hobbies*

To say that Sagittarians enjoy travelling in their spare time is to misunderstand the essence of the sign. Sagittarians travel as a way of life: they have jobs in their spare time, from nine to five, Monday to Friday.

The actual process of travelling is in itself exciting and rewarding for a Sagittarian. Stevenson, the man who said that 'to travel hopefully is a better thing than to arrive', was a Sagittarian. He also said, 'I travel for travel's sake. The great affair is to move', and wrote Treasure Island, of course—a Sagittarian story if ever there was one.

Methods of transport are often interesting in themselves to Sagittarians; many are devoted to open-top sports cars, old biplanes, or motorcycles. In each case, the attraction is the sensation of speed, the exhilaration of feeling yourself travel.

Naturally all forms of equestrian sport appeal, but so do all team games: Sagittarians are better team athletes than individual performers, because they like the friendly feeling of the team spirit.

On the rare days when he isn't active, the Sagittarian will sit and read, so that his mind does the exploring instead. He will read almost anything: history, biography, the lot. A Sagittarian likes novels which are full of action, and will seldom read romantic fiction, but apart from that absolutely anything goes.

# Capricorn

*Clothes*

There are two sorts of Capricorns—the super-smart high-profile fashion plate sort, and the total scruff. You will know which one you are: if you don't, ask your friends!

Capricorn, as we have noted before, is the sign concerned with the skin and the bones. This is because Saturn represents the outer limits of the universe, and its underlying structure. Your clothes are the outer limit of your body; they replace your skin, in that they are what people see of you. Therefore you are concerned to show that you are given the recognition you deserve for your position in life through that Capricornian outer layer—your clothes. In other words, you want to show your status through what you wear. If you are one of the scruffy Capricorns, it is probably because you are working so hard that you haven't given yourself time to consider this aspect of yourself, and you are probably overworking if that is the case.

Whatever you wear, it will reflect the influence of Saturn. That means that you will choose things in serious colours, such as greys and blacks. It also means that you will have a liking for heavy fabrics; lightweight stuff suggests flimsiness and lack of substance, which is not the sort of thing you want to be associated with at all. Finally, it means that you will choose traditional and conservative styles: not only does Capricorn like things which have stood the test of time, it also likes to show power and authority, and that is usually expressed through conservative but expensive taste.

Capricorn and money go together, and you are likely to look for ways to show your money through your clothes. Traditionally this has been done throughout history by the use of luxury fabrics—medieval noblemen didn't wear fur round their cloaks just to keep warm, they did it to show how wealthy and powerful they were, too. The twentieth-century equivalent, at least for Capricorn women, is a mink coat.

Leather is actually a Capricornian fabric, despite every astrology book you have ever read insisting that it is Scorpionic.

The reason is simple: it is strong, it is long-lasting, and when all's said and done, it's *skin*!

Capricorn men wear suits to work; some of them wear suits on their days off, too. The suit is the Capricorn garment *par excellence*; it is formal, it is standardized, it shows that you mean business, and it has a tradition behind it. Capricorn women have always liked suits, too: they have made quite a comeback in recent years, largely due to the influence of the planet Neptune, influencing society as a whole, which is currently in Capricorn. Whatever else they wear, Capricorn women wait for a style to become established before they wear it; they are not great experimenters. This is because you cannot increase your reputation by wearing something too new for society to have an opinion on.

Finally, the Capricorn's liking for hard, Saturnine fabrics and the extra skin of leather extends to the extremities of his body. Capricorn women love wearing high boots; it's not because they are trying to look sexy, but because they are trying to look powerful and elegant at the same time. They enjoy wearing gloves, too, for similar reasons.

## Food and Furnishings

A Capricorn's taste in food is very traditional. He eats the things that he has always eaten, and is particularly fond of any recipes which have been handed down in his family, because his sense of history and continuity add to his enjoyment of the dish itself. Despite the fact that he is likely, at least in later life, to be reasonably affluent, he isn't too keen on luxury foods; Capricorns are rather sparing in their treatment of themselves, and they see no reason why they should eat rich and rare delicacies when simpler food is just as nourishing. Sometimes this is taken to extremes, as in the cases which crop up from time to time of misers who starve themselves to death.

Capricorn houses are often impressive. It is true that the sort of Capricorn whose cares sit too heavily on him—the scruffy, careworn, undernourished sort—often has a home which seems empty of comforts and luxuries, but the rest of the sign does all that it can to make its home an advertisement for its status. Capricorns aren't fond of houses because they are family homes; they are fond of them because they are solid, lasting, impressive, and an appreciating asset.

Inside, they are furnished in a traditional style, but in the very finest quality materials. The overall purpose is for the visitor to wonder how much it must all have cost. Status symbols are all over the place. Although a lot of time and effort has been lavished on the place, unless there is the influence of another, non-Capricorn person around to add warmth and balance, the overall effect can be rather forbidding and cold.

### Hobbies

Capricorns work too hard and for too long to have any time for hobbies and recreation. When their doctors tell them to relax, though, they go out and do the sort of sports you would expect a Goat to do: walking in the hills, climbing, that sort of thing. The emphasis all the time is on cold, hard sports involving cold, hard rocks, suitable for a mixture of Saturn and an Earth sign.

When they stay indoors, they read history books. Biographies of famous people from the past appeal to Capricorns particularly—their sense of time helps them look at a whole life at once, and their sense of tradition and history helps them feel at home in the past.

# Aquarius

### Clothes

Aquarians don't dress in the same way as Capricorns at all. There's no reason why they should, since they are a different sign, but the two signs are ruled by the same planet, so you might expect a few similarities. There are some, but they will only become apparent later; for the moment, have a look at the surface effect of Aquarian dressing. What really characterizes Aquarian dressing is the desire to look different from everybody else.

Dressing so that you stand out in the crowd does two things, both of which an Aquarian is keen to achieve. Firstly, it marks you as an individual, somebody who thinks, and probably acts, in a manner apart from everyone else. Secondly, it isolates you; nobody can feel that he is similar to you because his clothes don't say the same things as yours; in addition, if your clothes have a message which is new or unfamiliar to those who see it, then it says nothing about the individual inside. What you have managed to do by dressing unconventially is to say that you are different, and that you are unknowable, at the same time. This is exactly what you are like, of course; you like to stay impersonal, slightly removed from the jostle of everybody else's emotional traffic.

Here is the similarity between Capricorn and Aquarius. The principle is that of enclosure and separation, which seems reasonable when you remember that Saturn is behind it. Capricorn wears formal and expensive clothes, to set himself apart by his status and position; Aquarius wears unusual clothes, to separate himself from the crowd he is usually part of.

In your actual choice of clothes, you are very varied. Often you will choose something which shows your allegiance to a particular set of ideas, rather than anything about you personally. The result is something of a uniform, something that other people from your group can recognize. It may be the working clothes of your profession, or it may be the scarf and hat of your favourite football team. It may represent some identifiable political group, such as the natural earth tones favoured by most environmentalists, or the red tie which used to be so popular with Socialists.

Left to your own devices, you will probably choose things which come in neat, small shapes, without much fussy detailing. At the same time, you will be looking for something different in the cut or the decoration—something which will say 'the wearer of this garment is very different from what you think'. For this reason you are likely to go for asymmetric designs, or zigzag lines. Aquarians of both sexes like clothes with diagonal lines in the design, and also anything which is recognizably futuristic; there is a sort of impersonal, scientific look to most clothes like that which has a great deal of appeal to you.

You're not fussy about the feel of the fabric, unlike, say, the Taureans; you are far more likely to make a logical choice on the grounds of how easy it is to wash, how long it will last, and things like that. You have no objection to modern fabrics, or even plastics; in fact you rather like them, because there is an element of enclosure and insulation associated with them, as well as a certain coldness. The plastic mac must be an Aquarian garment, then, but so is the boiler suit, and so, to a certain extent, are jeans: they were originally workwear, they came to symbolize a set of values, they were truly universal, transcending all barriers of class and sex, and they are—at least when new—indigo blue, the colour of the sign.

### Food and Furnishings

Aquarians have universal taste in food; they will usually eat absolutely anything, as long as everybody else is having the same thing. The idea is to be part of the group, as usual. Sometimes their choice in food represents their current interest; if they are campaigning to save the world's resources and to ban the use of chemical additives, they will change their diet to consist of organic wholefoods. Like the other Saturnine sign, Capricorn, they don't overeat, and they are not usually interested in food as a source of pleasure; they eat because they are hungry.

An Aquarian's home is likely to reflect his emotional tone; it will be cool and airy, full of interesting things, but not cluttered. The colour blue may predominate, but not so that you would really notice. Air signs like to circulate, and they like the air to move in their houses; consequently they leave doors open as they wander from room to room, involved in lots of things at once. Aquarians have strangely retentive tastes, in that they find something that they like and then stay with it for a long time; furniture is a fairly long-lasting item in anyone's home, but you may find things in an Aquarian home that you thought everybody had thrown out years ago. Often there is something in chrome and glass, such as a table, or a futuristic light fitting; the combination of cool, hard and transparent appeals to the person from the Lunar side of Saturn in the zodiac.

*Hobbies*

Aquarians are often too deeply immersed in what they are working at to take time off for pastimes. They tend to live their beliefs round the clock, especially if they have a political interest, or support some humanitarian cause. Those who do have time for other interests usually find something which gets them into their element, the air. Walking and climbing are popular, because the wind is usually noticeable, and so is driving an open-topped car. Hang-gliding and all forms of flying appeal for the same reason: you feel yourself moving in the air.

A lot of Aquarians have mechanical interests, such as fiddling with engines of one sort or another. This is a perfect combination of the hardness of Saturn and the logical thinking of Aquarius, and keeps them happy for hours. So does anything scientific, such as astronomy.

All Aquarians are great socializers, of course, and love going to parties: it's where their particular energy can be at its best. They are not, however, great sportsmen, probably because their interest in themselves is intellectual rather than physical. They might like badminton; you can see the effect of the air on the shuttlecock!

# Pisces

*Clothes*

Pisceans are in many ways the luckiest people in the zodiac as far as dressing goes, because they can look wonderful in anything at all. The reason for this lies partly in the strong character of most modern clothes, and partly in the Piscean's ability to match his surroundings. If a certain jacket is supposed to give you an image of being, say, strong and slightly menacing, then a Piscean wearing it will look exactly like that, because he will faithfully absorb and reflect the image of the jacket. Somebody with a stronger and more identifiable personality may not suit it; his own personality may shine through and clash with the image of the jacket. In such cases we say that the jacket doesn't suit him. There are no clothes which don't suit a Piscean though; the designer's intentions become the wearer's, and the image is complete.

The disadvantage to this peculiar talent is that you can't *not* be affected by what you wear. When you throw on your coat to go out, you put on a whole new personality; the rest of us just grab something to keep us warm, usually the one we have left our keys in from last time. It also means that everybody you meet is going to react to you differently according to what you wear; it happens to everybody else as well, but the messages put out in your case are clearer and stronger because they are not mixed in with the wearer's own signals.

Perhaps to lessen the effect you have on others, or perhaps to express the diffuse nature of your planetary energies, you tend to choose clothes of indefinite shape. You don't usually like things which are very close-fitting, and you certainly don't like anything which restricts movement in any way. You may need to escape from a tricky situation at some stage: how can you do that if your clothes prevent you from moving? For the same reasons you don't like clothes which have angular lines and a severe cut: it all looks too definite to you, and you like things to be undefined wherever possible.

Female Pisceans usually have at least one dress which is made of many layers of floaty fabric. Floatiness is not a quality that many people would deliberately choose in their clothes, but it has a special appeal to Pisceans, as does semi-transparency. Any fabric light and fine enough to be one is usually the other as well, so you should have no trouble finding what you want.

A lot of a Piscean's favourite clothes look rather unfinished, if not frayed at the edges. It is probably to do with not wanting the definite-ness of a hem or a border—to Pisceans such things are restrictive boundaries.

All colours which change or shimmer are Piscean, as are all the colours of the ocean. That gives an enormous range of greens and blues, and it extends into mauves and purples too, because Pisces is at the far end of the zodiac as violet is at the far end of the rainbow of colours. Whichever colour you choose to wear, you are likely to choose a paler version of it than anybody else would. Anybody who is as sensitive to colour as you are doesn't need to shout all the time, after all. Pastels are intense enough for many Pisceans; they leave the stronger colours to the other signs.

The one area where you really indulge yourself is in your choice of shoes. Pisces as a sign is associated with the feet, remember, and your own may well be remarkable—either very large or very small. Many Pisceans like going barefoot whenever they can, because it makes their feet feel better. Shoes, though, are an obsession with you. You probably have dozens of pairs, in all colours and styles, for all occasions, and you still think that you don't have enough. Plenty of Pisceans carry a few spare pairs around with them in the car, in case their mood changes during the day and they need to wear something different on their feet.

## Food and Furnishings

Pisceans eat fish, as you would expect, but their taste is wider than that. As always, the guiding principle is the emotional response, so you eat whatever appeals to you at any given moment, or anything which has a good feeling associated with it. You enjoy thick soups in winter, and ice-cream in summer. You enjoy birthday cake and Christmas cake not because the cake is good (though it usually is) but because of how happy everybody feels on such occasions. Jupiter, the planet behind the sign, will give you a taste for rich and spicy foods, which will surprise all those who think that you would like bland food to match your often pale complexion. Not so: food is something to be absorbed, and you would like the experience to be interesting and full of good associations. Association is the key to it all; if the food evokes a memory, a feeling, a mood, then you will like it. A Piscean home is somewhere soft and relaxing. There are no hard edges, and there are no formal arrangements. Furniture could be either very modern or very old, but it must evoke some sort of a mood, and it is likely to be soft and comfortable. The kind of home where hard straight chairs are formally arranged around a polished table is not Piscean. There is a lot of fabric in a Piscean home, arranged around things and over things, to round off edges and outlines, change the way the light falls, and generally add softness to the whole place. Ornaments and objects are not arranged or kept in any particular place, nor are they acquired because they match the furnishings or because of their value; they are all there because they have associations and memories for the owner, and that is their most important feature.

*Hobbies*

When a Pisces chooses to do something in his spare time it usually contains movement, but not in a forceful way. It is usually a solitary activity, too, so that he can take some time off from the constant barrage of other people's emotional states. If he likes being outdoors, he will be drawn towards the ocean or the river, and may well enjoy sailing or fishing.

Lots of Pisceans like to project their accumulated experiences outwards, and turn to Arts and the theatre, either at an amateur level or semi-professionally. Pisceans make good painters—they have an understanding of the perceived image—but far more of them are photographers, probably for the same reasons.

A lot of Pisceans like to lose themselves in voluntary work, usually doing something to help at a local hospital or institution. They may be active on behalf of their local church; Pisces is the most spiritual of the signs.

Many Pisceans relax simply by looking at new and exciting images. Cinema is the great Piscean entertainment form, and so are television and video, but to a lesser extent. Finally, they listen to music and read books. Favourites are romances and travel books, because the images they create are so vivid; and so are books on astrology, because they show a world of meaning behind our actions, to which Pisceans are sensitive.

# Zodiacal Luck

Being lucky isn't a matter of pure luck, you know; it can be engineered. What happens when you are lucky is that a number of correspondences are made between circumstances, people, and even material items, which eventually enable planetary energies to flow quickly and effectively to act with full force in a particular way. If you are part of that chain, or your intentions lie in the same direction as the planetary flow, then you say that things are going your way, or that you are lucky. All you have to do to maximize this tendency is make sure you are aligned to the flow of energies from the planets whenever you want things to work your way.

It is regular astrological practice to try to reinforce your own position in these things by attracting energies which are already strongly represented in you. For a Gemini, for example, this means Mercury, of course, and therefore any 'lucky' number, colour, or whatever for a Gemini is simply going to be one of the ones which correspond symbolically with the attributes of Mercury.

Each planet and sign has some colours associated with it; therefore these are your lucky colours, because by wearing them or aligning yourself to them, for example by betting on a horse whose jockey's silks are in your colours, or supporting a sporting team whose colours include your planet's, you align yourself to the energies of your planet and your sign, and thereby recharge the Solar energies that are already in you.

The zodiacal colours are as follows:

**Aries/Mars**: red.
**Taurus/Venus**: green.
**Gemini/Mercury**: yellow.
**Cancer/Moon**: white, silver.
**Leo/Sun**: gold, golden yellow.
**Virgo**: blue; **Mercury** as ruler of the sign gives yellow as well.
**Libra**: pink; **Venus** as ruler of the sign gives green as well.
**Scorpio/Mars**: black and red.
**Sagittarius**: pure blue.
**Capricorn**: black, grey, all sombre colours.
**Aquarius**: black and blue, indigo, electric blue.
**Pisces**: greeny-blues, ocean colours, mauves and violets.

As you can see, the definition of the colours gets more sophisticated as the zodiac progresses; the people from the later signs are also less straightforward than those from the early stages of the cycle.

Each zodiac sign has a gemstone associated with it, too. Gemstones are seen as being able to concentrate or focus magical energies, and the colour of the stone shows its propensity to the energies of a particular planet. Over the years, the list of stones associated with the signs has grown longer and longer; there are some stones now in the list, such as the opal, which were unknown in the ancient world, when the zodiac was devised. Sometimes you will find that the same stone is quoted for two different signs; in most of those cases the stone is associated with a planet, and you will recall that most of the planets have two signs to look after. If you are looking for a link between the various stones assigned to your Sun sign, then the most usual one is their colour, though that isn't true in every case.

The most usually quoted stones are:

**Aries**: ruby, bloodstone, red haematite.
**Taurus**: emerald, topaz.
**Gemini**: yellow topaz, amethyst, agate.
**Cancer**: pearl, moonstone, quartz.
**Leo**: diamond, chrysolite.
**Virgo**: green onyx, olivine.
**Libra**: sapphire.
**Scorpio**: jasper, bloodstone, malachite.
**Sagittarius**: amethyst, zircon.
**Capricorn**: black onyx, jet.
**Aquarius**: lapis lazuli, sapphire.
**Pisces**: amethyst, opal, turquoise.

The business of lucky numbers is a science in itself, but there are two which are easy to remember and which you can use to good effect. The first one is simply the number of your zodiac sign: Aries is 1, Taurus is 2, and so on up to Pisces, which is 12. The circular diagram in the first chapter (p.16) will remind you of the sequence of the signs, if you can't remember. The second one is the number associated with the planet of your sign (see 'The Planets and the Horseshoe', p.18, if you've forgotten). Here the sequence of numbers is a little irregular, but there is a certain logic to it nonetheless. They are:

**Sun**: 6.
**Moon**: 9.
**Mercury**: 8.
**Venus**: 7.
**Mars**: 5.
**Jupiter**: 4 (strictly, though some say 3).
**Saturn**: 3 (strictly, though some say 4).

All combinations of numbers which add up to your lucky number by reduction are lucky for you too, so you have a range to choose from. Reducing a number is done by adding its digits until you can go no further. As an example, take 678: $6 + 7 + 8 = 21$, and then $2 + 1 = 3$. There you are—678 is a lucky number for anybody whose lucky number is 3, such as a Gemini (third sign), remember), so for him to buy a car with those digits in its registration plate would make it a car which, while he had it, he was very fond of and which served him well. If you are very quick, you will have noticed that the tenth, eleventh and twelfth zodiac signs can have their own numbers reduced to 1, 2 and 3 respectively, giving them further lucky numbers to use.

The days of the week are each assigned a planet, too; their names, especially in French, will give you a clue:

| | | |
|---|---|---|
| **Sunday** | = *Sun's day* | = Sun. |
| **Monday** | = *Moon's day* | = Moon. |
| **Tuesday** | = *French mardi (Mars' day)* | = Mars. |
| **Wednesday** | = *French mercredi (Mercury's day)* | = Mercury. |
| **Thursday** | = *French jeudi (Jupiter's day)* | = Jupiter. |
| **Friday** | = *French vendredi (Venus' day)* | = Venus. |
| **Saturday** | = *Saturn's day* | = Saturn. |

The way to use all this is to combine influences that are favourable to you. If you are a Taurean (sign number 2, planet

Venus, planetary number 7) and you have something important to do, then get it started on Friday 2 July (month number 7); that way you will have made sure that you will get the result best suited to you, by aligning youself to your own planet and helping its energies flow unimpeded through you and your activity.

Each planet also has a metal associated with it, and in the Middle Ages people wore jewellery, made of their planetary metals, for luck or self-alignment and emphasis, whichever way you want to describe it. Some of them are quite surprising:

**Sun**: gold.
**Moon**: silver.
**Mercury**: mercury.
**Venus**: copper.
**Mars**: iron, steel.
**Jupiter**: tin.
**Saturn**: lead.

Now you can see why your Leo friends seem to have a lot of gold bracelets, rings, and the like. It isn't possible to make anything from the metal mercury, since it is not only highly toxic, but also a liquid at normal temperatures, and so Gemini and Virgo people tend not to wear a lot of jewellery. What they do have, though, and feel to be very necessary, is a good watch. Time speeding by is a Mercurial thing, and so these people from Mercury's sign find themselves living their life by the clock. Their watches are usually very accurate, and often have extra features such as a stop-watch or some such mechanism.

Sagittarians and Pisceans won't find much tin jewellery on sale, but they might find a pewter tankard, and pewter is almost pure tin these days. Alcohol is associated with Jupiter, too; the Sagittarian side is the fun and laughter, while the Piscean side is when everything gets blurred and the room starts to revolve.

The people from the signs of Mars and Saturn don't have to have bracelets and rings made of iron and lead—they have their cars instead. Cars are the jewellery of the twentieth century, and it isn't hard to see them embodying planetary principles. Big saloons, like Mercedes, are Saturnine: they give an impression of weight, wealth, and influence. Sports cars are to do with Mars: they are all about speed and power. The most desirable of these pieces of iron jewellery often combine the qualities of Saturn and Mars in the same vehicle: Porsche is a good example. Mars people like red cars, on the whole, and Saturn's folk like black ones.

There are also plants for each planet, and foods too. The list goes on and on, but here are a few to give you an idea:

**Sun**: oranges, lemons, ginger, saffron.
**Moon**: cabbage, lettuce, onions, mushrooms.
**Mercury**: beans (all kinds), filbert nuts, marjoram.
**Venus**: apples, figs, peaches, walnuts.
**Mars**: basil, coriander, garlic, tobacco.
**Jupiter**: daises, gooseberries, raisins, cloves, nutmeg.
**Saturn**: deadly nightshade(!), spinach, parsnip, sage.

There is almost no end to the list of correspondences between the planets and everyday items, and many more can be made if you have a good imagination. They are lucky for you if you know what makes them so, and if you believe in them too; the essence of the process lies in thinking yourself and the object of your intent with some identifiable token of your own planet, such as its colour or number, and strengthening yourself thereby. The stronger you are, then the more frequently you will be able to achieve the result you want—and that's all that luck is, isn't it?

# A Final Word

By the time you reach here, you will have learnt a great deal more about yourself. At least, I hope you have.

You will probably have noticed that I appear to have contradicted myself in some parts of the book, and repeated myself in others, and there are reasons for this. It is quite likely that I have said that your Sun position makes you one way, while your Ascendant makes you the opposite. There is nothing strange about this; nobody is consistent, the same the whole way through—everybody has contradictory sides to their character, and knowing some more about your Sun sign and your Ascendant will help you to label and define those contradictory elements. It won't do anything about dealing with them, though—that's your job, and always has been. The only person who can live your horoscope is you. Astrology won't make your problems disappear, and it never has been able to; it simply defines the problems more clearly, and enables you to look for answers.

Where I have repeated myself it is either to make the point for the benefit of the person who is only going to read that section of the book, or because you have a double helping of the energy of your sign, as in the instance of the Sun and Ascendant in the same sign.

I hope you found the relationships section useful; you may well find that the Sun-to-Ascendant comparison is just as useful in showing you how you fit in with your partner as the usual Sun-to-Sun practice.

Where do you go from here? If you want to learn more about astrology, and see how all of the planets fit into the picture of the sky as it was at your birth, then you must either consult an astrologer or learn how to do it for yourself. There is quite a lot of astrology around these days; evening classes are not too hard to find and there are groups of enthusiasts up and down the country. There are also plenty of books which will show you how to draw up and interpret your own horoscope.

One thing about doing it yourself, which is an annoyance unless you are aware of it in advance: to calculate your horoscope properly you will need to know where the planets were in the sky when you were born, and you usually have to buy this data separately in a book called an ephemeris. The reason that astrology books don't have this data in them is that to include enough for everybody who is likely to buy the book would make the book as big as a phone directory, and look like a giant book of log tables, which is a bit off-putting. You can buy ephemerides (the plural) for any single year, such as the one of your birth. You can also buy omnibus versions for the whole century.

So, you will need two books, not one: an ephemeris, and a book to help you draw up and interpret your horoscope. It's much less annoying when you *know* you're going to need two books.

After that, there are lots of books on the more advanced techniques in the Astrology Handbook series, also from the Aquarian Press. Good though the books are, there is no substitute for being taught by an astrologer, and no substitute at all for practice. What we are trying to do here is provide a vocabulary of symbols taken from the sky so that you and your imagination can make sense of the world you live in; the essential element is your imagination, and you provide that.

Astrology works perfectly well at Sun sign level, and it works perfectly well at deeper levels as well; you can do it with what you want. I hope that, whatever you do with it, it is both instructive and satisfying to you—and fun, too.

# THE AQUARIAN BOOK OF FORTUNE-TELLING

Can a set of playing cards tell you what the future has in store?

———— ★ ————

Can numbers reveal your hidden character traits?

———— ★ ————

Can Tarot cards foretell your money and health prospects?

———— ★ ————

Can runes predict your love life?

———— ★ ————

The answer to all of these questions is YES.

This fascinating compilation volume of four of the best-selling *Aquarian Fortune-Telling By . . .* series — Playing Cards, Numbers, Tarot, and Runes — provides all you need to know to start using these divinatory methods to enhance your life *today*.

Introduced by Sasha Fenton, with an extensive glossary of techniques, *The Aquarian Book of Fortune-Telling* provides a fascinating insight into the modern approach to predicting the future.